The Complete Idiot'

MW01174687

General Windows

Press	To
Alt+Print Screen	Copy the active window's image to the Clipboard.
Print Screen	Copy the entire screen image to the Clipboard.
Ctrl+Alt+Delete	Display the Close Program dialog box.
Ctrl+Esc	Open the Start menu.
Ctrl+Z	Undo the most recent action.

Keyboard Shortcuts for Programs

Press	To
Working with Program Windows	
Alt+Esc	Cycle through the open program windows.
Alt+Tab	Cycle through the active programs.
Alt+F4	Close the active program window.
F1	Display context-sensitive Help.
Working with Documents	
Ctrl+N	Create a new document.
Ctrl+O	Display the Open dialog box.
Ctrl+P	Display the Print dialog box.
Ctrl+S	Save the current file. If the file is new, display the Save As dialog box.

Keyboard Shortcuts for Working with Data

Press	To
Backspace	Delete the character to the left of the insertion point.
Delete	Delete the selected data, or the character to the right of the insertion point.
Ctrl+A	Select all the data in the current window.
Ctrl+C	Copy the selected data.
Ctrl+X	Cut the selected data.
Ctrl+V	Paste the most recently cut or copied data.

Keyboard Shortcuts for Dialog Boxes

Hold Down	To
Tab	Move forward through the dialog box controls.
Shift+Tab	Move backward through the dialog box controls.
Ctrl+Shift+Tab	Move backward through the dialog box tabs.
Ctrl+Tab	Move forward through the dialog box tabs.
Alt+Down arrow	Display the list in a drop-down list box.
Spacebar	Toggle a check box on and off; select the active option button or command button.
Enter	Select the default or active command button.

Keys to Hold Down While Dragging-and-Dropping

Hold Down	To
Ctrl	Copy the dragged object.
Ctrl+Shift	Display a shortcut menu after dropping a dragged object.
Esc	Cancel the current drag.
Shift	Move the dragged object.

Windows Explorer Keyboard Shortcuts

Press	To
+ (numeric keypad)	Display the next level of subfolders for the current folder.
– (numeric keypad)	Hide the current folder's subfolders.
* (numeric keypad)	Display all levels of subfolders for the current folder.
Backspace	Navigate to the parent folder of the current folder.
Delete	Delete the selected object.
Ctrl+A	Select all the objects in the current folder.
Shift+Delete	Delete the currently selected objects without sending them to the Recycle Bin.
F2	Rename the selected object.
F3	Display the Find dialog box with the current folder displayed in the Look In list.
F4	Open the Address toolbar's drop-down list.

Internet Explorer Keyboard Shortcuts

Press	To
Alt+Left arrow	Navigate backward to a previously displayed Web page.
Alt+Right arrow	Navigate forward to a previously displayed Web page.
Ctrl+A	Select the entire Web page.
Ctrl+B	Display the Organize Favorites dialog box.
Ctrl+D	Add the current page to the Favorites list.
Esc	Stop downloading the Web page.
F4	Open the Address toolbar's drop-down list.
F5	Refresh the Web page.
F11	Toggle between full screen mode and the regular window.

Shortcuts That Use the Windows Logo (⊞) Key

Press	To
[⊞]	Open the Start menu.
[⊞]+E	Open Windows Explorer.
[⊞]+F	Find a file or folder.
[⊞]+M	Minimize all open windows.
[⊞]+Shift+M	Undo minimize all.
[⊞]+R	Display the Run dialog box.

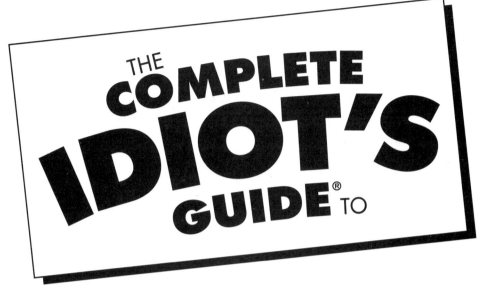

THE COMPLETE IDIOT'S GUIDE® TO

Windows Millennium

Paul McFedries

A Division of Macmillan USA
201 W. 103rd Street, Indianapolis, Indiana 46290

The Complete Idiot's Guide to Windows Millennium

International Standard Book Number: 0-7897-2407-3

Library of Congress Catalog Card Number: 00-102232

Printed in the United States of America

First Printing: July, 2000

02 01 00   4   3   2

Trademarks

Warning and Disclaimer

Associate Publisher
Greg Weigand

Senior Acquisitions Editor
Jenny Watson

Development Editor
Todd Brakke

Technical Editor
Jim Kelly

Managing Editor
Thomas F. Hayes

Project Editors
Leah Kirkpatrick
Pamela Woolf

Copy Editor
Julie A. McNamee

Indexer
Aamir Burki

Proofreaders
Harvey Stanbrough
Tricia Sterling

Illustrator
Judd Winick

Team Coordinator
Sharry Gregory

Interior Designer
Nathan Clement

Cover Designer
Michael Freeland

Copywriter
Eric Borgert

Production Team
Heather Hiatt Miller
Ayanna Lacey
Timothy Osborn
Stacey Richwine-DeRome

Contents at a Glance

Contents

Part 3: Making It Work: Useful Windows Millennium Chores   217

About the Author

Paul McFedries is a freelance writer who has worked with (yelled at, kicked) computers since 1975, yet still manages to keep his sanity relatively intact. He is the author of more than three-dozen computer books that have sold over two million copies worldwide. His other titles include the Que books *The Complete Idiot's Guide to Windows 98*, *The Complete Idiot's Guide to Windows 2000 Professional*, *The Unauthorized Guide to Windows Millennium*, and *The Complete Idiot's Guide to Creating a Web Page*.

Paul accepts compliments and other forms of flattery at his email address: cigwindows@mcfedries.com.

He also encourages all readers to drop by his Web site and poke around: www.mcfedries.com.

Dedication

To Karen, of course.

Acknowledgments

The editors are always right. Don't argue with them.

—Mark Skousen

Like Winnie-the-Pooh, "My spelling is Wobbly. It's good spelling but it Wobbles, and the letters get in the wrong places." Unlike Winnie-the-Pooh, however, I have editors to put the letters back where they belong. Near the front of the book, you'll see a page that runs through the roster of folks who had a hand in getting this book from vapor to paper. I extend my warmest thanks to all of them for a job well done.

While I'm in back-slapping mode, I'd also like to fire off a few kudos to the people I worked with directly. Great gobs of gooey gratefulness go to Associate Publisher Greg Wiegand, Acquisitions Editor Jenny Watson, Development Editor Todd Brakke, Project Editors Pamela Woolf and Leah Kirkpatrick, Tech Editor Jim Kelly, and Copy Editor Julie McNamee.

I'd also like to thank my friends and family for being, well, friendly and familiar. And, of course, no acknowledgments section would be complete without acknowledging all the welcome feedback I've received from my readers over the years. Keep those cards and letters coming!

Tell Us What You Think!

As the reader of this book, *you* are our most important critic and commentator. We value your opinion and want to know what we're doing right, what we could do better, what areas you'd like to see us publish in, and any other words of wisdom you're willing to pass our way.

As Associate Publisher for Que, I welcome your comments. You can fax, email, or write me directly to let me know what you did or didn't like about this book—as well as what we can do to make our books stronger.

Please note that I cannot help you with technical problems related to the topic of this book, and that due to the high volume of mail I receive, I might not be able to reply to every message.

When you write, please be sure to include this book's title and author as well as your name and phone or fax number. I will carefully review your comments and share them with the author and editors who worked on the book.

Fax: 317-581-4666

Email: consumer@mcp.com

Mail: Associate Publisher
        Que
        201 West 103rd Street
        Indianapolis, IN 46290 USA

Introduction

Imagine if every Thursday your shoes exploded if you tied them the usual way. This happens to us all the time with computers, and nobody thinks of complaining.

—Jef Raskin

Want to make my blood boil? Just tell me that someday, in the not-too-distant future, my refrigerator will include a computer that alerts me when I'm low on milk. Just tell me that someday my microwave oven will feature a computer that "senses" what's inside and cooks it accordingly. Just tell me that someday my car will include a computer that lets it repair itself by "downloading" some kind of software off the Internet.

The crazy thing is that there are scientists and engineers actually working on these kinds of pie-in-the-sky ideas. Don't these eggheads know that our regular computers are still too hard to use and are still too unreliable? Why can't they work on fixing *that*?

So, want to make my heart sing? Just tell me that someday, in the not-too-distant future, Microsoft will release a version of Windows that's truly simple to use; a version of Windows that doesn't make everyday tasks as easy as herding cats; a version of Windows that doesn't crash if you happen to breathe out through both nostrils at once; a version of Windows that, in other words, doesn't make otherwise-smart people—people who *know* how much milk they have in the fridge—feel like complete idiots.

Until that day comes, we have to content ourselves with trying to live with the Windows we have. And that's why I wrote *The Complete Idiot's Guide to Windows Millennium*. My aim is to show you that although Windows Millennium can be downright ornery at times, anyone with the regular complement of gray matter can soothe the savage Windows beast.

This book shuns anything and everything about Windows Millennium that is hopelessly technical. If it has a "For Geeks Only" label on it, I walk right on by it. Instead, this book concentrates only on those Windows tasks that you're likely to use most often. I present Windows concepts in clear, jargon-free language, and I teach you how to use Windows' features in a simple, step-by-step fashion.

After reading this book, you will not by any stretch of the imagination be a Windows expert. That's a good thing because I've talked to many a Windows expert in my day, and they are almost always dishwater-dull. What you will have, instead, is the competence to handle any day-to-day Windows task and the confidence to tackle any other Windows chore that comes your way.

The Parts Department: What's in the Book

You don't need to read *The Complete Idiot's Guide to Windows Millennium* cover-to-cover, although by all means you're free to do so. Instead, most of the book's chapters are self-contained, so you can usually just dive in and start learning. (In those sections that require some background, I've put in pointers back to the relevant material.) However, if you're just starting out with Windows, you'll get the most out of this book if you tackle Chapters 2 through 6 first to gain some basic know-how.

Just so you know what to expect, here are some quickie summaries of the major sections of the book:

Part 1: Getting Comfy with Windows Millennium

The half-dozen chapters that open the book are designed to help you get your Windows Millennium travels off on the right foot. Chapter 1, "The New ME: What's New in Windows Millennium," runs through what's noteworthily new in Windows Millennium. New Windows users will want to start with Chapter 2, "The Shallow End of the Pool: Some Windows Basics," which gives you a tour of the Windows Millennium screen and offers some mouse and keyboard basics. From there, you learn about controlling programs (Chapter 3, "Making Your Programs Do What You Want Them to Do"), working with windows (Chapter 4, "Your 20-Minute Windows Workout"), dealing with documents (Chapter 5, "Saving, Opening, Printing, and Other Document Lore"), and fiddling with files and folders (Chapter 6, "Using My Computer to Fiddle with Files and Folders").

Part 2: Jumping on the Internet Bandwagon

We live in an Internet-obsessed world, so it's no surprise that Windows Millennium includes a lot of features for the would-be-wired. It's also no surprise that Part 2 is the largest section in the book, comprising no less than seven chapters that take you through the basic Net gizmos in Windows Millennium. You learn step-by-step how to get connected (Chapter 7, "Getting Yourself Online"); how to surf the World Wide Web with Internet Explorer (Chapters 8, "It's a Small Web After All: Using Internet Explorer," and 9, "The Savvy Surfer: More Internet Explorer Fun"); how to exchange Internet email with Outlook Express (Chapters 10, "Sending and Receiving Email Missives," and 11, "More Email Bonding: Extending Outlook Express"); how to participate in newsgroups (Chapter 12, "Spreadin' the News: Participating in Newsgroup Conversations"); and how to send instant messages and make Internet-based "phone calls" (Chapter 13, "Real-Time Conversations: Instant Messages, Net Phone Calls, and Chat").

Part 3: Making It Work: Useful Windows Millennium Chores

This section of the book covers a hodgepodge of topics that will help you get the most out of your Windows Millennium investment. The first two chapters concentrate on some of the freebie programs that are part of the Windows Millennium. I discuss Notepad (a text editor) and WordPad (a word processor) in Chapter 14, "From Word Amateur to Word Pro: Windows' Writing Programs"; I show you how to wield

Paint (a drawing and painting program) and work with scanners and digital cameras in Chapter 15, "Image Is Everything: Windows Millennium's Graphics Tools"; I run through Windows Millennium's multimedia features in Chapter 16, "The Sights and Sounds of Windows Millennium Multimedia"; and I tell you all about Windows Millennium's notebook computer gadgets in Chapter 17, "Windows Millennium and Your Notebook Computer."

Part 4: "A Style of One's Own": Customizing Windows Millennium

Like people living in row houses who paint their doors and windowpanes to stand out from the crowd, most Windows users like to personalize their computing experience by adjusting the screen colors, changing the background, and performing other individualistic tweaks. The four chapters in Part 4 show you how to perform these customizations in Windows Millennium. You learn how to customize the desktop (Chapter 18, "Refurbishing the Desktop"), the Start menu and taskbar (Chapter 19, "Remodeling the Start Menu and Taskbar"), and the My Computer program (Chapter 20, "Renovating My Computer"). I also show you how to install (and uninstall) software and hardware (Chapter 21, "Installing and Uninstalling Programs and Devices").

Part 5: When Good Data Goes Bad: Millennium Maintenance and Repair

Thanks to higher-quality parts and improved manufacturing, modern computers are fairly reliable and will often run for years without so much as an electronic hiccup. However, that doesn't mean some disaster—be it a nasty computer virus, an ill-timed power failure, or some other spawn of Murphy's Law—can't strike at any time. The two chapters in Part 5 can help you prepare for problems. You get the goods on using Windows Millennium's collection of system maintenance tools (Chapter 22, "Smooth System Sailing: Wielding the System Tools") and on backing up your precious-as-gold data (Chapter 23, "Getting a Good Night's Sleep: Backing Up Your Precious Data").

Part 6: Networking with Windows Millennium

The final part of the book takes you into the mysterious and arcane world of networking. However, you'll see that for the small networks that Windows Millennium is ideally suited for, networking doesn't have to be an esoteric pursuit. On the contrary, I even take the fairly radical step of actually showing you how to put together your own small network (Chapter 24, "Using Windows Millennium to Set Up a Small Network"). From there, you learn how to use the Windows Millennium networking features (Chapter 25, "Using Windows Millennium's Networking Features") and how to dial up your network from remote locations (Chapter 26, "Remote Network Connections with Dial-Up Networking").

A Field Guide to This Book's Features

In a book such as this, I believe it's not only important *what* you say, but also *how* you say it. So I've gone to great lengths to present the info in easy-to-digest tidbits that can be absorbed quickly. I've also liberally sprinkled the book with features that I hope will make it easier for you to understand what's going in. Here's a rundown:

➤ Stuff you have to type will appear in a `monospaced font`, like that.

➤ Menus, commands, and dialog box controls that you have to select, as well as keys you have to press, appear in a **bold font**.

➤ Whenever I tell you to select a menu command, I separate the various menu and command names with commas. For example, instead of saying "click the **Start** button, then click **Programs**, and then click **Internet Explorer**," I just say "select **Start, Programs, Internet Explorer**."

➤ Many Windows Millennium commands have equivalent keyboard shortcuts, and most of them involve holding down one key while you press another key. For example, in most Windows programs, you save your work by holding down the **Ctrl** key, pressing the **S** key, and then releasing **Ctrl**. I'm *way* too lazy to write all that out each time, so I'll just plop a plus sign (+) between the two keys, like so: **Ctrl+S**.

I've also populated each chapter with several different kinds of sidebars, some in the middle of the page and others in the margin:

Windows Wisdom

These asides give you extra information about the topic at hand, provide you with tips for making things work easier, and generally just make you a more well-rounded Windows Millennium user.

Jargon Jar

These notes give you definitions of Windows words suitable for use at cocktail parties and other social gatherings where a well-timed *bon mot* can make you a crowd favorite.

Look Out!

These notes warn you about possible Windows Millennium pitfalls and tell you how to avoid them.

Each of these elements points you to another section of the book that contains related material.

New Knickknack

As you see in Chapter 1, there's a lot that's brand-spanking new in Windows Millennium. I use these sidebars throughout the book to alert you that something new is coming your way.

Part 1

Getting Comfy with Windows Millennium

My overall goal in this book is to help you get productive with Windows Millennium. By "getting productive" I mean not only getting your work done, but also getting online, getting creative, and just generally getting your ya-ya's out. Now I'll let you in on a not-so-little secret: The key to getting productive in Windows Millennium is getting comfortable with a few basic operations and features. After you're familiar with these fundamentals, everything else you do in Windows will be significantly easier.

So getting comfy with the nuts and bolts of Windows Millennium is what happens here in Part 1. You learn what's new with Windows Millennium, basic tasks such as using the mouse and keyboard, how to work with programs and windows, how to create and save documents, how to deal with files and folders, and much more.

The New ME: What's New in Windows Millennium

There was a scant two-year gap between the release of Windows 98 and the release of Windows Millennium Edition, which is a virtual eye-blink in the normally glacial pace of operating system updates. You usually expect to wait three or four years between major versions of Windows. Does this mean, then, that Windows Millennium isn't a major version of Windows? Is this just some kind of upgrade cash grab on Microsoft's part?

The answer to both questions is a definite *maybe*. Yes, a cursory glance tells you that Windows Millennium looks almost identical to Windows 98 and, yes, most of the Windows programs available in both versions work more or less the same. So is it the same old, same old? Well, not quite. The Jolt-cola-fuelled Microsoft programmers were doing *something* over those two years. What they were doing was adding some spit and polish: tweaking the interface to make it a bit easier to use; speeding up the startup and shutdown marathons; and adding new programs and features in a few key areas, such as the Internet, networking, and graphics.

No one with a lick of sense will tell you that Windows Millennium is an earth-shattering achievement that will revolutionize computing (Microsoft marketing types excepted, of course). But as you see in this chapter, Windows Millennium does have a fairly long laundry list of new and improved doodads that make it worth checking out.

New to Windows?

If you're new not only to Windows Millennium but to Windows in general, this chapter will probably sound like so much gibberish and jabberwocky. You hereby have my permission to leap right over the entire chapter and land squarely at the beginning of Chapter 2, "The Shallow End of the Pool: Some Windows Basics." That chapter is a much better place to begin your Windows education.

The "Look-and-Feel" Looks and Feels a Bit Different

When you fire up your machine for the first time after Windows Millennium has been foisted upon it, you notice a few differences right off the bat (see Figure 1.1):

➤ The most obvious change is the desktop, where the old teal motif has been painted over with a rather nice slate blue.

➤ The desktop's icon collection has changed, as well. There are several brand-new icons (such as My Network Places and Windows Media Player) and old icons such as My Computer and Recycle Bin have a fancier look.

Other look-and-feel tweaks become evident after you start messing around a bit. For example, on most systems, menus and ToolTips (the little yellow banners that appear when you hover the mouse over icons and toolbar buttons) fade in and out. Here's a list of a few other changes you'll be tripping over:

➤ **Personalized menus**   After you've used Windows Millennium for a while (usually a few days), the various Start menus will suddenly shrink to the point where they show only those commands that you've used so far. Chapter 19, "Remodeling the Start Menu and Taskbar," has the details.

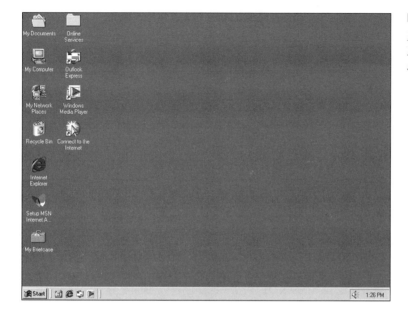

Figure 1.1

First looks: Windows Millennium sports a slightly different desktop.

➤ **Easier Start menu customizing**   Rearranging the Start menu is a great way to improve your productivity. Windows Millennium helps by giving you even more ways to customize the Start menu, most of which are simple check box toggles. Again, I cover this in Chapter 19.

My Computer is your Windows Millennium tool-of-choice for fooling around with files and folders. To help out with those chores, My Computer comes with some useful new features:

➤ **My Computer's toolbars**   My Computer gives you a choice of toolbars to display. Also, the main toolbar is now fully customizable. Chapter 20, "Renovating My Computer," has the details.

➤ **My Computer's Explorer bars**   My Computer comes with several panels that appear on the left side of the window and give you access to more features. For example, the Folders bar displays a tree-like list of the drives and folders on your computer. Again, head for Chapter 20.

➤ **Easier file searching**   One of those Explorer bars is called Search and it offers an easier file and folder searching experience (see Figure 1.2). I show you how it works in Chapter 6, "Using My Computer to Fiddle with Files and Folders."

11

Figure 1.2

My Computer's new Search bar cuts a couple of steps from the process of finding files.

Search bar

➤ **Easier file copying and moving** Although you can still use the standard cut-and-paste or drag-and-drop methods to copy and move files, Windows Millennium offers new Copy to Folder and Move to Folder commands that I think are a bit more straightforward for new users. I talk about them in Chapter 6.

➤ **A simpler Control Panel** Control Panel has always intimidated beginners with its horde of who-the-heck-knows-what-they-do icons. To reduce the confusion factor, Windows Millennium presents a kinder, gentler Control Panel that sports a mere seven icons, as shown in Figure 1.3.

Figure 1.3

In its default guise, Control Panel presents a simpler set of icons.

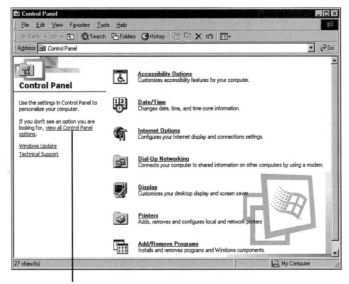

Click this link to see the rest of the icons

Newfangled Internet and Networking Doohickeys

Most of the major improvements in Windows Millennium are associated with those twin towers of connectivity, the Internet and networking. That's not surprising because those two areas are what everyone seems to be talking about these days.

Let's begin with the new Internet features:

Cross Reference

See "Toggling Some Start Menu Settings On and Off," p. 302.

Check out "Customizing the Standard Buttons Toolbar," p. 313.

See "Toggling My Computer's Bars On and Off," p. 310.

See "Finding a File in That Mess You Call a Hard Disk," p. 90.

Head for "Copying and Moving a File or Folder," p. 85.

➤ **A streamlined Internet Connection Wizard**   Windows 98's Internet Connection Wizard was a welcome addition because it took you step-by-step through the often tricky process of connecting your computer to the Internet. But were there ever a lot of steps! The Windows Millennium incarnation of this wizard has a drastically reduced number of dialog boxes to wade through, so getting connected to the Net is easier than ever. I show you how it works in Chapter 7, "Getting Yourself Online."

➤ **Internet Explorer 5.5**   This version of Microsoft's World Wide Web browser is faster and has a lot of little improvements (better searching, easier Favorites, and so on). I take you through all the new features (and plenty of the old ones, too) in Chapter 8, "It's a Small Web After All: Using Internet Explorer" and Chapter 9, "The Savvy Surfer: More Internet Explorer Fun."

➤ **Outlook Express 5.5**   This is Windows Millennium's Internet email program. Among many other improvements, it offers easier methods for handling multiple accounts, blocking and filtering messages, and working with stationery and signatures. It also lets you set up separate "identities" so that people who share the same computer can keep their messages private. See Chapter 10, "Sending and Receiving Email Missives" and Chapter 11, "More Email Bonding: Extending Outlook Express." Outlook Express also handles newsgroups, which I cover in Chapter 12, "Spreadin' the News: Participating in Newsgroup Conversations."

➤ **Easier Internet connection sharing**   Windows 98 Second Edition introduced the world to Internet Connection Sharing—the capability to share a single Internet connection among multiple, networked machines. Setting this up is a bit easier in Windows Millennium because the details are handled automatically by the new Home Networking Wizard (discussed in a sec).

➤ **Keeping in touch with the MSN Messenger Service**   Instant messaging

13

involves sending a typed message to another person who's online, that person immediately sending a response back to you, and so on. It's the latest Net craze, and it's now part of Windows Millennium thanks to the inclusion of the MSN Messenger program (see Figure 1.4). I show you how it works in Chapter 13, "Real-Time Conversations: Instant Messages, Net Phone Calls, and Chat."

Figure 1.4

Use the new MSN Messenger program to send instant messages to impatient types the world over.

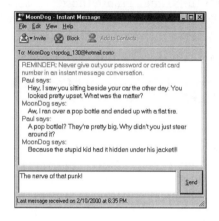

Cross Reference

Check out "Using MSN Messenger to Fire Off Instant Messages," p. 202.

See "Using the New Automatic Updates Feature," p. 357.

See "Setting Up Your Network," p. 385.

➤ **"Look ma, no hands!" updates with Automatic Updates** The Windows Update Web site has been around for a while now. It works fairly well as long as you remember to check it for updates! If you always forget, then you'll certainly appreciate the new Automatic Updates feature that checks for new stuff automatically, and can even download updates behind-the-scenes without interfering with your regular online duties. Automatic Updates is part of Chapter 22, "Smooth System Sailing: Wielding the System Tools."

On the networking side of things, Windows Millennium offers new tools that not only make it easier to make a computer network-savvy, but also make it easier to work with network resources:

➤ **The Home Networking Wizard** For my money, this addition to the wizard family is one of the best new Windows Millennium features. Its claim to digital fame is that it reduces what used to be an arcane and difficult network setup process down to a relatively simple step-by-step procedure. It ensures that all your networked machines can talk to each other, it sets up shared folders and printers (see Figure 1.5), it configures Internet Connection Sharing, and it can even create a version of itself that will install on Windows 95 and Windows 98 machines. I take you through the wizard's dialog boxes in Chapter 24, "Using Windows Millennium to Set Up a Small Network."

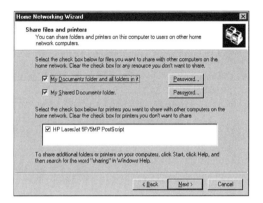

Figure 1.5

The new Home Networking Wizard: a godsend for amateur network administrators.

➤ **My Shared Documents**   This is a folder created by the Home Networking Wizard. You use it to store documents that you want to share with other folks on your network. This is handy because it means you don't have to share any of your other folders, which may contain data you don't want your peers to see.

➤ **Network places**   These are icons that represent shared resources from other computers on your network. They're handy because they let you access resources without having to wade through endless network folders. They're all stored in the new My Network Places folder, which takes over for the now retired Network Neighborhood. It's all described in not-too-gory detail in Chapter 25, "Using Windows Millennium's Networking Features."

Cross Reference

See "Your Starting Point: The My Network Places Folder," p. 394, and "Setting Up Network Places," p. 399.

I cover both the My Pictures folder and the thumbnails view (see the next item) in "Checking Out the New My Pictures Folder," p. 247.

New Tricks for Pics

If the right side of your brain is wondering, "Yo, what's in this for me?" tell it to hold its artistic horses because Windows Millennium has a few new graphical goodies it can play with:

➤ **The My Pictures folder**   This special, graphics-aware folder not only displays a preview of the currently highlighted image file, but also festoons the preview with tools for manipulating the image (zooming in and out, rotating, and more). Figure 1.6 shows the folder in action. Chapter 15, "Image Is Everything: Windows Millennium's Graphics Tools," tells you more.

Figure 1.6

The My Pictures folder has special graphics features built in.

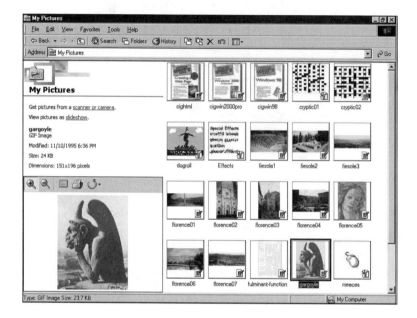

➤ **Easier image thumbnails**   If you have some folders that contain tons of images, you probably love My Computer's Thumbnails view. What's that? You've never heard of it? I'm not surprised because Windows 98 hid this oh-so-useful feature in an obscure dialog box. Windows Millennium remedies that by making thumbnails an easily accessible command on My Computer's View menu. You learn about thumbnails in Chapter 15.

Cross Reference

See "Graphics Gadgetry: Working with Scanners and Digital Cameras," p. 249.

See "Is That All There Is? Windows Millennium's Other System Tools," p. 354.

➤ **Scanner and digital camera improvements** Windows 98 understood that scanners and digital cameras exist, but support for them was spotty at best. Windows Millennium improves things somewhat by recognizing more types of scanner hardware, by making scanner installation a bit easier, and by giving you more ways to scan. For example, you can now scan an image directly into the Paint program. I talk about scanners and digital cameras in Chapter 15.

Other New Features to Write Home About

To close out this litany of Windows Millennium's newly-minted features, here are a few more to file under the "Miscellaneous" category:

➤ **System Restore**   This feature protects your system by taking periodic "snapshots" of the current system configuration. If you then install some software or hardware that makes your machine go kaput, you can revert to the pre-installation configuration to make everything well again. I discuss this tool briefly in Chapter 22.

➤ **A slicker Media Player**   Windows Millennium's Media Player is a big improvement over the one in Windows 98, as you can see in Figure 1.7. It looks a heckuva lot nicer, supports lots more media (including audio CDs and Internet radio), and it enables you to download music and artist information from the Internet. You learn how to work it in Chapter 16, "The Sights and Sounds of Windows Millennium Multimedia."

Figure 1.7
Windows Millennium's improved Media Player.

➤ **Games galore**   With all of Windows Millennium's work-related programs, it can often feel like a relentless taskmaster that requires your nose to be grindstone-bound at all times. That, of course, would be a recipe for acute dullness. To avoid that, the Microsoft programmers stuffed the Millennium box with 11 games. These include the timeless classics Solitaire, Minesweeper, and FreeCell, as well as a

Cross Reference

Check out "Installing Microsoft Backup," p. 362.

Hearts game, another solitaire game, and the remarkably realistic Pinball game. If you're online, there are even some Net-based games—such as backgammon and checkers—that let you play against other Net denizens.

➤ **Backup is out in left field**   The Backup program is the same as it was in Windows 98. The difference is that Windows Millennium now hides Backup in a hard-to-find section of the CD. It's dumb, I know. I tell you how to find and install it in Chapter 23, "Getting a Good Night's Sleep: Backing Up Your Precious Data."

➤ **DriveSpace doesn't do hard drives**   DriveSpace is the program that more or less doubles a drive's capacity by squeezing files down as far as they'll go. In Windows Millennium, DriveSpace only works its compression magic on removable drives; hard drives are out of the loop.

➤ **MS-DOS mode is toast**   Windows 95 and Windows 98 had a version of DOS called MS-DOS mode that you could use to run DOS programs that resolutely refused to run under Windows. Microsoft, eager to leave these recalcitrant programs behind, cut MS-DOS mode from Windows Millennium.

The Least You Need to Know

This chapter gave you the lowdown on the new Windows Millennium features that are of interest to non-nerds. I gave you a preview of those features in four categories: the interface, the Internet and networking, graphics, and miscellaneous.

Chapter 2

The Shallow End of the Pool: Some Windows Basics

In This Chapter

➤ Checking out the Windows Millennium screen

➤ Handy mouse and keyboard techniques

➤ A cautionary tale about shutting down Windows

➤ A few lengths around the Windows pool

Thrill-seeking types enjoy diving into the deep end of any new pool they come across. The rest of us, however, prefer to check things out first by dipping a toe or two into the waters and then slipping ever-so-gently into the shallow end. The latter is the most sensible approach when it comes to Windows waters, which can be cold and murky to the uninitiated. You need to ease into the pool by learning a few basics about the layout of the screen and about a few useful mouse and keyboard techniques. That's exactly what we'll do in this chapter.

Note, however, that this chapter assumes your Windows Millennium pool has already been built and filled with water. That is, I assume that either your computer came with Windows Millennium already installed or else you have (or a nearby computer wonk has) upgraded your computer to Windows Millennium.

Starting Windows Millennium

After you flick your computer's power switch, Windows Millennium begins pulling itself up by its own bootstraps. This takes a few minutes on most machines, so this is an excellent time to grab a cup of coffee or review your copy of *Feel the Fear and Do It Anyway*.

Booting Your Computer

The idea of Windows pulling itself up by its own bootstraps is actually a pretty good way to describe the whole process of Windows starting itself up from scratch. In fact, it's the source of the verb *to boot*, which means "to start a computer."

After your machine has churned through a few behind-the-scenes (and eminently ignorable) chores, Windows Millennium just *might* cough up a box like the one shown in Figure 2.1. What's happening here is that Windows Millennium wants you to supply the appropriate password before going any further (this is especially likely to happen if you use Windows Millennium at work). If so, you have three possibilities:

➤ If you don't have a password, leave the Password box blank and just press **Enter**. This means you won't be pestered with this dialog box again.

➤ If you do have a password (and assuming that you know it; the person at work who administers your computer system should have told you what it is), go ahead and type your password in the **Password** box. (The letters you type will appear as asterisks [*], but that's okay. It's a security feature that prevents some snoop from eyeballing your password.) Then press **Enter** to continue loading Windows Millennium.

➤ If you're really not sure what to do, press **Esc** to bypass the dialog box and move on.

Figure 2.1

This box might come your way while Windows Millennium loads.

A few seconds later, the dust clears and—voilà!—Windows Millennium is ready to roll.

What's What in the Windows Screen

The screen shown in Figure 2.2 is typical of the face that Windows Millennium presents to the world. (Note, however, that your screen might appear slightly different.)

If you're new to Windows Millennium, you need to get comfortable with the lay of the Windows land. To that end, let's examine the vista you now see before you, which I divide into two sections: the desktop and the taskbar.

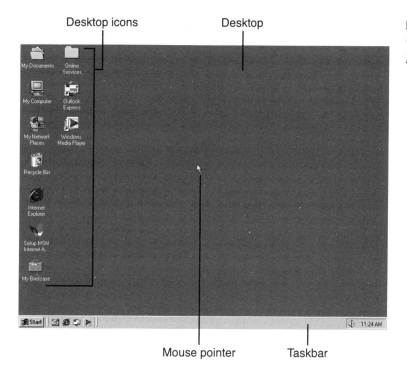

Desktop icons   Desktop

Mouse pointer   Taskbar

Figure 2.2

The Windows Millennium landscape.

The Desktop

The desktop is the vast blue expanse that takes up the bulk of the screen. Although the desktop is mostly empty right now, it's not entirely barren. The left side of the screen boasts a few little pictures, called *icons* in Windowspeak. These icons represent various features of Windows Millennium. In most cases, you open an icon by using your mouse to double-click it. (I explain this "double-clicking" business a bit later in this chapter.)

I discuss each of these icons as we progress through the book, so you don't need to worry about them just now. For the curious, however, Table 2.1 presents a quick synopsis of what each one represents (these are just the default icons in Windows Millennium; your mileage might vary).

Why the Heck Do They Call It *Desktop*?

That's just Microsoft indulging in a bit of metaphorical license. The idea is that just as you pull out real documents and work with them on the top of a real desk, in Windows you "pull out" electronic documents and work with them on the desktop.

Table 2.1   Windows Millennium's Desktop Icons

Desktop Icon	What It Does	More Info
My Documents	Represents a storage area (called a *folder*) that Windows Millennium sets up on your computer's hard disk. You use the My Documents area to store the various documents and files you create while working with Windows applications.	Chapter 5
My Computer	Opens the My Computer window.	Chapter 6
My Network Places	Gives you access to resources on your local area network. This friendly sounding icon appears only if your computer is part of a larger network of computers.	Chapter 25
Recycle Bin	Represents, literally, the Windows Millennium garbage can. When you delete files from your computer, Windows Millennium tosses them into this Recycle Bin.	Chapter 6
Internet Explorer	Launches the Internet Explorer Web browser.	Chapters 8 and 9
Setup MSN Internet Access	Sets you up with Microsoft's online service: MSN.	Chapter 7

Desktop Icon	What It Does	More Info
My Briefcase	A special storage area that makes it easy to move files between a desktop computer and a notebook computer.	Chapter 17
Online Services	Takes you to a collection of programs that you can use to set up accounts with some of the major online service providers.	Chapter 7
Outlook Express	Launches Outlook Express so that you can send and read email messages.	Chapter 10
Windows Media Player	Fires up the Windows Media Player program, which you use to play sounds, videos, and more.	Chapter 16
Connect to the Internet	Runs a wizard that helps you set up an Internet connection.	Chapter 7

The Taskbar

The gray strip along the bottom of the Windows Millennium screen is called the *taskbar*. In its basic guise, the taskbar sports four distinct features (pointed out in Figure 2.3).

Start button   Clock

Quick launch icons   System tray

Figure 2.3

The features of the taskbar.

➤ **Start button**   Believe it or not, this tiny chunk of screen real estate is one of the most important features of Windows Millennium. As its name implies, the Start button is your starting point for most of the Windows Millennium features and goodies. I discuss the Start button in depth in Chapter 3, "Making Your Programs Do What You Want Them to Do."

Cross Reference

"How to Start a Program," p. 32.

23

➤ **Quick Launch**   This area boasts a few more of those icon things. As with the desktop icons, these Quick Launch icons give you easy access to common features. Here's a summary of what each one does:

 This is the Show Desktop icon, and it hides any open programs, which gives you a pristine view of the desktop.

 This is the Launch Internet Explorer Browser icon, and it offers yet another way to start up Internet Explorer.

 This is the Launch Outlook Express icon, and it starts up Outlook Express, which is Windows 2000's Internet email program.

 This is the Windows Media Player icon, and it cranks up the Windows Media Player program for playing multimedia files.

Displaying the Date

The system tray's clock can also show you the date. To try it, move your mouse pointer until it sits over the time. After a second or two, the date miraculously appears. If you ever need to change the time or date, double-click the clock.

➤ **System tray**   Windows Millennium populates this area with even more icons. In this case, these icons tell you a bit about what's happening with your machine. For example, an icon that looks like a small, yellow speaker shows up if your computer has sound capabilities.

➤ **Clock**   The clock's purpose is obvious enough: It simply tells you the current time.

The rest of the taskbar is empty right now, but that will change soon enough. As you'll see in the next chapter when I show you how to start programs, Windows Millennium uses the taskbar to keep track of all your running programs. You can use the taskbar to switch between the programs, shut them down, and do other handy things.

Some Mouse and Keyboard Fundamentals

Okay, so Windows Millennium has icons up the wazoo. How do I get at 'em?

Ah, that's where your mouse and keyboard come in. You use them as "input devices" to give Windows Millennium its marching orders. The next few sections show you the basic mouse and keyboard techniques you need to do just that.

Basic Mouse Maneuvers

If you're unfamiliar with Windows, there's a good chance that you're also unfamiliar with the mouse, the electromechanical mammal attached to your machine. If so, this section presents a quick look at a few mouse moves, which is important because much of what you do in Windows will involve the mouse in some way. Don't worry, it won't bite, bogart your cheese, or scare the neighbor's kids.

For starters, be sure the mouse is sitting on its pad or on your desk with the cord facing away from you. Rest your hand lightly on the mouse with your index finger on (but not pressing down) the left button and your middle finger on the right button (or the rightmost button). Southpaws need to reverse the fingering.

Figure 2.2, displayed earlier, showed you the *mouse pointer*. Find the pointer on your screen and then slowly move the mouse on its pad. As you do this, notice that the pointer moves in the same direction (although it will stop dead in its tracks when it hits the edge of the screen). Take a few minutes to practice moving the pointer to and fro using slow, easy movements.

Slow and Steady Wins the Race

All this emphasis on slow and deliberate mouse movements isn't accidental and, in fact, should be the hallmark of *everything* you do with your computer. There's an old saw that says, "Never let a computer know you're in a hurry." That's good advice because, otherwise, some twisted new variant on Murphy's Law inevitably comes into play to ruin your day.

To new users, the mouse seems an unnatural device that confounds common sense and often reduces the strongest among us to tears of frustration. The secret to mastering the mouse is twofold. First, use the same advice as was given to the person who wanted to get to Carnegie Hall: practice, practice, practice. Fortunately, with Windows Millennium being so mouse-dependant, you'll get plenty of chances to perfect your skills.

Second, understand all the basic mouse moves that are required of the modern-day mouse user. There are a half-dozen in all:

➤ **Point**   Move the mouse pointer so that it's positioned over some specified part of the screen. For example, "point at the Start button" means move the mouse pointer over the taskbar's Start button.

➤ **Click**   Press and immediately release the left mouse button to initiate some kind of action. Need a fer instance? Okay, point at the Start button and then click it. Instantly, a menu sprouts up in response to the click. (This is Windows Millennium's Start menu. I'll discuss it in detail in the next chapter. For now, you can get rid of the menu by clicking an empty section of the desktop.)

25

➤ **Double-click** Press and release the left mouse button *twice*, one press right after the other (there should be little or no delay between each press). To give it a whirl, point at the time in the lower-right corner and then double-click. If all goes well, Windows Millennium will toss a box titled Date/Time Properties onto the desktop, as shown in Figure 2.4. You use this box to change the current date and time. To return this box whence it came, click the button labeled **Cancel**. If nothing happens when you double-click, try to click as quickly as you can, and try not to move the mouse while you're clicking.

Figure 2.4

Double-clicking the time tells Windows to fire up the Date/Time Properties dialog box.

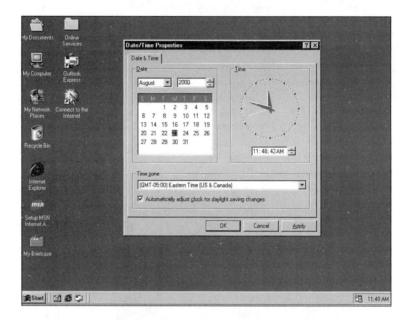

Click Confusion

Okay, so clicking initiates some kind of action, but so does double-clicking. What's the diff?

The whole single-click versus double-click conundrum is one of the most confusing and criticized traits in Windows, and I'm afraid there's no easy answer. Some things require just a click to get going, whereas other things require a double-click. With experience, you'll eventually come to know which clicking technique is needed.

➤ **Right-click** Press and immediately release the *right* mouse button. In Windows Millennium, the right-click is used almost exclusively to display a creature called the *shortcut menu*. To see one, right-click an empty part of the desktop. Windows Millennium displays a menu with a few common commands related to the desktop. To remove this menu, *left*-click the desktop.

➤ **Drag** Point at some object, press and *hold down* the left mouse button, move the mouse, and then release the button. You almost always use this technique to move an object from one place to another. For example, try dragging any of the desktop icons. (To restore apple-pie order to the desktop, right-click the desktop, click **Arrange Icons** in the shortcut menu, and then click **By Name**.)

➤ **Scroll** Turn the little wheel that's nestled in between the left and right mouse buttons. In programs that support scrolling, you can use this technique to move up and down within a document. The wheel is a relatively new innovation, so your mouse might not have one. If not, never fear, as Windows provides other ways to navigate a document. I tell you about those other ways in Chapter 4, "Your 20-Minute Window Workout."

Cross Reference

See "Window Weightlifting: Using Scrollbars," p. 57.

Common Keyboard Conveniences

I mentioned earlier that getting comfy with your mouse is crucial if you want to make your Windows Millennium life as easy as possible. That's not to say, however, that the keyboard never comes in handy as a timesaver. On the contrary, Windows Millennium is chock-full of keyboard shortcuts that are sometimes quicker than the standard mouse techniques. I tell you about these shortcuts as we go along. For now, let's run through some of the standard keyboard parts and see how they fit into the Windows way of doing things.

➤ **The Ctrl and Alt keys** If you press **Ctrl** (it's pronounced "control") or **Alt**, nothing much happens, but that's okay because nothing much is supposed to happen. You don't use these keys by themselves, but as part of *key combinations*. (The Shift key often gets into the act as well.) For example, hold down the **Ctrl** key with one hand, use your other hand to tap the **Esc** key, and then release **Ctrl**. Like magic, you see a menu of options sprout from the Start button. (To hide this menu again, press **Esc** by itself.)

Shortcut Shorthand

Windows Millennium has all kinds of keyboard combo shortcuts, so they pop up regularly throughout the book. Because I'm *way* too lazy to write out something like "Hold down the **Ctrl** key with one hand, use your other hand to tap the **Esc** key, and then release **Ctrl**" each time, however, I use the following short-hand notation instead: "Press *key1+key2*," where *key1* is the key you hold down and *key2* is the key you tap. In other words, instead of the previous long-winded sentence, I say this: "Press **Ctrl+Esc**." (On rare occasions, a third key joins the parade, so you might see something like "press **Ctrl+Alt+Delete**." In this case, you hold down the first two keys and then tap the third key.)

➤ **The Esc key**   Your keyboard's Esc (or Escape) key is your all-purpose get-me-the-heck-out-of-here key. For example, you just saw that you can get rid of the Start menu by pressing Esc. In many cases, if you do something in Windows Millennium that you didn't want to do, you can reverse your tracks with a quick tap (or maybe two or three) on Esc.

➤ **The numeric keypad**   On a standard keyboard layout, the numeric keypad is the separate collection of numbered keys on the right. The numeric keypad usually serves two functions, and you toggle between these functions by pressing the **Num Lock** key. (Most keyboards have a Num Lock indicator light that tells you when Num Lock is on.)

When Num Lock is on, you can use the numeric keypad to type numbers.

See "Getting It Right: Text Editing for Beginners," p. 67.

When Num Lock is off, the other symbols on the keys become active. For example, the 8 key's upward-pointing arrow becomes active, which means you can use it to move up within a program. Some keyboards (called *extended keyboards*) have a separate keypad for the insertion point movement keys, and you can keep Num Lock on all the time.

For more information about using the numeric keypad keys to move the cursor, head for Chapter 5, "Saving, Opening, Printing, and Other Document Lore."

Quittin' Time: Shutting Down Windows

When you've stood just about all you can stand of your computer for one day, it's time to close up shop. Please tape the following to your cat's forehead so that you never forget it: *Never, I repeat, never, turn off your computer's power while Windows Millennium is still running*. Doing so can lead to data loss, a trashed configuration, and accelerated hair loss that those new pills don't help.

Now that I've scared the daylights out of you, here are the steps to follow to properly shut down your computer:

1. Click the **Start** button to pop up the Windows Millennium Start menu.

2. Click the **Shut Down** option. Windows Millennium then displays a little box, as shown in Figure 2.5. (This is an example of a *dialog box*. I tell you all about dialog boxes in Chapter 3, "Making Your Programs Do What You Want Them to Do.")

Cross Reference

"Dealing with Dialog Boxes," p. 41.

Figure 2.5

When you shut down Windows Millennium, this dialog box shows up to ask whether you're sure you want to.

3. Use the **What do you want the computer to do?** list to select one of the following options (click the downward-pointing arrow to see the choices):

   ➤ **Shut Down**   Choose this option if you're going to turn off the computer's power.

   ➤ **Restart**   Choose this option if you want to start Windows Millennium all over again. For example, if you find that Windows is acting strangely, restarting can often put things right.

   ➤ **Hibernate**   Choose this option (which is only available on some computers) if you're going to shut down your computer, but you also want Windows Millennium to remember all your open windows and documents and restore them the next time you crank things up. If you go this route, it takes a bit longer for Windows Millennium to prepare itself for bed, but your machine will rouse from its slumbers much faster the next time you start it.

4. Click **OK**. Windows Millennium shuts down all its systems, which takes a few seconds.

5. If you chose the **Shut Down** option, wait until you see a message that says It is now safe to turn off your computer. If you chose the **Hibernate** option, wait until you hear a beep. When you do, switch off the power.

The Least You Need to Know

This chapter gave you a just-the-basics look at Windows Millennium. You took a tour of the Windows Millennium screen and saw sights such as the desktop, taskbar, Start button, and lots of inscrutable icons. From there, you found out a few mouse and keyboard basics, as well as how to shut down Windows Millennium. Here's a summary of what you now know:

Crib Notes

➤ **Screen anatomy**   The Windows Millennium screen is carved into two main areas: the *desktop*—the sea of blue that covers most of your monitor—and the *taskbar*—the gray strip along the bottom of the screen.

➤ **Desktop convenience**   The desktop's gang of icons provide you with double-clickable shortcuts to Windows Millennium features. For example, double-clicking the My Documents icon whisks you to the My Documents folder.

➤ **Taskbar features**   The taskbar consists of the Start button, the Quick Launch area, a space for program icons (see the next chapter), and the system tray.

➤ **Standard mouse dance steps**   The three most-used mouse movements are the *click* (quickly pressing and releasing the left mouse button), the *double-click* (two quick clicks), and the *drag* (holding down the left button and moving the mouse).

➤ **Keyboard shorthand**   A *key combination* involves holding down one key, pressing a second key, and then releasing the first key. I signify such a combo with the notation *First+Second* (where *First* is the key you hold down and *Second* is the key you tap). For example, **Ctrl+Esc**.

➤ **Shutting down Windows**   Click **Start**, click **Shut Down**, select the **Shut down** option, and then click **OK**.

G'WAN BOY!!

Chapter 3

Making Your Programs Do What You Want Them to Do

In This Chapter

➤ A couple ways to get a program off the ground

➤ Learning about pull-down menus, toolbars, and dialog boxes

➤ Getting the hang of the taskbar

➤ Techniques for switching between programs

➤ Shutting down a program

➤ A lot of useful tidbits for dealing with programs within Windows Millennium

The previous chapter's tour of the desktop had its moments, but it didn't exactly scream, "Productivity!" However, your computer is a digital domestic designed (at least in theory) to help you get your work done better and faster. (And, recognizing the all-work-and-no-play factor, your electronic lackey can also help you surf the Web and play games.)

The thing is, if you want to get your computer to do anything even remotely nonpaperweight-like, you need to launch and work with a program or three. For example, if you want to write a memo or a letter, you need to fire up a word processing program; if you want to draw pictures, you need to crank up a graphics program.

Fortunately, Windows Millennium comes with a decent collection of programs that enable you to perform most run-of-the-mill computing tasks. This chapter shows you how to get at those programs as well as how to mess with them after they're up and running.

How to Start a Program

In Chapter 2, "The Shallow End of the Pool: Some Windows Basics," I told you about the various icons that reside on the Windows Millennium desktop. You learned that most of those icons represent programs that come with Windows Millennium, and that you can start them by double-clicking the corresponding icon. However, those icons represent only a small subset of the programs that Windows Millennium has available. How do you get at the other ones?

Although it isn't the only method, the Start button is the most obvious point of attack; it is, in fact, your royal road to most of the Windows Millennium world. So, without further ado, let's head down that road. Use your mouse to point at the Start button and then click. As you can see in Figure 3.1, Windows Millennium responds by bringing up a list of options—called the Start menu—up the screen. (Note that the specific items displayed on the Start menu depend on how Windows Millennium is set up. Therefore, the items you see on your Start menu might be a bit different from the ones shown in Figure 3.1.)

Figure 3.1

The Start menu—your Windows Millennium launch pad.

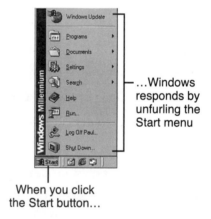

...Windows responds by unfurling the Start menu

When you click the Start button...

Maneuvering Around the Start Menu

To select one of the items shown on the Start menu, click it with your mouse. What happens next depends on which item you clicked:

➤ If the item represents a built-in Windows command or a program (such as Shut Down or Help), Windows Millennium launches the command or program without further ado.

➤ On the other hand, some of the Start menu items represent *submenus*. Specifically, these are the four items (Programs, Documents, Settings, and Search) with the little arrow on the right. Here's a bonus: You don't even need to click these items. When you move your pointer over the arrow, a new menu automatically slides out to the right of the Start menu (see Figure 3.2).

Other Ways to Uncover the Start Menu

Clicking the Start button is probably the most common way to get at the Start menu, but Windows Millennium also offers a couple of keyboard methods that you should have in your arsenal:

➤ Press **Ctrl+Esc**.

➤ If you have the Microsoft Natural Keyboard—the one with the alphanumeric keys split down the middle and the curvaceous, left-the-darn-thing-too-long-in-the-microwave-again look—press the key with the Windows logo on it (▓▓). Note, as well, that most recent keyboards sport the Windows logo key. In almost all cases, the key is located between the Ctrl and Alt keys.

When you click Programs...

Figure 3.2

The Start menu is loaded with all kinds of sub-menus.

...Windows yanks out this submenu

Don't be surprised if you find yourself wading through two or three of these sub-menus to get the program you want. For example, here are the steps you would follow to fire up WordPad, the Windows Millennium word processor:

1. Click the **Start** button to display the Start menu.
2. Click **Programs** to open the submenu.
3. Click **Accessories** to open yet another submenu.
4. Click **WordPad**. Windows Millennium launches the WordPad program.

Cross Reference

See ""From Word Amateur to Word Pro: Windows' Writing Programs," p. 219.

See "Launching a Program with the Run Command," p. 94

In the future, I abbreviate these long-winded Start menu procedures by using a comma (,) to separate each item you click, like so: "Select **Start, Programs, Accessories, WordPad**." Windows Millennium offers another way to launch programs: the Run command on the Start menu. I tell you all about it in Chapter 6, "Using My Computer to Fiddle with Files and Folders."

A Start Menu Summary

Table 3.1 provides a summary of each item on the main Start menu.

Table 3.1   The Standard Start Menu Items and What the Heck They Do

Start Menu Item	What It Does	More Info
Windows Update	Launches Internet Explorer and takes you to the Windows Update Web page.	Chapter 22
Programs	Displays a submenu that takes you to a collection of programs and Windows Millennium components. People upgrading from Windows 3.1 should note that their old Program Manager program groups appear on this submenu.	Throughout book
Documents	Opens a list of the last 15 documents you worked with in any of your applications. When you select a document from this folder, Windows automatically launches the appropriate program and loads the document.	Chapter 5
Settings	Displays a submenu with several options. For example, you use Control Panel to play around with various Windows Millennium settings; you use Printers to set up and work with a printer; and	Chapters 5, 19, and 26

Start Menu Item	What It Does	More Info
	you use Taskbar & Start Menu to customize—you guessed it—the taskbar and Start menu.	
Search	Contains tools that help you find things on your computer, the Internet, and the Windows Address Book.	Chapters 6 and 8
Help	Starts up the Windows Millennium Help system.	
Run	Enables you to run a program by typing its name and location.	Chapter 6
Log Off	Logs the current user off Windows or the network.	Chapter 25
Shut Down	Tells Windows Millennium that you've had enough for one day and want to return to the real world.	Chapter 2

Now You See 'Em, Now You Don't: Personalized Menus

After you've used Windows Millennium for a few days, you could get a "What the heck!?" moment when you see that several Start menu commands have up and disappeared on you. In their stead, you see only a mysterious double arrow, as shown in Figure 3.3. What the heck, indeed.

What's happened here is that you've run headlong into one of Windows Millennium new features: *personalized menus.* The idea behind them is that Windows Millennium sneakily keeps tabs on which items you choose in your daily Start menu travels. When it has gathered enough data (which usually takes several days), Windows reconfigures the various Start menus to show only those items that you used the most. So you end up with Start menus that are less cluttered, which is a good thing.

New Knickknack

Personalized Menus

This is a new feature in Windows Millennium.

Unfortunately, the other Start menu stuff is gone, which is a bad thing. Not to worry, though, because it just takes an extra step to get at those kidnapped Start menu commands: Click the double arrow that appears at the bottom of each menu. (If you're feeling particularly lazy, you don't have to click; instead, just hover the mouse pointer over the double-arrow.) If you're keyboard-bound, press the down-arrow key until you hit the double-arrow. Fortunately, it's easy to turn the personalized menus feature off if you don't like it (see Chapter 19).

Figure 3.3

After a few days, Windows stealthily hides unused menu commands.

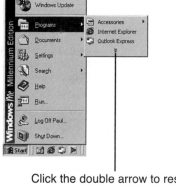

Click the double arrow to rescue the other Start menu items

Now What? Getting a Program to Do Something Useful

Okay, so I know how to get a program running. What's next?

Ah, now you get to go on a little personal power trip, because this section shows you how to boss around your programs. Specifically, you learn how to work with pull-down menus, toolbars, and dialog boxes.

Making It Go: Selecting Commands from Pull-Down Menus

See the "Toggling Some Start Menu Settings On and Off," p. 302.

Each program you work with has a set of commands and features that define the majority of what you can do with the program. Most of these commands and features are available via the program's *drop-down menus*. Oh sure, there are easier ways to tell a program what to do (I talk about some of them later in this chapter), but pull-down menus are special because they offer a complete road map for any program. This section gets you up to speed on this crucial Windows topic.

I'm going to use the My Computer program as an example for the next page or two. If you feel like following along, go ahead and launch the program by double-clicking the desktop's **My Computer** icon.

The first thing you need to know is that a program's pull-down menus are housed in the *menu bar*, the horizontal strip that runs just beneath the blue title bar. Figure 3.4 points out the menu bar in My Computer.

The various items that run across the menu bar (such as File, Edit, and View in My Computer) are the names of the menus. To see (that is, *pull down*) one of these menus, use either of the following techniques:

➤ Use your mouse to click the menu name. For example, click **View** to pull down the View menu.

➤ Hold down the **Alt** key and press the underlined letter in the menu name. In Windows Explorer, for example, the "V" in View is underlined, so you pull down this menu by pressing **Alt+V**.

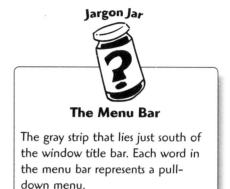

Jargon Jar

The Menu Bar

The gray strip that lies just south of the window title bar. Each word in the menu bar represents a pull-down menu.

When you click View
Menu bar   in the menu bar...

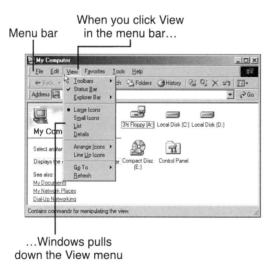

...Windows pulls
down the View menu

Figure 3.4
My Computer's View menu.

The various items you see in the menu are called *commands*. From here, you use any of the following techniques to select a command:

➤ Use your mouse to click the command you want.

➤ Use the up and down arrow keys to highlight the command, and then press **Enter**.

➤ Press the underlined letter in the command. For example, the "R" in the View menu's Refresh command is underlined, so you can select this command by pressing **R**. (Go ahead and try this example; you won't hurt anything.)

Throughout this book, I tell you to select a pull-down menu command by separating the menu name and command name with a comma (,) like this: "Select the **View, Refresh** command."

Bailing Out of a Menu

What do you do if you pull down a menu and then discover that you don't want to select any of its commands? You can remove the menu by clicking any empty part of the program's window, or you can pull down a different menu by clicking its name in the menu bar.

From the keyboard, you have two choices:

➤ To get rid of the menu, press **Alt** by itself.

➤ To pull down a different menu, press **Alt** plus the underlined letter of the new menu.

What happens next depends on which command you picked. Here's a summary of the various possibilities:

➤ **The command runs without further fuss**   This is the simplest scenario, and it just means that the program carries out the command, no questions asked. For example, clicking the Refresh command updates My Computer's display automatically.

➤ **Another menu appears**   As shown in Figure 3.5, if you click the View menu's Arrange Icons command, a new menu—called a *submenu* —appears on the right (similar to what you saw when learning to navigate the Start menu). You then click the command you want to execute from the new menu.

➤ **The command is toggled on or off**   Some commands operate like light switches: They toggle certain features of a program on and off. When the feature is on, a small check mark appears to the left of the command to let you know (see the Status Bar command in Figure 3.5). Selecting the command turns off the feature and removes the check mark. If you select the command again, the feature turns back on and the check mark reappears.

➤ **An option is activated**   Besides having features that you can toggle on and off, some programs have features that can assume three or four different states. (I call them the "Three or Four Faces of Eve" features.) My Computer, for example, gives you four ways to display the contents of your computer, according to your choice of one of the following View menu commands: Large Icons, Small Icons, List, and Details. Because these states are mutually exclusive (you can select only one at a time), you need some way of knowing which of the four commands is currently active. That's the job of the *option mark*: a small dot that appears to the left of the active command (see the Large Icons command in Figure 3.5).

➤ **A dialog box appears**   Dialog boxes are pesky little windows that show up whenever the program needs to ask you for more information. You learn more about them in the "Dealing with Dialog Boxes" section later in this chapter.

Select a command
that has an arrow...

The check mark
indicates an
activated feature

...and Windows
coughs up a
submenu

Figure 3.5

A few pull-down menu features.

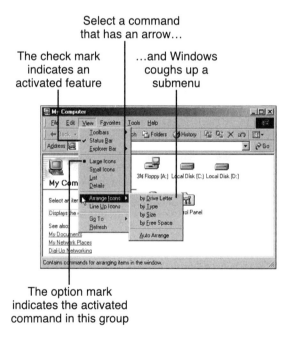

The option mark
indicates the activated
command in this group

Your Click Is My Command: Toolbar Basics

Pull-down menus are a handy way to access a program's commands and features. A click-click here, a click-click there, and you're off to the digital races. However, it probably won't take very long before you start resenting the few clicks you need to get at the menu commands you use most often. This has certainly happened to the world's programmers, because they keep inventing easier ways to make things happen in a program.

Shortcut Menus

Many Windows programs (and Windows Millennium itself) use *shortcut menus* to give you quick access to oft-used commands. The idea is that you right-click something and the program pops up a small menu of commands, each of which is somehow related to whatever you right-clicked. If you see the command you want, great: just click it (the left button this time). If you don't want to select a command from the menu, either left-click an empty part of the window or press **Esc**.

One of their most useful inventions has to be the *toolbar*. This is a collection of icons designed to give you push-button access to common commands and features. No unsightly key combinations to remember; no pull-down menu forests to get lost in.

Toolbars play a big role in Windows Millennium, and you can reap some big dividends if you get to know how they work. Although most Windows Millennium components have a toolbar or two as standard equipment, let's stick with My Computer. As you can see in Figure 3.6, the toolbar is the horizontal strip located just south of the menu bar. (Your toolbar may look a bit different than this one. I tell you how to make it look this way in just a sec.)

Figure 3.6

Like most Windows Millennium components, My Computer comes with a toolbar.

Toolbar

Click the arrow to display the "menu"

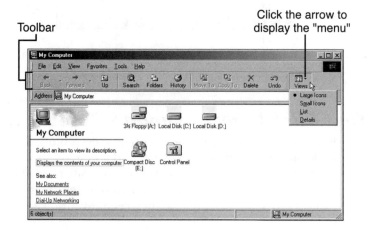

Most toolbar icons are buttons that represent commands you'd normally access by using the pull-down menus. All you have to do is click a button, and the program runs the command, no questions asked.

Here's a summary of a few other toolbar-related techniques you ought to know:

➤ **Toolbar text**   Most toolbar buttons advertise what they do using nothing more than an icon. Rather than trying to decipher the icon, some toolbars let you display text that at least gives you the name of each button. In My Computer, for example, select **View**, **Toolbars**, **Customize** to display the Customize Toolbar dialog box. Now use the **Text options** list to select **Show text labels**, and then click **Close**.

➤ **Button banners**   If the toolbar doesn't offer text labels, you can still find out the name of a particular button by pointing at it with your mouse. After a second or two, a banner (sometimes called a *ToolTip*) with the button name pops up.

➤ **Hiding and showing toolbars**   In most programs, you toggle a toolbar on and off by selecting the **View**, **Toolbar** command. If a program offers multiple toolbars (as does My Computer), select the **View**, **Toolbars** command to display a submenu of the available toolbars, and then select the one you want.

➤ **Drop-down buttons**   You'll occasionally come across toolbar buttons that are really drop-down menu wannabes. In My Computer, the View "button" is an example of the species. As shown in Figure 3.6, you click the downward-pointing arrow to see a list of commands.

Dealing with Dialog Boxes

I mentioned earlier that after you select some menu commands, the program might require more info from you. For example, if you run a Print command, the program might want to know how many copies of the document you want to print.

In these situations, the program sends an emissary to parley with you. These emissaries, called *dialog boxes*, are one of the most ubiquitous features in the Windows world. This section preps you for your dialog box conversations by showing you how to work with every type of dialog box control you're likely to encounter. (They're called *controls* because you use them to manipulate the different dialog box settings.) Before starting, it's important to keep in mind that most dialog boxes like to monopolize your attention. When one is on the screen, you usually can't do anything else in the program (such as select a pull-down menu). Deal with the dialog box first, and then you can move on to other things.

Conveniently, the WordPad program offers a wide variety of dialog boxes, so I use it for most of the examples in this section. If you're following along, launch the program by selecting **Start, Programs, Accessories, WordPad**. Begin by selecting WordPad's **View**, **Options** command to have the Options dialog box report for duty, as shown in Figure 3.7.

Figure 3.7

I use WordPad's Options dialog box for the first example.

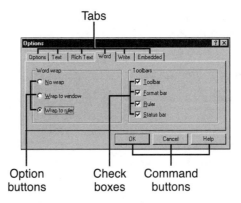

Tabs

Option buttons

Check boxes

Command buttons

Okay, let's get started:

➤ **Command buttons**   Clicking one of these buttons executes whatever command is written on the button. The three examples shown in the Options dialog box are the most common. You click **OK** to close the dialog box and put the settings into effect; you click **Cancel** to close the dialog box without doing anything; you click **Help** to open the program's Help system.

➤ **Check boxes**   Windows uses a check box to toggle program features on and off. Clicking the check box either adds a check mark (meaning the feature will get turned on when you click **OK**) or removes the check mark (meaning the feature will get turned off when you click **OK**).

➤ **Option buttons**   If a program feature offers three or four possibilities, the dialog box will offer an option button for each state, and only one button can be activated (that is, have a black dot inside its circle) at a time. You activate an option button by clicking it.

➤ **Tabs**   Click any of the tabs displayed across the top of some dialog boxes and you see a new set of controls. (At this point, you no longer need the Options dialog box, so click **Cancel** to shut it down.)

➤ **Text boxes**   You use these controls to type text data. To see some examples, select WordPad's **Format**, **Paragraph** command to get to the Paragraph dialog box, shown in Figure 3.8. The **Left**, **Right**, and **First line** controls are all text boxes. (The Paragraph dialog box has served its purpose, so click **Cancel**.)

➤ **List boxes**   These controls display a list of items; you select an item by clicking it. An example can be seen if you select WordPad's **Insert**, **Date and Time** command, shown in Figure 3.9. (After you've played around a bit, click **Cancel** to close this dialog box.)

➤ **Combo boxes**   These hybrid controls combine a list box and a text box. You can either select the item you want from the list or type it in the text box. In Figure 3.10, WordPad's Font dialog box shows several examples (select **Format**, **Font** to get there).

42

If you see highlighted text, it means this
text box is currently the active control

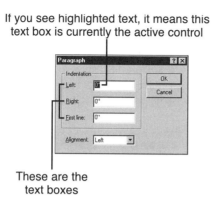

These are the
text boxes

Figure 3.8

*This shows some sample
text boxes.*

The highlight shows you
the currently selected item

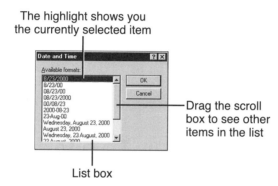

Drag the scroll
box to see other
items in the list

List box

Figure 3.9

*As its name implies, a list
box presents a list of
choices.*

Some combo boxes

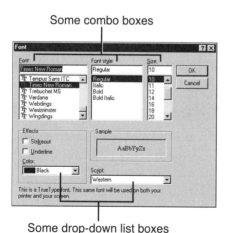

Some drop-down list boxes

Figure 3.10

*WordPad's Font dialog
box offers several exam-
ples of both combo boxes
and drop-down list boxes.*

➤ **Drop-down list boxes** These controls represent yet another example of the
list box genre. In this case, at first you see only one item. However, if you click
the downward-pointing arrow on the right, the full list appears and it becomes
much like a regular list box. (That's enough of the Font dialog box, so click
Cancel.)

➤ **Spin boxes**   These controls enable you to cycle up or down through a series of numbers. To see an example, select WordPad's **File**, **Print** command to wake up the Print dialog box, shown in Figure 3.11. The spin box is named **Number of copies**. The left part of the spin box is a simple text box into which you can type a number; however, the right part of the spin box has tiny up and down arrow buttons. You click the up arrow to increase the value, and you click the down arrow to decrease the value. (When you're finished, click **Cancel** to return the Print dialog box whence it came.)

Figure 3.11

Click the spin box arrows to cycle up or down through a range of values.

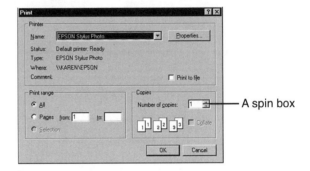

A spin box

Switching from One Program to Another

When you fire up a program, Windows Millennium marks the occasion by adding a button to the taskbar. If you then coax another program or two onto the screen (remember, Windows Millennium is capable of *multitasking*—running multiple programs simultaneously), each one gets its own taskbar button.

For example, Figure 3.12 shows Windows Millennium with two programs up and running: WordPad and Paint. (To run the latter, select **Start**, **Programs**, **Accessories, Paint**.) It looks as though Paint has lopped off a good portion of the WordPad window, but in reality Windows Millennium is just displaying Paint "on top" of WordPad. In addition, the taskbar has changed in two ways:

➤ There are now buttons for both WordPad and Paint in the taskbar.

➤ In the taskbar, the *active* program's button (the Paint button in this figure) looks as though it's been pressed. (The active program is the one you're currently slaving away in.)

The taskbar has another trick up its digital sleeve: You can switch from one running program to another by clicking the latter's taskbar button. For example, when I click the WordPad button, the WordPad window comes to the fore, as shown in Figure 3.13.

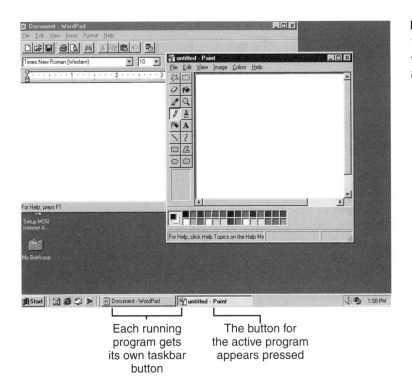

Figure 3.12

Windows Millennium with two programs on the go.

Each running program gets its own taskbar button

The button for the active program appears pressed

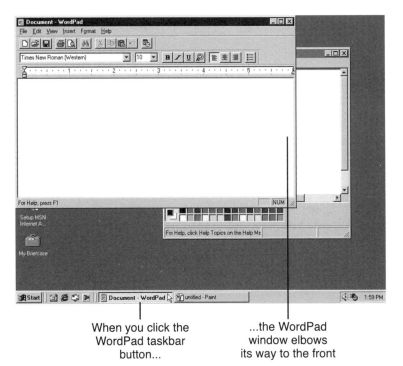

Figure 3.13

You can use the taskbar buttons to switch from one program to another.

When you click the WordPad taskbar button...

...the WordPad window elbows its way to the front

45

Multitasking Is Slick, But...

Although it's true that Windows Millennium is happy to deal with multiple run-ning programs—think of it as the electronic equivalent of walking and chewing gum at the same time—that doesn't mean you can just start every program you have and leave them running all day. The problem is that because each open program usurps a chunk of Windows' resources, the more programs you run, the slower each program performs, including Windows itself. The number of applica-tions you can fire up at any one time depends on how much horsepower your computer has. You probably need to play around a bit to see just how many applications you can launch before things get too slow.

When Enough's Enough: Quitting a Program

When you're finished with a particular program, you should close it to keep your screen uncluttered and to reduce the load on Windows' resources. The easiest way to do this is to click the Close button—the X in the upper-right corner of the program's window.

You can also use a few other methods, which you may find faster under certain cir-cumstances:

➤ Press **Alt+F4**.

➤ Pull down the program's **File** menu and select the **Exit** command (or, more rarely, the **Close** command).

➤ Right-click the program's taskbar button and then click Close in the little menu that appears.

See "The All-Important Save Command" on p. 63.

Depending on the program you're closing and the work you were doing with it, you might be asked whether you want to "save" some files. I tell you how to handle saving documents in Chapter 5, "Saving, Opening, Printing, and Other Document Lore."

Other Ways to Switch Programs

Besides clicking the taskbar buttons, Windows Millennium gives you three other ways to leap from one running program to another:

➤ **Click the program's window** This is perhaps the simplest and most obvious method. All you do is point the mouse inside the program's window and then click. This method is most useful if your hand is already on the mouse and you can see at least part of the window you want to activate.

➤ **Hold down Alt and tap Tab** When you do this, Windows Millennium displays a box that boasts an icon for each running program. Each time you press Tab, the next icon gets highlighted. After you highlight the icon for the program you want, release the Alt key; Windows Millennium then switches to the program. This technique is useful if your hands are on the keyboard and you have only a few programs running.

➤ **Hold down Alt and tap Esc** This method is similar to the Alt+Tab method in that Windows Millennium cycles through the open programs. The difference is that with each tap of the Esc key, Windows Millennium brings each program window to the fore. Use this method when you want to check out the contents of each window before you decide which program you want to work with.

The Least You Need to Know

This chapter showed you how to make Windows Millennium actually do something useful for a change. You learned how to start programs; how to boss around programs using their drop-down menus, toolbars, and dialog boxes; how to switch between running programs; and how to quit a program. Here's the Reader's Digest condensed version of what happened:

Crib Notes

➤ **Starting a program**   Click the **Start** button to display the Start menu, and then click the command or submenus required to launch the program.

➤ **Selecting a pull-down menu command**   First display the menu by clicking its name in the menu bar, and then click the command.

➤ **Dialog box command buttons**   Click **OK** to put dialog box settings into effect; click **Cancel** to bail out of a dialog box without doing anything; click **Help** to view the program's Help system.

➤ **Switching between running programs**   Click the taskbar buttons. Alternatively, click the program window if you can see a chunk of it or press **Alt+Tab**.

➤ **Quitting a program**   Click the **Close** (**X**) button. You can also usually get away with selecting the program's **File, Exit** command or pressing **Alt+F4**.

Your 20-Minute Window Workout

Windows gets its name because, as you saw in the previous chapter, each program that you launch shows up on the screen in a box, and that box is called a *window*. Why they named them "windows" instead of, say, "boxes" or "frames," I can't imagine. After all, have *you* ever seen a window on the top of a desk? I thought not.

Nincompoop nomenclature concerns aside, you're going to have to build up some window stamina because they'll come at you from the four corners of the screen. Fortunately, such stamina can be had without resorting to smelly sweats or Stairmasters. As you'll see in this chapter, all that's required is practicing a few handy mouse techniques.

See "Text Editing with Notepad" section, p. 221.

Warming Up: A Window Walkabout

Your average window is a kind of mini Nautilus machine brimming with various gadgets that you push and pull. The secret to a successful window workout is to get to know where these gadgets are and what you use them for. To that end, let's take a tour of a typical window, as shown in Figure 4.1. (This is a Notepad window. To get it onscreen, select **Start**, **Programs**, **Accessories**, **Notepad**.) To learn the ins and outs of the Notepad program, check out Chapter 14, "From Word Amateur to Word Pro: Windows' Writing Programs."

Figure 4.1

The Notepad window will be our "gym" for this chapter's exercise regimen.

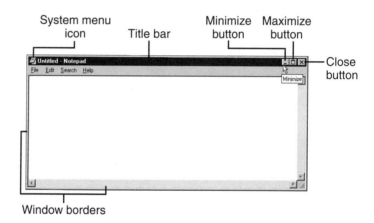

Here's a rundown of the various trinkets pointed out in Figure 4.1:

➤ **Title bar**   This is the blue band that forms the top portion of the window. As its name implies, the title bar's job is to tell you the name of the currently open document. (In Figure 4.1, the document is new, so it has the temporary—and decidedly uninspiring—name "Untitled." See Figure 4.7 for a better example.) The title bar also usually shows the name of the program (with a dash in between the two names).

➤ **Buttons, galore**   The right side of the title bar is populated with three buttons: Minimize, Maximize, and Close. I'll fill you in on what they do a bit later.

➤ **Borders**   Most windows are surrounded by four borders that you can manipulate with your mouse to change the size of the window (I show you how to do this later in this chapter).

➤ **System menu icon**   The system menu sports several commands that enable keyboard users to perform routine window maintenance. If you're dealing with a program window, you drop down the system menu by pressing **Alt+spacebar**; for a document window, the system menu sprouts in response to **Alt+- (hyphen)**.

Button Bedlam: The Tooltips Can Help

With all those buttons crowded into the upper-right corner of a window, it's tough keeping them straight. To help us out, Windows Millennium has a feature that tells you the name of each button. To check it out, move your mouse pointer over a button. A second or two later you see a little banner (known as a *tooltip*) with the button's name (as shown in Figure 4.1 by the word "Minimize").

Now just hold on a cotton-picking second. What's the diff between a "program window" and a "document window"?

Gee, you *are* paying attention, aren't you? Here you go:

➤ **Program window** This is the window in which the program as a whole appears.

➤ **Document window** This is a window that appears inside the program window and it contains a single, open document. This isn't something you have to worry about if you run only the programs that come with Windows Millennium, because they're only capable of opening one document at a time. However, lots of other programs—such as those that come with Microsoft Office—are capable of working with two or more documents at once. In this case, each document appears inside its own window.

Breaking a Sweat: Window Exercises

That's all well and good, Oh Nerdish One, but why bother with any of this? Why go through a window conditioning program when there are plenty of mouse potatoes in the world who seem to get their work done?

Good point. And, although I'm sure there are many competent folk whose window muscles have grown flabby through lack of use, there *are* advantages to making the effort. Let's see how the four main window techniques—minimizing, maximizing, moving, and sizing—can solve some niggling Windows problems and help you work better:

Look Out!

Moving Violation

You can't move or size a window if it's either maximized or minimized.

➤ **Problem #1   You have an open program that you know you won't need for a while. It's taking up desktop space, but you don't want to close it.** The solution is to *minimize* the program's window, which means that it's cleared off the desktop, but it remains open and appears only as a taskbar button.

➤ **Problem #2   You want the largest possible work area for a program.** The solution here is to *maximize* the program's window. This enlarges the window so that it fills the entire desktop area.

➤ **Problem #3   You have multiple programs on the go and their windows overlap each other so some data gets covered up.** The way to fix this is to *move* one or more of the windows so that they don't overlap (or so that they overlap less).

➤ **Problem #4   No matter how much you move your windows, they still overlap.** In this case, you need to resort to a more drastic measure: *sizing* the windows. For example, you can reduce the size of less important windows and increase the size of windows in which you do the most work.

The next few sections discuss these techniques and a few more, for good measure.

Minimizing a Window

When you click a window's Minimize button, the window disappears from view. The window isn't closed, however, because its taskbar button remains in place, as you can see in Figure 4.2.

Maximizing a Window

Clicking a window's Maximize button is a whole different kettle of window fish. In this case, the window grows until it fills the entire desktop, as you can see in Figure 4.3. Note that the Maximize button has, without warning, morphed into a new entity: the Restore button. I talk about this new creature in the next section.

Restoring a Window

In Windows parlance, *restoring* a window means you put the window back exactly the way it was before you minimized or maximized it. How you do this depends on what action you inflicted on the window:

➤ If you minimized the window, click its taskbar button.

➤ If you maximized the window, click the **Restore** button (pointed out in Figure 4.3).

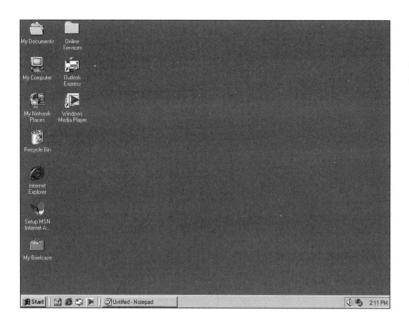

Figure 4.2

When you minimize a program's window, the program remains running, but all you see is its taskbar button.

Restore button

Figure 4.3

When you maximize a window, it takes over the entire desktop.

The taskbar remains
conveniently visible

Bigger Targets

The Minimize, Maximize, Restore, and Close buttons are tiny targets. Here are some techniques that can help:

➤ Minimize the current window by clicking its taskbar button.

➤ Maximize a window by double-clicking its title bar.

➤ Restore a maximized window by double-clicking its title bar.

➤ Close a window by double-clicking its system menu icon.

Moving a Window

Moving a window from one part of the desktop to another takes a simple mouse maneuver. Here are the steps to follow:

1. Make sure the window isn't maximized (or that it's not, duh, minimized).
2. Position the mouse pointer inside the window's title bar (but not over the system menu icon or any of the buttons on the right).
3. Press and hold down the left mouse button. You can now drag the title bar. As you drag, the window moves along with your mouse. (It may lag behind slightly if you have a slower system.)
4. When the window is in the position you want, release the mouse button.

Sizing a Window

If you want to change the size of a window instead, you need to plow through these steps:

1. Make sure the window isn't maximized or minimized.
2. Point the mouse at the window border you want to adjust. For example, if you want to expand the window toward the bottom of the screen, point the mouse at the bottom border. When you've positioned the pointer correctly, it becomes a two-headed arrow, as shown in Figure 4.4.
3. Drag the border to the position you want.

4. Release the mouse button to set the new border position.

5. Repeat steps 2–4 for any other borders you want to size.

Figure 4.4

You resize a window by dragging the window borders hither and yon.

At a window border, the mouse pointer
morphs into a two-headed arrow

Two-Sided Sizing

If you want to change both the height and width of a window, you can save yourself a bit of effort by sizing two sides in one fell swoop. To do this, move the mouse pointer over a window corner. (The pointer will change to a diagonal two-sided arrow.) When you drag the mouse, Windows Millennium sizes the two sides that create the corner.

Cascading and Tiling Windows

All these window calisthenics become a real aerobics session if you happen to have a lot of windows open on your desktop. However, if you're pressed for time, you may not want a full workout. In that case, you can take advantage of some Windows Millennium features that can save you a ton of time.

To get at these features, right-click an *empty* section of the taskbar. The shortcut menu that slides into view contains (among others) the following commands:

➤ **Cascade Windows**   This command automatically arranges all your nonminimized windows in a diagonal pattern that lets you see the title bar of each window. Figure 4.5 shows three cascaded windows.

55

Figure 4.5

The Cascade Windows command arranges your windows neatly in a diagonal pattern.

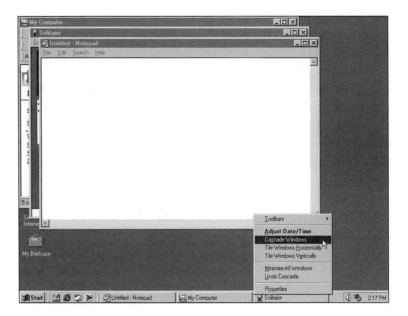

➤ **Tile Windows Horizontally**   This feature automatically arranges all your nonminimized windows into horizontal strips so that each of them gets an equal amount of desktop real estate without overlapping each other. Figure 4.6 shows the same three windows arranged horizontally.

Figure 4.6

The Tile Windows Horizontally command carves out equal-size horizontal desktop chunks for your windows.

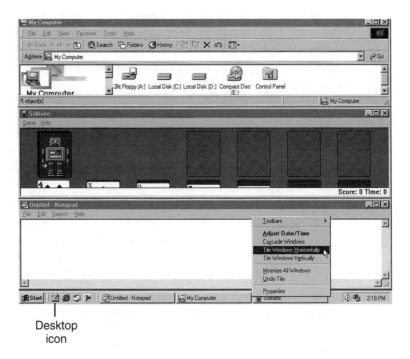

Desktop
icon

➤ **Tile Windows Vertically**   This command is similar to the Tile Windows Horizontally command, except that it arranges the windows into vertical strips.

➤ **Minimize All Windows**   This feature minimizes every open window in one shot. This is handy whenever you need to see what's on your desktop.

Easier Multiple Minimizing

The Minimize All Windows command is a handy way to clear the deck, but Windows Millennium offers an even easier way: Clicking the Show Desktop icon in the Quick Launch toolbar (pointed out in the taskbar in Figure 4.6).

Window Weightlifting: Using Scrollbars

Depending on the program you're using, you often find that the document you're dealing with won't fit entirely inside the window's boundaries, even when you maximize the window. When this happens, you need some way to move to the parts of the document you can't see.

From the keyboard, you can use the basic navigation keys (the arrow keys, Page Up, and Page Down). Mouse users, as usual, have all the fun. To navigate through a document, they get to learn a new skill: how to use scrollbars. The *scrollbar* is the narrow strip that runs along the right side of most windows. Using the Notepad window shown in Figure 4.7, I've pointed out the major features of the average scrollbar. Here's how to use these features to get around inside a document:

➤ The position of the scroll box gives you an idea of where you are in the document. For example, if the scroll box is about halfway down, you know you're somewhere near the middle of the document.

➤ To scroll down through the document one line at a time, click the down scroll arrow. To scroll continuously, press and hold down the left mouse button on the down scroll arrow.

➤ To scroll up through the document one line at a time, click the up scroll arrow. To scroll continuously, press and hold down the left mouse button on the up scroll arrow.

➤ To leap through the document one screen at a time, click inside the scrollbar between the scroll box and the scroll arrows. For example, to move down one screen, click inside the scrollbar between the scroll box and the down scroll arrow.

➤ To move to a specific part of the document, drag the scroll box up or down.

Figure 4.7

Mouse fans get to use the scrollbar to traipse through a document.

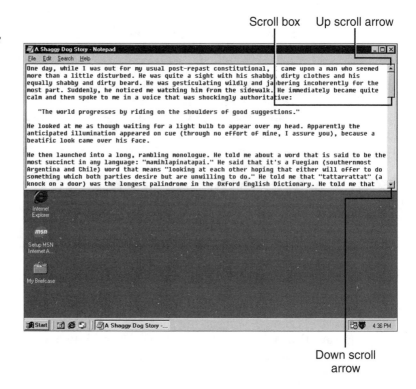

Scroll box   Up scroll arrow

Down scroll
arrow

Note, as well, that many of the windows you work in will also sport a second scrollbar that runs horizontally along the bottom of the window. Horizontal scrollbars work the same as their vertical cousins, except that they let you move left and right in wide documents.

Scrolling with the IntelliMouse

In early 1997, Microsoft introduced a radical new mouse design that incorporates a little wheel between the two buttons. If you're lucky enough to have one of these rotary rodents (or one of the knockoffs that some other mouse makers have put out), you can scroll up and down through a document by rotating the wheel forward or backward.

Some applications (such as Microsoft's Internet Explorer and the Office 97/Office 2000 programs) also support a feature called *panning* that lets you scroll automatically through a document and control the speed. To enable panning, click the wheel button. The application will then display an *origin mark* (the position of this mark varies from application to application). Drag the pointer above the origin mark to scroll up; drag the pointer below the origin mark to scroll down. Note also that the farther the pointer is from the origin mark, the faster you scroll. To turn off panning, click the wheel again.

The Least You Need to Know

This chapter led you through a workout with the windows that give Windows Millennium its name. I started by showing you the various odds and ends that comprise a window's anatomy. From there, you learned how to work with a window, including how to minimize, maximize, restore, move, and size a window. I also gave you the scoop on getting Windows to cascade and tile, and I closed by giving you a lesson on using scrollbars.

These window machinations will stand you in good stead as you work with documents in Chapter 5, "Saving, Opening, Printing, and Other Document Lore." But first, here's a fond look back at some of the highlights from this chapter:

Crib Notes

➤ **Minimizing a window**   This means that the window disappears from the desktop, although the program continues to run. You minimize a window by clicking the Minimize button in the upper-right corner.

➤ **Maximizing a window**   This means that the window expands to fill the entire desktop. You maximize a window by clicking the Maximize button in the upper-right corner.

➤ **Moving a window**   Use your mouse to drag the title bar to and fro.

➤ **Sizing a window**   Use your mouse to drag any of the window's borders.

➤ **Letting Windows do the work**   Right-click an empty part of the taskbar to eyeball several commands for cascading, tiling, and minimizing all windows.

Chapter 5

Saving, Opening, Printing, and Other Document Lore

In This Chapter

➤ Forging a fresh document

➤ Saving a document for posterity

➤ Closing a document and opening it again

➤ Handy document editing techniques

➤ Printing a document

➤ A blow-by-blow description of a dozen document deeds

Part I of this book is called "Getting Comfy with Windows Millennium," and if you've been following along and practicing what you've learned, you and Windows should be getting along famously by now. However, there's another concept you need to immerse yourself in before you're ready to fully explore the Windows universe: documents.

This chapter plugs that gap in your Windows education by teaching you all the basic techniques for manipulating documents. This will include creating, saving, closing, opening, editing, and printing documents, plus much more.

"What's Up, Doc(ument)?"

Hold on a sec, Pardner! What the heck is a document, anyway?

That's an insightful question because it's not at all obvious what a document is. When they think about it at all, most folks think a document is a word processing file. That's certainly true, as far as it goes, but I'm talking about a bigger picture in this chapter. Specifically, when I say "document," what I really mean is *any* file that you create by cajoling a program into doing something useful.

Jargon Jar

Document

A document is any file that you create (or can edit) yourself.

So, yes, a file created within the confines of a word processing program (such as Windows' WordPad) is a document. However, these are also documents: text notes you type into a text editor; images you draw in a graphics program; email missives you compose in an email program; spreadsheets you construct with a spreadsheet program; and presentations you cobble together with a presentation graphics program.

In other words, if you can create it or edit it yourself, it's a document.

Manufacturing a New Document

Lots of Windows programs—including WordPad, Notepad, and Paint—are courteous enough to offer up a new, ready-to-roll, document when you start the program. This means you can just dive right in to your typing or drawing or whatever.

Later on, however, you may need to start another new document. To do so, use one of the following techniques:

➤ Select the **File, New** command.

➤ Click the **New** button in the program's toolbar, pointed out in Figure 5.1. (This is the WordPad program. If you want to follow along, open WordPad by selecting **Start, Programs, Accessories, WordPad**.)

➤ In many Windows programs, you can spit out a new document by pressing **Ctrl+N**.

Figure 5.1

Most Windows programs offer toolbar buttons for easy access to document commands.

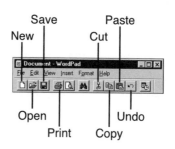

In most cases, the program will then toss a fresh document onscreen. Some programs (WordPad is one) display a dialog box that asks you what kind of new document you want.

Another Way to Craft New Documents

Windows Millennium also enables you to create a new, empty document without even opening the appropriate program. To accomplish this seemingly miraculous feat, run My Computer (discussed in the next chapter) and then open the folder in which you want to store the new document. Right-click an empty part of the folder, click **New** in the shortcut menu that appears, and then click the type of document you want. Type a name for the new document and press **Enter**.

At this point, the document you created is just an empty shell. To add stuff to the document, double-click the new icon you just created.

The All-Important Save Command

If this book were a multimedia product, this section would be festooned with flashing lights, warning signs, blinking arrows, and other "Hey, you! Listen up! This is important" indicators. With just plain old text at my disposal, I must resort instead to a simple message, italicized for emphasis:

Save your work as soon as you can and as often as you can.

Without even a jot of hyperbole, I'm telling you right here and now that this deceptively simple slogan is probably the single most important piece of advice that you'll stumble onto in this book.

Why all the fuss? Because when you work with a new document (or with an existing document), all the changes you make are stored temporarily in your computer's memory. The bad news is that memory is a fickle and transient medium that coughs up all its contents when you shut down Windows. If you haven't saved your document to your hard disk (which maintains its contents even when Windows isn't running and even if your computer is turned off), you lose all the changes you've made and it's impossible to get them back. Scary!

To guard against such a disaster, remember my "saving slogan" from before and keep the following in mind:

> ➤ When you create a new document, save it as soon as you've entered any data that's worth keeping.

> ➤ After the new document is saved, keep right on saving it as often as you can. When I'm writing a book, I typically save my work every 30 to 60 seconds!

More Reasons to Fret

If your computer's memory doesn't go into clean slate mode until you shut down Windows, you may be wondering why you can't just wait to save until you're ready to close up shop for the night. The reason is that you often don't get that chance. If a power failure shuts off your system, or if Windows crashes (and it *will* crash, believe me), all your unsaved work is toast. By saving constantly, you greatly lessen the chance of that happening (and of developing the ulcers and gray hairs that go along with it).

Saving a New Document

Saving a new document takes a bit of extra work, but after that's out of the way, subsequent saves require only a mouse click or two. To save a new document, use either of the following techniques:

> ➤ Select the **File, Save** command.

> ➤ Click the **Save** button in the program's toolbar (see Figure 5.1).

Most programs will display a Save As dialog box like the one shown in Figure 5.2.

Figure 5.2

The Save As dialog box appears when you're saving a new document.

From here, there's an easy road and a hard road you can take to get your document saved:

The easy road is when you see **My Documents** in the **Save in** list (as shown in Figure 5.2). As its name implies, My Documents is a built-in folder that Windows provides for storing your documents. If you want to use it (which I highly recommend), all you need to do is enter a name for the document in the **File name** text box, and then click **Save**. Note, however, that Windows places a few restrictions on filenames; see Step 3 in the steps that follow.

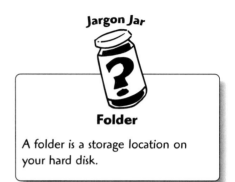

Jargon Jar

Folder

A folder is a storage location on your hard disk.

The hard road is when you want to use some other folder to store you document. Here are the steps you need to walk through to get your document safely stowed somewhere else:

1. The Save In drop-down list tells you the name of the current folder. To choose a different folder, first drop down the list and choose the disk drive that contains the folder you want to use to store the file.

2. The Save As dialog box then shows you a list of the folders on the selected disk drive. Double-click the folder you want to open. You may need to repeat this several times to get to the folder you want.

3. Use the **File name** text box to enter a name for your document. Note that the name you choose must be different from any other document in the folder. Also, Windows Millennium lets you enter filenames that are up to 255 characters long. Your names can include spaces, commas, and apostrophes, but not the following characters: \ , ? : * " < >

4. Now use the **Save as type** drop-down list to choose the type of document you want to create. In the vast majority of cases you won't have to bother with this because the default type is best. Many programs can create different document types, however, and this capability often comes in handy.

5. Click the **Save** button. The program makes a permanent copy of the document on your hard disk. (Confused about folders? Don't worry, I tell you all about them in Chapter 6, "Using My Computer to Fiddle with Files and Folders.")

Here are some notes about saving new documents:

➤ Happily, you won't have to go through the rigmarole of choosing a folder every time you save a new document. Most programs are smart enough to "remember" the most recent folder you worked with and will select it for you automatically the next time you're in the Save As dialog box. (Unfortunately, this only applies to the current session with the program. If you exit the program and then restart it, you have to reselect the folder.)

➤ If you want your new document to replace an existing document, open the folder that contains the document and then click the filename. The program will ask whether you want to replace the document, and you then click **Yes**.

➤ The rub with long filenames is that only programs written specifically for Windows 95, Windows 98, or Windows Millennium can take advantage of them. DOS programs and those meant to work with Windows 3.1 will scoff at your attempts to break through the old "8.3" filename barrier (eight characters for the filename and a three-character extension). What happens if you create a document with a long name, using a Windows Millennium program, and then try to open that document in an older program? Well, the document will probably open just fine, but you'll notice that the filename has been knocked down to size. You see, Windows Millennium actually keeps track of *two* names for each document: the long name and a shorter DOS-compatible name. The latter is just the first six characters of the long name (sans spaces), followed by a tilde (~), followed by a number. For example, a file named Fiscal 2001 - First Quarter Budget Spreadsheet would also use the DOS alias FISCAL~1.

Simpler Saves

If you're a fan of keyboard short-cuts, here's one to memorize for the ages: Press **Ctrl+S** to save your document. If you're a fan of toolbar buttons, click the **Save** toolbar button that you saw in Figure 5.1.

For more information about how to back up your documents, see Chapter 23, "Getting a Good Night's Sleep: Backing Up Your Precious Data," p. 361.

Saving an Existing Document

After all that hard work saving a new document, you'll be happy to know that subsequent saves are much easier. That's because when you select the **File**, **Save** command, the program simply updates the existing hard disk copy of the document. This takes just a second or two (usually) and no dialog box shows up to pester you for information. Because this is so easy, there's no excuse not to save your work regularly.

Taking Advantage of the My Documents Folder

I mentioned earlier that I highly recommend you use the prefab My Documents folder, which is designed to be a central storage area for all your documents. Using this folder is a good idea for three reasons:

➤ It makes your documents easy to find because they're all stored in one place.

➤ When you want to back up your documents, you need only select a single folder rather than hunting around your hard disk for all your documents.

➤ It's easy to get to: Just open the My Documents icon on the desktop. (You can also get there by selecting the My Documents folder within My Computer or Windows Explorer.)

Using the Save As Command to Make a Copy of a Document

As you slave away in Windows Millennium, you sometimes find that you need to create a second, slightly different, copy of a document. For example, you might create a letter and then decide that you need a second copy to send to someone else. Rather than create the entire letter from scratch, it's much easier to make a copy of the existing document and then change just the address and salutation.

The easiest way to go about this is to use the Save As command. This command is a lot like Save, except that it enables you to save the document with a new name or to a new location. (Think of it as the don't-reinvent-the-wheel command.) To use Save As to create a new document, follow these steps:

1. Open the original document (not a new one). (If you're not sure how to go about this, skip ahead to section titled, "Opening an Existing Document," to find out.)

2. Select the **File**, **Save As** command. The program displays the same Save As dialog box that you saw earlier.

3. Either select a different storage location for the new document or enter a different name (or both).

4. Click **Save**. The program closes the original document, makes a copy, and then opens the new document.

5. Make your changes to the new document (see the next section).

Getting It Right: Text Editing for Beginners

As you create your document, you have to delete text, move text chunks to different locations, and so on. To make your electronic writing life easier, it's crucial to get these basic editing chores down pat. To that end, here's a summary of some editing techniques you can use in most any program that deals with text (including Notepad, WordPad, and Outlook Express):

➤ **Highlighting text with the mouse** Before you can work with text, you need to *highlight* it. To highlight text with a mouse, simply drag the mouse over the characters you want. That is, you first position the mouse pointer ever so slightly to the left of the first character you want to highlight. Then you press and hold down the left mouse button and move the mouse to the right. As you do, the characters you pass over become highlighted. While you drag, you can also move the mouse down to highlight multiple lines. When you release the mouse button, the text remains highlighted.

Accidentally Deleting Highlighted Text Is Really Easy

If you highlight some text and then press a character on your keyboard, you'll be dismayed to see your entire selection disappear and be replaced by the character you typed! (If you press the Enter key, the highlighted text just disappears entirely.) This, unfortunately, is normal behavior that can cause trouble for even experienced document jockeys. To get your text back, immediately select the **Edit, Undo** command or press **Ctrl+Z**. (I talk a bit more about the life-saving Undo command a little later in this list.)

➤ **Highlighting text with the keyboard**   To highlight text by using the keyboard, position the cursor to the left of the first character, hold down the **Shift** key, and then press the right-arrow key until the entire selection is highlighted. Use the down-arrow key (or even Page Down if you have a lot of ground to cover) when you need to highlight multiple lines.

➤ **Copying highlighted text**   To make a copy of the highlighted text, select the **Edit, Copy** command. (Alternatively, you can also press **Ctrl+C** or click the **Copy** toolbar button, shown in Figure 5.1). Then position the cursor where you want to place the copy, and select the **Edit, Paste** command. (Your other choices are to press **Ctrl+V** or click the **Paste** toolbar button; again, see Figure 5.1). A perfect copy of your selection appears instantly.

➤ **Moving highlighted text**   When you need to move something from one part of a document to another, you *could* do it by making a copy, pasting it, and then going back to delete the original. If you do this, however, your colleagues will certainly make fun of you because there's an easier way. After you highlight what you want to move, select the **Edit, Cut** command (the shortcuts are pressing **Ctrl+X** or clicking the **Cut** toolbar button; see Figure 5.1). Your selection disappears from the screen, but don't panic; Windows Millennium saves it for you. Position the cursor where you want to place the text, and then select **Edit, Paste**. Your stuff miraculously reappears in the new location.

Where Does Cut and Copied Stuff Go?

All this cut, copy, and paste moonshine is a bit mysterious. Where does cut text (or whatever) go? How does Windows Millennium know what to paste? Does Windows Millennium have some kind of digital hip pocket that it uses to store and retrieve cut or copied data? Truth be told, that's not a bad analogy. This "hip pocket" is actually a chunk of your computer's memory called the Clipboard. Whenever you run the Cut or Copy command, Windows Millennium heads to the Clipboard, removes whatever currently resides there, and stores the cut or copied data. When you issue the Paste command, Windows Millennium grabs whatever is on the Clipboard and tosses it into your document.

➤ **Deleting text**   Because even the best typists make occasional typos, knowing how to delete is a necessary editing skill. Put away the Wite-Out, however, because deleting a character or two is easier (and less messy) if you use either of the following techniques:

> Position the cursor to the right of the offending character and press the **Backspace** key.

> Position the cursor to the left of the character and press the **Delete** key.

If you have a large chunk of material you want to expunge from the document, highlight it and press the **Delete** key or the **Backspace** key.

➤ **To Err Is Human, to Undo Divine**   What do you do if you paste text to the wrong spot or consign a vital piece of an irreplaceable document to deletion purgatory? Happily, Notepad, WordPad, and many other Windows Millennium programs have an Undo feature to get you out of these jams. To reverse your most recent action, select the **Edit, Undo** command to restore everything to the way it was before you made your blunder. (I've had some relationships where an Undo command would have come in *very* handy!) And, yes, there are shortcuts you can use: Try either pressing **Ctrl+Z** or clicking the **Undo** toolbar button (pointed out, as usual, in Figure 5.1).

Do Undo First!

It's important to remember that the Undo command usually only undoes your most recent action. So if you delete something, perform some other task, and then try to undo the deletion, chances are the program won't let you do it. Therefore, always try to run Undo immediately after making your error. Note, however, that some programs are more flexible and will let you undo several actions. In this case, you just keep selecting the Undo command until your document is back the way you want it.

Closing a Document

Some weakling Windows programs (such as WordPad and Paint) allow you to open only one document at a time. In such programs, you can close the document you're currently working on by starting a new document, by opening another document, or by quitting the program altogether.

Quicker Closing

In most programs that support multiple, open documents, you can close the current document by pressing **Ctrl+F4**.

Most full-featured Windows programs let you open as many documents as you want, however. In this case, each open document appears inside its own window—called a *document window*, not surprisingly. These document windows have their own versions of the Minimize, Maximize, Restore, and Close buttons. Also, the name of each document appears on the program's Window menu, which you can use to switch from one document to another.

Because things can get crowded pretty fast, though, you probably want to close any documents you don't need at the moment. To do this, activate the document you want to close and select the **File**, **Close** command, or click the document window's **Close** button. If you made changes to the document since last saving it, a dialog box appears asking whether you want to save those changes. Click **Yes** to save, **No** to discard the changes, or **Cancel** to leave the document open.

Opening an Existing Document

After you've saved a document or two, you often need to get one of them back onscreen to make changes or review your handiwork. To do that, you need to *open* the document by using any of the following techniques:

➤ **Use the Open dialog box**　Select the program's **File**, **Open** command. (Alternatively, press **Ctrl+O** or click the **Open** toolbar button as shown in Figure 5.1.) The Open dialog box that appears is similar to the Save As dialog box you messed with earlier. Find the document you want to open, highlight it, and then click **Open**.

➤ **Use the My Documents folder**　If you're using the My Documents folder to store your stuff, you can open a document by displaying My Documents and then double-clicking the document's icon. You can also highlight the document and then select **File**, **Open**. If the appropriate application isn't running, Windows Millennium will start it for you and load the document automatically.

➤ **Use My Computer or Windows Explorer**　You can also use My Computer or Windows Explorer (located under **Start**, **Programs**, **Accessories**) to open a document. Again, find the document you want and launch its icon.

➤ **Use the Documents menu**　This menu maintains a list of the last 15 documents you opened. To open one of these documents (and, of course, launch the program you used to create the document), select **Start**, **Documents**, and then click the document you want.

Sending a Document to the Printer

The nice thing about printing in Windows Millennium is that the basic steps you follow are more or less identical in each and every Windows program. After you learn the fundamentals, you can apply them to all your Windows applications. Okay, enough jawing. Here are the steps you need to follow: Before you can print, you may need to tell Windows Millennium what type of printer you have. I tell you how to go about this in Chapter 21, "Installing and Uninstalling Programs and Devices."

1. In your program, open the document you want to print.

2. Select the **File, Print** command. You see a Print dialog box similar to the one shown in Figure 5.3 for the WordPad word processor.

Cross Reference

See "Installing Specific Devices," p. 338.

Putting the Pedal to the Printing Metal

If your fingers are poised over your keyboard, you may find that in most applications pressing **Ctrl+P** is a faster way to get to the Print dialog box.

If you just want a single copy of the document, click the **Print** toolbar button (see Figure 5.1) to bypass the Print dialog box and print the document directly.

Figure 5.3

WordPad's Print dialog box is a typical example of the species.

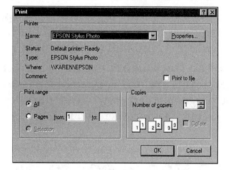

3. The options in the Print dialog box vary slightly from application to application, but you almost always see three things:

   ➤ A drop-down list for selecting the printer to use. In WordPad's Print dialog box, for example, use the **Name** drop-down list to select the printer.

   ➤ A text box or spin box to enter the number of copies you want. In the WordPad Print dialog box, use the **Number of copies** spin box.

   ➤ Some controls for selecting how much of the file to print. You normally have the option of printing the entire document or a specific range of pages. (WordPad's Print dialog box also includes a **Selection** option button that you can activate to print only the currently highlighted text.)

4. When you've chosen your options, click the **OK** button to start printing (some Print dialog boxes have a **Print** button, instead).

Keep watching the information area of the taskbar (the area to the left of the clock). After a few seconds (depending on the size of the document), a printer icon appears, as shown in Figure 5.4. This tells you that Windows Millennium is hard at work farming out the document to your printer. This icon disappears after the printer is finished with its job. If you have an exceptionally speedy printer, this icon may come and go without you ever laying eyes on it.

Printer icon

Figure 5.4

The printer icon tells you that Windows Millennium is printing.

The Least You Need to Know

This chapter showed you the power of the practical. You learned all kinds of handy techniques for creating, saving, editing, opening, printing, and closing documents. To help it all sink in, here a rehash of what just happened:

Crib Notes

➤ **Forging a new document**   Select the **File, New** command or press **Ctrl+N**.

➤ **Saving a document**   Select the **File, Save** command or press **Ctrl+S**. If you're saving a new document, use the Save As dialog box to pick out a location and a name for the document.

➤ **Make My Documents your own**   You'll simplify your life immeasurably if you store all your files in the My Documents folder.

➤ **Editing a document**   Press **Backspace** to delete the character to the left of the cursor; press **Delete** to wipe out the character to the right; press **Ctrl+Z** to undo your most recent mistake.

➤ **Shutting down a document**   Select the **File, Close** command or press **Ctrl+F4**.

➤ **Opening a document**   Select the **File, Open** command or press **Ctrl+O**.

➤ **Printing a document**   Select the **File, Print** command or press **Ctrl+P**.

Chapter 6

Using My Computer to Fiddle with Files and Folders

In This Chapter

➤ Navigating your system using My Computer

➤ Creating, selecting, copying, moving, renaming, and deleting files and folders

➤ Searching for long–lost files

➤ Understanding this Web integration business

➤ A fistful of useful file and folder factoids

In Chapter 5, "Saving, Opening, Printing, and Other Document Lore," you learned that it's off-the-scale crucial to save your documents as soon and as often as you can. That way, you preserve your documents within the stable confines of your computer's hard disk. You also learned that it's best to use your hard disk's My Documents folder as a central storage location for your documents.

You learned, in other words, that your hard disk is a vital chunk of digital real estate. So, as a responsible landowner, it's important for you to tend your plot and keep your grounds well maintained. That's the purpose of this chapter as it shows you how to use some of Windows Millennium's built-in tools to work with your hard disk's files and folders. You get the scoop on creating new folders, copying and moving files from one folder to another, renaming and deleting files and folders, and much more.

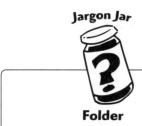
My, Oh, My: Learning About Your Computer Using My Computer

Windows Millennium has an annoying habit of appending the word "My" onto the front of things. On the desktop alone you can probably spy three or four of these exercises in self-absorption: My Documents, My Computer, My Network Places, and perhaps My Briefcase as well. This "My-opic" point of view is a bit cutesy, but it serves a more serious purpose: To remind you that what's truly important on your system is what you create yourself.

With that in mind, let's take a closer look at the main "My" machine: My Computer. From the name, you might be tempted to think it represents your entire computer caboodle. Well, that's close, but there's no cigar for you. My Computer really represents only the areas of your computer where files can be stored: your hard disk, your floppy disk, your CD-ROM or DVD-ROM drive, "removable" disks such as those that work with Zip or Jaz drives, folders on a network, and so on.

You can prove this for yourself by double-clicking the desktop's **My Computer** icon. You end up eyeballing a window that looks something like the one shown in Figure 6.1. (Your version of My Computer may look a bit different if your computer has a different configuration than mine.)

Figure 6.1

Double-click the My Computer icon on the desktop to check out your computer's goodies.

Name of current folder

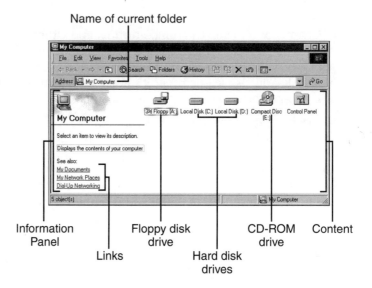

Information Panel

Links

Floppy disk drive

Hard disk drives

CD-ROM drive

Content

My Computer's job is to display the contents of a given folder so you can check out what's in the folder or muck about with those contents in some way (such as renaming one of your files). So the My Computer window is set up to help you do just that. After you get below the usual window suspects (the title bar, the menu bar, and the toolbar), the My Computer window boasts three sections to get excited about:

Address   This giant text box tells you the name of the current folder. You always see "My Computer" at first, but the text changes as you jump from folder to folder.

Jargon Jar

Folders Again

Although my earlier definition of a folder as a slice of a disk used for storage is accurate, you can see that Windows takes this idea of storage to great lengths. That is, in the Windows worldview, anything that can store anything is considered a folder. So even though My Computer isn't technically a slice of any disk, it's treated as a folder because it stores various icons.

Contents   The right side of the window displays the contents of the current folder. The My Computer folder stores your computer's disk drives, so that's mostly what you see in the contents area. (The Control Panel icon is used to customize and tweak various aspects of Windows Millennium; I'll talk about it throughout this book.) Under each icon, you see the type of disk (or, in some cases, the name of the disk), followed by the letter used by the disk drive. For example, Local Disk (C:) tells you the disk is a hard disk (don't ask me why on earth they use "local disk" instead of "hard disk") and that its drive letter is C.

Information panel   The left side of the window is used as an information area. For example, if you highlight drive C, the information panel shows you the capacity of the disk and how much free space you have left. This area is also usually sprinkled with *links*. A link is blue, underlined text that, when clicked, takes you to a specific folder. For example, clicking the **My Documents** link takes you to the My Documents folder.

To see the contents of a disk drive, double-click it. (If you plan to do this for a floppy drive, CD or DVD drive, or a removable disk drive, be sure you have a disk inside the drive or Windows Millennium will reprimand you with an error message.) For example, Figure 6.2 shows the contents of my drive C.

Figure 6.2

Opening a disk drive reveals the contents of that drive.

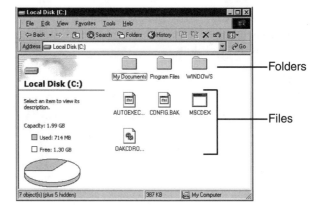

As you can see, this drive contains some files as well as a few folders (storage locations). To see what's inside one of these folders, just double-click its icon. For example, Figure 6.3 shows the contents of the Windows folder (which is where Windows Millennium stores most of its possessions).

Look Out!

An Extra Step for the Windows Folder

Microsoft would rest easier at night knowing the likes of you and I weren't poking around in its precious Windows folder. Therefore, when you first try to open the Windows folder, you see a warning message. The sky won't fall if you view the Windows folder, so go ahead and click the **View the entire contents of the folder** link. Note, however, that unless you're given specific instructions, under no circumstances should you play around with any of the files in the Windows folder.

File type   File stats   Subfolders

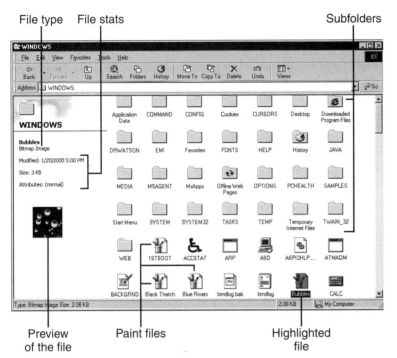

Figure 6.3
The Windows folder: more subfolders and more files.

Preview   Paint files   Highlighted
of the file   file

Icons, Icons, and More Icons

Every item you trip over in the My Computer window has both a name and an icon. You no doubt have noticed by now that there are all kinds of different icons. For example, most folders have a yellow icon that looks suspiciously like a file folder. Makes sense. Files are another kettle of icon fish, however, because they have all kinds of different icons. The reason is that each icon tells you what kind of file you're dealing with. For example, as shown in Figure 6.3, files that can be opened by Windows Millennium's Paint program have their own icon.

Note, in particular, that when you highlight a file, the information panel lights up with all kinds of data: the full name of the file; the type of file; and some stats about the file, such as when it was last modified and its size. For some files—particularly images—the information panel also shows a preview of the file.

Getting Around in My Computer

Here are a few pointers for navigating from folder to folder in My Computer:

➤ To go back to the previous folder, either click the **Back** button in the toolbar or select **View**, **Go To**, **Back**. (There's also a keyboard shortcut you can use: **Alt+Left Arrow**.)

Better Button Recognition

My Computer's toolbar is chock-full of one-click wonders, but it's sometimes difficult to tell which button does what. To help out, you can force My Computer to display the name of each button (see Figure 6.3). To do this, select **View**, **Toolbars**, **Customize** (or right-click the toolbar and then click **Customize**). In the Customize Toolbar dialog box, use the **Text Options** list to choose **Show text labels**, and then click **OK**.

➤ After you've gone back to a previous folder, you can move forward again either by clicking the **Forward** button or by selecting **View**, **Go To**, **Forward**. (The keyboard shortcut for this is **Alt+Right Arrow**.)

➤ Rather than stepping back and forward one folder at a time, you can leap over multiple folders in a single bound. To do this, click the downward-pointing arrow beside either the **Back** or **Forward** toolbar button. In the list that appears (see Figure 6.4), click the folder you want to visit. (You also can do this by selecting **View**, **Go To** and then choosing the folder from the list at the bottom of the menu.)

Figure 6.4

The Back and Forward buttons maintain lists of the places you've been.

Click this arrow to display this list

Click this arrow to display the Address list

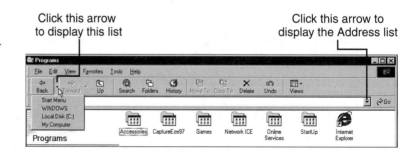

➤ The Address bar also does double-duty as a list. To see the list, click the downward-pointing arrow on the right side of the Address bar (or press **F4**). Note, too, that if you know the full name of the folder you want to see, you can type it in the Address bar and then click **Go** (or press **Enter**).

Folder Paths

When I say the "full name of the folder," what I really mean is what computer mavens call the folder's *path*. You can think of this as the path that you would take if you were travelling to the folder by first going to the hard disk, then to the main folder, then to the appropriate subfolder, and so on until you reach your destination. Here's how the geeks write such a path:

    drive:\folder

Here, *drive* is the letter of the disk drive (such as C) and *folder* is the name of the folder. For example, on most systems the folder that contains most of the Windows Millennium files is C:\Windows. For a subfolder, you add another backslash (\) and the folder name, such as C:\Windows\Media.

➤ If a folder has subfolders, the folder is called the *parent* and each subfolder is called a *child*. (Strange terms, I know. The irony is that they were probably made up by some geek who couldn't even get a date.) If you're viewing a child folder, you can go to its parent folder either by clicking the **Up** button in the toolbar or by selecting **View**, **Go To**, **Up One Level**. (Keyboard fans can press **Backspace**, instead.)

Taking Advantage of the Handy Folders List

The thing I dislike the most about My Computer is that it shows only one folder at a time, so you often end up "drilling down" through a series of subfolders to get where you want to go. Too slow! To speed things up, activate My Computer's Folders list either by clicking the Folders toolbar button or by selecting **View**, **Explorer Bar**, **Folders**. (To get rid of the Folders list, repeat the same procedure.)

As you can see in Figure 6.5, the result is a list of folders on the left side of the window. When you highlight a folder in this list, the folder's contents appear on the right side of the window. To view subfolders within the Folders list, use the following techniques:

➤ **To view subfolders**   Click the **plus sign** (+) beside the folder name. The plus sign changes to a minus sign (–).

➤ **To hide subfolders**   Click the **minus sign** (–) beside the folder name.

Figure 6.5

My Computer, modified to show the handy Folders list.

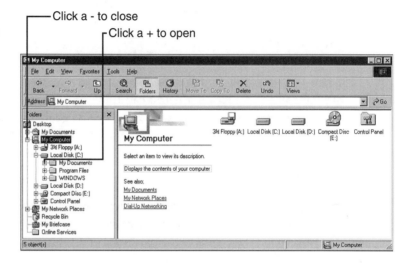

Workaday File and Folder Maintenance

Now that you and My Computer are getting along famously, it's time to put this digital domestic to good use. Specifically, I show you how to use My Computer to perform no fewer than five workaday chores for files and folders: creating, copying, moving, renaming, and deleting.

Creating a New File or Folder

If you want to manufacture a shiny new file for yourself, the best way to go about it is to run the appropriate application and select that program's **File**, **New** command. (Note, too, that most programs—including Windows Millennium's WordPad and Notepad accessories—create a new file for you automatically when you start them.) You then select the **File**, **Save** command to save the file to your hard disk.

However, it *is* possible to create a new file within My Computer. Here's how:

1. Open the folder in which you want to create the file. If you're not sure which folder to use, open the handy My Documents folder.

2. Select the **File**, **New** command. This displays another menu with a selection of file types, including Bitmap Image, WordPad Document, and Text Document.

3. Select the type of file you want. Windows Millennium creates the new file and displays a generic (read: boring) name—such as "New Text Document"—in a text box.

4. Edit the name and then press **Enter** or click some of the blank real estate inside the window. If you had any problems entering the name (such as a spelling error), just hold tight and I'll teach you how to change the filename later in this chapter.

To create a new folder, follow the preceding steps, but when you get to step 3, select the item named **Folder** in the menu.

My Computer + Folders List = Windows Explorer

When you combine My Computer with the Folders list, the resulting window is exactly the same as the one you see when you launch another Windows Millennium program: Windows Explorer. You fire up the latter by selecting **Start, Programs, Accessories, Windows Explorer**.

Don't Mess with the Rest

Three of these chores—moving, renaming, and deleting—ought to have a "For Your Stuff Only" label on them. That's because you should only use these techniques on files or folders that you create yourself. Otherwise, Windows Millennium or one of your programs might blow a gasket and refuse to run. See the next section to learn how to create your own files or folders.

Selecting Files and Folders

Before getting to the rest of the file-maintenance fun, you need to know how to select the files or folders that you want to horse around with.

Let's begin with the simplest case: selecting a single file or folder. How you do this depends on whether you're using Windows Millennium's Web integration feature (see "My Computer and Web Integration," later in this chapter). How do you know if

Web integration is on or off? The easiest way is to look at the file and folder names. If they're underlined, Web integration is on; otherwise, it's off.

Here's how you select a file or folder:

➤ If Web integration isn't turned on, click the file or folder you want to work with.

➤ If Web integration is on the job, you select a file or folder just by pointing at it with your mouse.

So far, so good. However, there will be plenty of times when you need to deal with two or more files or folders. For example, you might want to herd several files onto a floppy disk. Rather than doing this one item at a time, you can do the whole thing in one fell swoop by first selecting all the items and then moving (or copying, or whatever) them as a group. Windows Millennium offers the following methods:

Selecting the Whole Shebang

If you want to select everything inside a folder, choose the **Edit**, **Select All** command.

➤ **Selecting consecutive items** If the files or folders you want to select are listed consecutively, say "Ooh, how convenient!" and then do this: Select the first item, hold down the **Shift** key, select the last item, and then release **Shift**. Windows Millennium kindly does the dirty work of selecting all the items in between.

➤ **"Lassoing" items** Rather than trying to coordinate the mouse with one hand and the Shift key with the other, Windows Millennium offers a mouse-only technique in which you "lasso" a group of files or folders. To try it, first move the mouse pointer just to the left of the first item. Now hold down the left mouse button and then move the pointer down and to the right. As you do this, a box appears, and every item touched by the box gets selected (see Figure 6.6). When you've selected everything you need, release the mouse button.

➤ **Selecting nonconsecutive items** If the files or folders you want to select are listed willy-nilly, say "Oy!" and then do this: Select the first item, hold down the **Ctrl** key, select each of the other items, and then release **Ctrl**.

Begin dragging to the
left of the first item...

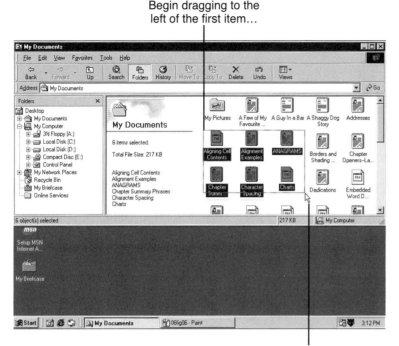

Figure 6.6
*Yee haw! The "lasso"
technique offers a mouse-
only method for selecting
consecutive files or folders.*

...then drag down and right

*Windows
Wisdom*

Lassoing Depends on the View

This lassoing technique works if My Computer is in Large Icons view (select **View**, **Large Icons**). However, if you're in Small Icons, List, or Details view, My Computer uses a slightly different lassoing technique (just to keep us all thoroughly confused, I guess). In this case, you have to start to the *right* of the first item, and then drag the mouse down and to the *left*.

Copying and Moving a File or Folder

A copy of a file or folder is an exact replica of the original that you store on another part of your hard disk or on a removable disk (such as a floppy disk). Copies are useful for making backups or if you want to transport a file or folder to another computer.

Note, too, that the location of the files and folders you create isn't set in stone. If you're not happy with the current location, there's no problem moving a file or folder somewhere else.

Windows Millennium offers two basic methods for copying and moving files and folders: the Copy to Folder and Move to Folder commands, and the "drag-and-drop" mouse technique.

Copy To Folder and Move To Folder

These two commands are new additions to the Windows Millennium family of features.

To use the Copy To Folder or Move To Folder command, follow these steps:

1. Select the files or folders you want to transport.

2. Pull down the **Edit** menu and choose one of the following commands:

   Copy To Folder   This is the command to choose if you're copying files or folders. Alternatively, click the **Copy To** toolbar button.

   Move To Folder   This is the command to choose if you're moving files or folders. Another route you can take is to click the **Move To** toolbar button.

3. Either way, you end up with a version of the Browse For Folder dialog box onscreen. Use the folder "tree" to locate and select the destination folder or disk drive.

4. Click **OK**.

Using the Send To Menu to Copy Quickly

Windows Millennium has a special Send To menu that contains commonly used destinations, such as your floppy disk or your My Documents folder. To see this menu, either select **File, Send To** or right-click an item and then click **Send To**. Now select the destination you want and Windows Millennium copies the selected items lickety-split.

Mouse fans will enjoy the alternative drag-and-drop method:

1. Use the contents list to select the files or folders you want to copy or move.

2. Move the mouse pointer over any selected item and hold down the right mouse button (yes, you read that correctly: the *right* mouse button).

3. With the button held down for dear life, move the mouse pointer toward the destination folder in the Folders list (this is the "dragging" part).

4. Position the mouse pointer over the destination folder (wait until you see it highlighted) and then release the mouse button (this is the "dropping" part). Windows Millennium displays the shortcut menu shown in Figure 6.7.

Figure 6.7

When you right-drag a file or folder and then drop it, Windows Millennium offers a shortcut menu.

5. Click **Copy Here** or **Move Here**, as appropriate.

Renaming a File or Folder

Windows Millennium supports file and folder names up to about 255 characters long, so you don't have to settle for boring monikers on the files and folders you create. If you don't like a name, feel free to rename it.

Follow these simple steps to rename a mismonikered file or folder:

1. Select the file or folder you want to rename. (You can work with only one item at a time for this.)

2. Run the **File**, **Rename** command (or press **F2**). Windows Millennium creates a text box around the name.

3. Edit the name as you see fit.

4. When you're done, press **Enter**.

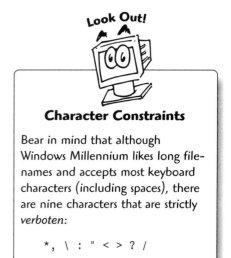

Look Out!

Character Constraints

Bear in mind that although Windows Millennium likes long file-names and accepts most keyboard characters (including spaces), there are nine characters that are strictly *verboten*:

*, \ : " < > ? /

Bring the Destination Folder into View

To get the most out of this drag-and-drop method, you need to first set up the My Computer window so your destination folder is visible in the Folders list. If you're in mid-drag and realize you forgot to do this, here are two tips that can help:

➤ If you need to scroll the Folders list down, drag the mouse and highlight the bottom item in the Folders list; similarly, you can scroll the list up by dragging the mouse so that it highlights the top item in the list.

➤ If the destination is a subfolder in an unopened folder, drag the mouse into the Folders list and place it over the folder. After a few seconds, Windows kindly opens the folder.

Deleting a File or Folder

Although most of today's hard disks boast a mammoth amount of real estate, you could still run out of room one day if you don't delete the debris you no longer use.

Drag to the Recycle Bin

Another way to delete a file or folder is to drag it from My Computer and drop it on the desktop's Recycle Bin icon.

Deleting unwanted files and folders is fairly easy:

1. Select the files or folders you want to blow away.

2. Run the **File**, **Delete** command, or click the **Delete** toolbar button (or just press **Delete**). Windows Millennium asks whether you're sure you want to consign these poor things to the cold, cruel Recycle Bin.

3. Say, "But of course, my good fellow!" and click **Yes**.

What happens if you nuke some crucial file or folder that you'd give your right arm to have back? Assuming you need your right arm, Windows Millennium offers an alternative method to save your bacon: the Recycle Bin.

You should know, first off, that if the deletion was the last thing you did, you don't have to bother with the Recycle Bin. Just pull down the **Edit** menu and select the **Undo Delete** command to salvage the file. In fact, Windows Millennium is only too happy to let you reverse the last *ten* actions you performed. Again, you pull down the **Edit** menu and select the **Undo *Whatever*** command (where *Whatever* is the name of the command, such as Delete).

Otherwise, you have to trudge through these steps:

Jargon Jar

Recycle Bin

This is the place where Windows Millennium stores deleted files. If you trash a file accidentally, you can use the Recycle Bin to recover it.

1. Open the desktop's **Recycle Bin** icon. The folder that appears contains a list of all the stuff you've expunged recently.

2. Select the files or folders you want to recover.

3. Select the **File**, **Restore** command (or click the **Restore** button in the information panel). Windows Millennium marches the items right back to where they came from. Whew!

Windows Wisdom

The Inner Mysteries of the Recycle Bin

Holy Lazarus! How the heck can the Recycle Bin restore a deleted file?

Good question. You can get part of the answer by looking at the Recycle Bin icon on your Windows Millennium desktop (or the icon of the Recycle Bin folder in Windows Explorer). It looks like a garbage can, and that's sort of what the Recycle Bin is. Think about it: If you toss a piece of paper in the garbage, there's nothing to stop you from reaching in and pulling it back out. The Recycle Bin operates the same way: It's really just a special hidden folder (called Recycled) on your hard disk. When you delete a file, Windows Millennium actually moves the file into the Recycled folder. So restoring a file is a simple matter of "reaching into" the folder and "pulling out" the file. The Recycle Bin handles all this for you (and even returns your file *sans* wrinkles and coffee grounds). However, just like when you hand your trash out to the garbage man, after you empty the Recycle Bin (covered later) there is no retrieving the lost files.

For more information about the Open and Save As dialog boxes, refer to Chapter 5, "Saving, Opening, Printing, and Other Document Lore," p. 61.

Dialog Box-Based File and Folder Maintenance

Often when you're working in an application, you'll need to perform one or two quick file-maintenance jobs (such as renaming or deleting a file or creating a new folder). It's overkill, however, to have to crank up My Computer, find the folder you want, select the file, and then run the necessary commands. Fortunately, Windows Millennium gives you a more convenient way to handle these kinds of quickie tasks.

In most modern programs, you can handle a good chunk of your file labors in the program's Open and Save As dialog boxes. All you do is open either dialog box, find the file you want to work with, and then right-click it. As you can see in Figure 6.8, the shortcut menu that appears sports all kinds of file-related commands, including Send To, Cut, Copy, Delete, and Rename. Note, too, that both dialog boxes have a Create New Folder button that enables you to pound out a new folder on-the-fly (see Figure 6.8).

Figure 6.8

In the Open or Save As dialog boxes, right-click a file to get a handy menu of file-maintenance commands.

Create New Folder button

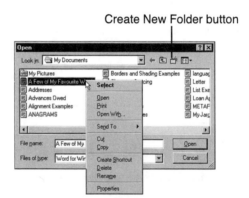

Finding a File in that Mess You Call a Hard Disk

Bill Gates, Microsoft's Big Cheese, used to summarize his company's mission of easy access to data as "information at your fingertips." We're still a long way off from that laudable goal, but there are a few things you can do to ensure that the info you need is never far away:

➤ **Use the My Documents folder** The most inefficient way to store your documents is to scatter them hither and yon around your hard disk. A much better approach is to plop everything in a single place so you always know where to look for things. The perfect place for this is the My Documents folder that Windows Millennium provides for you.

➤ **Use subfolders to organize your documents** Using My Documents is a good idea (if I do say so myself), but you shouldn't just cram all your stuff into that one folder. Instead, create subfolders to hold related items. Windows Millennium starts you off with a My Pictures subfolder, which is the ideal place for your graphics files. Feel free to add other subfolders for things such as letters, memos, projects, presentations, spreadsheets, and whatever other categories

Cross Reference

See "Checking Out the New My Pictures Folder," p. 247.

you can think of. The My Pictures folder has a few interesting properties that help you deal with graphics files. I tell you about them in Chapter 15, "Image Is Everything: Windows Millennium's Graphics Tools."

➤ **Give your files meaningful names** Take advantage of Windows Millennium's long filenames to give your documents useful names that tell you exactly what's inside each file. A document named "Letter" doesn't tell you much, but "Letter to A. Gore Re: Inventing the Internet" surely does.

➤ **Dejunk your folders** Keep your folders clean by deleting any junk files that you'll never use again.

If you're like most people, you'll probably end up with hundreds of documents, but if you follow these suggestions, finding the one you need shouldn't be a problem. Even so, there will be times when you don't remember exactly which document you need, or you might want to find all those documents that contain a particular word or phrase. For these situations, Windows Millennium offers a new Search feature that can help you track down what you need.

New Knickknack

Search Bar

Although Windows has long had the capability to find files, the Search bar is a new feature in Windows Millennium.

To get started, you have two choices:

➤ To search within the current folder in My Computer, either select the **View**, **Explorer Bar**, **Search** command, or click the **Search** toolbar button. (Pressing **Ctrl+E** also works.)

➤ To search all of My Computer (that is, all your disk drives), select **Start**, **Search**, **For Files or Folders**.

Figure 6.9 shows the window that appears if you use the former technique.

Figure 6.9

Windows Millennium's new search feature helps you find AWOL files.

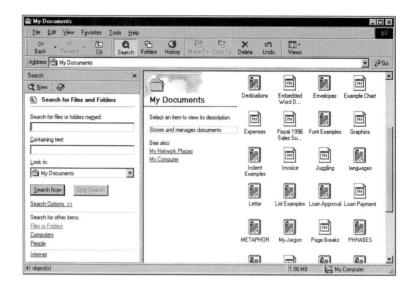

Let's see what happens from here:

1. Use the **Search for files or folders named** box to search for a file by name. Note that you don't have to enter the entire name of the file; just a word or even a few letters will do.

2. Use the **Containing text** box to search for a file by content. Enter a word or part of a word that the desired file contains.

3. Use the **Look in** list to select the folder or disk drive in which you want to search (if the displayed folder isn't the one you want).

4. Search also provides the following options that might occasionally come in handy. Click the **Search Options** link to see the following check boxes:

   Date   If you activate this check box, Search displays some extra controls that enable you to specify a date range for the file you want to find.

   Type   If you activate this check box, Search displays a drop-down list from which you can select the type of file you want to find (such as a Text Document).

   Size   If you activate this check box, Search provides a couple of controls that enable you to locate a file according to its size in kilobytes.

   Advanced Options   If you activate this check box, you get two more check boxes for your searching pleasure. Activating the **Search Subfolders** check box tells Search to examine not only the folder shown in the **Look in** list, but also all of its subfolders; activating the **Case sensitive** check box tells Search to match the exact uppercase and lowercase letters you use in the **Containing text** box.

5. When you're ready to roll, click the **Search Now** button. Search scours your machine and then uses the right side of the window to display the Search Results: the list of files that match your criteria. (If the file you want comes up right away, click **Stop Search** to tell Search to hold its horses.)

My Computer and Web Integration

The purpose of Windows Millennium's Web integration feature—theoretically, at least—is to make your computer easier to use by incorporating certain features from the Internet's World Wide Web. For our purposes in this chapter, Web integration affects three things:

➤ **How you view folders**   As you've seen, Windows Millennium's folders appear with an information panel on the left, and that panel contains images, text, and even links to other folders. In other words, the folder acts more or less like a Web page.

➤ **How you launch files and icons**   You normally launch something (such as a document or a desktop icon) by double-clicking it. Web integration changes that, so you launch files and icons by single-clicking them.

➤ **How you select a file or folder**   As you saw earlier, selecting a file or folder using Web integration involves just hovering the mouse pointer over the item.

Happily, you can toggle these Web-integration features on and off. To do this, select My Computer's **Tools**, **Folder Options** command to display the Folder Options dialog box. The General tab, shown in Figure 6.10, offers these Web-integration settings:

Enable Web content in folders   Activate this option to get the information panel when you view a folder.

Use Windows classic folders   Activate this option to do away with the information panel.

Single-click to open an item (point to select)   Activate this option to crank up the single-click launching and no-click selecting features. If you do this, the following option buttons arise from their slumbers:

➤ **Underline icon titles consistent with my browser**   Activate this option to tell Windows Millennium to underline all the filenames and icon titles using the same style as defined within Internet Explorer. This usually means that file and folder names and icon titles appear in blue, underlined text. This is a good idea because it gives you a visual reminder that Web integration is on.

➤ **Underline icon titles only when I point at them**   Activate this option to have Windows Millennium underline filenames and icon titles only when you point at them. This is a bit tidier-looking than having everything underlined.

Double-click to open an item (single-click to select) Activate this option to use the old-fashioned mouse techniques for launching and selecting stuff.

Figure 6.10

Use the General tab to set various Web-integration options.

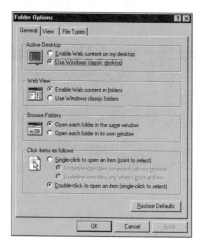

Launching a Program with the Run Command

Now that you're well versed in the arcane arts of files and folders, let's put all that to good use. This section shows you how to use Windows Millennium's Run command, which offers an alternative to the Start menu for launching programs.

Cross Reference

My Computer is loaded with options and settings that you can use to customize it to suit the way you work. I tell you all about them in Chapter 20, "Renovating My Computer," p. 309.

See the "Adding Stuff to the Start Menu sections," p. 304 and 306.

In rare cases, the program you want to run might not appear on any of the Start menus. This is particularly true of older DOS programs that don't do Windows. For the time being, you can use the Run command to get these old geezer programs under way. In Chapter 19, "Remodeling the Start Menu and Taskbar," I show you how to add your own Start menu commands for launching such programs.

This isn't for the faint of heart, however, because it requires a bit more work, as the following steps show:

1. Select **Start**, **Run**. Windows Millennium displays the Run dialog box.

2. In the **Open** text box, type the name of the disk drive where the program resides (for example, **d:**), its folder (such as **\install**), and then the name of the file that starts the program (for example, **setup.exe**). With these examples used, you'd enter **d:\install\setup.exe**.

3. Click **OK** to run the program.

Whew! Compared to the Start menu, that's true, calluses-on-the-fingertips manual labor. Bear these points in mind when you're working with the Run dialog box:

➤ Instead of typing the command, you can click the **Browse** button and choose the program from the Browse dialog box that appears.

➤ If any part of the filename or folder name contains spaces or is longer than eight characters, you have to surround the whole thing with quotation marks. If you're not sure about this, go ahead and add the quotation marks anyway.

➤ Although you normally use Run to enter program files, you can also use Run to enter the name and location of documents, folders, and even World Wide Web addresses. In each case, Windows Millennium launches the appropriate program and loads the item you specified.

➤ Windows Millennium "remembers" the last few commands you entered in the Run dialog box. If you need to repeat a recent command, drop down the **Open** list and select the command.

➤ If you have a keyboard with the Windows logo key on it, press **⊞+R** to display the Run dialog box.

The Least You Need to Know

This chapter closed out your look at Windows Millennium basics with a look at My Computer and how you can use it to perform routine maintenance chores such as copying, moving, renaming, deleting, and creating new files and folders. Here are a few highlights to discuss over dinner:

Crib Notes

➤ **What *not* to do**   Don't muck about with anything inside the sacred Windows folder (unless someone, like me, has given you very explicit instructions) and don't move, rename, delete, fold, spindle, or mutilate any files that you didn't create yourself.

➤ **Selecting a file or folder**   If Web integration isn't on, you select an item by clicking it; otherwise, you select an item by moving the mouse pointer over it.

➤ **Drag 'til you drop.**   To drag and drop a file or folder, move the mouse pointer over the item, hold down the right mouse button, move the mouse pointer over the destination, and then release the button. In the shortcut menu that pops up, click either **Copy Here** or **Move Here**.

➤ **Rename restrictions**   When renaming a file (or naming a new file), don't use the following characters:

   *, \ : " < > ? /

➤ To search for a file in My Computer's current folder, either select the **View**, **Explorer Bar**, **Search** command, or click the **Search** toolbar button. To search all of My Computer (that is, all your disk drives), select **Start**, **Search**, **For Files or Folders**.

Part 2

Jumping on the Internet Bandwagon

In late 1999, the number of Internet users in the U.S. alone topped the 100 million mark. 100 million! So it's probably safe to say that the Internet has long since passed the "fad" stage and is now firmly ensconced in the "fact-of-life" stage. (With all the "dot-com" ads we're seeing nowadays, some would call it the "in-your-face" stage.) There are all kinds of rhymes and reasons why the Internet is enjoying such relentless growth, but here's the main one: It's useful. Why phone or write to a company for a brochure when you can go to their Web site and see it (and more) right away? Why send a letter to someone that takes a week to get there when you can send an email that gets there in five minutes? Why root around dusty library stacks for hours to do your research when you can search any of the Web's billion (yes, that right, billion) Web pages from the comfort of your home or office? If you answered "Beats the heck outta me" to any of these questions, then it's time to get you online, which is what happens here in Part 2.

Getting Yourself Online

Okay, so you're convinced that the Internet is, as a certain domestic maven would say, "a good thing." What you're not so sure about is just how to go about it. After all, the way some Internet geeks carry on with their "http" this and their "dot-com-slash" that, you might think an Internet connection requires a Ph.D. in electrical engineering.

Not true! Getting on the Internet can actually be a fairly painless process because Windows Millennium automates much of the drudgery. Even if you're forced to bypass that automation and set up the connection with your bare hands, it's still very doable as long as you follow the required steps to the letter. In any case, I tell you everything you need to know in this chapter.

What to Look for in an Internet Service Provider

If you've got a hankering for, say, a Cubic Zirconium Bangle Bracelet or a Three Stooges Bean Bag Set, all you have to do is call up the Home Shopping Network and lay down your plastic. Just like that, you're de-hankered.

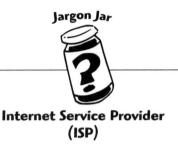

Jargon Jar

Internet Service Provider (ISP)

A company that takes your money in exchange for an Internet account, which you need to get online.

If you've got a hankering to see some *Web pages* about Cubic Zirconium Bangle Bracelets or Three Stooges Bean Bag Sets, however, things aren't quite so easy. That's because the route to the Internet isn't a direct one. Instead, you can only get there by engaging the services of a middleman or, more accurately, a middle-company: an *Internet service provider* (ISP, for short).

An ISP is a business that has negotiated a deal with the local telephone company or some other behemoth organization to get a direct connection to the Internet's highways and byways. These kinds of connections cost thousands of dollars a month, so they're out of reach for all but the most well-heeled tycoons. The ISP affords it by signing up subscribers and offering them a piece of the ISP's Internet connection. After you have an account with an ISP, the connection process works as follows:

1. You use your computer's modem to dial up the ISP.
2. The ISP's computer verifies that you're one of their subscribers.
3. The ISP's computer sets up a connection between your computer and the Internet.
4. You go, girl (or boy, as the case may be).

So before you can do anything on the Internet, you have to set up an account with an ISP and then you need to give Windows the details. Before we get to that, let's take a second to run through a few pointers to bear in mind when deciding which ISP to use:

➤ Most ISPs charge a monthly fee, which typically ranges from US $5 to US $30. Decide in advance the maximum that you're willing to shell out each month.

➤ When comparing prices, remember that ISP plans usually trade off between price and the number of hours of connection time. For example, the lower the price, the fewer hours you get.

➤ It's important to note that most plans charge by the minute or the hour if you exceed the number of hours the plan offers. These charges can be exorbitant (a buck or two an hour), so you don't want to get into that. Therefore, you need to give some thought to how much time you plan to spend online. That's hard to do at this stage, I know, but you just need to ballpark it. If in doubt, get a plan with a large number of hours (say, 100 or 150). You can always scale it back later on.

➤ Most major ISPs offer an "unlimited usage" plan. This means you can connect whenever you want for as long as you want, and you just pay a set fee per month (usually around US $20). This is a good option to take for a few months until you figure out how often you use the Internet.

➤ If you have a newish modem, it probably supports a faster connection speed called 56K. If so, make sure the ISP you choose also supports 56K.

➤ Make sure the ISP offers a local access number to avoid long-distance charges. If that's not an option, make sure they offer access via a toll-free number. (Note: Watch out for extra charges for the use of the toll-free line.) Even better, some nationwide ISPs offer local access in various cities across the land. This is particularly useful if you do a lot of traveling.

Internet Use Changes Over Time

Most people find that they spend a ton of time on the Internet for the first few months as they discover all the wonder and weirdness that's available. After they get used to everything, their connection time drops dramatically.

➤ Make sure the ISP offers a local or toll-free number for technical support.

➤ I recommend only dealing with large ISPs. There are plenty of fly-by-night operations out there, and they're just not worth the hassle of dropped connections, busy signals, lack of support, going belly-up when you most need them, and so on.

➤ If you can't decide between two or more ISPs, see what extra goodies they offer: space for your own Web pages, extra email accounts, Internet software bundles, and so on.

To help you compare major ISPs, Windows Millennium's Internet Connection Wizard has a feature that can display rates and special offers from the companies that provide Internet access in your area. For more on this, see "Signing Up for a New Internet Account," later in this chapter.

The Step-By-Step Net: Using the Internet Connection Wizard

Windows Millennium offers three different routes to Internet connection glory. Whichever avenue you pursue, you start things up the same way: by launching the desktop's **Connect to the Internet** icon. (If you don't see that icon anywhere, don't sweat it because you can still get things started by selecting **Start**, **Programs**, **Accessories**, **Communications**, **Internet Connection Wizard**.) The Internet

Connection Wizard fades in and offers you options for the three routes right off the bat. Here's a summary of the three options along with pointers to the relevant sections of this chapter:

➤ **I want to sign up for a new Internet account** This is the path to take if you don't currently have an Internet account and you want to sign up for one through Windows Millennium. In this case, see the section titled "Signing Up for a New Internet Account."

➤ **I want to transfer my existing Internet account to this computer** If you already have an Internet account, you can (in some cases, anyway) get Windows Millennium to transfer the account settings to your computer. This route is covered in the section titled "Transferring an Existing Internet Account."

Cross Reference

See "Installing Specific Devices," p. 338.

➤ **I want to set up my Internet account manually, or I want to connect through a local area network (LAN)** If you already have an existing account but Windows Millennium can't transfer it, then you need to take a walk on the wired side and set up the account yourself. For modem connections, see "Manually Setting Up an Existing Internet Account." This chapter assumes that you already have your modem installed and ready for the rigors of the Internet. (If that hasn't happened yet, forge ahead to Chapter 21, "Installing and Uninstalling Programs and Devices.")

Make your choice and then click **Next**.

Rates and Stuff

Each time you select a provider, the **Provider information** box gives you the goods on the provider's rates and special offers.

Signing Up for a New Internet Account

If you activated the **I want to sign up for a new Internet account** option, Windows Millennium walks you through the process of choosing and setting up the new account. Here's what happens:

1. If your area has multiple Internet Referral Service phone numbers, the wizard displays them in a list. Click the one your want and then click Next. The Internet Connection Wizard makes your modem dial a number. When connected, the wizard downloads a list of ISPs in your area. The wizard then displays a list of these ISPs, as shown in Figure 7.1.

2. Use the **Internet service providers** list to select the provider you want.

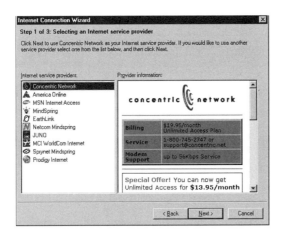

Figure 7.1

You eventually see a list of possible providers.

3. After you've chosen a provider, click **Next**.

4. In the next wizard dialog box, enter your vital statistics (name, address, and so on). The provider needs all this information before you can sign up with them. When you're done, click **Next**.

5. The rest of the steps vary from provider to provider, but most of the time you're asked for some or all of the following:

   ➤ Credit card information

   ➤ The access plan you want to use

   ➤ A username and password for your account

6. When the sign-up is complete, the wizard will likely show you the particulars of your account (such as your email address). Make a note of this info in case you need it later on.

7. The last wizard dialog box offers a check box that, when activated, connects you to the Internet immediately. Let's hold off on that for a minute, so deactivate that check box. Click **Finish** to complete the wizard. You can now skip down to the "Making the Connection" section, later in this chapter.

Transferring an Existing Internet Account

If you activated the **I want to transfer my existing Internet account to this computer** option, Windows Millennium attempts to grab your account data from your existing ISP. This option works almost exactly like the new account setup covered in the previous section:

1. The wizard dials the modem and retrieves a list of providers in your area.

2. If your provider is listed, highlight it and click **Next**. The wizard connects to the provider and then prompts you for some account data, as shown in Figure 7.2.

Figure 7.2

The Internet Connection Wizard prompts you to enter your username, password, and other account data.

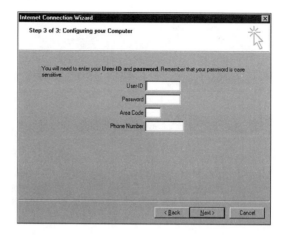

3. Enter your **User-ID** and **Password**, as well as the ISP's **Area code** and **Phone number**.

4. Click **Next**. The wizard logs in to your account, retrieves your settings, and then sets up your Internet connection in Windows Millennium. You eventually see a wizard dialog box with your account data.

5. Click **Next**.

6. In the last wizard dialog box, deactivate the check box that offers to connect you to the Internet immediately. I show you how to connect in the "Making the Connection" section later in this chapter. Click **Finish** to dismiss the wizard.

Manually Setting Up an Existing Internet Account

If your existing Internet account can't be transferred, you need to build the connection with the sweat of your own brow. This section runs through the data you need and takes you through the rest of the Internet Connection Wizard's steps.

Tidbits You Need to Know

To successfully set up a connection to your Internet account, you need to have the proper bits of information from your ISP. When you sign up, the ISP should send you an information sheet or booklet that details everything you need to know. (If something's missing, any good ISP will have a customer service number you can call to fill in the gaps.)

Here's a list of the basic items required for a connection and that should be supplied by your ISP:

➤ The phone number you have to dial to connect to the ISP.

➤ The username (which might also be called your logon name or your user ID) and password that you use to log on to the ISP.

➤ The username and password for your email account. (These are almost always the same as your logon name and password.)

➤ The type of server the ISP uses for incoming email: POP3, IMAP, or HTTP. If you don't have this, assume it's POP3.

➤ The Internet name used by the ISP's incoming mail server. (This often takes the form of `mail.`*`provider`*`.com`, where *provider* is the Internet name of your ISP.)

➤ The Internet name used by the ISP's outgoing mail server. (This is almost always the same as the incoming email server.)

Some ISPs also require some or all of the following advanced settings:

➤ The type of connection the ISP requires. This is usually PPP, but SLIP is sometimes used.

➤ Whether you need to log on to the ISP manually by connecting and then typing in your username and password (relatively rare these days).

➤ Whether your ISP provides you with a "script" for automating the logon procedure.

➤ Whether your ISP assigns you a permanent IP address. If so, you need to know the address.

➤ Whether your ISP provides you with IP addresses for their Domain Name Servers (DNS). If so, you need to know the addresses for the primary and alternate servers.

Didn't I tell you this was finicky stuff? Don't worry if you find all this gobbledygook to be completely meaningless. You need to hold it in your brain only for as long as it takes to set up your connection, and then you can forget it for all time (or at least until you get your next computer and have to start everything from scratch once again; doh!).

Jargon Jar

Log On

To provide your ISP with your username and password, and so gain access to the wonder that is the Internet.

Jargon Jar

Mail Server

A computer that your ISP uses to store and send your email messages.

Jargon Jar

IP Address

A crazy-looking series of numbers and dots (such as 123.234.56.78) that serves as your computer's address when you're connected to the Internet.

Feeding Those Tidbits to the Wizard

With all that info at your side, you're now ready to set up the account. Here are the rest of the steps to trudge through:

1. The next wizard dialog box presents you with your first choice. I'm assuming in this chapter that you're going online using your trusty modem, so be sure the **I connect through a phone line and a modem** option is selected and then click **Next**.

2. The wizard now asks you for the phone number of your ISP. Enter the **Area code**, **Telephone number**, and **Country/region name and code**. If the call doesn't require the country code or area code, deactivate the **Use area code and dialing rules** check box.

3. Now you come to a fork in the wizard's road: whether you need to enter advanced settings to set up the connection. These advanced settings include the following: the connection type (PPP or SLIP), whether you need to log on manually, your IP address, and your ISP's DNS server addresses. If your ISP didn't provide you with any of this information, you don't need to enter these settings, so click **Next** and skip to step 7. Otherwise, click **Advanced** to display the Advanced Connection Properties dialog box (see the next figure) and proceed to step 4.

Figure 7.3

Click Advanced to get to this dialog box. Note that most ISPs don't require you to set any of these options.

4. On the **Connection** tab, you have two groups to deal with:

   ➤ **Connection type**   Activate the appropriate connection type option: **PPP** or **SLIP**.

   ➤ **Logon Procedure**   Activate **None** if you don't have to log on to your ISP; if you have to type some information to log on, activate **Log on manually**; if your ISP provided you with a "script" that automates the logon, activate **Use logon script** and then enter the location of the script. (Click the **Browse** button to use the Open dialog box to select the script file.)

5. On the **Addresses** tab, you have another couple of groups to overcome:

> ➤ **IP address**   If your ISP assigns you an IP address automatically, activate **Internet service provider automatically provides one**. Otherwise, activate **Always use the following** and then enter your IP address in the **IP Address** text box.

> ➤ **DNS server address**   If your ISP assigns DNS addresses automatically, activate **My ISP automatically provides a Domain Name Server (DNS) address**. Otherwise, activate **Always use the following** and then enter the DNS server addresses in the **Primary DNS server** and **Alternate DNS server** text boxes.

6. Click **OK** to return to the Internet Connection Wizard, and then click **Next**.

7. In the next wizard dialog box, enter your **User name** and **Password** (the latter appears only as asterisks, for security), and then click **Next**.

8. The wizard now asks you to name your new connection. It suggests something excruciatingly dull such as **Connection to 555-1234**, but you don't have to stand for that. Enter your own creative name, and then click **Next**.

More Morsels: Setting Up Your Internet Email Account

You thought you were done, didn't you? Hah! There are still a few more wizard queries to answer before you're free to go. The next stage of the process involves setting up your Internet email account. Here's what happens:

1. When the Internet Connection Wizard asks whether you want to set up your Internet mail account, be sure **Yes** is activated, and then click **Next**.

2. The wizard asks for your display name, which is the name other folks see when you send them a message. Enter the name you want to use in the **Display name** text box (most people just use their real name), and click **Next**.

3. Now the wizard pesters you for your email address. Enter your address in the **E-mail address** text box, and click **Next**.

4. Next on the wizard's to-do list is gathering info about your ISP's mail server. You have three things to fill in (as usual, click **Next** when you're done):

> ➤ **My incoming mail server is a**   Use this list to specify the type of email server your ISP uses. Most are POP3.

> ➤ **Incoming mail (POP3, IMAP, or HTTP) server**   Enter the name of the server that your ISP uses for incoming mail.

> ➤ **Outgoing mail (SMTP) server**   Enter the name of the server that your ISP uses for outgoing mail (usually the same as the incoming mail server).

5. The next items on the agenda are your account details: your **Account name** and your **Password**. If you don't want to be pestered for your password each time you connect, leave the **Remember password** check box activated. Click **Next** after that's finished.

6. Don't look now but, at long last, you're done. Woo hoo! In the final wizard dialog box, deactivate the check box that offers to connect you to the Internet immediately. You learn how to connect in the "Making the Connection" section later in this chapter. Click **Finish** to get outta there.

Another Route: The Online Services Folder

Another way to get your Internet connection happening is to sign up with one of the big *online services*, such as America Online (AOL), the Microsoft Network (MSN), or Prodigy. These services offer not only a path to the goodies on the Internet, but also lots of useful and interesting attractions (and, of course, a few useless and dull ones, too) assembled by the company that owns the service. You normally have to pay a monthly fee (and sometimes additional hourly charges) to hook up to an online service.

In most cases, the connection to the service is handled by special software supplied the company, so you need to contact the company to get everything you need. However, Windows Millennium boasts a couple of shortcuts:

➤ If you want to try the Microsoft Network on for size, double-click the desktop's **Setup MSN Internet Access** icon and then follow the instructions that come your way.

➤ For the other available online services, double-click the desktop's **Online Services** icon. This drops you off at the Online Services folder shown in Figure 7.4. Double-click one of the icons to set up a trial account with a service.

Figure 7.4

Opening Windows Millennium's Online Services desktop icon displays this Online Services folder.

Making the Connection

Now that you have your account details down pat, it's time to put that account to good use by connecting to the Internet. The easiest way to get the connection going is to crank up any of the Internet programs mentioned later in this chapter (see "What the Heck Do I Do Now? The Windows Millennium Internet Programs"). For example, you can launch the Internet Explorer Web browser. Windows Millennium, ever eager to please, offers tons of ways to do this, but the following three are the most common:

➤ Double-click the desktop's **Internet Explorer** icon.

➤ Click the **Launch Internet Explorer Browser** icon in the taskbar's Quick Launch section.

➤ Select **Start**, **Programs**, **Internet Explorer**.

This gets you to the Connect To dialog box, shown in Figure 7.5.

Figure 7.5

When you start an Internet program, you end up at this dialog box, which is the launch pad for your Internet forays.

This dialog box offers the following toys:

➤ The list at the top of the dialog box should show the name of the connection you made earlier. If you happen to have multiple connections, use this list to select the one you want.

➤ **User name**   This is the username you use to log on to your ISP.

➤ **Password**   This is the password you use to log on to your ISP.

➤ **Save password**   When this check box is activated, Windows Millennium is kind enough to enter your password automatically. If you're worried about somebody else monkeying around with your account, you'll sleep better at night if you deactivate this option.

➤ **Connect automatically**   If you activate this option, Windows Millennium bypasses the Connect To dialog box entirely. Instead, it just leaps right into the connection. This is a real timesaver if you never have to change any of the data in this dialog box.

➤ **Connect**   Click this button to get the connection process going.

➤ **Properties**   Click this button to adjust your connection settings.

➤ **Work Offline**   Click this button if you change your mind about connecting.

Adjust the data as necessary and, when you're ready, click **Connect**. Windows Millennium taps your modem on the shoulder, passes it the phone number, and the connection process begins in the usually noisy modem fashion. If your ISP requires you to log on manually, a screen appears and the ISP's prompts (such as "User Name" and "Password") appear. Type in whatever information you're asked for. (Press **Enter** after you've entered each item.)

After a few more seconds of navel-gazing, Windows Millennium finally lets you know that you're now up and online by adding a connection icon to the system tray.

Severing the Connection

When you've stood just about all you can stand of the Internet's wiles, you can log off by right-clicking the connection icon in the taskbar's system tray, and then clicking **Disconnect** (see Figure 7.6). When Windows Millennium asks you to confirm the disconnect, click **Yes**.

Figure 7.6

Right-click the connection icon to disconnect from the Internet.

You see this icon when you're connected

Another Disconnection Route

Another way to disconnect is to shut down all running Internet programs. When you do that, Windows Millennium drags the Auto Disconnect dialog box in by the scruff of the neck. Click **Disconnect Now** to bail out of the connection.

On the other hand, many people find this feature annoying because they may be exiting one running Internet program and are planning to start up another one right away. If this happens to you, you can remain online by clicking the **Stay Connected** button. If you don't want Windows Millennium to use this feature at all, activate the **Don't use Auto Disconnect** check box before clicking a button.

What the Heck Do I Do Now? The Windows Millennium Internet Programs

Okay, so you've managed to get your Internet connection up and surfing. Where do you go from here? Ah, you'll be happy to know that the Net is your oyster because Windows Millennium offers just about everything you need to make things happen online. Here's a quick review of all the Windows Millennium features, and where to find out more about them:

➤ **Internet Explorer** As I said, this is Windows Millennium's World Wide Web browser. The Web is a vast storehouse of information presented in *pages* located on computers all over the world. These pages are created by individuals, corporations, and agencies, and they usually contain *links* that, when clicked, take you directly to other pages. See Chapter 8, "It's a Small Web After All: Using Internet Explorer," and Chapter 9, "The Savvy Surfer: More Internet Explorer Fun."

➤ **Outlook Express email** This is Windows Millennium's Internet email program. Email is a system that enables you to exchange electronic messages with other email users, whether they're across town or across the ocean. See Chapter 10, "Sending and Receiving Email Missives" and Chapter 11, "More Email Bonding: Extending Outlook Express."

➤ **MSN Messenger** This is Windows Millennium's instant messaging program, which enables you to send notes to other online folk that they'll see immediately. I show you how it works in Chapter 13, "Real-Time Conversations: Instant Messages, Net Phone Calls, and Chat."

➤ **Outlook Express newsgroups** Outlook Express also doubles as Windows Millennium's newsgroup reader. A newsgroup is a kind of electronic message board devoted to a particular topic. People "post" questions and comments to the newsgroup (there are thousands to choose from), other folks respond to those posts, and still others respond to the responses. It will all become clear in Chapter 12, "Spreadin' the News: Participating in Newsgroup Conversations."

➤ **NetMeeting** You use this program to place "telephone calls" over the Internet. NetMeeting also can be used to "chat" (exchange typed messages in real time), collaborate with other people on a program, and more. Chapter 13 is the place to go to learn how all this is done.

The Least You Need to Know

This chapter showed you how to go from tired to wired by getting Windows Millennium connected to the Internet. I first ran through the two easiest connection routes: setting up a new account and transferring an existing account. The bulk of the chapter was spent on the third route: setting up an existing account under your own power. After all that, I showed you how to make the connection and then went through a summary of Windows Millennium's Net tools.

111

Crib Notes

➤ **Running the Internet Connection Wizard**   After you create your account, the desktop's Internet Connection Wizard disappears in an invisible cloud of smoke. If you need to run this wizard again, select **Start, Programs, Accessories, Communications, Internet Connection Wizard**.

➤ **Manual connection info**   If you're setting up your connection by hand, your ISP should provide you with the settings and data you need: the access phone number, your username and password, the type of mail server, the address of the mail server, and so on.

➤ **Getting connected**   Making the leap to the Internet is as easy as starting any Internet program, such as Internet Explorer. When the Dial-up Connection dialog box wanders in, click **Connect**.

➤ **Getting disconnected**   To return to the real world, right-click the connection icon in the taskbar's system tray, and then click **Disconnect**.

Chapter 8

It's a Small Web After All: Using Internet Explorer

In This Chapter

➤ Becoming fast friends with the Internet Explorer window

➤ How to navigate from one Web page to another

➤ Searching the Web for the information you want

➤ Keeping track of your favorite Web sites

➤ A no muss, no fuss primer that'll have you up and surfing in no time flat

What is the World Wide Web? Well, I could sit here and tell you, as does the *American Heritage Dictionary of the English Language,* that it's "an information server on the Internet composed of interconnected sites and files, accessible with a browser." I *could* do that, but I'm afraid your initial impression of the World Wide Web would be that it's excruciatingly *boring.* And if the Web is anything, it's not boring. It's fascinating, frustrating, informative, infuriating, colossal, and corny—but dull? Never.

So, again, what is the World Wide Web? For starters, only pedants with overly-pursed lips and fussbudgets with overly-starched collars call it "the World Wide Web." The rest of us prefer just "the Web," which is the less tongue-twisting short form that I'll use throughout this chapter. The Web (ah, that's better) is a vast collection of documents called *pages.* How vast? Oh, there are now about a *billion* or so pages (give or take a few million). So you can imagine that these pages cover just about every topic under the sun (and a few over the sun, to boot). You'll find everything from humble personal pages to humongous corporate sites, what-I-did-on-my-summer-vacation essays to entire newspapers, and in-depth info for fans of The Cars to test-drive data for car fans.

The Web may sound like just some giant encyclopedia, but it boasts something that you won't find in any encyclopedia printed on mere paper: interaction. For example, almost every Web page in existence comes equipped with a few *links*. Links are special sections of the document that, when clicked, immediately whisk you away to some other page on the site or even to a page on another site (which may be on the other side of town or on the other side of the planet). You can also use the Web to play games, post messages, buy things, sell things, grab files and programs, and much more.

Your chariot for these Web adventures is a program called a Web browser. In Windows Millennium, the chariot-of-choice is Internet Explorer, and it's the subject of this chapter. You learn the nuts and bolts of the Internet Explorer window, how to use Internet Explorer to navigate Web pages, and how to wield some Internet Explorer tools designed to make your Web wandering easier.

Internet Explorer Nuts and Bolts

Windows Millennium offers a ton of ways to get Internet Explorer up and surfing. Here's the basic method:

1. If you're looking to burn off a few extra calories after dinner, here's the long way to start Internet Explorer: select **Start, Programs, Internet Explorer**. Otherwise, Windows Millennium gives you two quicker ways to launch Internet Explorer:

   ➤ Double-click the desktop's **Internet Explorer** icon. (Remember to single-click if you have Web integration turned on.)

   ➤ Click the **Launch Internet Explorer Browser** icon in the taskbar's Quick Launch toolbar at the bottom of the screen.

Cross Reference

To learn about signing up with an ISP, check out Chapter 7, "Getting Yourself Online," p. 99.

2. If you don't have a connection established with your Internet service provider, the Connect To dialog box shows up at this point. Go ahead and click **Connect** to reunite Windows Millennium and the Internet.

The first time you launch Internet Explorer, you end up at a page that gives you the opportunity to learn more about the program and about the Web. If you get there but you don't feel comfortable enough to take the various tours, that's okay because you learn all that stuff in this chapter. Instead, select the **View, Go To, Home Page** command.

You arrive at the MSN.com Web site, shown in Figure 8.1. (You see MSN.com automatically each subsequent time you run Internet Explorer.) Note that this screen changes constantly, so the one you see will almost certainly look a bit different than the one shown in Figure 8.1.

Page title   Address bar   Links

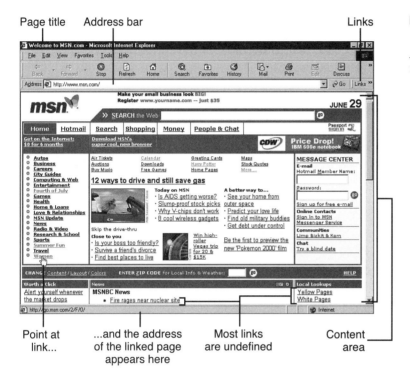

Point at   ...and the address   Most links   Content
link...   of the linked page   are undefined   area
                appears here

Figure 8.1

When you launch Internet Explorer, you end up at the MSN.com Web site.

MSN.com is Microsoft's Internet starting point. (This kind of site is known as a *portal* in the Web trade.) Fortunately, not all the sites you see in your travels will be as cramped-looking and as ugly as the MSN.com page.

Before I show you how to use this page to see more of the Web, let's take a minute or two and get our bearings by checking out the main features of the Internet Explorer window:

➤ **Page title**   The top line of the screen shows you the title of the current Web page.

➤ **Address bar**   This area shows you the address of the current page. Web page addresses are strange beasts, indeed. I help you figure them out a bit later in this chapter.

115

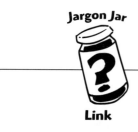

Jargon Jar

Link

A section of text or an image that, when clicked, takes you to another Web page.

➤ **Links bar**   This barely visible toolbar has various buttons that each represent a predefined link. I explain the buttons later on.

➤ **Content area**   This area below the Address and Links bars takes up the bulk of the Internet Explorer screen. It's where the body of each Web page is displayed. You can use the vertical scrollbar to see more of the current page.

➤ **Links**   The content area for most Web pages also boasts a link or two (or 10). These links come in two flavors: images and text. (The latter are usually underlined or in a different color than the rest of the text.) When you put the mouse pointer over a link, Internet Explorer does two things: it changes the pointer into a hand with a pointing finger, and it displays, in the status bar, the address of the linked page.

Web Page Navigation Basics

Now that you're familiar with the lay of Internet Explorer land, you can start using it to navigate sites. This section takes you through the various ways you can use Internet Explorer to weave your way through the Web.

As you saw earlier, Internet Explorer displays links either as text in an underlined font that's a different color from the rest of the text, or as an image. If everything seems hunky-dory, click the link to toddle off to the new page. What could be simpler?

Windows Wisdom

Some Images Are All Show and No Go

Just to keep us all confused, not all the images you see on a Web page are necessarily links. Some are there strictly for show—you can click them until your finger falls off, and nothing will happen. How can you tell links from non-links? The only surefire way is to point your mouse at the picture. If the mouse pointer turns into the little hand with the pointing finger, then you know you're dealing with a link.

If you happen to know the address of the Web page you want to visit, you can strike out for this new territory by following these easy steps:

1. Click inside the Address bar.
2. Delete the current address.
3. Type the address for the new site.
4. Press **Enter** or click **Go**.

The Weirdness of Web Addresses

Internet addresses, with their "http" this and slash (/) that, are obvious geek creations that now find themselves at large in the real world. You'll deal with them a lot, so let's see if we can knock some sense into them. Here's an example that illustrates the general format:

```
http://www.mcfedries.com/books/index.html
```

`http://`	This part identifies this as a Web address.
`www.mcfedries.com`	This is the "domain name" (think of it as the address) of the host computer where the Web page resides (`www.mcfedries.com` is my Web home).
`/books/`	This is the directory that contains the Web page.
`index.html`	This is the filename of the Web page.

More Address Bar Fun

Besides showing you the address of the current page and letting you enter a new page address, the Address bar has a few other tricks up its digital sleeve:

➤ The Address bar also moonlights as a drop-down list that holds the most recent addresses you typed in. So you can save a bit of typing by dropping down this list and selecting the address you want. You drop down the list either by clicking the downward-pointing arrow on the right or by pressing **F4**.

Jargon Jar

URL

You often hear folks using the acronym URL (sometimes pronounced "earl") to refer to Web addresses. URL stands for *uniform resource locator*, a phrase that could warm the cockles of only the most nerdish heart.

➤ The Address bar comes with an AutoComplete feature that monitors the address as you type. If a previously entered address matches your typing, the rest of that address is displayed automatically. Press **Enter** to select that address, press **Delete** to remove the rest of the address, or just keep typing to specify something different.

➤ Internet Explorer assumes any address you enter is for a Web site. Therefore, you don't need to type the http:// prefix because Internet Explorer adds it for you automatically.

➤ Internet Explorer also assumes that most Web addresses are of the form http://www.whatever.com. Therefore, if you simply type the "whatever" part and press **Ctrl+Enter**, Internet Explorer automatically adds the http://www prefix and the com suffix. For example, you can get to my home page (http://www.mcfedries.com) by typing **mcfedries** and pressing **Ctrl+Enter**.

More Address Bars

The Address bar isn't just part of the Internet Explorer window. In fact, you can use it in two other places:

➤ All folder windows in Windows Millennium have an Address bar just like the one in Internet Explorer. For example, you see one if you open My Computer. Go right ahead and type a Web site address in this Address Bar and press **Enter**. In this case, the My Computer window magically transforms itself into the Internet Explorer window and the Web page appears.

➤ The taskbar also has its own Address bar. To display it, right-click an empty section of the taskbar, click **Toolbars** in the menu, and then activate the **Address** command. Again, you type the Web site address and press **Enter**. In this case, Windows Millennium loads Internet Explorer and displays the page.

To and Fro: More Web Navigation Techniques

After you start leaping and jumping through the Web's cyberspatial byways, you often want to head back to a previous site, or even to your start page (the first page you see when you launch Internet Explorer). Here's a rundown of the various techniques you can use to move back and forth in Internet Explorer:

➤ To go back to the previous page, either click the **Back** toolbar button or select the **View, Go To, Back** command. (Pressing **Alt+Left Arrow** also does the job.)

➤ After you've gone back to a previous page, you can move forward again either by clicking the toolbar's **Forward** button or by selecting **View, Go To, Forward**. (For a change of pace, you can also press **Alt+Right Arrow**.)

Making Toolbar Buttons Make Sense

Internet Explorer's toolbar is a mish-mash of text and non-text buttons. Who's the genius who came up with *that*? The buttons would be much easier to decipher if they all displayed text. Fortunately, that's not a problem. Select **View, Toolbars, Customize** to request the presence of the Customize Toolbar dialog box. Use the **Text options** list to select **Show text labels**, and then click **Close**.

➤ Both the Back and Forward buttons do double duty as drop-down lists. When you click the little arrow to the right of each button, Internet Explorer displays a list of the sites you've visited. You can then click the site you want and jump straight there. Note that these lists are cleared when you return to the start page.

➤ To return to the start page, either click the **Home** button or select **View, Go To, Home Page**.

➤ To return to a specific document you've visited, select **View, Go To** and then select the page title from the menu.

The Links Bar Links

If you're not sure where you want to go on the Web, Internet Explorer's Links bar contains a few prefab sites that you can try out to get your Web feet wet. To see the buttons, you have two choices:

➤ Click the Links bar's right-pointing double arrow.

➤ View the entire toolbar by moving the mouse pointer over the left edge of the Links bar and then dragging it below the Address bar.

Here's a summary of each link:

➤ **Best of the Web**   This is a great place to start your Web explorations. Clicking this link takes you to the MSN Search page, which contains even more links arranged by category: Entertainment, Finance, News, Sports, and much more.

➤ **Channel Guide**   Click this link to display a page that gives you access to sites that feature audio and video.

➤ **Customize Links**   This link takes you to a page that tells you how to customize the Links bar.

➤ **Free Hotmail**   This button takes you to a page where you can sign up for a free email account with Microsoft's Hotmail service.

See "Getting Latest and Greatest from the Windows Update Web Site," p. 355.

➤ **Internet Start**   This link returns you to Internet Explorer's startup page.

➤ **Is Your Operating System Genuine**   This strange link drops you off at the Microsoft Piracy page, so you can see if your copy of Windows Millennium is legal(!).

➤ **Microsoft**   This button takes you to the Microsoft home page.

➤ **Windows Media**   This link takes you to the same page as the Channel Guide link. Go figure.

➤ **Windows Update**   Click this link to go to the Windows Update Web site. I describe Windows Update in Chapter 22, "Smooth System Sailing: Wielding the System Tools."

➤ **Windows**   This link takes you to the Windows home page.

Plucking Page Needles from the Net's Haystack: Searching for Sites

The navigation approaches you've tried so far have encompassed the two extremes of Web surfing: randomly clicking on links to see what happens, and entering addresses to display specific sites. What if you're looking for information on a particular topic, but you don't know any appropriate addresses and you don't want to waste time clicking aimlessly around the Web? In this case, you want to put the Web to work for you. That is, you want to crank up one of the Web's search engines to track down sites that contain the data you're looking for.

Conveniently, Internet Explorer contains a special Search feature that gives you easy access to a few of the Web's best search sites. Here's how you use this feature to perform a search:

1. Either click the toolbar's **Search** button or select **View, Explorer Bar, Search**. Internet Explorer adds a Search screen to the left of the content area, as shown in Figure 8.2.

When you press this button…

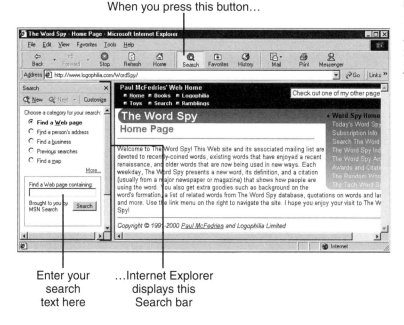

Figure 8.2

Windows Millennium's Internet Explorer has a new Search bar that gives you access to some of the Web's top search engines.

Enter your
search
text here

…Internet Explorer
displays this
Search bar

Dealing with Files in Internet Explorer

As you click your way around the Web, you find that some links don't take you to other pages but are, instead, tied directly to a file. In this case, Internet Explorer throws the File Download dialog box at you and asks whether you want to **Open this file** or **Save this file to disk**. Make sure that the latter option is activated, and then click **OK**. In the Save As dialog box that shows up next, choose a location for the file, and then click **Save**.

This is as good a place as any to warn you that you need to be careful about downloading files because they can contain viruses that can wreck your system. To be safe, you should only download from reputable sites or from sites that you trust explicitly. If you plan to live dangerously and download files willy-nilly, at least get yourself a good antivirus program such as McAfee (www.mcafee.com) or Norton (www.symantec.com).

Search Know-How

If you enter two or more words as your search text, the search site looks for Web pages that contain *all* the words anywhere within the page. If you want to search for a specific phrase, instead, enclose the words in quotation marks.

2. In the Search bar, use the text box to enter a key word (or two) that represents the type of information you want to find.

3. Click the **Search** button to get things underway. The search site rummages through its database of Web sites and then, hopefully, it displays a list of sites that contain the word or words you entered.

What happens next depends on what the search site's digital bloodhounds turn up:

➤ If the search site finds any matching pages, it displays a list of the page titles in the Search bar. If you see one that looks interesting (hint: you can get a bit more info by putting your mouse pointer over the title), click the title. Internet Explorer then displays the page in the content area, as shown in Figure 8.3.

Figure 8.3

If the search site finds sites that contain your search text, it displays a list of links to those sites.

Click this button to try different search sites

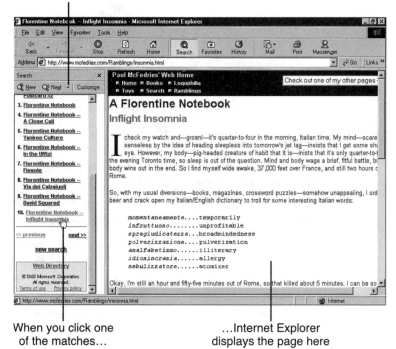

When you click one of the matches…

…Internet Explorer displays the page here

➤ If the search site found more than 10 matching pages, you see a **next>>** link near the bottom of the Search bar. Click this link to see more results.

➤ If no matches are found, try running another search using different (or perhaps just fewer) search terms.

➤ A more likely scenario is that your search will return thousands of sites. If that's the case, check out the first 10 or 20 to see if you find what you want. If not, run another search using more search terms to try to narrow things down a bit.

➤ The Search bar is on friendly terms with quite a few search sites, all of which have a different take on the Web's wonders. So if you didn't find what you're looking for, try running your search again using a different search site. To do that, click the Search bar's **Next** button (the one that appears near the top of the Search bar).

➤ The Next button is also a list of search sites. To head directly to a particular site, click the downward-pointing arrow and then click the one you want.

Customizing the Search Bar's Search Sites

The Search bar offers a snippet of flexibility as far as the available search sites go. Specifically, you can control which search sites appear on the Next list and the order in which they appear when you click the Next button. You do this by clicking the Search bar's **Customize** button. In the **Find a Web page** section, activate the check boxes of the search sites you want in the list. (If there are any search sites that you don't like, feel free to deactivate their check boxes to get them out of your life.) Use the up- and down arrows to change the order of the search sites.

The Favorites Folder: Sites to Remember

One of the most common experiences that folks new to Web browsing (and even some of us old-timers) go through is stumbling on a really great site, and then not being able to find it again later. They try to retrace their steps, but usually just end up clicking links furiously and winding up on the wrong side of the Net tracks.

123

To help prevent this kind of toss-the-#$%*&-monitor-out-the-window experience, you should become adept at using Internet Explorer's Favorites feature. In Internet Explorer land, a *favorite* is a "shortcut" to a specific Web page. You just select the shortcut and Internet Explorer handles the hard part of navigating back to the page. The Favorites feature keeps track of these shortcuts and even lets you organize them into separate folders.

Here's how you tell Internet Explorer to remember a Web page as a favorite:

1. Use Internet Explorer to display the page.

2. Select **Favorites, Add to Favorites** to get the Add Favorite dialog box onscreen.

3. The **Name** text box shows the name of the page, which is what you'll select from a menu later when you want to view this page again. If you can think of a better name, don't hesitate to edit this text. (This is as good a place as any to tell you that I'm going to recklessly ignore the **Make available offline** check box for the time being. Not to worry, however: You learn all about it in Chapter 9, "The Savvy Surfer: More Internet Explorer Fun.")

4. Most people end up with dozens or even hundreds of favorites, so it's a good idea to organize them into folders. To save a favorite in a folder, click **Create in**. (If you don't want to bother with this, skip to step 7.)

Another Way to Get to Your Favorites

If you find yourself constantly pulling down the Favorites menu to get at your favorite pages, you might prefer to have the Favorites list displayed full-time. You can do that by clicking the **Favorites** button in the toolbar. Internet Explorer then sets aside a chunk of real estate on the left side of the window to display the Favorites list.

5. The Favorites feature has only two folders at the start: Links and Media, neither of which you should use for this. Instead, click **New Folder**, enter a name for the new folder in the dialog box that comes up, and then click **OK**.

6. Click the folder in which you want to store your favorite.

7. Click **OK** to wrap things up.

After you have some pages lined up as favorites, you can return to any one of them at any time by pulling down the **Favorites** menu and clicking the page title. (If the favorite is stored in a folder, click that folder to open its submenu, and then click the page.)

If you need to make changes to your favorites, you can do a couple of things right from Internet Explorer's Favorites menu. Pull down the menu and then right-click the item you want to work with. In the shortcut menu that slinks in, click **Rename** to change the item's name, or click **Delete** to blow it away.

For more heavy-duty adjustments, select the **Favorites**, **Organize Favorites** command. Not surprisingly, this pushes the Organize Favorites dialog box into view, as shown in Figure 8.4. You get four buttons to play with:

➤ **Create Folder** Click this button to create a new folder. (Tip: If you click an existing folder and then click this button, Internet Explorer creates a subfolder.) Internet Explorer adds the folder and displays New Folder inside a text box. Edit to taste, and then press **Enter**.

➤ **Move to Folder** Click this button to move the currently highlighted favorite into another folder. In the Browse for Folder dialog box that saunters by, highlight the destination folder, and then click **OK**.

➤ **Rename** Click this button to rename the currently highlighted favorite. Edit the name accordingly, and then press **Enter**.

➤ **Delete** Click this button to nuke the currently highlighted favorite. When Windows Millennium asks whether you're sure about this, click **Yes**.

When you're done, click **Close** to return to Internet Explorer.

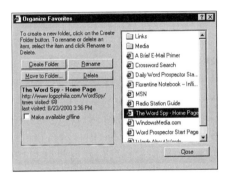

Figure 8.4

Use the Organize Favorites dialog box to put your favorites in apple-pie order.

The Way You Were: Using the History List

I showed you earlier how you can click the Back and Forward buttons to follow in your own Web footsteps. Internet Explorer wipes those lists clean, however, when you return to the start page or exit the program. What do you do when you want to revisit a site you checked out a few days ago? Well, you'll be happy to know that Internet Explorer keeps track of the addresses of all the pages you've perused during the last 20 days!

Here's how it works:

1. Click the **History** button in the toolbar. By this time, you won't be surprised to see a History bar show up on the left side of the window, as shown in Figure 8.5.

Figure 8.5

The History list keeps track of all the Web addresses you called on during the last 20 days.

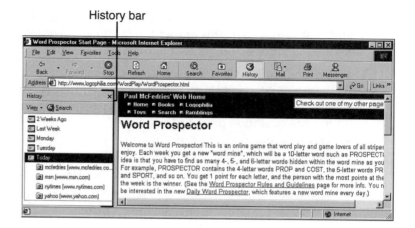

History bar

The Fickle Web

Time, tide, and the Internet wait for no one, so Web page addresses are in a constant state of flux. Therefore, after a while you'll probably find that some of your favorite sites may no longer be available. Bummer. All is not lost, however. The page may simply be renamed, so try deleting the filename portion of the address from the Address bar and pressing **Enter**. This should get you to the site's main page. If that doesn't work, the page may have moved to an entirely new site, so try searching for the page.

2. Do one of the following:

   ➤ If the date you want to work with is in this week, click the day (such as **Monday**).

   ➤ If the date you want is in a previous week, click the week (such as **2 Weeks Ago**) and then click the day.

3. Internet Explorer displays a list of the sites you visited on that day. Click the site you want. This gives you a list of the pages you visited on that site.

4. Click the page you want to see. Internet Explorer displays the page in the rest of the content area.

Internet Explorer also offers a couple of methods for dealing with the History bar's links:

➤ **Sorting the list**   Click the History bar's **View** button and then click a sort option (such as **By Most Visited**).

➤ **Searching the list**   If you do a lot of surfing, your History bar will be crammed to the gills with links. To find the one you want, click the History bar's **Search** button, enter a word or phrase in the **Search for** text box, and then click **Search Now**.

When you're done with the History bar, you can hide it by clicking the **History** toolbar button once again.

The Least You Need to Know

This chapter showed you the basics of using Internet Explorer to ply the electronic highways and byways of the World Wide Web. I gave you a quick tour of the Internet Explorer screen, and then ran through the standard Web navigation techniques. You then learned about three features that make your surfing more efficient: Search, Favorites, and History.

That was quite a chapter, but you're not done yet, not by a long shot. Internet Explorer is loaded with other useful trinkets and I've devoted another whole chapter to checking them out. See Chapter 9, "The Savvy Surfer: More Internet Explorer Fun." Before moving on, however, here are a few pointers to pack up and take along for the ride:

Crib Notes

➤ **Going Internet Exploring**   To start Internet Explorer, click the **Launch Internet Explorer Browser** icon in the taskbar's Quick Launch section. (Alternatively, you can either double-click the desktop's **Internet Explorer** icon or select **Start, Programs, Internet Explorer**.)

➤ **Navigation for novices**   To light out for another page, either click a link or type a URL in the Address bar and then press **Enter**. Use the toolbar's **Back** button to return to the previous page, and use the **Forward** button to head the other way.

➤ **Site searching**   To scour the Web for a particular topic, click the **Search** button to get the Search bar onscreen, enter a word or two, and then click **Search**.

➤ **Playing favorites**   Run the **Favorites, Add Favorites** command to save a page on the Favorites menu.

➤ **Studying history**   To return to any site you visited during the last 20 days, open the History bar by clicking the **History** toolbar button.

Chapter 9

The Savvy Surfer: More Internet Explorer Fun

In This Chapter

➤ Working with Web pages offline

➤ Taking advantage of the Links bar

➤ Understanding Internet Explorer security

➤ Customizing, converting, and otherwise cajoling Internet Explorer into doing what you want it to do

Like electrons passing in the night, Web users never see each other as they surf sites. If they could, however, there might be a mutual flash of recognition between them because most Web users seem to fall into one of three categories:

Clickstreamers   Users who spend their online time wandering aimlessly from site to site, hoping for serendipitous finds (a new word: surfendipity!). By the way, *clickstream* is Web jargon for the "path" a person takes as they navigate through the Web by clicking links.

Nooksurfers   People who keep going to the same sites over and over and rarely check out new sites.

Researchers   People who use the Web exclusively for gathering information.

Whatever kind of Web user you are, your online time will be vastly more fun and productive if you can play your browser like a virtuoso. To that end, this chapter presents a master class for Internet Explorer. You learn how to read pages while you're offline, how to customize the Links bar, how to set up security, how to work with Internet Explorer's options, and much more.

Reading Pages Offline

Many Web fans have a few pages that they check out regularly because the content is always changing. Let's say you have 12 such pages and it takes you an average of five minutes to read each one. That's an hour of online time you've used up. Wouldn't it be better if Internet Explorer could somehow grab those pages while you weren't around (at night, for example), and then let you read them while you're not connected?

Well, *sure* it would! That's probably why the Windows Millennium programmers added the Synchronize feature to Internet Explorer. This feature lets you designate Web pages to be available offline (that is, when you're not connected to the Internet). Then, when you run the Synchronize command, Internet Explorer absconds with the latest version of those pages and stores them on your hard disk. Internet Explorer also is happy to set up an automatic synchronization that can be scheduled to run any time you like.

To make a page available offline, begin by using either of the following techniques:

➤ **If the page is set up as a favorite** Pull down the **Favorites** menu and display the shortcut for the page. Then right-click that shortcut and click **Make available offline**.

➤ **If the page isn't yet set up as a favorite** Display the page and then select **Favorites**, **Add to Favorites** to meet up with the Add Favorite dialog box. Activate the **Make available offline** check box and then click **Customize**.

Whichever route you take, you end up with the Offline Favorite Wizard staring you in the face. Here's how it works:

1. The first wizard dialog box just offers an introduction, so click **Next**. (You can save yourself this step down the road by activating the **In the future, do not show this introduction screen** check box.) You end up at the dialog box shown in Figure 9.1.

Figure 9.1

Use the Offline Favorite Wizard to set up a page for offline reading.

2. This wizard dialog box wonders whether you want any pages that are linked to the favorite to be downloaded, as well. If you don't care about the linked pages, activate **No**; otherwise, activate **Yes** and then use the **Download pages *x* links deep from this page** spin box to specify how many levels of links you want grabbed. Click **Next** when you're ready to proceed.

Look Out!

Don't Go Too Deep!

If you elect to download pages that are linked to the favorite page, you can choose to go 1, 2, or 3 levels deep. Going 1 level deep means just the pages linked to the favorite page are downloaded. Going 2 levels deep means that you also get any pages that are linked to the pages that are linked to the favorite page. For example, if the favorite page has 10 links, and each of those linked pages also has 10 links, you'll end up downloading 100 pages! And because any of those pages could be from completely different sites, you never know what you're going to get. Obviously, you want to exercise some caution here because you could end up with a massive download on your hands.

3. The wizard asks how you want the page synchronized:

   ➤ **Only when I choose Synchronize from the Tools menu**   Select this option if you want to control when the synchronization occurs. If you choose this option, click **Next** and then skip to step 5.

   ➤ **I would like to create a new schedule**   Activate this option if you want Internet Explorer to perform the synchronization automatically on a preset schedule. If you select this option, click **Next** and then continue with step 4.

Jargon Jar

Synchronize

To download a copy of a Web page so that the version you have stored on your computer is the same as (that is, is synchronized with) the version on the Web.

131

4. If you elected to set up a synchronization schedule, you'll see a dialog box with scheduling options. Here's a rundown of the controls you get to mess with (click **Next** when you're ready to move on):

➤ **Every *x* days**   Specify the number of days between synchronizations.

➤ **at**   Specify the time you want the synchronization to happen.

➤ **Name**   Enter a name for this synchronization schedule.

➤ **If my computer is not connected...**   Activate this check box to have Internet Explorer connect your computer to the Internet to download the page (or pages). Note that this option works only if you don't have to log on manually to your ISP.

5. The final wizard dialog box wants to know whether the Web page requires you to log on. If not (most sites don't), activate **No**; if so, activate **Yes** and then fill in your **User name** and **Password** (twice). Click **Finish** to complete the synchronization setup.

6. If you're adding a new favorite, you'll end up back in the Add Favorite dialog box. Select a folder for the favorite (if necessary) and then click **OK**.

At this point, Internet Explorer performs the initial synchronization: It connects to the page and hauls in a copy that it stores on your system.

If you elected to go the manual synchronization route, you can download the pages for offline perusing at any time by selecting the **Tools**, **Synchronize** command. In the Items to Synchronize dialog box (see Figure 9.2), deactivate the check boxes for any items you don't want to synchronize, and then click **Synchronize**.

Figure 9.2

Deactivate the check box beside any page you don't want synchronized.

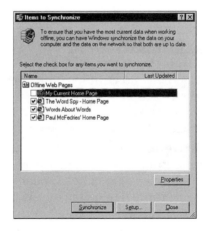

The Items to Synchronize dialog box also enables you to make some adjustments to your items and to the Synchronize feature:

➤ **To adjust the settings for a synchronized item** Highlight the item in the Items to Synchronize dialog box, and then click **Properties**. The dialog box that appears has three tabs:

Web Document Deactivate the **Make this page available offline** check box to stop synchronizing this page.

Schedule Use this tab to change the synchronization schedule for the page.

Download Use this tab to change the number of link levels you want downloaded. A very handy feature on this tab is the **When this page changes, send e-mail to** check box. If you activate this and then fill in your **E-mail address** and **Mail Server (SMTP)** (the Internet name of your ISP's outgoing mail computer), Internet Explorer will send you an email to let you know that the page has changed.

➤ **To adjust the settings for the Synchronize feature as a whole** Click **Setup** to project the Synchronization Settings dialog box onto the screen. Once again, you have three tabs to play with:

Logon Use this tab to set up a synchronization every time you log on to Windows Millennium.

On Idle Use this tab to set up a synchronization when your computer hasn't been used for a while. To control when this synchronization happens, click the **Advanced** button.

Scheduled Use this tab to adjust the synchronization schedules that you've defined so far.

Customizing the Handy Links Bar

I like Internet Explorer's Links bar because, in my never-ending quest to minimize mouse clicks and keystrokes, it gives me one-click access to a few sites. The problem, however, is that I don't use the Links bar's predefined sites all that often. The solution? I just gave the default links the heave-ho and replaced them with my most frequently accessed sites. Here's a rundown of some of the things you can do to remake the Links bar:

➤ **Seeing hidden Links bar buttons** By default, the Links bar is crammed into the right side of the window so that only the "Links" label is in view. Dumb! However, you can still get to the other buttons by clicking the double arrow that appears on the right side of the Links bar.

➤ **Sizing the Links bar**   A better way to get to those hidden buttons is to change the size of the Links bar. To give this a whirl, position the mouse pointer over the **Links** label, then drag the label left or right.

➤ **Moving the Links bar**   To see the entire Links bar, move your mouse over the **Links** label and then drag it down until the Links bar snaps into place below the Address bar.

➤ **Changing button positions**   The positions of the Links bar buttons are not set in stone. To move any button, use your mouse to drag the button left or right along the Links bar.

Here are a few methods you can use to manipulate individual Links bar buttons:

➤ **Changing a button's address**   If you right-click a button and then click **Properties**, Internet Explorer displays the Properties dialog box for an Internet shortcut. Use the **URL** text box to edit the button's address.

➤ **Creating a button for the current page**   To add a new Links bar button for the current page, drag the page icon from the Address bar and drop it on the Links bar.

➤ **Creating a button from a hypertext link**   If a page has a hypertext link, you can create a button for that link by dragging the link text into the Links bar.

➤ **Renaming a button**   Right-click the button and then click **Rename** in the menu. In the Rename dialog box that barges in, enter the new name and then click **OK**.

➤ **Deleting a button**   To blow away a button from the Links bar, drag the button and then drop it in the Windows Millennium Recycle Bin. (You can also right-click the button and then click **Delete**.)

Caveat Surfer: Internet Explorer and Security

Tons of people are flocking to the Web, and tons of content providers are waiting for them there. Still, the Web is by no means in the mainstream. That is, although millions of people surf the Web, that's still only a small percentage of the hundreds of millions of potential Web denizens that remain resolutely unwired. There are many reasons for this, but one of the biggest is the security issue. There are two issues, actually:

➤ **Protecting the data that you send to the Web**   Many Web page forms ask you to supply sensitive data, such as your credit card number. You wouldn't leave credit card receipts lying in the street, but that's more or less what you're doing if you submit a normal Web form that has your Visa number on it. The solution here is to enter sensitive data only on Web pages that are secure (more on this in a sec).

➤ **Being protected from the data that the Web sends to you**   The nature of the Web means that all kinds of items—text, graphics, sounds, Java applets (a kind of mini-program), ActiveX controls (another mini-program), and more—get deposited on your computer, at least temporarily. How do you know all that stuff is safe? And if you're not sure about something, how do you refuse delivery?

Internet Explorer offers quite a number of features that tackle these issues directly. For example, the Internet Explorer window gives you visual cues that tell you whether a particular document is secure. Figure 9.3 shows Internet Explorer displaying a secure Web page. Notice how a lock icon appears in the lower-right corner, and that the address of a secure page uses **https** up front rather than **http**. Both of these features tell you that the Web page has a security certificate that passed muster with Internet Explorer.

Figure 9.3

An example of a secure Web document.

Lock icon

Internet Explorer also displays security warning dialog boxes. These seemingly paranoid notes are actually quite useful most of the time. They warn you about all kinds of potentially nefarious activities:

➤ Entering a secure Web site.

➤ Browsing allegedly secure Web sites that don't have a valid security certificate.

➤ Leaving a secure Web site (see Figure 9.4).

➤ Being redirected to a page other than the one you specified.

➤ Downloading and running objects, including files, ActiveX controls, Java applets, and scripts.

➤ Submitting a form unsecurely.

135

Figure 9.4

Internet Explorer warns you when you're about to send data from an unsecure form.

A Note About eCommerce and "128-Bit" Security

Many folks want to try out these newfangled ecommerce and online banking sites that everyone's talking about, but they're concerned about security. That's smart, because financial data *must* be as secure as possible. When you investigate these kinds of sites, you often see them yammering on about "128-bit encryption" and similar-sounding gobbledygook. What's up with that? The details are interesting only to tall-forehead types, but the gist is that any Web browser that boasts 128-bit encryption can scramble your financial data to make it virtually uncrackable by nefarious nogoodniks. It used to be that you had to download a special update to get this super-duper security. That's a thing of the past now because Windows Millennium's version of Internet Explorer comes with 128-bit security built right in.

Note that these dialog boxes contain a check box that enables you to turn the warning off. You can also use the Security tab in the Internet Options dialog box (shown in Figure 9.5; select **Tools, Internet Options** to get there) to toggle these warnings on and off and customize the level of security used by Internet Explorer.

The way Internet Explorer handles security is to classify Web pages according to different security *zones*. Each zone is a collection of Web pages that implements a common security level. There are four zones:

➤ **Internet zone**   This is a catch-all zone that includes all Web pages that aren't in any of the other zones. The default security level is Medium.

➤ **Local intranet zone**   This zone covers Web pages on your local hard drives and on your local area network (intranet). The default security level is Medium-low.

136

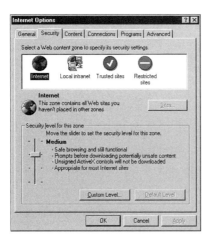

Figure 9.5

Use the Security tab to set the level of security you're comfortable with.

➤ **Trusted sites zone**   You use this zone to specify Web sites that you trust. That is, these are sites for which you're certain that any objects you download and run are safe. The default security level is Low.

➤ **Restricted sites zone**   You use this zone to specify Web sites that you don't trust, and so want to implement the tightest possible security. The default security level is High.

You can add sites to three of Internet Explorer's security zones: Local intranet, Trusted sites, and Restricted sites. Here's how you do it:

1. In the Security tab, click the icon of the zone you want to work with.

2. Click the **Sites** button.

3. If you're working with the Local intranet zone, you see a dialog box with three check boxes that determine the sites that are part of the default settings for this zone. Leave these as they are and click **Advanced**.

4. To add a site, enter the address in the **Add this Web site to the zone** text box, and then click **Add**.

5. To remove a site from the zone, highlight it in the **Web sites** list, and then click **Remove**.

6. If you want Internet Explorer to make sure each site's Web server is using the HTTPS security protocol (a good idea), activate the **Require server verification (https:) for all sites in this zone** check box.

7. Click **OK**

Internet Explorer has four predefined security levels: **High** (most secure), **Low** (least secure), **Medium-low**, and **Medium**. You can assign any of these levels within the Security tab by first using the **Zone** list to choose the security zone, and then dragging the slider to the security level you want. Note that Internet Explorer displays the types of security each setting provides next to the slider.

A Few More Useful Internet Explorer Options

It's probably safe to crown Internet Explorer the undisputed heavyweight customization champion of the Windows world. This baby is bursting at the seams with settings, options, dials, and widgets for changing the way the program works. The secret to the prodigious customizability is the Internet Options dialog box, part of which you saw in the previous section. To shove this dialog box into the fray, use either of the following techniques:

➤ In Internet Explorer, select **Tools, Internet Options**.

➤ Select **Start, Settings, Control Panel** and then launch the **Internet Options** icon.

Either way, you end up eyeball to eyeball with the Internet Properties dialog box shown in Figure 9.6.

Figure 9.6

Use the Internet Options dialog box to customize Internet Explorer to suit the way you work.

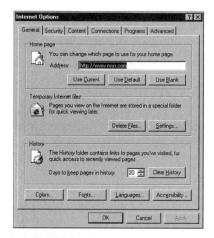

The **General** tab contains a mixed bag of options:

➤ **Home page**   To change the Internet Explorer home page (the page that first appears when you launch the browser), use the **Address** text box to enter the address of the page you prefer to use. (Alternatively, first navigate to the page you want to use, and then click **Use Current** in this group.) To revert to Internet Explorer's default home page, click the **Use Default** button. If you prefer that Internet Explorer not load a page at startup, click **Use Blank**.

➤ **Temporary Internet files**   The temporary Internet files folder is a storage area where Internet Explorer keeps the files associated with the sites that you visit. That way, when you revisit a page, Internet Explorer only has to pick up the local files, which means it can display the page contents much more quickly. You can click **Delete Files** to clear this cache, and you can click **Settings** to adjust a few parameters. I recommend leaving these options as they are, however.

Look Out!

Make Sure the Pages Are Up-To-Date

These temporary Internet files sound like the bees knees, but they have a downside. There's a chance that the page may have changed since your last visit, which means the version stored by Internet Explorer is out-of-date. If you want to make sure you're seeing the most recent edition of a page, either select **View**, **Refresh** or press **F5**.

➤ **History**   This group controls various options related to the History list I talked about in the previous chapter. Use the **Days to keep pages in history** spin box to set the maximum number of days that Internet Explorer will store an address in its History list. You can also click **Clear History** to remove all URLs from the History folder.

The **Content** tab, shown in Figure 9.7, boasts a wide array of settings for dealing with the content you come across on the Web.

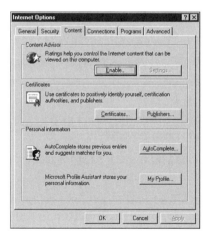

Figure 9.7

The Content tab lets you restrict access to certain Web sites as well as store information about yourself.

The buttons in the **Content Advisor** group let you control the type of content that appears in the browser:

➤ **Enable**   Clicking this button displays the Content Advisor dialog box, described next. When you click **OK**, you see the Create Supervisor Password dialog box, which you use to enter a password for the Content Advisor. After you've done this, the name of this button changes to Disable. You can turn off the ratings by clicking this button and entering your password.

➤ **Settings**   Clicking this button displays the Content Advisor, which you use to set site restrictions for people who don't know the password. The idea is that you select a category (such as Language or Nudity) and then move the slider to set the maximum level that users who don't have a password can view. If a site is rated higher, users must enter the supervisor password to download the site.

Other Ways to Restrict Content

The Internet is bursting with other tools that can help parents restrict the content their children can view. These packages come with names such as CyberSitter, Net Nanny, and KinderGuard —you get the idea. The Yahoo! Service has a list of these software packages at the following address:

```
http://www.yahoo.com/Business_and_Economy/Shopping_and Services/
Computers/Software/Internet/Blocking_and_Filtering/Titles/
```

The **Certificates** group deals with site certificates that act as positive identifications on the Web. This is advanced stuff, and it can be safely ignored.

The **Personal information** group gives you a place to store some data about yourself. Here are the options:

➤ **AutoComplete**   This feature enables Internet Explorer to automatically enter some data for you, including form data. Click this button and then activate the check boxes for the features with which you want to use AutoComplete.

➤ **My Profile**   Click this button to enter more data about yourself that a Web site can grab automatically.

More About AutoComplete

If AutoComplete is off, the first time you enter data into a Web form and then submit it, Internet Explorer sends in a dialog box asking if you want to turn AutoComplete on. Click **Yes** to activate AutoComplete, or click **No** to leave it be.

If you decide to go the AutoComplete route, *never* use it to automatically enter passwords for sensitive data such as online banking sites, stock trading, health sites, and so on.

The **Connections** tab stores most of the information you supplied to the Internet Connection Wizard. You can use the controls in this tab to change some of those settings, or you can click **Setup** to run the wizard all over again.

If you select Internet Explorer's **Tools, Mail and News** command, you see a menu of commands that enable you to send mail, view newsgroups, work with your address book, place a NetMeeting call directly from Internet Explorer, and more. The controls in the **Programs** tab, shown in Figure 9.8, determine which applications Internet Explorer launches when you select these commands. Again, you'll probably want to leave this as is.

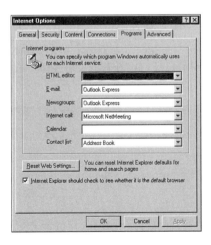

Figure 9.8

Use the Programs tab to set the default programs that Internet Explorer uses for things like email and reading newsgroups.

Finally, the **Advanced** tab boasts a huge list of check boxes and option buttons that controls how Internet Explorer interacts with the Web. For example, if you're sick of those lame MIDI files that so many Webmasters play when you visit their sites, you can turn them off by deactivating the **Play sounds** check box.

Unfortunately, there are just way too many options to go through here. If you want to get the lowdown on all these settings, check out the following page on my Web site:

```
http://www.mcfedries.com/wintelligence/IEAdvanced.html
```

The Least You Need to Know

This chapter took you through a whole host of beyond-the-basics Internet Explorer features. I showed you how to read pages offline, how to customize the Links bar, how to configure security, and how to set Internet Explorer's various options. Here's a quick review for tomorrow's pop quiz:

Crib Notes

➤ **Offline surfing** To get Internet Explorer to download a page for leisurely offline reading, select **Favorites, Add Favorites** and activate the **Make available offline** check box.

➤ **Links hi-jinks** Right-click a Links bar button to rename or delete the button or to change the link address. To add a button to the Links bar, either drag the Address bar icon into the Links bar or drag a link into the Links bar.

➤ **Feeling secure** Only submit sensitive data (such as your credit card number) to a secure site (that is, one that has a lock icon in the status bar).

➤ **Customizing Internet Explorer** Select the **Tools, Internet Options** command (or launch the Control Panel's **Internet Options** icon) to display the Internet Options dialog box.

Sending and Receiving Email Missives

The world passed a milestone of sorts a couple of years ago when it was reported that, in North America at least, more email messages are sent each day than postal messages. In fact, by early 2000, email message volume tripled that of "snail mail" (as regular mail is derisively called by the wired set), with well over a *billion* e-notes getting shipped out each day.

That's a staggering number, but it's not really a surprising one to anybody who has used email. Why? For the simple reason that email is just a better way to communicate. It's much faster than the post office (messages arrive in seconds or minutes instead of days or weeks), it's cheaper (email notes don't cost a nickel, other than your connection time), and it's easier on the tongue (is there anyone in the world who *likes* licking stamps and envelopes?).

The really good news is that email has become extremely easy to use because email programs have become much better over the years. An excellent example of this trend is Outlook Express, Windows Millennium's Internet email program. As you see in this chapter, shipping out messages and reading incoming messages is a painless affair, thanks to the admirable email capabilities of Outlook Express.

A Brief Email Primer

If you're new to the Internet email game, you should know a bit of email background before taking to the field. This section gives you the basics.

Email Addresses Deconstructed

The first thing you need to know is that each person on the Internet has a unique *email address*. Just like the full address of a house, your email address tells everyone the exact location they can use to send stuff to you. These addresses can be confusing, so let's look closely at an example, the email address for this book:

    cigwindows@mcfedries.com

This address has the following three parts:

cigwindows   This is the username. Most usernames are a single word representing either the person's first name, last name, or a combination of the two names. Some companies insist that the username be both the first name and last name separated by a period (for example, **paul.mcfedries**). Other email systems use different conventions. In America Online, for example, this part of the address is the user's screen name.

@   This symbol (it's pronounced "at") separates the "who" part of the address (the part to the left of the @ sign) and the "where" part (the part to the right of the @ sign).

mcfedries.com   This is my *domain name*, and it tells you where my e-mailbox is located. For most users, this part of the address is the domain name of their ISP. The part after the dot (.) tells you what type of organization you're dealing with. In this case, "com" represents a commercial business. Table 10.1 lists the other organization types you'll run into in your email travails.

Table 10.1   Post-Dot: Internet Organization Types

Code	What It Represents
com	Commercial business
edu	Educational institution
gov	Government
int	International organization
mil	Military
net	Networking organization
org	Non-profit organization

Finally, you should also know that many email addresses forego the old "type" designations in favor of geographical designations (or *geographical domains* as the pocket protector crowd calls them). Table 10.2 lists a few common geographical domains. (Note that, in a bit of geographical chauvinism, most U.S. email addresses don't bother with the country code.)

Table 10.2   Country Codes: Some Internet Geographical Domains

Code	The Country It Represents
at	Austria
au	Australia
ca	Canada
ch	Switzerland
de	Germany
dk	Denmark
es	Spain
fi	Finland
fr	France
jp	Japan
nz	New Zealand
uk	United Kingdom
us	United States

Complete Country Codes

The following Web page has a list of codes for all countries:

`http://www.iana.org/cctld.html`

Minding Your Email Manners

One of the first things you notice when you're drifting around the Net is that it attracts more than its share of bohemians, non-conformists, and rugged individualists. And despite all these people surfing to the beat of a different drum, the Net resolutely refuses to degenerate into mere anarchy. Oh sure, you get the odd every-nerd-for-himself hurly-burly, but civility reigns the majority of the time.

Usually most Netizens are just too busy with their researching and rubbernecking to cause trouble, but there's another mechanism that helps keep everyone in line: *netiquette* (short for *Internet etiquette*). Netiquette is a collection of suggested behavioral norms designed to grease the wheels of Net social discourse. Scofflaws who defy the netiquette rules can expect to see a few reprimands in their email inbox. To help you stay on the good side of the Internet community, this section tells you everything you need to know about the netiquette involved in sending email.

➤ **DON'T SHOUT!** When writing with your high-end word processor, you probably use italics (or, more rarely, underlining) to emphasize important words or phrases. But because most email just uses plain vanilla text (that is, no fancy formatting options allowed), you might think that, in cyberspace, no one can hear you scream. That's not true, however. In fact, many email scribes add emphasis to their epistles by using UPPERCASE LETTERS. This works, but please use uppercase sparingly. AN ENTIRE MESSAGE WRITTEN IN CAPITAL LETTERS FEELS LIKE YOU'RE SHOUTING, WHICH IS OKAY FOR USED-CAR SALESMEN ON LATE-NIGHT TV, BUT IS INAPPROPRIATE IN THE MORE SEDATE WORLD OF EMAIL CORRESPONDENCE.

➤ **Don't be "shiftless"** on the other hand, you occasionally see email messages written entirely in lowercase letters from lazy susans, toms, dicks, and harrys who can't muster the energy to reach out for the shift key. this, too, is taboo because it makes the text quite difficult to read. Just use the normal capitalization practices (uppercase for the beginning of sentences, proper names, and so on), and everyone will be happy.

➤ **Take your subject lines seriously** As you see a bit later, the message subject line is a heading that (theoretically, at least) describes the contents of the message. It's common for people to use the contents of the subject line to make a snap judgment about whether to bother reading a message. (This is especially true if the recipient doesn't know you from Adam.) The majority of mail mavens *hate* subject lines that are either ridiculously vague (for example, "Info required" or "Please help!"), or absurdly general (for example, "An email message" or "Mail"), and they'll just click the delete button without giving the message a second thought. (In fact, there's a kind of illicit thrill involved in deleting

146

an unread message, so don't give the person any excuse to exercise this indulgence.) Give your subject line some thought and make it descriptive enough so the reader can tell at a glance what your dispatch is about.

➤ **Don't send out someone else's words**   If you receive private email correspondence from someone, it's considered impolite to quote them in another message without their permission. (You're probably also violating copyright law, because the author of an email message has a copyright on any and all messages they send. There's even an acronym that covers this point with admirable succinctness: YOYOW—you own your own words; see the next section, "An Initial Look at Internet Acronyms," for more acronym fun.

➤ **Quote the original message when replying**   When replying to a message, include quotes from the original message for context. Few things are more frustrating in email than to receive a reply that just says "Great idea, let's do it!" or "That's the dumbest thing I've ever heard." Which great idea or dumb thing are they talking about? To make sure the other person knows what you're responding to, include the appropriate lines from the original message in your reply. You'll need to use some judgment here, though. Quoting the entire message is wasteful (especially if the message was a long one), and should generally be avoided. Just include enough of the original to put your response in context.

➤ **Don't expect an immediate reply**   Email can be extremely fast, and it's not unusual for missives to find their way to their destination within only a few minutes. However, that does *not* necessarily mean you'll get a reply just a few minutes later, so don't expect one. People are busier than ever, and you should assume your correspondents are wading through a huge stack of messages.

An Initial Look at Internet Acronyms

For most new users, acronyms are the bugbears and hobgoblins of computer life. They imply a hidden world of meaning that only the cognoscenti and those "in the know" are privy to. The Internet, in particular, is a maddeningly rich source of TLAs (three-letter acronyms) and other ciphers. To help you survive the inevitable onslaught of Internet acronymy, here's a list of the most commonly used initials in Net discourse:

AAMOF	As a matter of fact.
AFAIK	As far as I know.
BTW	By the way.
CU	See you (as in "see you later").
FAQ	Frequently Asked Questions. These are lists that appear in many Web sites and Usenet newsgroups to provide answers to questions that newcomers ask over and over.

FTF	Face-to-face.
FYA	For your amusement.
FYI	For your information.
IANAL	I am not a lawyer.
IMCO	In my considered opinion.
IMHO	In my humble opinion. (Although, in practice, opinions prefaced by IMHO are rarely humble. See IMNSHO, below.)
IMO	In my opinion.
IMNSHO	In my not so humble opinion. (This more accurately reflects most of the opinions one sees on the Internet!)
IOW	In other words.
LOL	laughing out loud.
NRN	No response necessary.
OTOH	On the other hand.
ROTFL	Rolling on the floor laughing.
ROTFLOL	Rolling on the floor laughing out loud.
SO	Significant other.
TFS	Thanks for sharing.
TIA	Thanks in advance.
TPTB	The powers that be.
TTFN	Ta-ta for now.
TTYL	Talk to you later.
WRT	With respect to.
YMMV	Your mileage may vary. This acronym means the advice/info/instructions just given may not work for you exactly as described.

Internet Hieroglyphics: Smileys

Email misunderstandings occur for a variety of reasons, but one of the most common reasons is someone misinterpreting a wryly humorous, sarcastic, or ironic remark as insulting or offensive. The problem is that the nuances and subtleties of wry humor and sarcasm are difficult to convey in print. *You* know your intent, but someone else (especially someone for whom English isn't their first language) may see things completely differently.

To help prevent such misunderstandings, and to grease the wheels of Net social interaction, cute little symbols called *smileys* (or, more rarely, *emoticons*) have been developed. The name comes from the following combination of symbols: :-). If you rotate this page clockwise so the left edge is at the top, you'll see that this combination looks like a smiling face. You would use it to indicate to your readers that the previous statement was intended to be humorous or, at least, not serious.

Acronyms Served Up Piping Hot (AFAIK)

If you come across an acronym that's not covered here, check out the WorldWideWeb Acronym Server, which lets you look up acronyms, or find acronyms whose expansion contains a particular word. Surf to the following page to check it out:

`http://www.ucc.ie/info/net/acronyms/index.html`

The basic smiley is the one you'll encounter most often, but there are all kinds of others to tilt your head over (some of which are useful, most of which are downright silly). Here's a sampling:

Smiley	Meaning
:-)	Ha ha, just kidding.
:-D	(Laughing) That's hilarious; I break myself up.
;-)	(Winking) Nudge, nudge, wink, wink; I'm flirting.
:-(	I'm unhappy.
;-(	I'm crying.
:-|	I'm indifferent; well whatever, never mind.
:-#	My lips are sealed.
:-/	I'm skeptical.
:->	I'm being sarcastic.
:-V	I'm shouting.
;^)	I'm smirking.
%-)	I've been staring at this screen too long!

Look Out!

Don't Get Too Cute

Smileys are an easy way to convey meaning in your online writings, but don't lean on them too heavily. Overusing smileys not only means your writing isn't as clear as it could be, but it'll also automatically brand you as a dreaded newbie or as terminally cute. One way around this is to use one or more of the following "non-smileys":

Symbol	What It Means
\<g>	Grinning, smiling
\<l>	Laughing
\<l>	Irony
\<s>	Sighing
\<jk>	Just kidding
\<>	No comment

Some Thoughts on Email Virus Hoaxes

After you're online, it probably won't take very long until you receive an email message along the following lines:

```
There is a computer virus that is being sent across the Internet. If
you receive an email message with the subject line "Good Times," DO
NOT read the message, DELETE it immediately. Some miscreant is send-
ing email and files under the title "Good Times." If you receive this
file, do not download it. It has a virus that rewrites your hard
drive, obliterating anything on it. Please be careful and forward
this mail to anyone you care about.
```

Heeding the last sentence, the sender will most likely have forwarded this warning to a few dozen friends, relatives, and colleagues. That's awfully thoughtful of him, but there's only one problem: *This message is a hoax!* There is no such virus, and the message is just some prankster's attempt to yank the Net's collective chain.

"Good Times" is the oldest (it's been around since 1994) and most famous of the email virus hoaxes. It is not, unfortunately, the only one. While writing this book, I received many "warnings" forwarded by concerned readers about an alleged email virus called "Win a Holiday." Other hoaxes include the "Penpal Greetings" virus, the "Deeyenda" virus, and the "Irina" virus. All these are variations on the "Good Times" theme.

Other email hoax annoyances take the form of chain letters. Some of these messages claim to be from malicious hackers who will do something nasty to your computer if you don't forward the message to ten of your friends. One of my favorites is the "Bill Gates $1,000" hoax, where a message allegedly from Bill Gates tells you to forward the message to everyone you know and, when 1,000 people have received it, you'll win $1,000.

The ironic thing about all this is that these messages act as a kind of virus themselves. With thousands of people naively forwarding tens of thousands of copies of the message all over the Internet, they end up clogging systems and wasting the time of those people who must refute their claims.

The Internet offers many sources of information on these virus hoaxes. Here are three of the best:

➤ **Computer Virus Myths** `http://www.kumite.com/myths/`

➤ **Internet ScamBusters** `http://www.scambusters.org/`

➤ **About.com's Urban Legends and Folklore**
   `http://urbanlegends.about.com/`

The Lay of the Outlook Express Land

Now that you're up to speed with the whole email thing, it's time to put all this knowledge to good use by learning how to use Outlook Express.

Windows Millennium gives you three ways to launch the program:

➤ **The easy way** Click the **Launch Outlook Express** icon in the taskbar's Quick Launch area.

➤ **The slightly harder way** Double-click the desktop's **Outlook Express** icon.

➤ **The hardest way** Select **Start**, **Programs**, **Outlook Express**.

If, when you were configuring your Internet connection back in Chapter 7, "Getting Yourself Online," you were negligent in your email account setup duties, Outlook Express asks the Internet Connection Wizard to step in for a moment to run through the necessary steps.

Cross Reference

To revisit configuring your Internet connection, see "More Morsels: Setting Up Your Internet Email Account" p. 107.

By default, Outlook Express is set up to go online and grab your waiting messages at startup. We'll get there eventually, so for now just close the Connect To dialog box if it shows up.

At long last, the Outlook Express window shows itself, and it looks much like the one in Figure 10.1.

Figure 10.1

Use Outlook Express to ship and receive Internet email messages.

The Folders list contains various Outlook Express storage areas

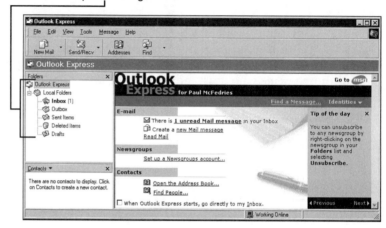

A More Sensible Startup

The default Outlook Express startup screen shows a collection of common chores (such as Create a new Mail message). Most people don't find this screen particularly useful, so they just click the **Inbox** folder (which is where all your incoming messages first get stored). If you want Outlook Express to open the **Inbox** folder automatically at startup, activate the **When Outlook Express starts, go directly to my Inbox** check box.

The Outbox: Sending an Email Message

Let's begin the Outlook Express tour with a look at how to foist your e-prose on unsuspecting colleagues, friends, family, and Brady Bunch cast members. This section shows you the basic technique to use, and then gets a bit fancier in discussing the Address Book, attachments, and other Outlook Express sending features.

The Basics: Composing and Sending a Message

Without further ado (not that there's been much ado to this point, mind you), here are the basic steps to follow to fire off an email message to some lucky recipient:

1. Click the **New Mail** button in the toolbar, or select **Message**, **New Message**. (Keyboard fans will be pleased to note that pressing **Ctrl+N** also works.) You end up with the New Message window onscreen, as shown in Figure 10.2.

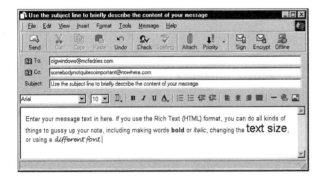

Figure 10.2

You cobble together an email message in the New Message window.

2. In the **To** text box, type in the email address of the recipient. (It's perfectly acceptable to enter multiple addresses in this text box. Use a semicolon (;) or a comma (,) to separate each address.)

3. The address you put in the To box is the "main" recipient of the message. However, it's common to shoot a copy of the message off to a "secondary" recipient. To do that, enter their email address in the **Cc** text box. (Again, you can enter multiple addresses, if you're so inclined.)

No Recipient? Just Try Me

If you don't yet know anyone's email address (or even if you do), feel free to toss a message my way by using the address **cigwindows@mcfedries.com**. I would love to hear from you!

Cc and Its Bcc Cousin

"Cc" stands for either *courtesy copy* or *carbon copy*; nobody really knows for sure. There's also an email creature called the *blind courtesy* (or *carbon*) *copy* (Bcc), which also delivers a copy of the message to a specified recipient. However, none of the other recipients see that person's address anywhere. To enter a Bcc address, activate the **View, All Headers** command to add a **Bcc** field to the New Message window.

4. Use the **Subject** line to enter a subject for the message. (The subject acts as a kind of title for your message. It's the first thing the recipient sees, so it should accurately reflect the content of your message, and it shouldn't be too long. Think *pithy*.)

5. Decide what type of message you want to send. You have two choices, both of which are commands on the Format menu:

   ➤ **Rich Text (HTML)** Choose this command to include formatting in your message. This enables you to make your message look its best. However, your recipient might have problems if his email program doesn't support this formatting. (Just so you know, HTML stands for Hypertext Markup Language. It's a series of codes used to format characters and things, and it's used to create Web pages. Don't worry, you don't have to know anything about HTML to use this feature.)

   ➤ **Plain Text** Choose this command to send out the message without any formatting. This makes life easier for your recipient if he doesn't have an email program that supports formatting. If you're not sure what your recipient is using, choose this command anyway.

6. Use the large, empty, area below the Subject line to type in the message text (also known as the *message body*).

7. If you chose the Rich Text (HTML) format, after you're inside the message text area, notice that the buttons on the Formatting bar suddenly become available, as do more of the Format menu commands. Use these buttons and commands to change the font, format paragraphs, add a background image, apply stationery, and more. (*Stationery* is a prefab set of formatting options.)

No Spell Check?

You might be intrigued that Outlook Express has a **Spelling** command on the **Tools** menu (as well as a **Spelling** toolbar button). However, you might also be bummed that you can't select it. That's because Outlook Express doesn't actually have its own spell checker. Instead, it just rides the spell checking coattails of other programs, such as Microsoft Word. So you can run the Spelling command only if you have a spell-check–equipped program installed.

8. When your message is fit for human consumption, you have two sending choices:

> ➤ **If you're working online** Click the **Send** toolbar button or select **File**, **Send Message** (or try **Alt+S** on for size). Outlook Express sends the message, no questions asked.

> ➤ **If you're working offline** Click the **Send** toolbar button or select **File**, **Send Later**. In this case, Outlook Express coughs up a dialog box that tells you the message will bunk down in the Outbox folder until you're ready to send it. This is good because it means you can compose a few messages before connecting to the Internet. When you're ready to actually ship the messages, select the **Tools**, **Send and Receive**, **Send All** command in Outlook Express. (You also can drop down the **Send/Recv** toolbar button, and then click **Send All**.)

Note that after your message is Net-bound, Outlook Express also is kind enough to save a copy of the message in the Sent Items folder. This is handy because it gives you a record of all the missives you launch into cyberspace.

Easier Addressing: Using the Address Book

If you find yourself with a bunch of recipients to whom you send stuff regularly (and it's a rare emailer who doesn't), you soon grow tired of entering their addresses by hand. The solution is to toss those regulars into the Windows Millennium Address Book. That way, you can fire them into the To or Cc lines with just a few mouse clicks.

Here's how you add someone to the Address Book:

1. In Outlook Express, click the **Addresses** button or select the **Tools, Address Book** command. (Keyboard diehards can get their kicks by pressing **Ctrl+Shift+B**. Note, too, that you also can work on your Address Book when Outlook Express isn't running. In this case, select **Start, Programs, Accessories, Address Book**.)

2. In the Address Book window that reports for duty, click the **New** toolbar button and then click **New Contact**. (Alternatively, either select **File, New Contact** or slam **Ctrl+N**.) The Address Book conjures up the Properties dialog box shown in Figure 10.3.

Figure 10.3

Use this dialog box to spell out the particulars of the new recipient.

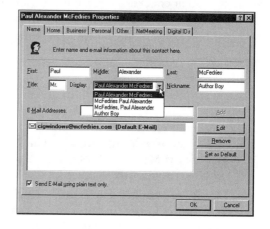

Using Nicknames

If you enter a value in the **Nickname** field, you can type in that value in the To or Cc box when sending a message.

3. In the **Name** tab, enter at least the person's **First** and **Last** names.

4. Use the **E-Mail Addresses** text box to enter the recipient's address, and then click **Add**.

5. If you want this person to receive only plain text messages, activate the **Send E-Mail using plain text only** check box.

6. Fill in the fields in the other tabs, if you feel like it.

7. When you're done, click **OK** to add the new recipient.

After you have contacts in your Address Book, Outlook Express gives you a ton of ways to get them a message. Here are my two favorite methods:

➤ In the New Message window, click **To** or **Cc** to get the Select Recipients dialog box. Click the contact name and then click **To** (or **Cc** or **Bcc**).

➤ The Outlook Express window has a Contacts area that lists everyone in the Address Book. Use this area to double-click the name of the recipient you want to use.

One final note. If you set up the recipient to receive only plain text messages, when you send the message, you see a dialog box asking what format you want to use. In this case, you'd click **Send Plain Text**.

Group Email Gropes

One of the Internet's most enduring pastimes is to send out jokes and trivia to a select group of friends and colleagues. (Some folks find this annoying, but most see it as all in good fun.) The best way to do this is to organize those recipients into a *group*. That way, you can send a message to all of them just by specifying the group name in the To line. To create a group, click the **New** button and then click **New Group**. (You can also select the Address Book's **File**, **New Group** command, or press **Ctrl+G**.) Enter a **Group Name** and then click **Select Members** to add recipients to the group.

Inserting Attachments and Other Hangers-On

Most of your messages will be text-only creations (with possibly a bit of formatting tossed in to keep things interesting). However, it's also possible to send entire files along for the ride. Such files are called, naturally enough, *attachments*. They're very common in the business world, and it's useful to know how they work. Here goes:

Jargon Jar

Attachment

A file that latches on to an email message and is sent to the recipient.

1. In the New Message window, either click the **Attach** toolbar button or select **Insert**, **File Attachment**. The Insert Attachment dialog box rears its head.

2. Find the file you want to attach and then highlight it.

3. Click **Attach**. Outlook Express returns you to the New Message window where you see a new **Attach** box that includes the name of the file.

The Inbox: Getting and Reading Email Messages

Some people like to think of email as a return to the days of *belles-lettres* and *billets-doux* (these people tend to be a bit pretentious). Yes, it's true that email has people writing again, but this isn't like the letter writing of old. The major difference is that email's turnaround time is usually much quicker. Instead of waiting weeks or even months to get a return letter, a return email might take as little as a few minutes or a few hours.

So, if you send out a message with a question or comment, chances are you get a reply coming right back at you before too long. Any messages sent to your email address are stored in your account at your ISP. Your job is to use Outlook Express to access your account and grab any waiting messages. This section shows you how to do that and shows you what to do with those messages after they're safely stowed on your computer.

Mailing Lists

Another good way to be sure your email Inbox stays populated is to subscribe to a *mailing list*. This is an email-based forum that discusses a particular topic. For example, in my Word Spy mailing list, I send out a new or recently coined word and its definition each day (see www.wordspy.com). There's a directory of mailing lists available at www.liszt.com.

Getting Your Messages

Here are the steps to stride through to get your email messages:

1. Outlook Express offers two different postal routes:

   ➤ **To only receive messages**   Either drop down the **Send/Recv** toolbar button and then click **Receive All**, or select **Tools, Send and Receive, Receive All**.

   ➤ **To send and receive messages**   If you have outgoing messages waiting in your Outbox folder, either drop down the **Send/Recv** toolbar button and then click **Send and Receive All**, or select **Tools, Send and Receive, Send and Receive All**. (Keyboardists can get away with pressing **Ctrl+M**.)

2. Outlook Express connects to your mail account, absconds with any waiting messages, and then stuffs them into your Inbox folder. If you were working offline previously, disconnect from the Internet if you no longer need the connection.

3. If it's not already displayed, click the **Inbox** folder so you can see what the e-postman delivered.

Reading Your Messages

Figure 10.4 shows the Inbox folder with a few messages. The first thing to notice is that Outlook Express uses a bold font for all messages that you haven't read yet. You also get info about each message organized with the following half-dozen columns:

Automatic Message Checking

When you're working online, Outlook Express automatically checks for new messages every 30 minutes. You can change that by selecting **Tools, Options**. In the **General** tab, use the spin box that's part of the **Check for new messages every x minute(s)** option to set the checking interval.

Attachment

Priority   Flag

Unread messages are shown in bold type

Figure 10.4

After you've pilfered your incoming messages from your ISP, they get stored in your Inbox folder.

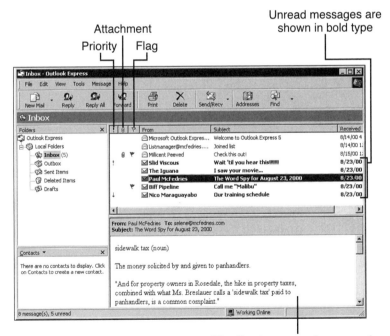

The Preview pane shows you the text of the highlighted message

159

➤ **Priority**   This column tells you whether the sender set up the message with a priority ranking. If you see a red exclamation mark, it means the message was sent with high priority (this is the "handle this pronto, buster!" symbol); if you see a blue, downward-pointing arrow, it means the note was sent with low priority (this is the "handle this whenever, man" symbol).

➤ **Attachment**   If you see a paper clip icon in this column, it means the message is accompanied by a file attachment. See "Attending to Attachments," later in this chapter.

➤ **Flag**   If you want to remind yourself to deal with a message, you can "flag" it for a future follow-up (a sort of digital string-tied-to-the-finger thing). You do this by highlighting the message and then selecting the **Message, Flag Message** command. This adds a flag icon in this column.

Jargon Jar

Conversation

A series of messages with the same subject line. It's also known as a *thread* in email circles.

➤ **From**   This column tells you the name (or occasionally, just the email address) of the person or company that sent you the message.

➤ **Subject**   This column shows you the subject line of the message which will, hopefully, give you a brief description of the contents of the message.

➤ **Received**   This column tells you the date and time the message was received.

Outlook Express offers two methods for seeing what a message has to say:

➤ Highlight the message in the Inbox folder. Outlook Express displays the text of the note in the Preview pane. After about five seconds, Outlook Express removes the bolding from the message to indicate that it has been read.

➤ Highlight the message in the Inbox folder and then double-click it or select **File, Open**. (For the heck of it, you also can press **Ctrl+O** or just **Enter**.) This method opens the message in its own window.

Windows Wisdom

Grouping Messages by Conversation

Before you can use the Next Unread Conversation command, you have to group all the messages from the same conversation. To do that, choose the **View, Current View, Group Messages by Conversation** command.

To read other messages, either repeat these procedures or use any of the following Outlook Express techniques:

➤ **To read the previous message in the list** Select **View, Previous Message**. (**Ctrl+<** works, as well; if you have the message window open, click the **Previous** toolbar button.)

160

➤ **To read the next message in the list**   Select **View**, **Next**, **Next Message**. (**Ctrl+>** also does the job; if you have the message window open, click the **Next** toolbar button.)

➤ **To read the next *unread* message**   Select **View**, **Next**, **Next Unread Message** (or press **Ctrl+U**).

➤ **To read the next unread conversation**   Select **View**, **Next**, **Next Unread Conversation** (or press **Ctrl+Shift+U**).

Attending to Attachments

As I mentioned earlier, if you get a message that has one or more files tied to it, you see a paper clip icon in the Inbox folder's Attachment column. You also see a larger paper clip icon in the upper-right corner of the preview pane. Outlook Express gives you a few ways to handle any attachments in the current message:

➤ **Saving the file**   Select **File**, **Save Attachments** to convince the Save Attachments dialog box to drop by. If there are multiple files, use the **Attachments To Be Saved** list to highlight the ones you want to save. Use the **Save To** text box to specify where you want the files to be stored (click **Browse** to choose the folder from a dialog box). Then click **Save** to dump the file (or files) onto your hard disk.

➤ **Saving the file from the preview pane**   Click the paper clip icon in the upper-right corner of the preview pane to see a list that includes the filename of the attachment. Click **Save Attachments** and follow the steps I just took you through.

➤ **Opening the file**   If you just want to see what's in the file, you can open it. To do that, click the paper clip icon in the upper-right corner of the preview pane, and then click the filename. This gets you to the Open Attachment Warning dialog box. From here, be sure the **Open it** option is activated, and then click **OK**.

What to Do with a Message After You've Read It

This section gives you a rundown of all the things you can do with a message after you've read it. In each case, you either need to have a message highlighted in the Inbox folder, or you need to have the message open. Here's the list:

➤ **Ship out a reply**   If you think of a witty retort, you can email it back to the sender either by selecting **Message**, **Reply to Sender**, or by clicking the **Reply** toolbar button. (The keyboard route is **Ctrl+R**.)

➤ **Ship out a reply to every recipient**   If the note was foisted on several people, you might prefer to send your response to everyone who received the original. To do that, either select **Message**, **Reply to All**, or click the **Reply All** button. (The keyboard shortcut is **Ctrl+Shift+R**.)

➤ **Forward the message to someone else** To have someone else take a gander at a message you received, you can forward it to him either by selecting **Message**, **Forward**, or by clicking the **Forward** button. (Keyboard dudes and dudettes can press **Ctrl+F**.)

"Melissa" and Other Attachment Nasties

Although Outlook Express makes it easy to deal with attachments, you should never just blithely open an attached file. The Internet is inundated with rogue messages that carry virus-infected programs as attachments. If you run such a program, it infects your system and then (usually) ships out more copies of itself to people in your Address Book! This is how the famous "Melissa" virus works. The rule of thumb with attachments is to open only those you receive from people you know and trust. Even then, if a friend unexpectedly sends you a program as an attachment, drop them a quick note to confirm that they really sent it.

Forwarding an Exact Copy of the Message

A forwarded message contains the original message text, which is preceded by an "Original Message" header and some of the message particulars (who sent it, when they sent it, and so on). If you want your recipient to see the message exactly as you received it, use the **Message**, **Forward As Attachment** command, instead.

➤ **Move the message to some other folder** If you find your Inbox folder is getting seriously overcrowded, you should think about moving some messages to other folders. To move a message, select **Edit**, **Move to Folder** (or press **Ctrl+Shift+V**). In the Move dialog box that shows up, highlight the destination folder and then click **OK**. (You can create a new folder by clicking the **New Folder** button, entering a name for the folder in the New Folder dialog box, and then clicking **OK**.)

➤ **Delete the message** If you don't think you have cause to read a message again, you might as well delete it to keep the Inbox clutter to a minimum. To delete a message, either select **Edit**, **Delete**, or click the **Delete** button. (A message also can be vaporized by pressing **Ctrl+D**).

The Least You Need to Know

This chapter showed you how to use Outlook Express to work with Internet email. You spent the first half of the chapter learning about sending messages. I showed you the basic steps for composing and sending a message, how to use the Address Book, and how to insert a file as an attachment. The rest of the chapter concentrated on receiving notes. You learned how to connect to your ISP and get your waiting messages, how to read messages, how to deal with attachments, and what to do with a message after you've read it. Here's a summary of what you need to know:

Retrieving Deleted Messages

Note that Outlook Express doesn't get rid of a deleted message completely. Instead, it just dumps it in the Deleted Items folder. If you later realize that you deleted the message accidentally (insert forehead slap here), you can head for Deleted Items and then move it back into the Inbox.

Crib Notes

➤ **Outlook Express takeoff**   Either click the **Launch Outlook Express** icon in the Quick Launch area, double-click the desktop's **Outlook Express** icon, or select **Start**, **Programs**, **Outlook Express**.

➤ **Go to the Inbox**   It's best to launch Outlook Express and go directly to the Inbox folder. To do that, activate the **When Outlook Express starts, go directly to my Inbox folder** check box.

➤ **Composing a message**   Click the **New Mail** button (or select **Message**, **New Message**), enter the address and a Subject line, fill in the message body, and then either select **File, Send Message** (if you're online) or **File, Send Later** (if you're offline).

➤ **Receiving messages**   Click the **Send/Recv** button and then click **Receive All** (or select **Tools, Send and Receive, Receive All**).

Chapter 11

More Email Bonding: Extending Outlook Express

In This Chapter

➤ Basic message folder maintenance

➤ Fonts, stationery, signatures, filtering, and other message techniques

➤ Sharing Outlook Express with others by creating separate email identities

➤ Searching for Internet email addresses

➤ A miscellany of mail methods to help you make the most of Outlook Express

After they're on the Net and comfortable with this whole cyberspace deal, most people turn into regular e-scribes barraging every wired person they know with e-letters, e-memos, and e-rants of all kinds. If you find this happening to you, you're probably also finding that you're spending great gobs of time inside Outlook Express. It may even be your most-used program (or at least in the top three or four).

But if all you're doing is pecking out your missives and then slamming the Send button, you're missing out on some of the most useful and fun features of Outlook Express. In this chapter, you go beyond the previous chapter's basics and learn many of the program's more interesting features and options. I show you how to manage message folders, work with stationery and signatures, create identities, filter incoming messages, search for Internet email addresses, and customize all kinds of Outlook Express options.

Taking Charge of Your Message Folders

Right out of the box, Outlook Express comes with five prefab folders: Inbox (in-coming messages), Outbox (messages waiting to be sent), Sent Items (messages that you've sent), Deleted Items (messages that you've blown away), and Drafts (saved messages that you're still working on). Surely that's enough folders for anyone, right?

Maybe not. Even if you're good at deleting the detritus from your Inbox folder, it still won't take long before it becomes bloated with messages and finding the note you need becomes a real needle-in-a-haystack exercise. What you really need is a way to organize your mail. For example, suppose you and your boss exchange a lot of email. Rather than storing all her messages in your Inbox folder, you could create a separate folder just for her messages. You could also create folders for each of the Internet mailing lists you subscribe to, for current projects on the go, or for each of your regular email correspondents. There are, in short, a thousand-and-one uses for folders and this section tells you everything you need to know.

To create a new folder, follow these steps:

1. Select the **File, Folder, New** command to display the Create Folder dialog box, shown in Figure 11.1. (Attention keyboardists: Pressing **Ctrl+Shift+E** also gets you where you want to go.)

Figure 11.1

Use this dialog box to create your new folder.

2. In the **Select the folder...** list, highlight the folder within which you want the new folder to appear. For example, if you want your new folder to be inside your inbox, click the Inbox folder.

3. Use the **Folder name** text box to enter the name of the new folder.

4. Click **OK**.

Here's a quick look at a few other folder maintenance chores you may need from time to time:

➤ **Renaming a folder** The names of the
five predefined Outlook Express folders are
set in stone, but it's easy to rename any
folder that you created yourself. To do so,
highlight the folder and then select **File,
Folder, Rename** (or press **F2**). In the
Rename Folder dialog box, enter the new
name and then click **OK**.

➤ **Compacting a folder** To help minimize
the size of the files that Outlook Express
uses to store messages, you should *compact*
the files regularly. To do this, select **File,
Folder** and then select either **Compact**
(to compact just the currently highlighted
folder) or **Compact All Folders** (to compact the whole shooting match). You
don't have to worry about this one too much because Outlook Express keeps an
eye peeled on your folders and offers to compact them automatically every once
in a while.

Look Out!

Can't Select the Folder Command?

If the Folder command is unavail-
able, it means you have the
Outlook Express "folder" selected in
the Folders list. To unlock this command, first click any other folder
(such as Local Folders or Inbox).

Windows Wisdom

Why Is Compacting Necessary?

You need to compact your folders because when you permanently delete messages (such as when you delete stuff from the Deleted Items folder), Outlook
Express lazily leaves gaps in its files where the messages used to be. Compacting
scrunches the files together to eliminate the gaps, which makes the files smaller
and saves disk space. The good news is that this has absolutely no effect on your
remaining messages and folders.

Rescuing a Deleted Folder

As with messages, folders that you delete are stuffed into the Deleted Items folder. If you made a horrible mistake when you deleted the folder, you can get it back by moving it out of Deleted Items.

➤ **Moving a folder**   If you want to move a folder to a different location, the easiest method is to use your mouse to drag the folder and drop it on the new location. (The harder method is to highlight the folder and select **File, Folder, Move**. In the Move dialog box, use the folder tree to highlight the new location for the folder, and then click **OK**.)

➤ **Deleting a folder**   To get rid of a folder you no longer need (and all the messages it contains), highlight the folder and then select **File, Folder, Delete**. (If your mouse is tired, the keyboard alternative is to press the **Delete** key.) Outlook Express then wonders if you're sure about this. Ponder your next move carefully and, if you still want to go ahead, click **Yes** to delete the folder. (Click **No** if you get cold feet and decide not to nuke the folder.)

Some Handy Message Maneuvers

You spend the bulk of your Outlook Express time shipping out messages to far-flung folks, and reading messages that those folks fire back at you. To help you get the most out of these sending and reading tasks, this section looks at the wide range of message options offered by Outlook Express.

Better E-Letters: Setting the Default Message Font

In Chapter 10, "Sending and Receiving Email Missives," you learned about the difference between Plain Text messages and Rich Text (HTML) messages. For the latter, you can use the Formatting toolbar to mess with, among other things, the font in which your typed characters appear. The font controls the typeface, the type style (bold or italic, for example), the type size, and the color.

If you have a particular font combo that you're particularly fond of, you can tell Outlook Express to use it automatically. Here's how:

1. Select **Tools, Options** to invite in the Options dialog box.
2. Click the **Compose** tab.
3. In the **Compose Font** group, click the **Font Settings** button that appears beside the **Mail** heading. This lands you smack dab in the middle of the Font dialog box, shown in Figure 11.2.

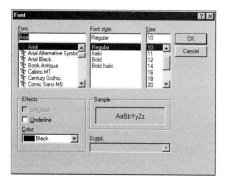

4. Use the various controls to pick the font options you want, and then click **OK** to get back to the Options dialog box.

5. Click **OK** to put the new settings into effect.

Working with Stationery

In the real world, stationery is paper that includes predefined text, colors, and images. Outlook Express lets you set up the electronic equivalent. That is, you can define email stationery that includes a background image and predefined text. This is essentially a Web page to which you can also add your own text. Outlook Express gives you three choices:

➤ Use any of the Outlook Express predefined stationery designs on an individual message.

➤ Set up a stationery as the default that gets applied to all your outgoing messages.

➤ Create your own stationery.

Let's begin with using one of the built-in stationery patterns on a single message. Outlook Express gives you two ways to do this:

➤ To start a new message using a specific stationery, select **Message, New Message Using** (you can also click the downward-pointing arrow in the **New Mail** toolbar button). When Outlook Express displays its menu of stationery options, click the one you want to use.

➤ If you've already started a message, you can choose stationery by selecting the **Format, Apply Stationery** command, and then picking out the stationery you want from the submenu that appears.

A Stationery Cautionary Tale

Keep in mind that your recipients may not have an email program that understands stationery. In fact, some email programs have been known to choke on messages that are festooned with stationery and other non-text frippery. So if a correspondent complains that he couldn't read your message, re-send it without the stationery.

If you find yourself using the same stationery over and over, perhaps it's time to set up that stationery so that Outlook Express applies it automatically whenever you start a new message. Here's what you have to do:

1. In Outlook Express, select **Tools, Options** to request the presence of the Options dialog box.

2. Click the **Compose** tab.

3. In the **Stationery** group, activate the **Mail** check box, and then click the **Select** button to the right of it. Outlook Express reaches into its bag of tricks and pulls out the Select Stationery dialog box.

4. Highlight the stationery file you want to use. (If you're not sure, make certain the **Show preview** check box is activated. This displays a preview of the highlighted stationery in the **Preview** box.)

5. When you've settled on a stationery, click **OK** to return to the Options dialog box.

6. Click **OK**.

Finally, Outlook Express is happy to use a stationery that you create yourself. It even provides a cheerful little wizard to take you through the steps. Here's what happens:

1. In Outlook Express, select **Tools, Options** to request the presence of the Options dialog box.

2. Click the **Compose** tab.

3. In the **Stationery** group, click **Create New**. The Stationery Setup Wizard comes bursting through the door.

4. The initial wizard dialog box just has some not-very-useful introductory material, so click **Next**. The wizard proffers its Background dialog box, shown in Figure 11.3.

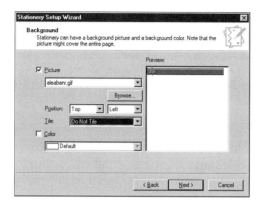

Figure 11.3

Use the Stationery Setup Wizard dialog box to pick out a background picture or color for your stationery.

5. You have two ways to set the stationery background (when you're done, click **Next**):

➤ If you want to have a picture as the background, leave the **Picture** check box activated and use the list box below it to select the picture file you want (or click **Browse** to pick out the picture using a dialog box). Use the **Position** lists to choose where the picture appears in the stationery, and use the **Tile** list to determine whether the picture appears just once (**Do Not Tile**) or is repeated until it covers the stationery.

➤ If you prefer (or also want) to use a solid color as the background, activate the **Color** check box and then use the list below it to choose a color that suits your fancy.

6. Next up are the stationery fonts. Choose the **Font** (typeface), **Size**, **Color**, and whether the text is **Bold** and/or **Italic**. Click **Next** to keep things moving.

7. The wizard's to-do list continues with setting the stationery margin widths. The margins determine where in the stationery your typing starts. Use the **Left Margin** spin box to set the distance from the left edge, and use the **Top Margin** spin box to set the distance from the top edge. Click **Next** to continue.

8. In the last of the wizard's dialog boxes, enter a **Name** for your funky new stationery (such as **Funky New Stationery**) and click **Finish** to send the wizard home.

After you've completed your stationery creation, you can use it in your messages just like any other stationery.

Online Stationery Storehouse

A few other stationery samples are available on the Web. To see them, select **Tools, Options** to get back to the Options dialog box, head for the **Compose** tab, and then click the **Download More** button in the Stationery group.

Setting Up a Signature

In email lingo, a *signature* is a chunk of text that appears at the bottom of all your messages. Most people use their signature to give contact information, and you often see sigs (that's the hip short form) adorned with witty quotations or sayings. Outlook Express even lets you create multiple signatures, so you can tailor them to various audiences.

Here are the steps to plow through to create a signature or two:

1. Select the **Tools, Options** command.
2. In the Options dialog box that climbs into the ring, display the **Signatures** tab.
3. Click **New**. Outlook Express adds a new item to the Signatures list.
4. Use the **Text** box to compose the signature.
5. Annoyingly, Outlook Express gives each signature a boring name such as Signature #1 (see Figure 11.4). A more meaningful name would be nice, so click the signature in the **Signatures** list, click **Rename**, enter a snappier name, and then press **Enter**.

Figure 11.4

Use the Signature tab to enter one or more signatures.

6. Repeat steps 3–5 to create more signatures, if you so desire.
7. If you want Outlook Express to tack on the default signature to all your messages, activate the **Add signatures to all outgoing messages** check box. If you don't want the signature to show up when you reply to a message or forward a message to someone, leave the **Don't add signatures to Replies or Forwards** check box activated.
8. When you're done, click **OK** to return to Outlook Express.

If you elected not to add your signature automatically, it's easy enough to toss it into a message that you're composing. In the New Message window, move the cursor to where you want the text to appear, and then select **Insert**, **Signature**. (If you have multiple signatures defined, a submenu with a list of the sigs slides out. Select the one you want to use.)

The Default Signature

The "default signature" is the first signature you create. To set up some other signature as the default, highlight it in the **Signatures** list, and then click **Set as Default**.

Seven Useful Sending Settings

Let's spend a little more time hanging out in the handy Options dialog box. In this section, I take you through a few settings related to sending messages. To see these options, select the **Tools**, **Options** command and then display the **Send** tab, shown in Figure 11.5.

Figure 11.5

The Send tab is loaded with ways to customize sending messages in Outlook Express.

Here's a once-over of what's available (click **OK** when you're done):

➤ **Save copy of sent messages in the 'Sent Items' folder**   Deactivate this check box to tell Outlook Express not to bother putting copies of your messages in Sent Items. I don't recommend doing this because you'll probably refer to previously sent notes on many an occasion.

➤ **Send messages immediately**   When this option is activated and you're working online, Outlook Express transmits your messages as soon as you send them (unless, of course, you select the Send Later command). If you want Outlook Express to hold its sending horses, deactivate this check box.

173

➤ **Automatically put people I reply to in my Address Book**   This option is on by default, which is downright silly because it means that every last person to whom you send a reply will get stuffed into your Address Book. That's dumb, so you might consider deactivating this one.

➤ **Automatically complete e-mail addresses when composing**   After you have some names in your Address Book, you can start typing a name and Outlook Express will "guess" the rest of the name based on the Address Book entries. If you don't like this feature, deactivate this check box to turn it off.

➤ **Include message in reply**   When this option is activated and you reply to a message, Outlook Express adds the original message to your reply message. This is a good idea because it reminds the recipient of what they said, so you should leave this option on.

➤ **Reply to messages using the format in which they were sent**   When this check box is activated, Outlook Express sets up your replies using the same format that the sender used. For example, if you get a plain text message and you reply to it, the reply will automatically be set up as plain text, as well. Again, I recommend leaving this one on.

➤ **Mail Sending Format**   These options determine the default format that Outlook Express uses for your messages. Select either **HTML** or **Plain Text**.

Dealing with the Onslaught: Filtering Messages

It's an unfortunate fact of online life that the email system is the source of many unwanted messages. Whether it's the scourge of unsolicited commercial email (also know whimsically as *spam*) or someone you've had a falling out with, you inevitably end up getting some messages that you instantly delete.

Jargon Jar

Spam

Unsolicited commercial email messages that advertise products, services, miracle cures, pyramid schemes, and GET RICH QUICK!!!! scams (recognizable by their unrelenting use of all-uppercase letters).

You can save yourself the bother by setting up Outlook Express to delete these annoyances for you. You can also go beyond this by having Outlook Express look for certain messages and then automatically move them to another folder, send out a reply, flag the messages, and much more.

Let's begin with the most straightforward case: blocking incoming messages from a particular email address. *Blocking* means that any message that comes in from that address is automatically relegated to the Deleted Items folder, so you never see the message. There are two ways to set up the block:

➤ **Block the sender of a message** If you already have a message from the address that you want to block, highlight the message and then select **Message**, **Block Sender**. Outlook Express displays a dialog box that tells you the address has been added to the "blocked senders list." It also asks whether you want to expunge any other messages from this address that are in the current folder (click **Yes** if you do).

➤ **Block a specified email address** If you don't have an email specimen from the address you want to block, select **Tools**, **Message Rules**, **Blocked Senders List**. This displays the Message Rules window with the **Blocked Senders** tab displayed. Click **Add**, enter the **Address** you want to block, and then click **OK**.

If you have a change of heart down the road, you can remove the block by selecting **Tools**, **Message Rules**, **Blocked Senders List**, highlighting the address in the **Blocked Senders** tab, and then clicking **Remove**. Click **Yes** when Outlook Express asks you to confirm.

If you need to filter messages based on conditions other than (or in addition to) the email address, or if you want to do something other than just delete a message, then you need to set up *message rules*. These rules tell Outlook Express exactly what to look for (such as specific words in the subject line or message body) and exactly what to do with any messages that meet those conditions (move them to a folder, forward them, and so on).

Here are the steps to follow to set up a message rule:

1. Select the **Tools**, **Message Rules**, **Mail** command. Outlook Express relinquishes the New Mail Rule dialog box.

2. In the **Select the Conditions for your rule** list, activate the check box beside a condition that you want to use to single out an incoming message. Outlook Express adds the condition to the Rule Description box.

3. In most cases, the condition includes some underlined text. For example, if you activate the **Where the Subject line contains specific words** condition, the "contains specific words" portion will be underlined, as shown in Figure 11.6. The idea here is that you click the underlined text to specify the exact condition (in this case, a word or two that specifies which subject lines are to be filtered).

4. Repeat steps 2 and 3 to set up other conditions, if necessary.

5. In the **Select the Actions for your rule** list, activate the check box beside an action you want Outlook Express to perform on the selected messages. Again, Outlook Express adds the action to the Rule Description box.

6. Many actions also have the underlined text, so be sure to click the text to enter a specific value.

7. Repeat steps 5 and 6 to set up other actions, if necessary.

175

Figure 11.6

Most conditions require you to add specific words or addresses.

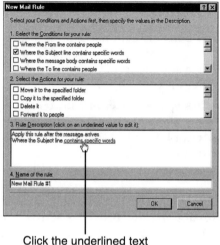

Click the underlined text
to complete the condition

8. Use the **Name of the rule** text box to enter a descriptive name for the rule.

9. Click **OK**. Outlook Express displays the Message Rules dialog box with your new rule shown in the **Mail Rules** tab.

Quick Address-Based Rules

If you're creating a rule based on the address of an existing message, you can save yourself a bit of time by highlighting the message and then selecting **Message**, **Create Rule from Message**. This displays the New Mail Rule dialog box with the **Where the From line contains people** condition activated and filled in with the address of the sender.

Sharing Outlook Express with Others: Setting Up Identities

Internet email is such a useful tool that *everyone* wants to get in on the act. That's fine because most ISPs let you set up multiple email accounts, so it's usually not a problem to set up an account for each person in your family or your small office.

Sounds good, but what happens if two or more people have to share a single computer? *Nobody* likes having someone else snooping around in their email, so how do you avoid fistfights?

The answer is a new Outlook Express feature called *identities*. The idea is simple: Each person who uses the computer sets up a distinct identity in Outlook Express. This gives each person his or her own set of folders and settings, and no one sees anyone else's. Each person's identity can be protected with a password to make extra sure that no one pokes around in his or her stuff.

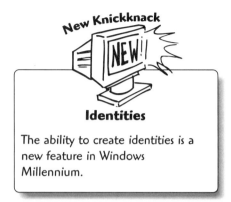

New Knickknack

Identities

The ability to create identities is a new feature in Windows Millennium.

Creating a New Identity

When you set up your Internet email account, Outlook Express created an identity called, boringly, Main Identity. Here are the steps to follow to set up another identity:

1. Select the **File, Identities, Add New Identity** command. Outlook Express whips out the New Identity dialog box.

2. Use the **Type your name** text box to enter a name for the new identity.

3. If you want the identity protected by a password, activate the **Require a password** check box. In the Enter Password dialog box that materializes, type in the password in both the **New Password** and **Confirm New Password** text boxes, and then click **OK** to return to the New Identity dialog box.

4. Click **OK**.

5. When Outlook Express asks if you want to switch to this new identity now, click **Yes**. Outlook Express shuts down and then restarts. Because no account info has been defined for this identity, the Internet Connection Wizard is called in to take down the details.

6. Run through the wizard to define the Internet email account data for the new identity. I took you through the Internet Connection Wizard's mail account setup duties in Chapter 7, "Getting Yourself Online."

Cross Reference

See "More Morsels: Setting Up Your Internet Email Account," p. 107.

Switching From One Identity to Another

After you've set up two or more identities, Outlook Express will always be "logged in" to one of those identities. How do you know which one? Check out the title bar. As shown in Figure 11.7, the name of the current identity appears to the right of "Outlook Express."

Figure 11.7

The Outlook Express title bar tells you the name of the identity currently logged in.

Identity name

To switch to a different identity, follow these steps:

1. Select **File, Switch Identity**. Outlook Express delivers the Switch Identities dialog box.
2. In the list of defined identities, highlight the one you want to use.
3. If the identity is protected by a password, enter it in the Password text box.
4. Click **OK**. Outlook Express shuts down and then restarts with the selected identity logged on.

Logging Off Your Identity

If you exit Outlook Express by selecting the usual **File, Exit** command (or by pressing **Alt+F4** or clicking the window's **Close** button), the current identity remains logged in. Therefore, the next time you crank up Outlook Express, that identity remains the current one.

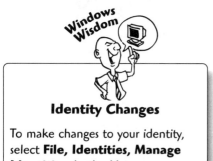

Identity Changes

To make changes to your identity, select **File, Identities, Manage Identities**. In the Manage Identities dialog box, highlight your identity and click **Properties**.

Chances are that this isn't what you want. After all, it means that if someone else launches Outlook Express, they start off in your identity. To prevent that from happening, be sure to exit Outlook Express by choosing the **File, Exit and Log Off Identity** command.

Having done that, the next time you or anyone else tries to start Outlook Express, the first thing that shows up is the Identity Login dialog box. From there, you choose your identity, enter a password, if necessary, and then click **OK** to get Outlook Express onscreen.

Finding Folks on the Internet

When you need to call a person or company and you don't know the phone number, you probably head for the white or yellow pages and look them up there. What if you need to track down an email address? One way would be to search for the person's or company's Web site and then snoop around the site for contact info.

If that's a no go, try using a *directory service*. A directory service is a database of names and email addresses that you can use to search for people you know (or would like to know). Conveniently, Outlook Express offers predefined accounts for several of the most popular directory services, including Bigfoot, InfoSpace, Verisign, and WhoWhere. (You can see a complete list of these accounts by selecting **Tools, Accounts** to display the Internet Accounts dialog box. Activate the **Directory Service** tab. Note, too, that you can also use this dialog box to add your own directory service accounts.)

To use one of the directory services to find someone on the Internet, follow these steps:

1. Select **Edit, Find, People** to display the Find People dialog box. (You might find that pressing **Ctrl+E** is a faster route.)

2. Use the **Look in** list to select the directory service you want to use. (You can also look for people in the Address Book.)

3. Use the **Name** text box to enter part or all of the name of the person you want to find.

4. If you know the person's email address, enter it in the **E-mail** text box.

5. Click **Find Now**. Outlook Express connects to the directory service. If it finds any matches, it displays them at the bottom of the dialog box.

Directory Service Info

If you want to find out more about a service before using it, click the **Web Site** button to load Internet Explorer and display the Web site for the selected directory service.

The Least You Need to Know

This chapter took you through a few beyond-the-basics Outlook Express email techniques. You learned how to work with message folders, how to change the message fonts and stationery, how to specify a signature, how to filter incoming messages, and how to find people on the Internet. We covered a lot of ground, so I think a quick review is in order.

Crib Notes

➤ **Folder folderol** Make liberal use of folders to organize your messages. You create new folders by selecting the **File, Folder, New** command (or by pressing **Ctrl+Shift+E**).

➤ **Default fonts and stationery** If you have fonts or stationery that you use all the time, set them up as the default by selecting **Tools, Options** and displaying the **Compose** tab.

➤ **Blocking boneheads and bores** To have Outlook Express automatically delete messages from a particular address, highlight one of that person's messages and select **Message, Block Sender**.

➤ **Keeping the email peace** If you share your computer with other people, set up separate identities for everyone by selecting the **File, Identities, Add New Identity** command.

➤ **Avoiding an identity crisis** To make sure that no one else accidentally logs in to Outlook Express with your identity, always exit by using the **File, Exit and Log Off Identity** command.

➤ **Finding far-flung folks** To find someone on the Internet, select the **Edit, Find, People** command (or press **Ctrl+E**).

Chapter 12

Spreadin' the News: Participating in Newsgroup Conversations

In This Chapter

➤ Understanding newsgroups

➤ Useful snippets of newsgroup jargon and etiquette

➤ Using Outlook Express to set up your news account

➤ Subscribing to newsgroups

➤ Reading and posting newsgroup messages

➤ Everything you need to make the leap from newsgroup newcomer to old-timer

If you enjoy the thrust-and-parry of a good conversation, you'll probably get a kick out of an Internet service called Usenet news (Windows Millennium just calls it "news") and its associated newsgroups. To understand what newsgroups are all about, think of a newspaper's Letters to the Editor section. The newspaper publishes an article or an editorial, and then someone writes to the editor to convey just how shocked and appalled they are. Yet another reader might write to rebut that letter, others might rebut the rebutter, and so on.

That's pretty much a newsgroup in a nutshell. Each one is devoted to a particular topic. People send messages to the newsgroup (this is called *posting* to the group), other people respond to those messages with posts of their own, and so on.

That's not to say, however, that a newsgroup is just one big argument. Plenty of debating goes on to be sure, but a newsgroup also is about sharing information, asking and answering questions, and generally just yakking about whatever topic interests you. And there are *thousands* of these newsgroup things, so there's bound to be *something* that interests you.

Unlike a Letters to the Editor section, however, there's usually no newsgroup "editor" to ensure messages pass muster. As a result, many newsgroups are a chaotic mass of spam (unsolicited commercial messages), flames (spiteful and insulting posts), and off-topic messages.

A Brief Newsgroup Primer

To get your newsgroups education off on the right foot, this section looks at a few crucial concepts that will serve as the base from which you can explore the rest of newsgroups.

News History

The Usenet news service began its life back in 1979 at Duke University. A couple of resident computer whizzes (James Elliot and Tom Truscott) needed a way to easily share research, knowledge, and smart-aleck opinions among Duke students and faculty. So, in true hacker fashion, they built a program that would do just that. Eventually, other universities joined in, and the thing just mushroomed. Today, tens of millions of people participate in Usenet and ship out millions of messages each day.

Some Words You Should Know

Let's start with a rundown of a few newsgroup terms you need to be familiar with:

➤ **Article**   An individual message in a newsgroup discussion.

➤ **Follow up**   To send a response for an article to the newsgroup.

➤ **Newsreader**   The software you use to read a newsgroup's articles and to post your own articles. In Windows Millennium, the newsreader software is built in to Outlook Express.

➤ **Post**   To send an article to a newsgroup.

➤ **Subscribe**   To add a newsgroup to the list of groups you want to read. If you no longer want to read the group, you unsubscribe from the group.

➤ **Thread**   A series of articles related to the same subject line. A thread always begins with an original article and then progresses through one or more follow-ups.

Jargon Jar

Conversation

Although *thread* is the official term for a series of articles with the same subject, just to be a pain, Outlook Express prefers to use the term *conversation*.

Figuring Out Newsgroup Names

When most people encounter newsgroups for the first time, they're thrown for a loop by the weird names used by the groups. Before moving on, let's take a second and see whether we can pound some sense into those names.

All newsgroup names use the following general format:

```
category.topic
```

Here, `category` is the general classification to which the group belongs, and `topic` is the subject discussed in the newsgroup. For example, consider the following newsgroup name:

```
rec.pets
```

This group is part of the `rec` category, which contains groups related to recreational activities. The `pets` part tells you that this group's topic is general discussions about pets. (News aficionados would pronounce `rec.pets` as "reck dot pets.")

Note, however, that most newsgroup names are quite a bit longer because newsgroups usually cover specific topics. This means that a group's name often has one or more subtopics. Here's an example:

```
rec.pets.dogs.breeds
```

For the category part of the name, you mostly see the following seven:

comp	Computer hardware and software topics
misc	Miscellaneous topics
news	Topics related to newsgroups news and newsgroups

`rec`	Recreational topics: entertainment, hobbies, sports, and so on
`sci`	Science and technology topics
`soc`	Social topics: sex, culture, religion, politics, and so on
`talk`	Topics used for debates about controversial political and cultural ideas

You also see tons of newsgroups in the `alt` (alternative) hierarchy. As the name implies, these newsgroups cover non-mainstream topics.

Understanding Articles and Threads

Articles, as you can imagine, are the lifeblood of newsgroups. Every day millions of articles are posted to the different newsgroups. Some newsgroups might get only one or two articles a day, but many get a dozen or two, on average. A few very popular groups—`rec.humor` is a good example—can get a hundred or more postings in a day.

Happily, newsgroups generally place no restrictions on article content. (However, as I explain in a bit, a few newsgroups have *moderators* who decide whether an article is worth posting.) Unlike, say, the heavily censored America Online chat rooms, newsgroups articles are the epitome of free speech. Articles can be as long or short as you like (although extremely long articles are frowned upon because they take so long to retrieve), and they can contain whatever ideas, notions, and thoughts you feel like getting off your chest (within the confines of the newsgroup's subject matter). You're free to be inquiring, informative, interesting, infuriating, or even incompetent—it's entirely up to you. Having said all that, however, I don't want you to get the impression that this system is total anarchy. If you want to get along with your fellow news hounds, you should follow a few guidelines. See the section "Some Netiquette Niceties for Newsgroups," later in the chapter, to get some pointers on minding your newsgroups p's and q's.

Getting a Handle on Newsgroup Jargon

Newsgroups, as you'll soon find out, boast a lot of buzzwords and a wealth of colorful lingo and jargon. To help you decipher what some people are talking about, this section introduces you to the jargon you encounter most often in your newsgroup voyages:

➤ **Cross-post**   To post an article in multiple newsgroups.

➤ **Expired article**   An article that no longer appears in a newsgroup because it was deleted by your service provider's system administrator. The volume of newsgroup news is so huge that the only way most service providers can keep their heads above water is to purge articles after a certain period (usually anywhere from two to seven days). The moral of the story is that you should check your favorite newsgroups as often as you can. Otherwise, an interesting article could come and go, and you'd never know it.

Expiration = Confusion

Article expiration is the principal cause of one of the biggest frustrations for newsgroup rookies: the feeling that you've stepped into the middle of a conversation. That's because many of the articles you see at first are either follow-ups to an expired article or original posts commenting on some previous state of affairs. The best thing you can do is muddle through and keep reading. In particular, concentrate on reading original posts (that is, posts with Subject lines that don't begin with "Re:"). After a while, you'll catch on to new threads, and you'll be an old hand before you know it.

➤ **Holy war**   A never-ending, unchanging (and very boring for the rest of us) argument in which the opinions of combatants on both sides of the issue never budge an inch. Common holy-war topics include religion, abortion, which operating system is superior, and the optimum way to dispense toilet paper.

➤ **Lurk**   To read articles without posting any of your own. This behavior is considered *de rigueur* for newsgroup neophytes, but because newsgroups thrive on participation, everyone is expected to post eventually. (This is known as *delurking*.)

Newsgroups are a haven for acronyms and smileys as well, so you should also be sure to read "An Initial Look at Internet Acronyms," p. 147.

➤ **Moderator**   An overworked, underpaid (read *volunteer*) news jockey who reads all submissions to a particular newsgroup and selects only the best (or most relevant) for posting.

➤ **Ob-**   This prefix means *obligatory*. For example, it's traditional that each post to `rec.humor` includes a joke. If someone writes in with some non-joke material, they usually finish with an *objoke*, or *obligatory joke*.

➤ **Signal-to-noise ratio**   This electronics term is used ironically to compare the amount of good, useful information ("signal") in a newsgroup with the amount of bad, useless dreck ("noise"). The best groups have a high signal-to-noise ratio, whereas groups that have a lot of flame wars and spam rate low on the signal-to-noise ratio totem pole. For example, the group `rec.humor` has a low signal-to-noise ratio because most of the jokes are bad and many of the posts comment on how bad the jokes are. By contrast, the moderated newsgroup `rec.humor.funny` has a relatively high signal-to-noise ratio because only jokes that are at least mildly amusing make the moderator's cut and appear in the group.

➤ **Spoiler**   An article that gives away the ending to a movie or book, or contains the answer to a puzzle or riddle. Proper Netiquette requires that you put the word **spoiler** somewhere in the subject line of such an article. (The next section gives you many more pointers on newsgroup politeness.)

Some Netiquette Niceties for Newsgroups

In newsgroup lingo, a *newbie* is someone new to the Net. Although the term sounds sort of cute, it's actually an insult you want to avoid at all costs. How do you do that? Easy. Just read this section and take its news Netiquette lessons to heart, and in everyone's eyes you'll appear to be a true Net veteran (which, of course, you will be before long). Most Netiquette applies to *all* newsgroupies, but there are a few guidelines aimed specifically at rookies. These are covered in the next few sections.

Lurk Before You Leap

You might sorely be tempted to dive right in to the deep end of a newsgroup and start posting articles left, right, and center. However, you should first get the lay of the group's land by limiting yourself to just reading articles posted by others. This gives you a chance to gauge the tone of the group, the intellectual level of the articles, and the interests of the various group members. Then, after you feel comfortable with the newsgroup (which could take as little as a few days or as long as a few weeks, depending on how often you're on the Net), you can start posting some original articles and following up on articles written by your group colleagues.

Check Out the Newcomer Newsgroups

The news hierarchy contains over two dozen newsgroups devoted exclusively to the news system. There are, however, two groups you should read religiously when you're just starting out:

➤ **news.announce.newusers**   This group posts regular articles (these are called *periodic postings*) that explain news concepts to beginners. Some good articles to look for include "What Is Usenet?," "Hints on Writing Style for Usenet," and "A Primer on How to Work with the Usenet Community."

➤ `news.newusers.questions`   This is the group in which news rookies ask questions about Netiquette, newsreaders, groups, and a lot more. News old-timers monitor this group and are usually pretty quick to chime in with the appropriate answers.

Don't Forget to Delurk

Introverted types, or those uncomfortable with their writing skills, might decide to become full-time lurkers, never posting their own articles. That's their decision, of course, but it's considered bad form in newsgroups circles. Why? Well, newsgroups thrive on participation and the constant thrust and parry of post and follow-up. Mere rubbernecking adds no value whatsoever to a group, so everyone is expected to post sooner or later. If you're really reluctant, wait until you come across a post that offers an easy or short follow-up opportunity, and then go for it. You'll be amazed at the pride and sense of accomplishment you feel when you see your first post appear in a newsgroup.

Read the Frequently Asked Questions Lists

In your travels through the `alt` hierarchy, you might come across, say, the newsgroup `alt.buddha.short.fat.guy` (really!). This group could be described as "Buddhism with an attitude," and it can be a lot of fun. So you check it out for a while, and when you decide to post, the first question that comes to mind is "Who the heck was the Buddha, anyway?" That's a good question, but the problem is that most of the other readers of this group probably asked the same question when they were newcomers. You can imagine how thrilled the group regulars are to answer this question for the thousandth time.

To avoid these kinds of annoyingly repetitive queries, many newsgroups have a Frequently Asked Questions list, or FAQ (pronounced *fack*). Before you even think about posting to a newsgroup for the first time, give the group's FAQ a thorough going over to see whether your question has come up in the past.

How do you get a FAQ for a group? There are many methods you can use, but the following three are the most common:

➤ Check out the newsgroup itself. Some newsgroups post their own FAQs regularly (usually monthly).

➤ Look in the answers group under each mainstream hierarchy (such as `rec.answers` or `comp.answers`). These groups are set up to hold nothing but FAQ lists for the various groups in the hierarchy. Alternatively, the `news.answers` group contains periodic FAQ postings from most groups that have them.

➤ Use anonymous FTP to log in to `rtfm.mit.edu` and head for the `/pub/usenet-by-group/news.answers` directory. This directory contains the archived FAQ for every group that has one.

What the Heck Is Anonymous FTP!?

Ah, I thought you might be wondering about that. First off, FTP (File Transfer Protocol) is an Internet service that's used to ship files from one computer to another. Most FTP sites require a username and password. However, some sites allow *anonymous* FTP, which means you need to enter only anonymous as the username and your email address as the password. Happily, Internet Explorer can do all this for you automatically. For the `rtfm.mit.edu` site, for example, enter the following address in Internet Explorer's Address bar:

`ftp://rtfm.mit.edu/pub/usenet-by-group/news.answers`

By the way, the news system has its own FAQ called "Answers to Frequently Asked Questions About Usenet." It's posted monthly in both `news.announce.newusers` and `news.answers`. If you can't find it there, FTP to `rtfm.mit.edu` and grab the file named `part1` in the `/pub/usenet-by-group/news.answers/usenet/faq` directory.

Follow Proper Posting Procedures

Okay, you've had a lengthy lurk in your favorite newsgroups, you've faithfully scoured `news.announce.newusers` and `news.newusers.questions`, and you've studied the appropriate FAQ files. Now you can just plow ahead and start posting willy-nilly, right? Wrong. There's a whole slew of Netiquette niceties related to posting, which isn't surprising because posting is what the news system is all about. To get you prepared, here are a few pointers that tell you everything you need to know:

➤ **Use subject line warnings**   Use the subject line of your article to warn others of material that might be offensive. In brackets, write **Offensive to X**, where *X* is the group your article is slamming (such as computer book authors). Similarly, if your article gives away an ending to a movie, TV show, or book, or if it contains the answer to a riddle, include **Spoiler** in the subject line so that everyone knows what's coming.

➤ **Pick your newsgroup with care**   If you put together a list of the top newsgroup pet peeves, "articles posted to inappropriate groups" would be a shoo-in to appear on the list. For whatever reason, newsgroup participants always seem to blow a gasket when they come across an article that doesn't fit into their group's theme. To keep the Net on your good side, think carefully about which newsgroup would welcome your article with open arms. Not only will you avoid some wrathful replies, but also you'll be more likely to get a good response to your post.

➤ **Watch your cross-posting**   Although cross-posting is occasionally useful, you should rarely need to do it. If you're debating about sending an article to a couple of closely related groups, keep in mind that the same people probably read both groups, so your potential audience won't be any bigger. (And, believe me, nobody likes to read the same article twice!)

➤ **Route test posts properly**   If you want to run a test to see whether Outlook Express is posting articles properly, be sure to use one of the test newsgroups (such as misc.test). Do not—I repeat, do *not*—use any of the regular newsgroups, unless you want your email inbox stuffed with angry complaints.

➤ **Don't post ads**   If you want to advertise a product, don't use a regular newsgroup. Instead, use the groups in the biz category (for example, biz.comp.software).

➤ **Practice posting patience**   If you post an article and it doesn't show up in the newsgroup five minutes later, don't resend the article. A posted article goes on quite a journey as it wends its way through the highways and byways of the Internet. As a

> **Windows Wisdom**
>
> **Avoiding Automatic Test Replies**
>
> Many news sites have programs that automatically fire off email messages to you when they receive your test posts. If you prefer not to receive these messages, include the word **ignore** in the subject line of your test article.

result, it can often take a day or two before your article appears in the newsgroup. (This is why it's also considered bad newsgroups form to post articles "announcing" some current news event. By the time the article appears, the event is likely to be old news to most readers, and you end up looking just plain silly. If you're aching to discuss it with someone, try the `misc.headlines` group.)

Avoid Follow-Up Faux Pas

One of the best ways to get your newsgroup feet wet is to respond to an existing article with a follow-up message. You can answer questions, correct errors, or just weigh in with your own opinions on whatever the topic at hand happens to be. Following up has its own Netiquette rules, however, and I've summarized the most important ones here:

➤ **Read any existing follow-ups first**   Before diving in, check to see whether the article already has any follow-ups. If so, read them to make sure that your own follow-up won't just repeat something that has already been said.

➤ **Use the Reply to Group command**   Don't respond to an article by posting another original article. Instead, use the Reply to Group command in Outlook Express (explained later in this chapter) to ensure your article becomes part of the appropriate thread.

➤ **Quote the original article sparingly**   To make sure that other folks know what you're responding to, include the appropriate lines from the original article in your follow-up. You need to use some judgment here, however. Quoting the entire article is wasteful (especially if the article was a long one) and should be avoided at all costs.

➤ **Reply by email when appropriate**   If you think your follow-up will have interest only to the original author and not the group as a whole, send your response directly to the author's email address.

➤ **Avoid "Me too" or "Thanks" replies**   Few newsgroups experiences are more frustrating than a follow-up that consists only of a brain-dead "Me too!" or "Thanks for the info" response (especially if the dope sending the follow-up has quoted the entire original article!). If you feel the need to send missives of this kind, do it via email to the sender.

Setting Up a News Account

Whew! What a whack of background info. Fortunately, the actual mechanics of working with newsgroups are much easier, thanks to the nicely configured news feature in Outlook Express. So it's time, at long last, to get down to the brass news tacks. Your first order of business is to start Outlook Express. (Remember that the quickest route is to click the **Launch Outlook Express** icon in the Quick Launch toolbar.) After you've done that, follow these steps to set up the news account supplied by your ISP:

Netiquette Isn't Universal, Unfortunately

Although this Netiquette stuff is second nature to many news participants, you'll find plenty of Netiquette-ignorant savages when you get out there yourself. Try to ignore those brutes and keep up your end of the Netiquette deal. At least you can take comfort in knowing that you're doing your bit to make the news system a more civilized place.

1. Select **Tools**, **Accounts**. Outlook Express slips the Internet Accounts dialog box under the door.

2. Display the **News** tab. If you already see an account listed here, pump your fist and say "Yes!" because it looks like your ISP set one up for you automatically. You have my permission to skip the rest of these steps.

3. Click **Add** and then click **News**. Outlook Express asks the Internet Connection Wizard to make a return engagement. The first wizard dialog box asks you for your display name.

4. Enter your name (you don't have to use your real name if you don't want to), and then click **Next**. The wizard asks for your email address.

No News Is Bad News

If your ISP doesn't provide access to newsgroups, there are plenty of *Usenet servers* on the Internet that are only too happy to give you that access. There's a good list of both free and commercial servers on Yahoo!. Go to www.yahoo.com and search for "usenet servers".

5. Enter your email address (again, this is optional) and click **Next**. The wizard mumbles something about an "NNTP" server. This is the name of the computer that your ISP uses to handle newsgroup traffic.

No Spam, Thank You Ma'am

If I might be so bold, I suggest that you don't enter your real email address in step 5. The most popular method that companies use to gather email addresses for spam purposes is to grab them from newsgroup posts. If you still want to give folks the capability to respond to you directly, "mung" your address by adding "NOSPAM" or some other text (for example, you@yourisp.com-NOSPAM).

6. Enter the name of the server in the **News (NNTP) Server** text box (your ISP has this information). If you have to sign in to the server, activate the **My news server requires me to log on** check box. Click **Next**.

7. If you told the wizard that you have to log on, use the next dialog box to enter your **Account name** and **Password**, and then click **Next**.

8. In the final wizard dialog box, click **Finish** to return to the Internet Accounts dialog box.

9. Click **Close** to return to Outlook Express. You're now asked whether you want to download a list of the account's newsgroups.

10. Click **Yes** to connect to the Internet and download the newsgroups from the server. Note that, because there are so many groups, this might take quite a while.

When the newsgroup download is done, you're dropped off at the Newsgroup Subscriptions dialog box. You learn more about this dialog box a bit later, so click **Cancel** for now. After you're back in Outlook Express, notice that the Folders list has grown a new branch, the name of which will be the name of your ISP's news server. Click that "folder" to highlight it. If Outlook Express asks whether you want to view a list of newsgroups, click **No** (you get there in a sec).

Newsgroup Subscribing and Unsubscribing

The first thing you need to do is subscribe to a newsgroup or two. *Subscribing* means that you add a particular newsgroup to your news account. After you do that, the newsgroup shows up in the Outlook Express Folders list as a subfolder of the news account (see Figure 12.2, later in this chapter).

Subscribing to a Newsgroup

Follow these steps to subscribe to a newsgroup:

1. In the Outlook Express Folders list, click the news account name to highlight it.
2. Either select the **Tools**, **Newsgroups** command, or click the **Newsgroups** toolbar button. (Pressing **Ctrl+W** also works.) You end up at the Newsgroup Subscriptions dialog box shown in Figure 12.1.

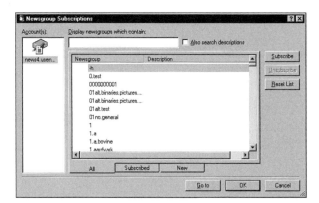

Figure 12.1

You use this dialog box to subscribe to newsgroups.

3. Click the name of the newsgroup you want to subscribe to.

Finding Newsgroup Needles

When confronted with a list that contains thousands of newsgroups, how the heck are you supposed to find something you like if you don't know the name? The best thing to do is use the **Display newsgroups which contain** text box to enter a word or part of a word that describes the subject you're interested in. In this case, Outlook Express filters the list to show only those groups that contain the text you entered.

Newsgroup Icon Guide

In the Newsgroup Subscriptions dialog box, two different icons appear beside the newsgroups. A newspaper icon indicates a subscribed group, whereas an asterisk icon appears beside groups that are new since you last connected. (You can also see the new groups by displaying the **New** tab.)

4. With the newsgroup highlighted, you now have two ways to proceed:

   ➤ **Go to**   Click this button if you just want to have a gander at the newsgroup without committing to a subscription. When you click this button, Outlook Express closes the dialog box.

   ➤ **Subscribe**   Click this button to subscribe to the newsgroup. Outlook Express adds an icon beside the newsgroup name to remind you that you're subscribed.

5. To continue subscribing, repeat step 2 *ad nauseam*.

6. When you're done, click **OK** to get back to Outlook Express.

Unsubscribing from a Newsgroup

If you get sick and tired of a newsgroup's carryings-on, you can unsubscribe at any time by using either of the following techniques:

➤ In the Newsgroups dialog box, display the **Subscribed** tab, highlight the newsgroup, and then click **Unsubscribe**.

➤ In the Outlook Express window, right-click the newsgroup and then click **Unsubscribe** in the shortcut menu. When Outlook Express asks if you're sure about this, say "Way!" and click **OK**.

Downloading Newsgroup Messages

As I mentioned earlier, subscribing to a newsgroup means the group's name appears as a subfolder of your news account in the Outlook Express Folders list. You're now ready to start reading the group's posts. With Outlook Express, this is a two-stage process:

1. Download the newsgroup's current list of message headers. A header contains only the name of the person who sent the post, the subject line, the date the post was sent, and the size of the post.

2. Choose one or more posts that you want to read and then download the message text for each one.

The next two sections take you through these two steps. Before we get to that, however, you need to understand that Outlook Express operates in two distinctly different modes:

➤ **Online**   Working online means you're logged on to your news account. If you have a full-time connection to the Internet, then you can leave Outlook Express in online mode all the time, which makes things much easier.

➤ **Offline**   Working offline means that you're not logged on to your account. If you connect to the Internet using a modem, then you probably want to minimize your connection time. Outlook Express enables you to do that by letting you go online temporarily to grab just what you need.

You toggle Outlook Express between these two styles by selecting the **File, Work Offline** command. When you see a check mark beside this command, it means that Outlook Express is in offline mode.

Step 1: Downloading the Message Headers

To grab the headers, first use the Outlook Express Folders list to click the name of the newsgroup you want to work with. You now have a couple of ways to proceed:

➤ **If you're working online**   Outlook Express kindly reaches out and takes the group's first 300 headers without further prompting.

➤ **If you're working offline**   In this case, you need to select the **Tools, Get Next 300 Headers** command. When Outlook Express asks you if you want to go online, click **Yes**.

The group may have more than 300 headers. If so, the total remaining to be downloaded appears in the status bar (see Figure 12.2). To get those headers, repeat the **Tools, Get Next 300 Headers** command as often as necessary.

Figure 12.2 shows the Outlook Express window with some downloaded headers.

More Headers, Please

You can control the number of headers that Outlook Express downloads at one time. Select **Tools, Options** and display the **Read** tab. Use the **Get *x* headers at a time** spin box to enter the number of headers you want downloaded each time. (The maximum number is 1,000.)

Figure 12.2

Outlook Express with a few newsgroup headers downloaded.

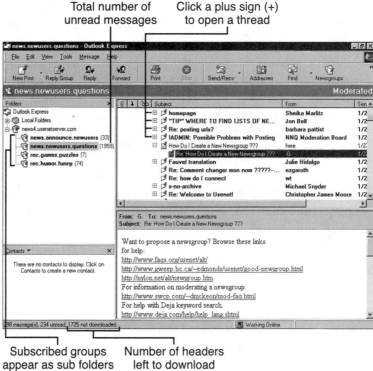

Total number of unread messages

Click a plus sign (+) to open a thread

Subscribed groups appear as sub folders

Number of headers left to download

Step 2: Downloading the Message Text

As you saw in Figure 12.2, groups such as news.newusers.questions often feature an intimidatingly large number of messages—in this case, there are over 2,000. You can see why Outlook Express downloads only the message headers. If it also took the time to hoist the text of every message onto your system, it could take an hour or two (depending on your connection speed, of course).

So the basic newsgroup modus operandi is to sift through the headers looking for interesting posts and ignoring all the others. (Although, if a group contains only a small number of posts, you may be able to get away with reading everything.) Again, how you do this depends on whether you're working offline or online.

Life is easiest if you're working online. In this case, just click the post you want to read and Outlook Express dutifully downloads the message text.

If you're working offline, you have to follow these steps:

1. Make sure the newsgroup you want to work with is highlighted in the Folders list.

2. You now need to "mark" which messages you want to download. You have three choices:

   ➤ **To mark a single message** Click the header of a message and then select **Tools, Mark for Offline, Download Message Later**.

   ➤ **To mark an entire thread** Click the header of any message in the thread and then select **Tools, Mark for Offline, Download Conversation Later**.

   ➤ **To mark every message** Select **Tools, Mark for Offline, Download All Messages Later**.

Unmarking Messages

If you change your mind about one or more of the marked messages, you can unmark them by highlighting them and then selecting **Tools, Mark for Offline, Do Not Download Message**.

3. To download the marked messages (which are indicated by a downward-pointing blue arrow), select the **Tools, Synchronize Newsgroup** command. The Synchronize Newsgroup dialog box (see Figure 12.3) books in.

Figure 12.3

Use this dialog box to tell Outlook Express to download all the marked messages.

4. Make sure the **Get messages marked for download** check box is activated, and then click **OK**. Outlook Express asks if you want to go online.

5. Click **Yes.** The **Connect To** dialog box appears.

6. Click **Connect.** After you're connected, Outlook Express displays a dialog box that shows you the progress of the message download.

7. Put Outlook Express offline by activating the **File, Work Offline** command.

8. Disconnect from the Internet.

At this point, the newsgroup becomes more or less like the Inbox folder. This means you can read any downloaded message just by highlighting it and viewing the text in the preview pane. (You also can double-click the message to open it.) Note, too, that Outlook Express organizes all the newsgroup messages by thread. That's why you see some messages with plus signs (+) beside them. Clicking the plus sign "opens" the thread so that you can see the other messages.

Posting a Message to a Newsgroup

When you think you're ready to delurk and post something yourself, Outlook Express gives you a few ways to do it:

➤ **Send a response to the newsgroup** Click the original message to highlight it, and then either select **Message, Reply to Group** or click the **Reply Group** toolbar button. (Keyboard connoisseurs might prefer to press **Ctrl+G**.)

➤ **Send a response to the message author only** If you prefer that your response go only to the author of a message (via email), click the message and then either select **Message, Reply to Sender** or click the **Reply** button. (**Ctrl+R** is the way to go from the keyboard.) Remember that many people monkey with their email address to avoid spam, so double-check the address before sending your response.

➤ **Send a response to the newsgroup and the author** Click the message and then select **Message, Reply to All**. (Pressing **Ctrl+Shift+R** also gets the job done.)

➤ **Sending a new message** Either select **Message, New Message** or click the **New Post** button. (You also can press **Ctrl+N**.)

Oops! Nevermind...

If you fire off a post and then decide that it wasn't fit for human consumption, Outlook Express lets you claw it back whence it came. Wait until you see the post show up in the newsgroup. Then highlight it and select **Message, Cancel Message**. Unfortunately, just as it may take a while for a message to appear in the group, it may also take a while for your cancel request to go through.

The Least You Need to Know

This chapter showed you how to get all the Usenet news that's fit to read (and some that's not). After a lengthy digression on newsgroups, news jargon, and news netiquette, you learned how to set up a news account, subscribe to newsgroups, download messages, and post your own messages. Here's a recap of today's headlines:

Crib Notes

➤ **Newsgroup names**   Newsgroups have monikers that use the form `category.topic`, where `category` is the general classification for the group (such as `rec` for recreation) and `topic` is the subject of the group (such as `pets`).

➤ **Newcomer netiquette**   Remember to lurk in a group before posting, read the periodic postings in `news.announce.newusers` and `news.newusers.questions`, and peruse a group's FAQ list (if it has one).

➤ **Creating a news account**   In Outlook Express, select **Tools, Accounts** and then click **Add, News**.

➤ **Offline/online**   Modem users toggle Outlook Express between offline mode and online mode by selecting the **File, Work Offline** command.

➤ **Subscribing to a newsgroup**   Select **Tools, Newsgroups** (or click the **Newsgroups** button), highlight the group, and then click **Subscribe**.

➤ **Reading a newsgroup**   First download the group's headers and then download the text of the messages you want to read.

Chapter 13

Real–Time Conversations: Instant Messages, Net Phone Calls, and Chat

The last few chapters have focused on conversation, an art that many a parlor-sitting pundit had thought was lost. Of course, the techniques we looked at—email and newsgroups—don't offer the back-and-forth, give-and-take repartee that you usually associate with the word conversation. In both cases, the lag time between message and reply—between post and riposte, if you will—is just too long. Sure, it may be as little as a few minutes, but it doesn't take someone a few minutes to chime in during a *real* conversation.

So if what you're pining for is a good old-fashioned chinwag (and that low-tech bastion of banter, the telephone, isn't available), the Internet and Windows Millennium can help. Together, they offer no less than three ways to start up a true conversation with someone: instant messages, Internet phone calls, and chat. I talk about all three in this chapter.

Using MSN Messenger to Fire Off Instant Messages

The Internet, once a craze itself, now goes through its own internal crazes. Java applets (mini-programs that run inside Web pages) were big for a while; portals (everything-including-the-kitchen-sink Web sites) were all the rage for a time; and MP3s (music files) continue to generate frenzies among certain copyright-challenged elements of the population.

The big craze nowadays is something called *instant messaging* (usually abbreviated IM by those in the know). Millions of people use it, and it has been estimated that nearly 200 million Netizens will be doing the instant messaging thing by 2002.

What's the big whoop? It's the real-time conversation hook. If someone sees that you're online (special software lets them know), they compose a quick note, ship it, and it pops up on your screen instantly (well, a few seconds later, anyway). You can then dash off a response, and it gets delivered immediately to your correspondent. Repeat to taste and voilà: an instant conversation.

Who's using instant messaging? At first, it seemed to be mostly those all-time champs of the gabfest world: teenagers. Now, however, many businesses have seen the benefits of instant messages, so they're jumping aboard as well. And the simple fact that Microsoft chose to include its own instant messaging software—called MSN Messenger—in Windows Millennium tells you that this thing is getting pretty big. The next few sections show you how to set up and use MSN Messenger.

More Instant Messengers

MSN Messenger isn't the only IM game in town. The most famous service is called ICQ ("I seek you"), and it can be found at www.icq.com. Note, however, that America Online (AOL) now owns ICQ, so its fate has to be considered up in the air. That's because AOL has its own IM service called AOL Instant Messenger. (If you're a member, the keyword is AIM.) The other major IM service is Yahoo! Messenger, which can be found at www.yahoo.com.

Setting Up MSN Messenger

Getting MSN Messenger fit for active duty doesn't take much effort on your part. Keep in mind, however, that to use MSN Messenger you need to have an account with Hotmail, Microsoft's free email service, or a "passport" from www.passport.com. (For the record, a *passport* is a Microsoft invention that enables you to quickly log in to Web sites that use the passport technology.)

Here's what you have to do:

1. Select **Start**, **Programs**, **Accessories**, **Communications**, **MSN Messenger Service**. A wizard flies in and lights upon the desktop.

2. The opening wizard window just offers an overview of the service, so click **Next** to move along.

3. The wizard now informs you that you need a Microsoft Passport to log on to MSN Messenger. (Microsoft Passport sounds a bit ominous, I know, but it will come in handy in a few years when Microsoft owns the planet.) You've come to a fork in the wizard's road:

   ➤ If you already have a Hotmail account or a Passport, click **Next**.

   ➤ If you don't have a Hotmail account or Passport, click the **Get a Passport** button. This launches Internet Explorer and takes you to a page where you can register for a Passport. Follow the instructions on the page. When you're done, close Internet Explorer and return to the wizard. Click **Next** to continue.

4. The wizard displays the dialog box shown in Figure 13.1. Enter your **Sign-in name** (your Hotmail address minus the "@hotmail.com" part, or your Passport name) and your **Password**. If you don't want to have to enter this info every time you log on to the MSN Messenger service, be sure to activate the **Remember my name and password on this computer** check box. Click **Next** to keep on keeping on.

5. In the final wizard dialog box, click **Finish** to put a cap on things.

At this point, the MSN Messenger Service window sets up camp on the desktop and logs you on to the MSN Messenger service. Figure 13.2 shows you the initial window.

Windows Wisdom

Logging On Is a Must

Unfortunately, you can't do anything useful in the MSN Messenger window unless you're logged on to the service. Therefore, you need to connect to the Internet and log on to perform any of the tasks described in the next few sections.

Figure 13.1

The wizard needs to know your sign-in name and password.

Figure 13.2

This is how the MSN Messenger Service window looks when it first shows its face.

Adding Contacts

The heart and soul of MSN Messenger is the *contacts list*, which is the list of lucky folks to whom you want to send your instant messages. (And who, of course, will be lobbing instant messages your way.)

Jargon Jar

Contacts List

The contacts list is the list of people with whom you want to exchange instant messages. In some circles (particularly AOL) this is known as a *buddy list*.

So on your metaphorical MSN Messenger to-do list, job number one is to add one or more contacts:

1. Click the **Add** button or select **File**, **Add a Contact**. The Add a Contact Wizard comes marching by, as shown in Figure 13.3.

2. How you proceed from here depends on what you know about the would-be contact:

   ➤ **If you know the person's Passport sign-in name** Activate the **By Passport** option and click **Next**. Then enter the contact's **Sign-in name** and click **Next**.

➤ **If you know the person's email address**   Activate the **By e-mail address** option and click **Next**. Then enter the contact's email address and click **Next**.

➤ **If you know only the person's name**   Activate the **Search for a contact** option and click **Next**. Then enter the person's **First Name** and **Last Name** (you can also specify the **City** or **State** if the person is in the United States) and click **Next**. If you get any matches, click the person you want and then click **Next**.

Figure 13.3

Use the Add a Contact Wizard to, well, add a contact.

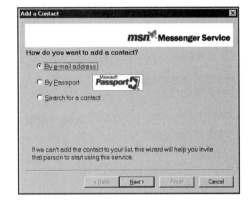

3. In each case, the wizard then offers to send an email message to the potential contact to explain to him how to install MSN Messenger. If you know the other person already uses the program, activate **No**. Otherwise, activate **Yes**. Click **Next**.

4. To add more contacts, click **Next** and then repeat steps 2 and 3 until you're done.

5. Click **Finish** to exit the wizard.

As you can see in Figure 13.4, the MSN Messenger window now lists your contacts and groups them according to whether each person is online (that is, logged on to the MSN Messenger service) or not. Note, too, that you also see the current status of the online folks.

Figure 13.4

MSN Messenger segregates contacts into two classes: online and not online.

Canceling a Contact

To get someone off your contacts list, click his name and then select **File**, **Delete Contact**. (You can also right-click his name and then click **Delete Contact**.)

What happens when someone else adds you to *her* contacts list? If you're logged on to the MSN Messenger service (or the next time you log on), you see a dialog box similar to the one shown in Figure 13.5. If this is okay with you, make sure the **Allow this person...** option is activated. You probably also want to leave the **Add this person to my contact list** check box activated. If this is just some stranger that you want to shun, activate the **Block this person...** option instead. (You can block them later if you're unsure.) Click **OK** to get rid of the dialog box.

Figure 13.5

This dialog box shows up if someone adds you to her contacts list.

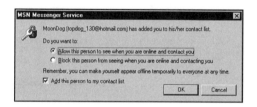

Changing Your Status

Unless you're one of the world's great extroverts, there will be times when you don't want to be bothered with any incoming messages. To that end, MSN Messenger offers various "Do Not Disturb" signs that you can hang on your electronic door. To choose one, click the **Status** button and then click one of the items in the menu (or select **File**, **Status** and then choose an item). If you really want to make sure you're not disturbed, either log off (select **File**, **Log off**) or choose the **Appear Offline** status.

Blocking Blockheads

If someone on your contacts list is behaving badly, tell MSN Messenger to prevent him from sending you messages or even seeing your online status. To do that, select **Tools**, **Privacy**. Highlight the contact's name in the **My Allow List** and then click **Block**. This tosses the boor into the purgatory of the **My Block List**.

Sending an Instant Message

With your contacts list on the go, it's time to do some actual contacting. You have two ways to get started:

➤ Click **Send** and then click the name of the online contact you want to converse with, or select **Tools**, **Send an Instant Message** and then select the contact from the menu that pops out.

➤ In the online contacts list, right-click the name of the person you want to parley with, and then click **Send an Instant Message**.

Either way, MSN Messenger drags the Instant Message window out into the open. Your instant message conversation now proceeds as follows:

1. In the message box at the bottom of the window (see Figure 13.6), type in the message you want to ship out.

2. Click **Send** or press **Enter**. The message wings its way to the contact and is also added to the conversation box that takes up the bulk of the window (again, see Figure 13.6).

3. When (or perhaps I should say if) the contact responds, his text appears in the conversation box below your message for your reading pleasure.

4. Repeat steps 2 and 3 to get a full-fledged conversation going. Figure 13.6 shows an example.

Instant Messages: Short and Sweet

Instant messages are meant to be short notes, not story–length essays. To keep things that way, MSN Messenger sets the maximum message size to only 400 characters.

Figure 13.6

This is an example of an MSN Messenger conversation in progress.

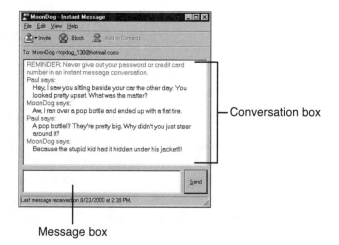

— Conversation box

Message box

Look Out!

Conversation Caveat

When you first open the Instant Message window, it displays a message warning you not to send your password or your credit card number in an instant message. That's excellent advice because these messages get shipped out over the cyber airwaves in plain sight, and it would be easy for a snoop with the right equipment to monitor traffic looking for telltale words and phrases (such as "password" and "credit card").

Here are a few notes to bear in mind when playing around in the Instant Message window:

➤ If you want someone else to join the fun, click **Invite**, **To Join This Conversation** and then click the contact name. (Alternatively, select **File**, **Invite**, **To Join This Conversation** and then select the contact.)

➤ If the person turns out to be a goofball, you can prevent him from continuing the conversation by clicking the **Block** button (or by selecting **File**, **Block**). If you're chatting with two or more people, you're presented with a list of their names, so you need to click the person you want to block.

➤ To change the size of the conversation text, select **View**, **Text Size** and then select one of the relative sizes from the submenu.

➤ For even more control over the conversation text, select **Edit**, **Set My Message Font** and then use the dialog box that comes in to change the typeface, style, size, and the other usual font suspects.

➤ If you end up with some particularly witty repartee, you can save it for posterity by selecting the **File**, **Save** command. Use the **Save As** dialog box to save the conversation to a text file.

➤ When you're talked (or typed) out, select **File**, **Close**. If there are only two of you in the conversation, MSN Messenger shuts down the Instant Message window without further ado. However, if there are three or more yakkers, the program presents you with an ambiguous dialog box that tells you that you won't receive future instant messages "from this session." This just means you won't get anymore messages from the conversation, so it's okay to click **Yes**.

MSN Messenger and Outlook Express

It's not obvious at first, but MSN Messenger and Outlook Express are in cahoots and have been cavorting together behind your back. Here are a few things you should know about the relationship between these two conversation cousins:

➤ Your MSN Messenger contacts list also appears in the Outlook Express window. The next time you run Outlook Express, look for the **Contacts** box just below the Folders list.

➤ When you run Outlook Express, it automatically logs you on to the MSN Messenger service. If you prefer to control the logon yourself, select **Tools**, **Options** and, in the **General** tab of the Options dialog box, deactivate the **Automatically log on to MSN Messenger Service** check box.

➤ You can control some MSN Messenger settings from Outlook Express. Select the **Tools**, **MSN Messenger Service** command, and a submenu slides out that gives you commands to send an instant message, log on or off the service, change options, or add a contact. You can also change your MSN Messenger status by selecting the **Tools**, **My Online Status** command.

In other words, after you have your MSN Messenger service particulars set up, you can do almost all your instant messaging chores from the friendly confines of Outlook Express.

Phone Free: Using NetMeeting to Place Calls Over the Internet

Instant messages are fast and fun, but they lack the subtleties and nuances of the human voice. What if I told you that it's possible to use your Internet connection to "call" someone and have a real live voice-to-voice powwow? It's true! You can turn the Internet into a giant phone booth that enables you to chat amiably with some-one across town, across the country, or even across the ocean. And get this: *no long-distance charges apply!* The "cost" of the call is just your Internet connection time.

Sounds radical, but you've gotta have some kind of high-falutin' equipment installed, right?

Nope. All you (and the person you're calling) need is the following:

➤ A sound card in your computer. (For best results, make sure that you have a sound card that supports something called *full-duplex audio*. This just means that the sounds—that is, your conversations—can travel both ways at the same time.)

➤ A microphone attached to the sound card.

➤ Windows Millennium's NetMeeting program.

The next few sections show you how it's done.

Getting NetMeeting Ready for Action

Assuming that your Internet connection is up and running, let's stroll through the steps necessary to configure NetMeeting:

1. Select **Start**, **Programs**, **Accessories**, **Communications**, **NetMeeting**. When you do this for the first time, the Microsoft NetMeeting Wizard materializes.

2. The initial dialog box merely summarizes what NetMeeting can do, so click **Next** to get to something more useful.

3. The next wizard dialog box pesters you for a few vital statistics. At the very least, you have to provide your **First name**, **Last name**, and **Email address**. (The other fields are optional.) Click **Next** to move on.

4. Now the wizard blathers on about a "directory server." The deal here is that Microsoft and other companies run computers that maintain lists of people who are using NetMeeting. This makes it easy to find other users, but it also might mean you get a crank call or two. If you don't need such a service (if you know who you want to call, for example), deactivate the **Log on to a directory server when NetMeeting starts** check box. Click **Next** when you're ready to continue.

5. Now the wizard wonders about the speed of your Internet connection. This is important because NetMeeting tailors the data that comes your way to match the speed of your connection. Activate the appropriate option and click **Next**.

6. The wizard now offers to populate your screen with a couple of NetMeeting shortcuts: one on the desktop and one in the taskbar's Quick Launch area. The latter is probably the more useful one, but activate or deactivate the check boxes as you see fit, and then click **Next**.

7. The next stage of the setup involves a beast called the Audio Tuning Wizard. This wizard's mission is to set up your sound card to handle the rigors of Net-based calling. The first dialog box is just an intro, so click **Next**.

Going Incognito

If you're shy, don't worry about using your real name and email address in step 3. NetMeeting works just fine if you use a pseudonym and a false address. The only time the latter might be a problem is when someone tries to email you from the directory server. If that's something you want other people to be able to do, then use your real email address.

If you want to log on to a directory server, but you don't want your name listed, it's possible to hide your listing. To do this, activate the **Do not list my name in the directory** check box in step 4.

8. The Audio Tuning Wizard's first chore is to ensure that the audio playback level (that is, the sound you hear) is acceptable. Click **Test** to get the wizard to start playing a very annoying sound. Adjust the **Volume** slider to taste, and then click **Stop** when the noise level feels right. Click **Next** to head for another dialog box.

9. Now the Audio Tuning Wizard wants to ensure that your voice won't be distorted. To do that, you get the dialog box shown in Figure 13.7. The idea is that you speak into the microphone using your normal chatting-on-the-phone voice. As you do, the wizard adjusts the **Recording Volume** level accordingly. When the level has stabilized, click **Next**.

Figure 13.7

Speak into the microphone to help the Audio Tuning Wizard tune your system to your voice.

10. Click **Finish** in the final Audio Tuning Wizard dialog box.

With that procedure thankfully done, NetMeeting finally shows up and you see the window in Figure 13.8. (If you chose not to log on automatically to a directory server, you can do so at any time by selecting **Call**, **Log On to Microsoft Internet Directory**. Note that NetMeeting won't prompt you to start your Internet connection. Therefore, you should always connect to the Net by hand before attempting to log on to any directory server.)

Figure 13.8

The NetMeeting window.

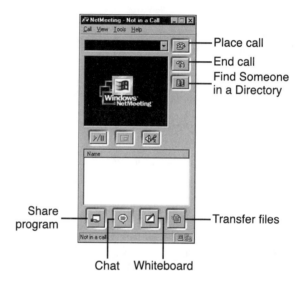

Place call

End call

Find Someone in a Directory

Share program

Transfer files

Chat   Whiteboard

Reach Out and Touch Someone: Placing NetMeeting Calls

Without further ado, let's get right to a NetMeeting phone call:

1. Select **Call**, **New Call**, or click the **Place Call** button. (Keyboard mavens can press **Ctrl+N**.) The Place A Call dialog box butts in, as shown in Figure 13.9.

Figure 13.9

Use this dialog box to get a NetMeeting call off the ground.

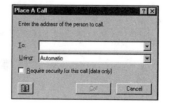

2. Use the **To** list to specify the person you want to call. You have three choices:

   ➤ If you're both logged on to the same directory server, enter the person's email address.

➤ Enter the other person's IP address, if you know it.

➤ If you're doing the NetMeeting thing over a network, enter the network name of the other person's computer.

3. Make sure that **Automatic** is selected in the **Using** list.

4. Click **Call**. (If NetMeeting detects that the other person is using a different version of NetMeeting, it displays a dialog box to let you know. In this case, click **OK**.)

5. On the other end, the person hears a telephone-like ring, and then sees a window like the one shown in Figure 13.10. The person you're calling has two choices:

➤ **Accept**   She can click this button to answer the call.

➤ **Ignore**   She can click this button to reject the call. If the ingrate clicks this button, NetMeeting lets know that you've been rejected and asks whether you want to send the person a message. If you do, click **Yes**.

Figure 13.10

This window pops up when someone tries to call you.

Automatic Accept and Ignore

If you're feeling particularly gregarious, you can tell NetMeeting to answer every incoming call automatically. To set this up, activate the **Call**, **Automatically Accept Incoming Calls** command.

On the other hand, if you're feeling introverted, you might not want to answer *any* incoming calls. That's no problem, too. Just pull down the **Call** menu and activate the **Do Not Disturb** command.

If the other person accepts your call, NetMeeting establishes the connection and then displays his name and your name in the **Name** list. Now just speak into your microphone and have yourself a rousing confab on the Net's nickel.

When you're done, you can end the call by selecting the **Call**, **Hang Up** command or by clicking the **End Call** button.

Other Things You Can Do After You're Connected

Internet phone calls are a lot of fun, but NetMeeting is no mere one-trick pony. After you've established a connection, there are all kinds of things you can do to take advantage of it. Here's a quick summary:

➤ **File transferring**   You can send the other person a file by selecting the **Tools**, **File Transfer** command or by clicking the **Transfer Files** button (poking **Ctrl+F** also works). In the File Transfer dialog box that bubbles up to the surface, select **File**, **Add Files**, highlight the file, and then click **Add**. Now select **File**, **Send All** (or click the **Send All** button). The other person sees a window that displays the progress of the transfer. He can click **Delete** if he doesn't want to accept the file. If he does accept the file, he can select **Tools**, **File Transfer** to open the File Transfer dialog box. He then selects **File**, **Open Received Folder** to see where it went.

➤ **Whiteboard collaborating**   NetMeeting's Whiteboard feature is really just a version of Paint that's been suitably modified. The idea is that you use the Paint tools to draw shapes and type text. Everything you do is reflected on the other person's Whiteboard, so you can collaborate on a project or idea. To get to the Whiteboard, select **Tools**, **Whiteboard** or click the **Whiteboard** toolbar button. (To give the mouse a breather, press **Ctrl+W** instead.)

➤ **Program sharing**   If you want to demonstrate a technique to the other person, or if you want to be able to collaborate on a document beyond what the Whiteboard can do, then you need to use NetMeeting's application sharing. This enables you to run a program on one machine and have the other user see exactly what you're doing. It's even possible for the other person to assume control of the program and run its commands, enter text, and so on. To use this feature, first start the program that you want to share. Then either select **Tools**, **Sharing** or click the **Share Program** button. (**Ctrl+S** is the keyboarder's way.) This gives you a list of the running programs, so click the program you want to work with and then click **Share**. If you want the other person to be able to manipulate the program, click the **Allow Control** button, and then click **OK**.

And as if all this wasn't enough, NetMeeting also lets you "chat" in real time, and that's the subject of the next section.

Using NetMeeting to Chat Over the Internet

If you don't have a sound card or microphone, or if you don't want other people to hear your conversation, NetMeeting's Chat feature might be the way to go. This feature enables you to type messages to the other person and have them type messages back to you. It's actually a lot like MSN Messenger, except you don't need a Hotmail account or a Passport: just a Net connection.

To get into the Chat feature, either select **Tools**, **Chat** or click the **Chat** button. (Pressing **Ctrl+T** also is a possibility.) A Chat window appears on both computers. Here's how it works:

1. If you have multiple people connected, use the **Send To** list to choose who participates in the chat.

2. To send some text, type it in the **Message** box, and then either press **Enter** or click the **Send Message** button.

3. When the other person sends a reply, read it in the area above the Message text box. Figure 13.11 shows the Chat window in mid-conversation.

Figure 13.11

NetMeeting's Chat window with a chat in progress.

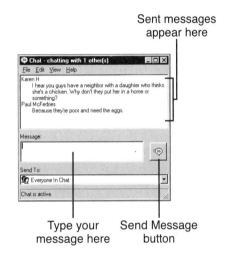

Sent messages appear here

Type your message here

Send Message button

4. Repeat steps 2 and 3 until you're done.

5. Select **File**, **Exit** to close the Chat window and return to NetMeeting.

The Least You Need to Know

This chapter closed out your look at Windows Millennium's Internet features by showing you three more ways to exchange pleasantries online. You began by learning how to use Outlook Express to get in on instant messages. From there, you learned how to use Phone Dialer to place "phone calls" over the Internet. I then showed you how to use NetMeeting to not only make Net-based calls, but also to transfer files, use a Whiteboard, and share programs. I finished the chapter by showing you how to use NetMeeting to exchange chat messages.

Crib Notes

➤ **Passport, please**   To use the MSN Messenger service, you need either a Hotmail email account or a Passport from www.passport.com.

➤ **Add some contacts first**   You can't do much of anything in MSN Messenger until you add a contact or three by clicking the **Add** button or by selecting **File, Add a Contact**.

➤ **Requirements for Net-based calls**   You need a sound card, a microphone attached to the card, and either Phone Dialer or NetMeeting on both ends.

➤ **Net calls via NetMeeting**   Select **Call, New Call**, enter the remote person's address, and click **Call**.

➤ **Chatting via NetMeeting**   Select **Tools, Chat** or click the **Chat** button.

Part 3

Making It Work: Useful Windows Millennium Chores

The Internet may be where all the glamorous action is these days, but people sometimes forget that there's plenty of good old non-wired work to be done as well. There are still memos to write, letters to compose, logos to create, and other workaday tasks to perform. So although everyone seems to talk about nothing but the Internet (and having just devoted no less than seven chapters to the subject myself, I plead guilty as charged on that count), there are other things of interest in the Windows Millennium package. Here in Part 3, you learn about some of the more practical elements of that package. They include Notepad and WordPad for writing, Paint for graphics, CD Player and Sound Recorder for multimedia, and Power Management and Briefcase for notebook computers.

Chapter 14

From Word Amateur to Word Pro: Windows' Writing Programs

> ### In This Chapter
>
> ➤ Using Notepad for "no-frills" writing
>
> ➤ Using WordPad for "fancy-schmancy" writing
>
> ➤ Handy techniques for finding and replacing text
>
> ➤ Inserting ¢, ©, and other oddball (but occasionally useful) characters
>
> ➤ Using Windows Millennium to turn your left brain into a "write" brain

Is there anyone who uses a computer regularly and *doesn't* do any writing? Perhaps the odd hard-core game addict or some of the less-fortunate members of the Partridge family, but that's about it. Everybody else is a writer in some form or another. Don't get me wrong: I'm not talking about writing Ph.D. theses, epic poems, or the Great (Insert Nationality Here) Novel. If that's what you're into, fine, but what I'm really talking about is the day-to-day prose that is the average person's literary bread-and-butter: to-do lists, memos, letters, recipes, résumés, ransom notes, and so on.

For these kinds of jottings and pencil pushings, Windows Millennium offers a couple of programs: Notepad and WordPad. Neither program will set the world of writing tools on fire, but they can handle the basics with a reasonable amount of aplomb. And, heck, they're free, so who's complaining? This chapter shows you how to use Notepad for simple text tasks, and how to use WordPad for full-bore word processing tasks.

What's in an Icon? Styles of Writing Files

Before getting started, you should know that the written documents you deal with will come in two flavors:

➤ **Plain**   This kind of document contains characters that have no special formatting: just plain, unadorned text. So, unshockingly, these types of documents are called *text files*. In the Windows Millennium world, you read, edit, and create text files by using the Notepad text editor.

➤ **Formatted**   This kind of document contains characters that have (or can have) formatting such as **bold** or *italic*. These types of documents are called *word processing files*. In Windows Millennium, you can read, edit, and create word processing files using the WordPad word processor.

Notepad is the subject of the first part of this chapter, and I discuss WordPad's eccentricities a bit later (see "Word Processing with WordPad.")

Keyboard Calisthenics

Typing teachers always suggest limbering up your fingers before you get down to heavy typing. One of the best ways to do this is to type *pangrams*—sentences that use all 26 letters of the alphabet. The standard pangram that everybody (sort of) knows is *The quick brown fox jumps over a lazy dog.* This is fine, but it's a bit dull. Try some of these on for size:

Pack my box with five dozen liquor jugs.
The five boxing wizards jump quickly.
Jackdaws love my big sphinx of quartz.
Five Windows wizards jump thru dialog box hoops quickly.

Text Editing with Notepad

If text files are so plain, why on earth would anyone want to use them? Here are a few good reasons:

➤ You just need a quick-and-dirty document without any formatting frills.

➤ You want to send a document to another person and you want to be sure they can open it. Most of the personal computers on the planet can deal with a text file, so that's your safest bet. If you used WordPad, on the other hand, your friend has to have WordPad (or a relatively recent version of Microsoft Word) installed to open the file.

➤ You want to create a document that *must* be plain text. For example, if you want to create a Web page from scratch, you have to save it as a text file; a word processing file won't work.

Windows Wisdom

Web Page Creation Made Easy

Creating your own Web page from scratch sounds like a daunting task, but it's really not that hard. In fact, I tell you everything you need to know in my book *The Complete Idiot's Guide to Creating a Web Page*. If you have Web access, you can find out more about the book here:

`http://www.mcfedries.com/books/cightml/`

Just about anyone using just about any PC can read a text file. This universality means that you'll get a lot of text files coming your way. For example, if you examine the installation disk of most programs, you'll almost always see at least one text file with a name such as "Readme" or "Setup." This file usually contains information about the installation process (such as how to prepare for the install and how the install operates), last-minute changes to the manual, and so on.

You can identify these and other text files by the icon they use in My Computer. Figure 14.1 points out a couple of text files. When you see the text file icon, double-click the file to open it in Notepad.

Figure 14.1

My Computer shows text files using a special icon.

Text files　WordPad files

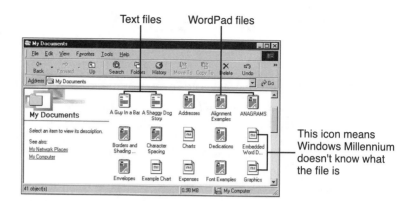

This icon means Windows Millennium doesn't know what the file is

Opening Any Text File in Notepad

Once in a blue moon, you'll come across a text file that doesn't have the proper icon and, in fact, has Windows Millennium's beats-me-what-the-heck-this-thing-is icon (pointed out in Figure 14.1). As long as you're sure it's a text file, you can still talk Notepad into opening the file. To do this, highlight the file and select **File**, **Open With** to get to the Open With dialog box. Highlight **Notepad** in the list, and then click **OK**.

If you need to create a text file, begin by opening Notepad: **Start**, **Programs**, **Accessories**, **Notepad**. Figure 14.2 shows the window that materializes on your screen.

Figure 14.2

Notepad: A simple window for a simple file.

As you can see, Notepad sports a plain, no-frills look that perfectly matches the plain, no-frills text files you work with. There's nary a bell or whistle in sight, and even the menus contain, for the most part, just a bare-bones collection of commands: New, Open, Save, Cut, Copy, Paste, and so on. Dullsville. That's okay, because that's the nature of the Notepad beast. You just fire it up and then read, type, and edit as necessary.

However, Notepad is not without its small quirks and one-of-a-kind features. Here's a summary:

➤ **Inserting the date and time**   To plop the current date and time into your text file, select the **Edit**, **Date/Time** command (or press **F5**).

➤ **Wrapping text**   When you type in most normal programs and the cursor hits the right edge of the window, the cursor automatically jumps down one line and starts again on the left edge of the window (this feature is known as *word wrap*), but not Notepad, no. It just blithely continues along the same line for exactly 1,024 characters, and only *then* will it wrap onto the next line. Dumb! To avoid this annoyance, activate the **Edit**, **Word Wrap** command.

➤ **Opening other files**   I mentioned earlier that some text files don't have the Notepad icon. Unfortunately, if you select Notepad's **File**, **Open** command, the Open dialog box only shows files with that icon. To see other text files, go to the **Files of type** drop-down list at the bottom of the dialog box and select the **All Files (*.*)** option.

➤ **Dialog boxless printing**   The **File**, **Print** command doesn't display a Print dialog box. Instead, without even so much as a how-do-you-do, it just fires the document right to the printer.

➤ **Tweaking the page**   The **File**, **Page Setup** command displays the dialog box shown in Figure 14.3. You can use this dialog box to set various page layout and printing options, including the paper size and orientation, the size of each margin, and text that you want printed in each page's Header and Footer. (The **&f** thingy tells Notepad to print the name of the file, and the **&p** combo tells it to print each page number. You can also enter **&d** to print the current date, **&t** to print the current time, and **&l**, **&c**, or **&r** to align the header or footer text on the left, center, or right, respectively.)

Figure 14.3

Use the Page Setup dialog box to spell out various page-layout and printing options for Notepad.

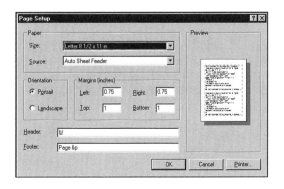

Word Processing with WordPad

Like Dorothy getting whisked from the black-and-white world of Kansas into the Technicolor world of Oz, we turn now to WordPad, Windows Millennium's word processor. To get this program down the yellow brick road, select **Start**, **Programs**, **Accessories**, **WordPad**. Figure 14.4 shows the WordPad window. Unlike the spartan expanse of Notepad, the WordPad window offers a well-appointed interior with lots of word processing amenities.

Figure 14.4

WordPad's window accessories include a couple of toolbars and a ruler.

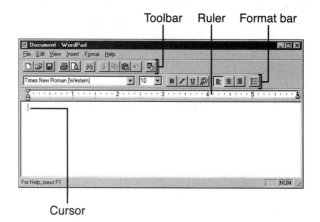

Toolbar   Ruler   Format bar

Cursor

WordPad and Word Processing Files

Here are a few notes to bear in mind when working with WordPad and its word processing files:

➤ **The WordPad file icon**   Like text files, WordPad files also have their own unique icon, as shown earlier in Figure 14.1. When you see a file with this icon, double-click it to load the file in WordPad.

➤ **What type of document do you want?**   When you select the **File**, **New** command, WordPad winds up and delivers the New dialog box to you. WordPad is wondering what type of document you want to create. You have four choices:

    Word 6 Document   This format is based on the one used by Microsoft Word, Microsoft's flagship word processing program. (In fact, WordPad's design and most of its features were taken directly from Word.) This is a good choice if you'll be sharing the document with other WordPad users or with Microsoft Word users.

    Rich Text Document   This produces a file in the Rich Text Format (RTF, for short), which accepts all kinds of formatting. It's a standard format in computing circles, so it's readable by many other word processing programs. This is a good choice if you'll be sending the document to someone and you're not sure what program they'll be using.

Text Document   This gets you a plain text file.

Unicode Document   This is a relatively obscure type of text file that can be safely ignored.

➤ **Opening documents: Are you my file type?**   As you've seen, several different types of files fall under the aegis of WordPad. Unfortunately, when you select the **File**, **Open** command, the Open dialog box only shows Microsoft Word files. If you're trying to open a different type (such as RTF or text), you need to open the **Files of type** list and select either the type you need—such as **Rich Text Format (*.rtf)** or **Text Documents (*.txt)**—or **All Documents (*.*)**.

➤ **Working on two files at once**   WordPad's one-track mind means that it can have only one file open at a time. However, there will be plenty of times when you need to work with *two* files at once. For example, you might want to compare text in the two files, or you might want to copy or move text from one file to the other. No problem. All you have to do is open up a second copy of WordPad and use it to open the second file.

Tip Sheet: Text-Selection Tricks

Before you can format, cut, or copy text, you first have to select it. I showed you the basic text-selection maneuvers in Chapter 5, "Saving, Opening, Printing, and Other Document Lore," but WordPad has a few extra techniques that can make your life a teensy bit easier:

➤ **To select a word**   Double-click it.

➤ **To select a line**   Click inside the narrow strip of whitespace to the left of the line (that is, between the line and the WordPad window's left border). In word processing circles, this strip is called the *selection area*.

➤ **To select a paragraph**   Double-click the selection area beside the paragraph. (Those with energy to burn also can select a paragraph by *triple*-clicking inside the paragraph.)

➤ **To select the whole document**   Hold down **Ctrl** and click anywhere inside the selection area. (You can also choose **Edit**, **Select All** or press **Ctrl+A**.)

Cross Reference

To find the basic text-selection techniques, see "Getting It Right: Text Editing for Beginners" section, p. 67.

Formatting Frippery I: Fonts

The whole point of using a word processor (as opposed to a text editor, such as our pal Notepad) is to turn dull-as-dishwater text into beautifully formatted prose that other people will be clamoring to read. Happily, WordPad offers quite a few formatting features that can turn even the plainest file into a document with text appeal.

In this section, you begin with the most common formatting makeover: the font. A *font* is a style of text in which a unique design and other effects have been applied to all the characters. To begin, you need to decide whether you want to format existing text or text that you're about to type:

➤ **To format existing text**   Select the text to which you want to apply the font.

➤ **To format new text**   Position the cursor at the spot where the new typing will appear.

With that done, here are the steps to follow to apply the font:

1. Select WordPad's **Format**, **Font** command. The Font dialog box puts in an appearance, as shown in Figure 14.5.

Figure 14.5

Use the Font dialog box to put some oomph in your text.

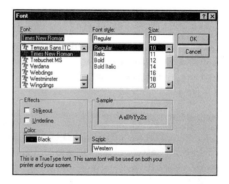

2. Use the **Font** list to choose a typeface. The *typeface* is what most people think of when they use the word "font." It represents the distinctive design applied to all the characters. See Figure 14.6 for some examples. (Wondering what's up with all those typefaces that have the stylized "TT" beside them? Those are *TrueType* typefaces and they generally display better than the other type-faces.)

3. Use the **Font style** list to select a style for the text (see Figure 14.6).

4. Use the **Size** list to choose the font height you want to use. The various values are measured in *points*, where 72 points equals an inch (see Figure 14.6 for an example or two).

5. The **Effects** group is populated with three controls: activate the **Strikeout** check box to get ~~strikeout~~ characters; activate the **Underline** check box to format characters with an underline; and use the **Color** list box to change the color of the text.

6. Click **OK** to put the new font into effect.

Note, too, that WordPad offers a few toolbar shortcuts for many of these font tricks. Figure 14.6 points out the relevant lists and buttons and shows a few fonts in action.

Serif and Sans Serif

A *serif* font has small cross strokes at the extremities of each character and is good for regular text in a document. A *sans serif* font doesn't have the cross strokes and is most often used for titles and headings that require a larger type size. In Figure 14.6, Arial is an example of a sans serif font and Times New Roman is an example of a serif font.

Figure 14.6

Some examples of the various font features.

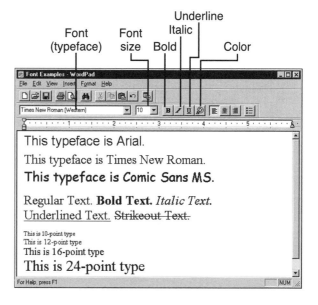

Speaking of shortcuts, you'll be pleased to hear that WordPad also offers a small collection of keyboard combos for easier font fiddling, as listed in Table 14.1.

Table 14.1   Shortcut Keys for Fonts

Press	To Format Text As
Ctrl+B	**Bold**
Ctrl+I	*Italic*
Ctrl+U	<u>Underline</u>

Installing New Fonts

Windows Millennium brings a few dozen fonts to the formatting table, which isn't bad. However, plenty of font collections are available on the market, and they generally cost only pennies a font. If you purchase one of these collections, you have to install it. To do that, first select **Start**, **Settings**, **Control Panel**. In the Control Panel window that shows up, click the **View all control panel options** link, and then launch the **Fonts** icon. When the Fonts folder appears, select **File**, **Install New Font** to open the Add Fonts dialog box. Insert the font disc and select the appropriate drive in the **Drives** list. After a few seconds, the available fonts on the disc appear in the **List of fonts**. Highlight the ones you want to install, and then click **OK**.

Formatting Frippery II: Paragraphs

Few things are as uninviting to read as a document that's nothing but wall-to-wall text. To give your readers a' break (literally), divide your text into separate paragraphs: Press **Enter** once to start a new paragraph; press **Enter** twice to give yourself a bit of breathing room between each paragraph.

As a further measure, consider formatting your paragraphs. WordPad enables you to indent entire paragraphs, indent only the first line of a paragraph, and align your paragraphs with the margins. Here's how it works:

1. Place the cursor anywhere inside the paragraph that you want to format.
2. Either select the **Format**, **Paragraph** command, or right-click the paragraph and then click **Paragraph**. WordPad coaxes the Paragraph dialog box onto the screen.
3. Use the **Left** text box to set how far (in inches) the text is indented from the left margin.

4. Use the **Right** text box to set how far (in inches) the text is indented from the right margin.

5. Use the **First line** text box to set how far (in inches) the first line of the paragraph is indented from the left margin.

6. Use the **Alignment** list to align the paragraph relative to either the **Left** margin or the **Right** margin. You can also select **Center**, which centers the paragraph evenly between both margins.

7. Click **OK**.

Figure 14.7 demonstrates a few of WordPad's paragraph-formatting options.

Figure 14.7

Some examples of WordPad's sundry paragraph formats.

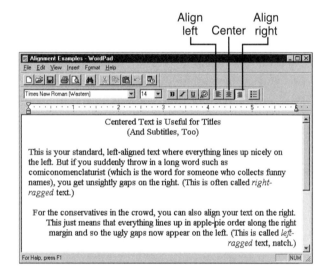

Rather than messing around with inches for the various paragraph indents, try WordPad's ruler. The ruler has various markers that set the paragraph indents (see Figure 14.8). Here's a rundown of what they do:

➤ **Left indent for first line**   Indents the paragraph's first line from the left margin.

➤ **Left indent for the rest of the paragraph**   Indents the rest of the paragraph from the left margin.

➤ **Left indent for entire paragraph**   Indents the entire paragraph from the left margin.

➤ **Right indent for entire paragraph**   Indents the entire paragraph from the right margin.

To use these markers to format a paragraph, place the text cursor inside the paragraph and then use your mouse to drag the appropriate marker left or right.

Figure 14.8

WordPad's ruler can make paragraph formatting a breeze.

Left indent for the rest of the paragraph

Left indent for first line

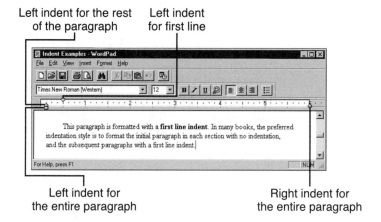

Left indent for the entire paragraph

Right indent for the entire paragraph

Formatting Frippery III: Bullets

When you need to include a list of points or items in your document, it's best to separate those items from the regular text by displaying each one in a separate paragraph. To make these items even easier to read, format them with a *bullet* out front, as shown in Figure 14.9. To use bullets, follow these steps:

1. If you want to turn an existing paragraph into the first item in a bulleted list, first place the cursor anywhere within the paragraph. If you want to convert several paragraphs to bullets, select the paragraphs.

2. Turn on bullets by activating the **Format**, **Bullet Style** command. (You can also click the **Bullets** toolbar button or right-click the paragraph and then click **Bullet Style**.)

3. To create a new bulleted item, move to the end of the last bulleted item and press **Enter**. WordPad dutifully creates another bullet.

4. Enter the text for the new bullet.

5. Repeat steps 3 and 4 until you've entered all your bulleted items.

6. Press **Enter** twice to tell WordPad to knock off the bulleted style.

Figure 14.9

An example of a bulleted list.

Bullets button

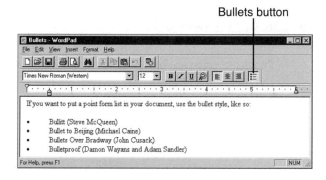

Formatting Frippery IV: Tabs

If you place the cursor on a blank line and press **Tab**, notice that the cursor leaps ahead by exactly half an inch. Press **Tab** again, and you get another half-inch jump. These half-inch intervals are known as *tab stops*, and they're great for making columns or tables that line up like a precision drill team.

WordPad goes one better by enabling you to set your own tab stops anywhere you like. To begin, place the cursor inside the paragraph that you want to mess with. Once that's done, use any of the following techniques:

➤ **To set a tab stop** Move your mouse pointer into the ruler at the spot where you want the tab stop to appear, and then click. WordPad adds what looks like a small "L" to the ruler; that's your tab stop.

➤ **To move a tab stop** Use your mouse to drag the tab stop marker left or right.

➤ **To delete a tab stop** Use your mouse to drag the tab stop marker off the ruler.

Just for the record, there *is* a hard way to set the tabs: Select the **Format**, **Tabs** command to display the Tabs dialog box. In this case, you enter the position (in inches) where you want the tab to appear, and then click **Set**.

Windows Wisdom

The Ruler Rules

Always use WordPad's ruler when setting indents and tabs. It's much easier to drag the indent markers or click and drag tab stops than to do everything via the dialog boxes.

Finding and Replacing Text

Back in Chapter 6, "Using My Computer to Fiddle with Files and Folders," I showed you how to use Windows Millennium's Search feature to find a file needle in a hard-disk haystack. However, what if the haystack is a huge, multipage document and the needle is a word or phrase? Not to worry: Windows Millennium has a solution. It's called the Find feature and it's part of both Notepad and WordPad.

Here's how it works:

1. In Notepad or WordPad, open the document you want to search, if it isn't already open.

2. Select the **Edit**, **Find** command (or press **Ctrl+F**). The Find dialog box appears (see Figure 14.10).

Cross Reference

See "Finding a File in That Mess You Call a Hard Disk," p. 90.

Figure 14.10

WordPad's Find dialog box.

3. Use the **Find what** text box to enter the word or phrase you want to find.

4. (WordPad only) Activate the **Match whole word only** check box to force Find to match only the exact word or phrase you entered in step 3. If you leave this option deactivated, Find looks for text that *includes* the word or phrase. For example, if your search text is waldo and this check box is deactivated, Find matches not only the name *Waldo*, but also words such as *Waldorf* and *Oswaldo*.

5. Activate the **Match case** check box if you want to run a *case-sensitive* search. This means that Find matches only those words or phrases that exactly match the uppercase and lowercase letters you used in your search text. For example, if your search text is **Bill** and you activate this check box, Find matches the name *Bill* and ignores the word *bill*.

6. Click the **Find Next** button to let Find loose. If it finds a match, it highlights the text. If that's not what you wanted, click **Find Next** again to resume the search; otherwise, click **Cancel** to shut down the dialog box. If Find fails to ferret out a match, it displays a dialog box to let you know the bad news.

7. If you end up back in the document and realize that the found text was not the instance you needed after all, you don't have to fire up the Find dialog box all over again. Instead, either select the **Edit**, **Find Next** command, or press **F3**. Find simply repeats your last search from the current position.

Look Out!

Replace All with Caution

The Replace All feature can save you oodles of time, but use it with care. For example, you might think it's safe to replace all instances of "St." with "Street," but the sentence "He went last." might end up as "He went lastreet." (This is a good example of when the Match case option would come in handy.)

Instead of merely finding some text, a more common editing chore is to find some text and then replace it with something else. For example, you might have written "St." throughout a document and you want to change each instance to "Street." WordPad's Replace feature (it's not available in Notepad, unfortunately) makes these kinds of adjustments a snap:

1. In WordPad, open the document you want to work with, if necessary.

2. Select the **Edit**, **Replace** command. (Alternatively, you can press **Ctrl+H**.) This gets you face-to-face with the Replace dialog box.

3. The Replace dialog box is pretty much the same as the Find dialog box, except that it has an extra **Replace with** text box. You

use this text box to enter the word or phrase with which you want to replace whatever's in the **Find what** text box.

4. Enter the other searching options, as needed.

5. You now have two choices:

➤ If you want to replace only selected matches, click **Find Next**. Again, Find highlights the text if it zeros in on a match. To replace the highlighted text with what's in the **Replace with** box, click **Replace**. Repeat this until you've finished all the replacements.

➤ If you prefer to replace every instance of the **Find what** text with the **Replace with** text, click **Replace All**.

Using Character Map for Foreign Letters and Other Symbols

If you need to use a symbol such as © or × in a document, or if you want to spell a word such as résumé with the requisite accent marks, don't go hunting around your keyboard because you won't find what you need. Instead, open the Character Map program and use it to copy all the strange and exotic symbols and characters you require. Here's how it works:

1. Select **Start**, **Programs**, **Accessories**, **System Tools**, **Character Map**. This opens the Character Map window shown in Figure 14.11.

2. Use the **Font** list to pick out a typeface to work with. (Hint: For foreign characters and some common symbols, select any regular typeface; for other symbols, try the Webdings, Wingdings, or Symbol typefaces.)

3. Select the symbol you want by clicking it and then clicking **Select** (you can also double-click the symbol). The symbol appears in the Characters to Copy box.

4. Click the **Copy** button to copy the character.

5. Return to WordPad or Notepad, position the cursor where you want the character to appear, and select the **Edit**, **Paste** command (or press **Ctrl+V**).

Figure 14.11

Use Character Map to get foreign characters, currency signs, zodiac signs, and many more silly symbols.

Clicking a symbol gets you this magnified view

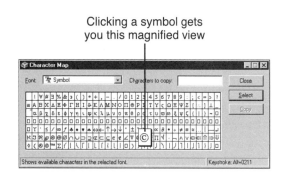

233

The Least You Need to Know

This chapter showed you how to get your thoughts down on paper (electronically, at least). You saw that this isn't your father's IBM Selectric you're dealing with. Even a humble program such as Notepad can run rings around a typewriter. And toss WordPad into the mix with its fonts and indents and bullets, and word-processed writing is the only way to go.

Crib Notes

➤ **Smooth versus crunchy**   Use Notepad (**Start, Programs, Accessories, Notepad**) for plain-text files, and use WordPad (**Start, Programs, Accessories, WordPad**) for formatted word processing files.

➤ **Wrap Notepad text**   To avoid frustration in Notepad, always activate the **Format, Word Wrap** command to ensure that text wraps inside the Notepad window.

➤ **The ruler rules**   Don't forget to use WordPad's ruler when setting indents and tabs. It's much easier to drag the indent markers or click and drag tab stops than to do everything via the dialog boxes.

➤ **Map those characters**   Use the Character Map program (**Start, Programs, Accessories, System Tools, Character Map**) whenever you need foreign characters or symbols that aren't on your keyboard.

Chapter 15

Image Is Everything: Windows Millennium's Graphics Tools

In This Chapter

➤ Navigating the Paint window

➤ Drawing lines, boxes, circles, and other funky shapes

➤ Taking a gander at the new My Pictures folder

➤ Scanning documents and pictures

➤ Importing photos from a digital camera

➤ Right–brain fun for those who just like to look at the pictures

Your left brain has a nice buzz going after all the writing you did in the previous chapter, but now your right brain is clamoring for some attention. Well, it will get plenty to chew on in this chapter as I take you through some of Windows Millennium's graphics goodies. The bulk of the chapter shows you how to use the Paint program to create digital masterpieces. To help you manage those masterpieces, I also tell you all about Windows Millennium's new My Pictures folder. And for those of you without an artistic bone in your body, you also learn how to use a scanner and digital camera to get images from out here to in there, and then to use Windows Millennium's Imaging program to mess around with those images.

The Art of Windows Millennium: Using Paint

If you're looking for some enjoyment of the my-how-time-flies-when-you're-having-fun variety, look no further than Windows Millennium's Paint program. What's that? Drawing was never your strong suit? Don't worry about it. Even if you're no Michelangelo, there are still plenty of wild things Paint can do to turn even the humblest drawing into a veritable *objet d'art*. This section gives you a brief explanation of Paint's basic drawing techniques, and then sends you to the master class so that you can play with Paint's *really* fun features.

A Look Around the Paint Canvas

To get your Paint studio open, select **Start**, **Programs**, **Accessories**, **Paint**. Figure 15.1 shows the Paint window that gets drawn onto the desktop.

Figure 15.1

A few key facts about the Paint window.

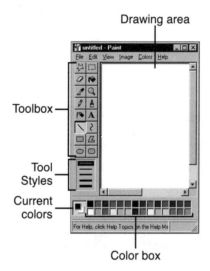

As you can see, the Paint window is chock full of artistic goodies you can play with:

➤ **Toolbox**   This area contains the tools you use to create or edit your drawings. You get a Pencil, a Brush, an Airbrush, an Eraser, and all kinds of utensils for drawing lines and shapes. I describe each tool in more detail a bit later.

➤ **Tool styles**   Some of the tools give you a selection of styles so that you can add some variety to your drawings. When you select one of these tools (such as the Brush tool or the Line tool), the available styles appear in the area below the toolbox.

➤ **Color box** This section shows the available colors and patterns you can use for drawing or filling shapes. Think of this as your own personal 28-box of Crayola crayons (minus that icky flesh-colored crayon) that never need sharpening.

➤ **Current colors** These two boxes display the currently selected foreground color (the top box) and background color (the bottom box). To select a new foreground color, left-click one of the color rectangles in the color box. To select a new background color, right-click a color.

➤ **Drawing area** This is the large blank area that takes up most of the Paint window. The drawing area is your Paint canvas: it's where you perform the mouse moves that lead to the creation of your digital drawings. It is, in short, where all the fun happens.

The Basic Paint Procedure

The best way to approach Paint is to have a good time fooling around with the various tools, styles, and colors. Go on, let loose; toss off those inhibitions, free yourself from the shackles of adult responsibilities, and allow yourself to revert to an immature, to-heck-with-it-I'm-going-to-be-at-one-with-my-inner-child state. (You may want to close the door for this.)

When you're suitably juvenile, you can pick a tool and start playing. There *is* a basic four-step method you use for each tool, however:

1. Select the tool you want to work with by clicking it in the toolbox.

2. Click one of the available tool styles (if the tool has any, that is).

3. Select a foreground and background color from the color box.

4. Move the pointer into the drawing area and draw the shape you want.

Windows Wisdom

Right-Drag for the Background Color

For most of the Paint tools, a left-drag or a left-click draws a shape using the current foreground color. If you prefer to use the current background color, right-drag or right-click, instead.

Bailing Out of Your Mistakes

Before you start, you probably should know how to get rid of the botched lines and mutinous shapes that inevitably appear when you learn to use each tool:

➤ If you make a mess during the drawing, you can start again by clicking the other mouse button *before* you release the button you're using.

➤ If you've already finished drawing the shape, select the **Edit, Undo** command (or press **Ctrl+Z**).

➤ If the drawing is a total disaster, you can start over by selecting the **Image, Clear Image** command (or by pressing **Ctrl+Shift+N**).

Wielding the Paint Tools

Paint's toolbox is stuffed with tools that will get your creative juices flowing. Here's a review of the drawing-related tools you can pluck out of the toolbox:

Pencil Use this tool to draw freehand lines. That is, after selecting this tool, you move the mouse into the drawing area, hold down the left mouse button, and then wiggle the mouse around. Paint draws a freehand line that mirrors your every twitch.

Brush You use this tool also to draw freehand lines. The difference between this tool and Pencil is that Brush gives you a selection of brush shapes and sizes.

Line Use this tool to draw straight lines of varying widths. Drag the mouse in the drawing area to create a line. To draw a perfect horizontal or vertical line, or to draw your line at an exact 45-degree angle, hold down the **Shift** key while dragging the mouse.

Rectangle This tool enables you to draw rectangles. To draw a perfect square, hold down the **Shift** key while dragging the pointer. The Rectangle tool gives you three styles to choose from: a "border only" style that draws only the border of the shape; a "border and fill" style that draws a border and fills it with a color; and a "no border" style that leaves off the shape's border and draws only the fill.

Ellipse   Use this tool for drawing ovals. To draw a perfect circle, hold down the **Shift** key while you drag the mouse.

Rounded Rectangle   This tool draws a rectangle that has rounded corners.

Curve   You use this tool for drawing wavy lines. To wield this tool, first drag the mouse until the line is the length you want, and then release the button. Now drag the mouse again to curve the line, and then release the button. If you want to add a second curve to the line, drag the mouse again and release the button when you're finished.

Polygon   Use this tool to create a polygon shape. (*Polygon* is a highfalutin' mathematical term for a collection of straight lines that forms an enclosed object, such as a triangle.) To give it a whirl, drag the pointer until the first side is the length and angle you want, and then release the mouse button. Now position the pointer where you want the next side to end, and then click. Paint draws a line from the end of the previous line to the spot where you clicked. Repeat to taste. To finish the shape, position the pointer where you want the final side to start, and then double-click. Paint automatically connects this point with the beginning of the first side.

Fill with Color   This tool fills any enclosed shape with whatever color you select. It's really easy to use, too: Just click the **Fill with Color** tool in the toolbox, and then click anywhere inside the shape. If you left-click, Paint fills the shape with the current foreground color; if you right-click, Paint uses the current background color.

Airbrush   This fun tool is like a can of spray paint and it's useful for satisfying those graffiti urges without breaking the law. When you drag the mouse in the drawing area, Paint "sprays" the current color.

Text   Use this tool to add text to your drawing. You first drag your mouse in the drawing area to create a box big enough to hold your text. When you release the mouse button, an insertion point cursor appears inside the box and the Fonts toolbar appears (see Figure 15.2) Use the drop-down lists and buttons on the Fonts toolbar to establish a format for your text; then type your text in the box. Note, too, that Paint offers two text styles:

➤ **Opaque**   This style displays the text with a background. The text color is the currently selected foreground color and the background is the currently selected background color.

➤ **Transparent**   This style displays the text without any background.

Pick Color   Use this tool if the drawing you're working on has a particular color you want to use. To set a color as the current foreground color, select this tool and then left-click the color you want. Right-clicking sets the color as the current background color.

239

Figure 15.2

You can add text to your drawing using either an opaque or transparent style.

Text Gets Set in Stone

You need to be extra careful when typing your text with the Text tool. Why? Because after you enter the text and then click outside the box to finish, the text becomes uneditable. If you try to click inside the box to make changes, Paint annoyingly ignores the existing text completely and starts a new text box. So, if you make a mistake, the only thing you can do is undo or erase the text and start over.

Eraser   Use this tool to erase parts of your drawing. You select a width for the eraser in the styles area, and then drag the mouse in the drawing area to wipe out everything in the mouse pointer's path. (This is not a tool to wield lightly!)

Erasing Colors

The Eraser tool has another personality: the *color eraser*. How does it work? Well, suppose you want to preserve the outlines of a drawing but wipe out the color that fills it, or suppose you want to replace one color with another. These sound like tricky operations, but the color eraser can do the job without breaking a sweat.

You use the color eraser just as you do the eraser, except that you right-drag the eraser box. When you drag the tool over your drawing, it replaces anything it finds in the current foreground color with the current background color.

Magnifier Use this tool to magnify your drawing so that you can get a closer look at a particular section. At the maximum magnification (a whopping 800%), you can even see the tiny individual elements (the *pixels*) that make up a Paint picture. To try this out, click the **Magnifier** tool and click a magnification from the choices that appear at the bottom of the toolbox. Paint zooms in, as shown in Figure 15.3.

Select Use this tool to select a rectangular area of the drawing. (A selected chunk is called a *cutout* in Paint lingo.)
You can then cut or copy the selected area. To use the Select tool, click the tool and move the pointer to the upper-left corner of the area you want to select. Drag the mouse until the box encloses the area you want to work with, and then release the mouse button.

Free-Form Select Use this tool to select any area that's not rectangular. After clicking the tool, move the pointer into the drawing area and drag the mouse around the area you want to select. Release the button when you've completely outlined the area.

Jargon Jar

Pixels

Pixels are the individual pinpoints of light that make up a Paint drawing (and, for that matter, everything you see on your screen). Pixel is short for picture element.

241

Figure 15.3

The Magnifier tool in action.

Thumbnail window

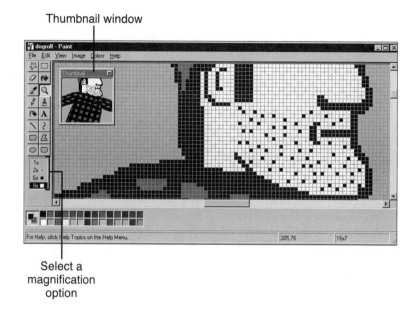

Select a
magnification
option

Pasting Cut or Copied Images

After you cut or copy your selected image (by using the **Edit** menu's **Cut** or **Copy** commands), you need to paste the image. When you select the **Edit, Paste** command, the image appears in the upper-left corner of the drawing. To position it, move the mouse pointer inside the image, drag the image to the location you want, and then click outside the image. Note that you can't move the image after you've clicked, so make sure the image is where you want it before clicking. If you make a mistake, press **Ctrl+Z** to undo the paste and try again.

Other Ways to Zoom

Here are a few other zoom-related techniques:

➤ To magnify the image to 400%, select the **View, Zoom, Large Size** command (or press **Ctrl+Page Down**).

➤ To return to the regular size, select **View, Zoom, Normal Size** (or press **Ctrl+Page Up**).

➤ You can also select the **View, Zoom, Custom** command, activate a magnification percentage in the Custom Zoom dialog box, and then click **OK**.

➤ You can see the individual pixels more easily if you activate the grid (refer to Figure 15.3) by activating **View, Zoom, Show Grid** (pressing **Ctrl+G** also works).

➤ You can display a separate "thumbnail image" that shows the drawing at regular size (again, refer to Figure 15.3) by activating **View, Zoom, Show Thumbnail**.

➤ **Select**   Use this tool to select a rectangular area of the drawing. (A selected chunk is called a cutout in Paint lingo.) You can then cut or copy the selected area. To use the Select tool, click the tool and move the pointer to the upper-left corner of the area you want to select. Drag the mouse until the box encloses the area you want to work with, and then release the mouse button.

➤ **Free-Form Select**   Use this tool to select any area that's not rectangular. After clicking the tool, move the pointer into the drawing area and drag the mouse around the area you want to select. Release the button when you've completely outlined the area.

A Master Class in Paint

Now that you're familiar with all the Paint tools, let's check out a few more techniques that enable you to take your Paint works of art to the next level.

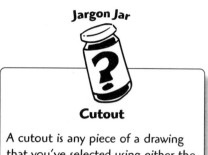

Jargon Jar

Cutout

A cutout is any piece of a drawing that you've selected using either the Select or the Free-Form Select tool.

Getting a Bigger Picture

Instead of using the Magnifier tool to see less of your drawing, you may prefer to see more of it. Here are a few Paint techniques for seeing the big (or, at least, bigger) picture:

➤ To expand the picture so that it takes up the entire screen, select the **View**, **View Bitmap** command (or press **Ctrl+F**). This view is useful for seeing the maximum amount of the drawing, but that's about it because you can't edit the drawing in this view. To return to Paint, click the mouse or press any key.

➤ You can create more elbow room by removing certain Paint features from the screen. Pull down the **View** menu and deactivate any or all of the following commands: **Tool Box** (or press **Ctrl+T**), **Color Box** (or poke **Ctrl+L**), and **Status Bar**.

➤ If you prefer to keep the tool and color boxes onscreen, you can still create more room by dragging them out of their normal locations. This turns the boxes into "floating" toolbars that sit on top of your drawing.

Dragging-and-Dropping a Cutout

If you need to move a cutout or make one or more copies of a cutout, don't bother with the Cut, Copy, and Paste commands. You can move a cutout just by dragging it with your mouse and dropping it in the new location. To copy the cutout, hold down the **Ctrl** key while you drag it.

Creating Sweeps

This one's a real crowd-pleaser. After selecting the cutout, hold down the **Shift** key and drag the cutout around the drawing area. Whoa! As you drag the mouse, Paint leaves multiple copies of the cutout in its wake, as shown in Figure 15.4.

Figure 15.4

Create sweeps by dragging cutouts while you hold down the Shift key.

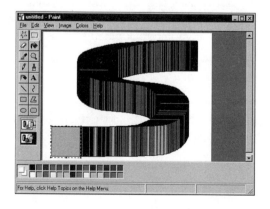

The next few techniques show you some of the other special effects you can create in Paint. Figure 15.5 shows you examples of these effects.

Figure 15.5

Examples of Paint's cutout special effects.

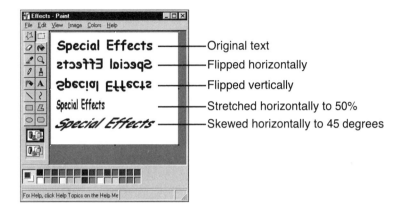

Flipping a Cutout

You can flip a cutout either horizontally (so that left becomes right, and vice versa) or vertically (so that up becomes down, and vice versa). Select **Image**, **Flip/Rotate** (or press **Ctrl+R**) to display the Flip and Rotate dialog box. Activate either the **Flip horizontal** or **Flip vertical** option. If you want more precise control over the rotation of your image, you can also activate **Rotate by angle** and then choose one of the angle options.

Inverting a Cutout's Colors

Inverting colors means that black changes to white, white changes to black, and the other colors change to their complementary colors. To invert the colors in a cutout, select the **Image**, **Invert Colors** command (or tap **Ctrl+I**).

Stretching and Skewing a Cutout

If you need to scale a cutout to either a smaller or larger size, or tilt a cutout at an angle, the **Stretch/Skew** command (or pressing **Ctrl+W**) can do the job. The Stretch and Skew dialog box has two groups:

➤ **Stretch** Use the **Horizontal** and **Vertical** text boxes to specify a percentage value that you want to use to stretch the cutout. Use values greater than 100% to get a larger image; use values less than 100% to get a smaller image.

➤ **Skew** Use the **Horizontal** and **Vertical** text boxes to enter the number of degrees by which you want the cutout tilted. You can enter values between –89 and 89.

Saving a Cutout to Its Own File

If you think you might need to use a cutout in other pictures, you can save it to its own file and then retrieve it when you need it. Select **Edit**, **Copy To**, enter a filename in the Copy To dialog box, and then click **Save**.

Pasting a File into Your Drawing

You can plop an entire file right into your drawing. To try this, select the **Edit**, **Paste From** command, highlight the file in the Paste From dialog box, and then click **Open**.

Setting the Image Attributes

Selecting the **Image, Attributes** command (or pressing **Ctrl+E**) displays the Attributes dialog box shown in Figure 15.6. These controls govern the size of your picture and whether it displays colors. The numbers displayed in the Width and Height text boxes reflect the measurement units selected in the Units group.

Figure 15.6

Use the Attributes dialog box to change the size of a picture and toggle colors on and off.

Creating Custom Desktop Wallpaper

After you've finished your drawing, you may like it so much that you want to use it as your desktop wallpaper. Paint makes this easy by including two commands on its **File** menu:

➤ **Set As Wallpaper (Tiled)**   If you select this command, Paint tells Windows Millennium to use this image as the desktop wallpaper, and that Windows Millennium should tile the image. (*Tiling* means that Windows Millennium displays multiple copies of the image so that it covers the entire desktop.)

➤ **Set As Wallpaper (Centered)**   If you select this command, Paint tells Windows Millennium to use this image as the wallpaper, and that the image should be centered on the screen.

Capturing a Picture of the Screen

Later in this chapter you learn how to get images into your computer by using a scanner and digital camera. Another way to get an image without having to draw anything is to "capture" what's on your screen. You have two ways to go about this:

➤ To capture the entire screen, lock, stock, and taskbar, press your keyboard's **Print Screen** key.

➤ If you want to capture only whatever is in the active window, press **Alt+Print Screen**.

Either way, you can then toss the captured image into Paint by selecting **Edit, Paste**. If Paint complains that the image you're pasting is too large, click **Yes** to enlarge your drawing area to fit the image.

Checking Out the New My Pictures Folder

After you have a collection of picture files on your system, you soon notice a problem: When you view the files using My Computer, looking at the filenames isn't enough—it would be better if you could see some kind of "preview" of each image. Happily, Windows Millennium gives you a couple of ways to do just that:

➤ Highlight the file. Windows Millennium then displays a smaller version of the image on the left side of the window, as shown in Figure 15.7.

Highlight a picture file...

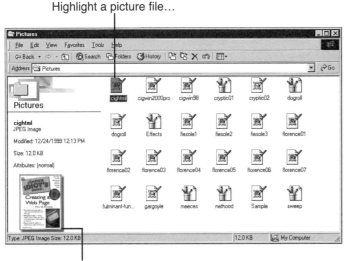

...and the picture appears here

Figure 15.7

Windows Millennium displays a preview of the selected graphics file.

➤ Turn on Thumbnails view by activating the **View**, **Thumbnails** command. As you can see in Figure 15.8, Windows Millennium replaces each file icon with a tiny version (called a *thumbnail*) of the image.

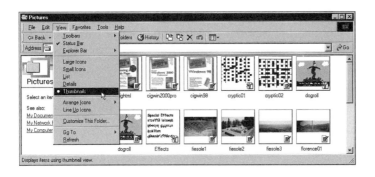

Figure 15.8

Activate View, Thumbnails to see thumbnail versions of each file.

Those are handy techniques, to be sure. However, Windows Millennium adds a new entry to the picture preview parade. It's called the My Pictures folder, and it sits (naturally enough) inside the My Documents folder. Figure 15.9 shows an example of the My Pictures folder in action.

Figure 15.9

The new My Pictures folder offers a few extra tricks for your pics.

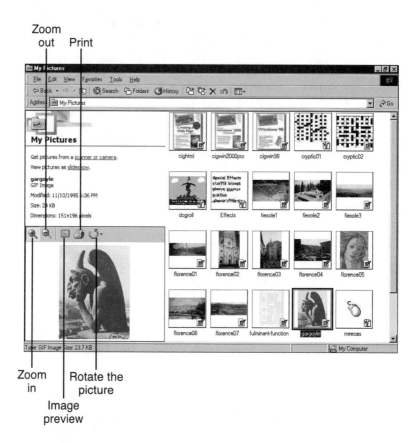

Two things are obvious right off the bat: My Pictures is automatically in Thumbnails view, and highlighting a picture file produces a preview on the left side of the window.

However, the preview is a bit different than the one you saw earlier. Specifically, the top part of the preview box is festooned with a few buttons. Here's what they do:

➤ **Zoom In** Click this button and then click the preview to get a closer look at the picture.

My Pictures

The My Pictures folder is a new feature in Windows Millennium.

➤ **Zoom Out**   Click this button and then click the preview to pull back from the picture.

➤ **Image Preview**   Click this button to display the image in a separate Image Preview window.

More Preview Sizing

The My Pictures folder offers two more ways to change the size of a preview. Right-click the file and then, in the shortcut menu that pops up, click either **Actual Size** (to see a life-sized preview) or **Best Fit** (to resize the preview so that it fits into as much of the available space as it can). Note, too, that these two features are also available in button form when you click the **Image Preview** button.

➤ **Print**   Click this button to print the image.

➤ **Rotate the picture**   Click this button and then click either **Rotate clockwise** or **Rotate counter clockwise** to rotate the image. Note that this rotation doesn't apply only to the preview; Windows Millennium applies it to the file itself.

For its final trick, the My Pictures folder also offers a "slideshow" view. This means that Windows Millennium displays a full-screen version of the first file, waits about 10 seconds, displays the second file, and so on. To activate the slideshow, click the **slideshow** link on the left side of the folder.

To learn more about installing scanners and digital cameras, see "Installing Specific Devices," p. 338.

Graphics Gadgetry: Working with Scanners and Digital Cameras

It used to be that the only way to get an image onto your computer was either to create it yourself or to grab a prefab pic from a clip art collection or photo library. If you lacked artistic flair, or if you couldn't find a suitable image, you were out of luck.

Now, however, getting images into digital form is easier than ever, thanks to two graphics gadgets that have become more affordable: document scanners and digital cameras.

➤ A *document scanner* is a lot like a photocopier, except that instead of processing the document onto a sheet of paper, you save it to a file on your hard disk.

➤ A *digital camera* is a lot like a regular camera, except that instead of film being exposed, the image is stored internally in the camera's memory. You can then connect the camera to your computer and save the images to your hard disk.

The big news is that Windows Millennium understands both types of devices. (Although it's good to remember that in the Windows world, both types of devices are known as "scanners.") In most cases, you can just install whatever software came with your scanner or camera, connect the cable, and then run the software to bring your images onto your hard disk.

On the other hand, after you've installed your scanner, Windows Millennium itself becomes scanner-savvy, so you can use it as a one-stop digital imaging shop. This section shows you how to do just that.

Unfortunately, Windows Millennium's scanner support is a bit confusing because it offers a different set of features depending on the scanner. The next two sections take you through the different routes.

Using the Imaging Program with Older Scanners

If you have an older scanner or camera, your only Windows Millennium option is to run the Imaging program (select **Start**, **Programs**, **Accessories**, **Imaging**) and then select the **File**, **Scan New** command.

What happens next depends entirely on the device you're using. Basically, Windows Millennium loads up whatever software the device uses to scan an image. For example, Figure 15.10 shows the window that appears for the Kodak DC120 digital camera. You then use that software to capture the image, which eventually appears inside the Imaging window. From there, you use Imaging's **File**, **Save** command to make a permanent copy of the image on your hard disk.

Figure 15.10

This window shows up if you're using the Kodak DC120 digital camera.

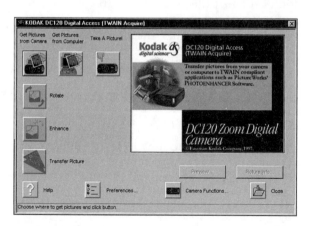

Using the Scanner and Camera Wizard with Newer Scanners

If you have a newer scanner or camera, Windows Millennium installs its own Scanner and Camera Wizard to give you a step-by-step method for capturing images. Here's how it works (note that these steps may vary from scanner to scanner):

1. Give the wizard a poke in the ribs by selecting **Start**, **Programs**, **Accessories**, **Scanner and Camera Wizard**.

2. When the initial wizard window appears, click **Next**. The wizard connects to the scanner and then displays a preview of the image, as shown in Figure 15.11.

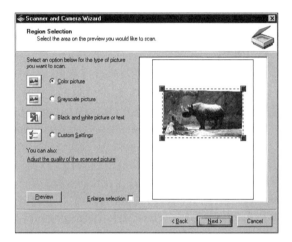

Figure 15.11

The new Scanner and Camera Wizard takes you through the scanning process.

3. Use the options on the left to set the type of picture. (You probably don't need to change this.) Also, use your mouse to change the size of the scanned area by dragging the borders of the box that surrounds the image preview. When you're ready to continue, click **Next**.

4. In the next wizard dialog box, use the **Save picture using this name** to enter the filename you want to use; use the **Save picture in this folder** list to choose a location for the file (the default is My Pictures, which is probably the best place); use the **Save file as** list to choose the type of image file you want. When you've done all that, click **Finish**.

Windows Wisdom

Third-Party Scanning

Any decent graphics program also comes with support for scanning stuff. So if you have a better program than Paint or Imaging, check to see if you can use it to scan pictures.

251

5. The wizard scans the picture and then opens the folder where you elected to store the file.

For your scanning convenience, Windows Millennium also gives you two other ways to scan pictures:

➤ In Paint, select **File, From Scanner or Camera**.

➤ In Imaging, select **File, Scan New**.

Either way, you end up at a window that looks much like the one shown in Figure 15.11. To see a preview of the scan, click **Preview**. When you're ready to scan for real, click the **Scan** button. Windows Millennium scans the image and then loads it into either Paint or Imaging.

The Least You Need to Know

This chapter showed you how to make good use of Windows Millennium's graphics features. You learned how to use Paint and its decent collection of tools and techniques; how to work with the fancy, new My Pictures folder; and how to use Paint, Imaging, and the new Scanner and Camera Wizard to get images from device to disk.

Crib Notes

➤ **The basic Paint method**   Click a tool, select a style (if applicable), choose the foreground and background colors, and then draw the shape. Most Paint tools operate by clicking and dragging within the drawing area.

➤ **Shift for accuracy**   Holding down **Shift** gets you a horizontal, vertical, or 45-degree angle line with the Line tool, a square with the Rectangle tool, or a circle with the Ellipse tool.

➤ **Grabbing screen shots**   Press **Print Screen** to capture an image of the full screen, or **Alt+Print Screen** to capture an image of just the active window.

➤ **Grabbing digital images**   If you have an older scanner, run Imaging and select **File, Scan New**. If you have a newer scanner, either select **Start, Programs, Accessories, Scanner and Camera Wizard** or else use Paint (**File, From Scanner or Camera**) or Imaging (**File, Scan New**).

Chapter 16

The Sights and Sounds of Windows Millennium Multimedia

In This Chapter

➤ Understanding multimedia files and hardware

➤ Playing multimedia files

➤ Listening to audio CDs and watching DVD movies

➤ Recording sounds

➤ Windows Millennium's multitudinous multimedia marvels

The graphics gadgetry you gawked at in the previous chapter represents only a selection of Windows Millennium's visual treats. There are actually quite a few more goodies that fall into the "sights for sore eyes" category, and even a few that could be called "sounds for sore ears." In this chapter, you see that Windows Millennium turns your lowly computer into a multimedia powerhouse capable of showing videos, playing audio CDs, making realistic burping noises, watching slick DVD movies, and even creating your own sound recordings.

Notes About Multimedia Files

Most of the multimedia your eyes will see and ears will hear resides in files on your hard disk, on a CD-ROM or DVD disc, or on the Internet. Just to keep us all thoroughly confused, the world's multimedia mavens have invented dozens of different file formats, each of which has its own incomprehensible two- or three-letter acronym. To help you make some sense of all this, I've grouped all the various formats into a mere five categories for easier consumption:

Jargon Jar

MIDI Sequence File

MIDI stands for Musical Instrument Digital Interface. It's a sound file that plays music generated by electronic synthesizers.

➤ **Sound files**   Files that contain sounds or music only. The two main types are Audio files and MIDI sequence files. You'll deal with audio files mostly, and you'll also hear them referred to using their specific formats, including WAV, AU, AIFF, and MP3. (The latter is a format that's used to play songs with near-CD quality. MP3 is an extremely popular and growing format on the Internet.)

➤ **Animation files**   Files that contain animated movies or shorts, and they might include sound. The three most popular formats are Video files (also called AVI files), MPEG files, and QuickTime files.

➤ **Movie files**   Files that contain live action movies or shorts, and they usually have a soundtrack. These files use the same formats as animation files.

➤ **Audio CD tracks**   Files that Windows Millennium uses to represent individual tracks on an audio CD; however, you rarely deal with them that way yourself. Instead, you can have Windows Millennium play some or all of a CD's tracks from your CD-ROM or DVD-ROM drive.

➤ **DVD movies**   Files that contain high-quality versions of feature films, documentaries, and other big-screen entertainment. Again, you never have to deal with these files directly.

Notes About Multimedia Hardware

More than most other computer features, multimedia is strongly tied to specialized hardware. In many (but not all) cases, your multimedia will be multimediocre if your computer isn't loaded down with the requisite devices. To help you get your computer multimedia ready, this section takes a quick look at the hardware side of things.

Audio Hardware

Take a stroll through any office these days and you're bound to hear all manner of boops, bips, and beeps emanating from cubicles and work areas. You might think that the body snatchers have replaced your colleagues with R2D2 clones; what you're actually hearing is evidence that today's modern Windows Millennium user is truly wired for sound.

If you're sick of carrying on a one-way conversation with your computer (if the yelling, cursing, and threatening that most of us direct at our digital domestics can be considered conversation), you can get into the sound thing by using a *sound card*.

This is an internal circuit board that's standard equipment on almost all new PCs. How can you tell if your system has a sound card? The easiest way is just to listen: if Windows Millennium plays a snippet of music at startup, then you've got sound.

Audio CD Hardware

If you want to listen to the soothing sounds of The Beastie Boys or Rage Against the Machine on your machine, you could just plop the appropriate CD into a nearby stereo. However, it may also be possible to play the CD directly from your computer. All you need is a sound card, some speakers, and either a CD-ROM drive or a DVD-ROM drive.

DVD Hardware

In the currency of computing power, the bells and whistles that comprise the Windows DVD experience don't come cheap. Pushing around all those pixels and belting out all those notes puts quite a strain on a machine. So as you can imagine, specialized hardware for DVD is a must.

Unfortunately, how Windows Millennium reacts to DVD hardware is weird and confusing. Let's start with the easy part—the basic requirements. The basic needs are a DVD-ROM drive and a sound card/speakers combo.

Not too bad, so far. Where things get twisted is in the add-on—called a *decoder*—that your system requires to process the video and audio torrent that the DVD drive sends its way. There are two kinds of decoders:

➤ **Hardware decoder** This is a device—usually a circuit board—that attaches to your computer. This is the kind Windows Millennium prefers.

Update Your Drivers

If Windows Millennium doesn't recognize your hardware decoder, you may need to get updated *device driver* files from the manufacturer. (A device driver is a little program that lets a device talk to Windows Millennium—and vice-versa.) The latest driver will either be on a disk that comes with the decoder or on the manufacturer's Web site.

➤ **Software decoder**   This is a program that performs the translation from DVD to video and audio output. This requires a reasonably powerful computer—at least a Pentium II machine running at 266 MHz or better. If your machine qualifies, your DVD-ROM drive should have a disc that includes a setup program for installing the decoder. In either case, DVP Player only plays DVD movies if your system has a decoder that Windows Milennium recognizes. If your decoder doesn't pass muster, you should still be able to watch DVD movies using the player that came with your DVD drive.

Media Player: The One-Stop Multimedia Shop

You saw earlier that Windows supports all kinds of multimedia formats. In previous versions of Windows, the bad news was that to play those formats you had to master a passel of player programs. In Windows Millennium, the good news is that (with the notable exception of DVD flicks) you now need to wrestle with only one program: Media Player. This is actually version 7 of this program, but it has been totally revamped not only externally (it looks completely different) but internally, as well. (It knows how to play far more multimedia files.)

Media Player

Media Player 7 is a new addition to the Windows Millennium cast of characters.

To try Media Player, you have a bunch of ways to proceed:

➤ Double-click the **Windows Media Player** icon on the desktop, or single-click the Windows Media Player icon in the taskbar's Quick Launch toolbar. If you prefer the road less traveled, select **Start**, **Programs**, **Accessories**, **Entertainment**, **Windows Media Player**.

➤ Insert an audio CD in your CD-ROM or DVD-ROM drive.

➤ Find a media file to play and then double-click the file. If you don't have any media samples kicking around, open My Computer, open the drive where Windows is stored (usually drive C), open the Windows folder, and then open the Media folder. Here you should find a few dozen sound files for your listening pleasure. Double-click any file; Media Player launches, cues up the file, and then starts playing.

➤ Download media from the Internet. In most cases, Media Player will launch right away and start playing the sound or movie or whatever. (This is called *streaming* the media.) Sometimes, however, you may have to wait for the entire file to download before Media Player will spring into action.

Figure 16.1 shows the Media Player window that shows up.

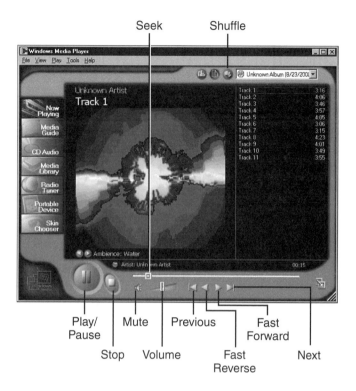

Seek   Shuffle

Figure 16.1
This is the window you see when you launch Media Player.

Play/Pause | Mute | Previous | Fast Forward

Stop   Volume   Fast Reverse   Next

Opening a Media File

To open a media file, you have two possibilities:

➤ **To open a file on your computer** Select the **File**, **Open** command (or press **Ctrl+O**), use the Open dialog box to highlight the file, and then click **Open**.

➤ **To open a file on the Internet** Select **File**, **Open URL** (or press **Ctrl+U**), use the Open text box to enter the Internet address of the file, and then click **OK**.

Playing a Media File

To control the playback of a file, Media Player offers the following buttons:

➤ **Play/Pause** Starts the media file; pauses the file while it's playing. Alternatives: Select **Play**, **Play/Pause** or press **Ctrl+P**.

➤ **Stop** Stops the media file and returns to the beginning of the file (or to the beginning of the current audio CD track). Alternatives: Select **Play**, **Stop** or press **Ctrl+S**.

257

➤ **Mute**   Turns off the sound playback. Alternatives: Select **Play**, **Volume**, **Mute** or press **F8**.

➤ **Volume**   Controls the playback volume. Drag the slider to the left to reduce the volume, or to the right to increase the volume. Alternatives: Select **Play**, **Volume**, **Up** or press **F10** to increase the volume; select **Play**, **Volume**, **Down** or press **F9** to decrease the volume.

➤ **Seek**   Drag this slider left to rewind, or right to fast forward.

➤ **Previous**   Returns you to the beginning of the file or track. Alternatives: Select **Play**, **Skip Back** or press **Ctrl+B**.

➤ **Fast Reverse**   Rewinds continuously through a media file (such as a streaming video file). Click Play/Pause to continue playing. Alternatives: Select **Play**, **Rewind**, or press **Ctrl+Shift+B**.

Play, Rewind, Repeat

If you want a media file to play over and over, activate the **Play**, **Repeat** command (or press **Ctrl+T**).

➤ **Fast Forward**   Fast forwards continuously through a media file (such as a streaming video file). Click Play/Pause to continue playing. Alternatives: Select **Play**, **Fast Forward**, or press **Ctrl+Shift+F**.

➤ **Next**   Sends you to the next file or track. Alternatives: Select **Play**, **Skip Forward**, or press **Ctrl+F**.

➤ **Shuffle**   Play's an audio CD's tracks in random order. Alternatives: Select **Play**, **Shuffle**, or press **Ctrl+H**.

Media Player and the Internet

Media Player does a fine job of playing local media files and audio CDs. However, Media Player has strong ties to the Internet, including support for streaming media files and Internet radio, the capability to download track and artist data for CDs, and much more. Here's a quick summary of Media Player Net niceties (note that all of these items assume you're connected to the Internet):

➤ **Downloading audio CD data**   Each audio CD has a unique identification code that enables Media Player to ask Web sites for the skinny on the CD: the artist, the CD title, and the track titles. To get this data for a CD, click the **CD Audio** button on the left (or select **View**, **Task Bar**, **CD Audio**). Click the **Get Names** button to download the data. Note, too, that you can also click **Album Details** to download extra data about the CD and the artist.

➤ **Using the Media Guide**   Click the **Media Guide** button or select **View**, **Task Bar**, **Media Guide**. This takes you to the WindowsMedia.com Web site, which gives you links to media for Music, Radio, Broadband (that is, video), and more. In most cases, you just click a link that looks interesting and the underlying file will load itself into Media Player and start cranking away.

➤ **Listening to Internet radio**   Hundreds of radio stations are sending their signals over the Net, and Media Player can tune in to many of them. First, click the **Radio Tuner** button or select **View**, **Task Bar**, **Radio Tuner**. The **PRE-SETS** list shows some stations defined by Media Player. To hear a station, double click.

Personal Presets

Media Player also enables you to create a custom list. To add your own stations, first select **My Presets** in the **PRESETS** list. Now move over to the **STATION FINDER** side of the window and use the **Find By** list to choose how you want to search for a station (such as by format or location). Use the controls that appear to enter your search criteria and run the search. Click the station you want and then click **Add** to put the station on your presets list.

➤ **Downloading visualizations**   In Media Player, a *visualization* is a psychedelic pattern that appears when you click **Now Playing** on the left (or select **View**, **Task Bar**, **Now Playing**). Media Player ships with over 50 built-in visualizations (select **View**, **Visualizations** to see them). If you want more, you can download them by selecting **Tools**, **Download Visualizations**.

Using DVD Player to Play DVD Movies

DVD stands for, well, nobody's really sure! Depending on whom you talk to, it either means Digital Versatile Disc or Digital Video Disc. (I suggest Dumb, Very Dumb or, depending on the kind of movie you're watching, Digital Viagra Dose.)

Acronymic quibbles aside, DVD is exciting news because it means that full-length feature films can now fit on a CD-size platter. Not only that, but thanks to the inclusion of the DVD Player in the Windows Millennium box, you can watch those films from the comfort(?) of your own PC. (As I mentioned earlier, however, remember that DVD Player is only available if your system has a software decoder or a hardware decoder device that Windows Millennium recognizes.)

At this point, all you have to do is plop a DVD movie disc into the DVD drive and then close the drive.

The first time you do this, you may see a dialog box named Select DVD Region, which you're supposed to use to select what part of the world you hang out in. (This is related to licensing agreements and other such gobbledygook.) Use the map to click your home country, click OK, and then click OK again when you're asked to confirm your selection.

Windows Millennium detects the disc's presence automatically, launches the DVD Player in response, and starts playing the movie. (If none of this happens for some reason, or if the disc was already in the drive when you started the computer, you can cue up the DVD Player by hand by using either of the following techniques:

➤ Select **Start**, **Programs**, **Accessories**, **Entertainment**, **DVD Player**.

➤ Select Start, Run to get to the Run dialog box, type **dvdplay** in the **Open** text box, and then click OK.

You end up at the DVD Player window, shown in Figure 16.2.

Figure 16.2

All you add is popcorn: Windows Millennium's DVD Player lets you watch big-time movies directly from your PC.

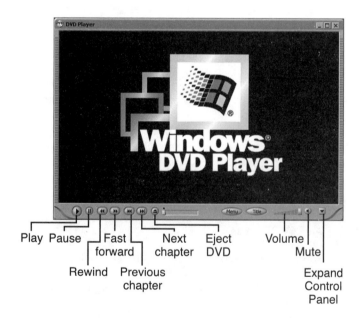

Play Pause Fast Next Eject Volume
forward chapter DVD Mute

Rewind Previous Expand
chapter Control
Panel

As pointed out in the figure, DVD Player has the standard controls for starting, stopping, rewinding, and fast forwarding.

Keeping It Down to a Dull Roar: Adjusting the Volume

If your colleagues or family start complaining about the noise pollution drifting from your computer, you'll want to turn down the volume of your sound files to keep the peace. On the other hand, if you can hardly hear what Windows Millennium is say-ing, you may need to pump up the volume a bit.

Media Player and DVD Player have their own volume controls built in. However, there is also a "master" Volume Control program you can use rather than fiddling with all those individual controls.

The easiest way to use the Volume Control is via the taskbar's Volume icon. As shown in Figure 16.3, clicking this icon pops up the Volume box, which enables you to do two things (which apply to all the sounds on your system):

➤ Drag the slider up (to crank up the volume) or down (to quiet things down a bit).

➤ Activate the **Mute** button to turn off the sound altogether.

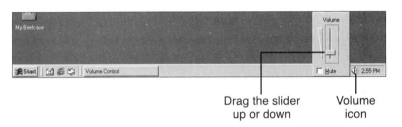

Figure 16.3

*Click the **Volume** icon to display this box and adjust the volume for all sound sources on your machine.*

Volume Control also comes in a beefier version that enables you to control the vol-ume for individual sound sources. To see this version, you have two choices:

➤ Double-click the taskbar's **Volume** icon.

➤ Select **Start**, **Programs**, **Accessories**, **Entertainment**, **Volume Control**.

Either way, the Volume Control window steps up to the mike, as shown in Figure 16.4.

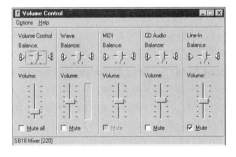

Figure 16.4

Use the Volume Control to set the volume and speaker balance for the various sound sources available on your machine.

261

The layout of the Volume Control window depends on how sound is structured in your computer, but the five sections shown in Figure 16.4 are typical:

➤ **Volume Control**   This is the Big Cheese section that controls the sound for all your sound devices.

➤ **Wave**   Controls the sound for regular sound files (those Wave sound file doo-dads I mentioned earlier).

➤ **MIDI**   Controls MIDI Sequence files.

➤ **CD Audio**   Controls the sound for audio CDs and DVD movies.

➤ **Line-In**   Controls the sound for devices that are attached to the back of your sound card. Examples include an external CD-ROM drive and a TV tuner card.

Controlling the Recording Volume

The volume controls you see at first are all related to playback. If you also want to mess with the record-ing volume, you need to display a different set of controls. To do this, select **Options**, **Properties** to call up the Properties dialog box. Activate the **Recording** option and then click **OK**.

In all cases, you have three ways to mess with the sound output. Use the **Balance** slider to adjust the balance between your speakers; use the **Volume** slider to turn the volume up or down; use the **Mute** check box to toggle sound on and off.

Note that all these settings go into effect right away. When you're done, select **Options**, **Exit** to make everything permanent.

Rolling Your Own: How to Record Sounds

If you have a sound card capable of recording sounds (and you have a microphone attached to the sound card), you can have hours of mindless fun creating your own sound files. Preserving silly sounds for posterity is the most fun, of course, but you can also create serious messages and embed them in business documents.

To record a sound file, follow these steps:

1. Select **Start**, **Programs**, **Accessories**, **Entertainment**, **Sound Recorder**. Figure 16.5 shows the Sound Recorder window that rushes in.

2. If Sound Recorder already has a sound file opened and you want to start a new file, select the **File**, **New** command. If you prefer to add sounds to an existing file, open it, and move to the position in the sound file where you want your recording to start.

3. Grab your microphone, clear your throat, get your script, and do whatever else you need to do to get ready for the recording.

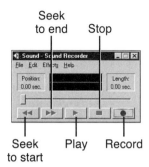

Seek to end Stop

Seek to start Play Record

Figure 16.5

Use the Sound Recorder program to compose your own sound files.

4. Click the **Record** button.

5. Speak (yell, groan, belch, whatever) into the microphone. Sound Recorder shows you the length of the file as you record. Note that you have a maximum of about 60 seconds (depending on the settings you use) to do your thing.

6. When you're finished, click the **Stop** button.

7. Click the **Seek to Start** button and then click the **Play** button to hear how it sounds. If you're happy with your recording, select the **File**, **Save** command, enter a name for the file in the Save As dialog box, and click **Save**.

As if letting you record your own sounds weren't enough, Sound Recorder also comes with a host of cool options for creating some really wild effects. Here's a summary:

➤ **Mixing sound files**   You can mix two or more sound files so that they play at the same time. For example, you can combine one sound file that contains narration with another that has soothing music. To try this, open one of the sound files and move to where you want the second file to start. Select the **Edit**, **Mix with File** command, highlight the other sound file in the Mix With File dialog box, and then click **Open**.

➤ **Changing the volume**   If you recorded your sound file too loudly or too softly, pull down the **Effects** menu and select either **Increase Volume** (to make the sound louder by 25%) or **Decrease Volume** (to make the sound softer by 25%).

➤ **Altering the playback speed**   You can make your voice recordings sound like Alvin and the Chipmunks or Darth Vader by adjusting the speed of the playback. Pull down the **Effects** menu and choose either **Increase Speed** (to double the speed) or **Decrease Speed** (to halve the speed).

➤ **Adding an echo...echo...echo**   The **Effects**, **Add Echo** command creates a neat echo effect that makes your sound files sound as though they're being played in some cavernous location.

➤ **Reversing a sound**   Playing a sound file backward can produce some real mind-blowing effects. To check it out, select the **Effects**, **Reverse** command.

263

The Least You Need to Know

This chapter took you on a tour of Windows Millennium's multimedia marvels. I began by giving you a bit of background about multimedia files and hardware. From there, you learned how to operate a couple of media file player programs: Media Player and DVD Player. You also learned how to use the Volume Control to adjust Windows Millennium's noise level, and how to record your own sounds for presentations or posterity. Here's this chapter's highlight reel:

Crib Notes

➤ **Multiple multimedia formats**   Multimedia files come in five generic flavors: sound files (such as wave, MIDI, and MP3), animation files, movie files, audio CD tracks, and DVD movies.

➤ **Media Player is the workhorse**   The Media Player program can handle most kinds of multimedia files. To use it, launch the desktop's **Windows Media Player** icon or double-click a file.

➤ **Automatic CD playing**   In most cases, your audio CDs will start playing automatically after you insert the disc.

➤ **Quick volume change**   The fastest way to adjust the volume is to click the **Volume** icon in the system tray, and then use the slider that pops up to set the noise level.

Chapter 17

Windows Millennium and Your Notebook Computer

In This Chapter

➤ Using power management to preserve notebook battery life

➤ Using Briefcase to tote files around

➤ Inserting and removing PC Card devices

➤ Using Direct Cable Connection to exchange files between machines

➤ A complete look at the best of the Windows Millennium notebook toys

---

If you have a notebook computer, you know full well that these machines are fundamentally different from their desktop cousins and that the difference goes well beyond mere luggability. There are batteries to monitor, weird "PC Card" wafers to slide in and out, files to exchange between desktop machines, and direct cable connections to furrow your brow over.

The Windows Millennium programmers must have had to wrestle with notebooks a time or two themselves, because they've put together a passel of portable perks. This chapter fills you in on four of these notebook niceties: power management, PC Cards, the Briefcase, and Direct Cable Connection.

Power Management Techniques for Preserving Batteries

A certain level of anxiety is always involved with running your notebook on its batteries, especially if no AC outlet is in sight. You know that you have only a limited amount of time to get your work done (or play your games, or check your email, or whatever), and the pressure's on. To help change road worriers back into road warriors, all notebooks support some kind of *power management*. This means that the system conserves battery life by shutting down things like the display and hard drive after the computer has been idle for a specified interval.

When your notebook is running on batteries, Windows Millennium displays a Power Meter icon in the taskbar's information area, as shown in Figure 17.1.

Figure 17.1

When your notebook is running on batteries, Windows Millennium displays a Power Meter icon in the taskbar.

Power Meter
icon

When the notebook battery has a full complement of juice, the Power Meter icon is completely blue. As you mess with your computer and deplete the battery power, the Power Meter's "level" decreases. For example, if the battery power is down to half, the Power Meter displays half blue, half gray. To see the current level, you have two options:

➤ Point your mouse at the Power Meter icon. Windows Millennium displays a banner showing the percentage of battery life available.

➤ Double-click the Power Meter icon to display a dialog box with the battery life stats.

Setting Battery Alarms

The last thing you want to do is run out of power in the middle of a major memo. Windows Millennium monitors the power level and sounds two battery alarms when things get tense:

➤ **Low** This alarm is set off when the power level reaches 10%.

➤ **Critical** This alarm is set off when the power level reaches 3%.

To control the power levels at which these alarms are sounded, follow these steps:

1. Select **Start**, **Settings**, **Control Panel** and, when the Control Panel window appears, click the **view all Control Panel options** link.

2. Double-click the **Power Options** icon to crack open the Power Options Properties dialog box, and then display the **Alarms** tab, which is shown in Figure 17.2.

Figure 17.2

Use the Alarms tab to set options for the battery alarms.

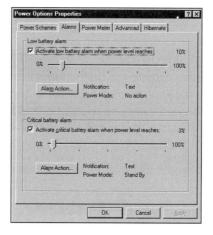

3. All the low battery alarm doodads are in the **Low battery alarm** group, which won't come as too much of a shock. You have three things to play with:

   ➤ Use the **Activate low battery alarm...** check box to toggle the alarm on and off.

   ➤ Use the slider to set the power level at which the alarm is set off.

   ➤ Click the **Alarm Action** button to configure the alarm. When Windows Millennium projects the Low Battery Alarm Actions dialog box onto the screen, you see the following options (click **OK** when you're done):

   Sound alarm   Activate this check box to have Windows Millennium beep your computer's speaker when the alarm is triggered.

   Display message   Activate this check box to have Windows Millennium display a warning message when the alarm is triggered.

   When the alarm goes off, the computer will   Use this list to choose the action taken by Windows Millennium when the alarm is triggered: **Standby** or **Power Off**. (Newer notebooks may also have a **Hibernate** option.)

4. Use the controls in the **Critical battery alarm** group (which are almost identical to those in the Low battery alarm group) to set up the critical alarm.

5. Click **OK**.

267

Look Out!

Low Battery? Save Your Work!

It's been my experience that when battery power gets low, it tends to go south in a hurry. So although you might think the low battery alarm still gives you a few minutes to keep working, don't believe it! Instead, you should immediately save all your work and either get to an AC outlet right away, or exit Windows Millennium until a power source comes your way.

Specifying a Power Scheme

As I mentioned earlier, Windows Millennium offers power management features that help preserve notebook battery power. These include the ability to shut off the monitor and the hard disk, and to go into something called *standby mode*. The latter means that Windows reduces power consumption for all the notebook's components.

Not only that, but Windows Millennium also lets you choose or create a *power scheme* that controls the time intervals that the notebook must be idle before the various power management features kick in. Here's how you work with these schemes:

1. As described in the previous section, display the Power Options Properties dialog box. Make sure the **Power Schemes** tab is displayed, as shown in Figure 17.3.

Figure 17.3

Use the Power Schemes tab to choose a power management scheme for your computer.

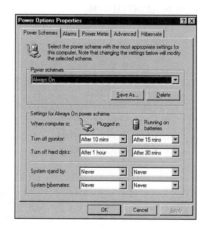

2. Use the **Power schemes** list to choose one of Windows Millennium's predefined power schemes (such as **Portable/Laptop**).

3. To adjust the power scheme time intervals, use the following lists in both the **Plugged in** and **Running on batteries** columns:

Turn off monitor   Sets the number of minutes the notebook must be idle before Windows Millennium shuts off the monitor.

Turn off hard disks   Sets the number of minutes the notebook must be idle before Windows stops your hard disk (or disks) from spinning.

System stand by   Sets the number of minutes the notebook must be idle before Windows puts the notebook into standby mode.

System hibernation   Sets the number of minutes the notebook must be idle before Windows puts the computer into hibernate mode. (Hibernate mode means Windows shuts down the computer but preserves all your open winodws. To set it up, go to the Hibernate tab [if you have one] and activate Enable hibernate support.)

4. If you made changes in step 3 and you want to save those changes under a different scheme name, click **Save As**, enter a new name for the scheme, and then click **OK** to return to the Power Options Properties dialog box.

5. Click **OK**.

Expanding Your Notebook's World with PC Card Devices

One of the problems that originally caused notebooks to be relegated to a lower status on the PC totem pole was their lack of expandability. Desktop systems had all kinds of internal "slots" and "drive bays" that intrepid hobbyists and power users could use to augment the capabilities of their systems. Notebook configurations, however, were generally set in stone; what you bought was what you got.

That all changed with the advent of the absurdly named *Personal Computer Memory Card International Association* (PCMCIA) and the standards it developed for notebook expansion boards. These PC Card standards (as they're now called) let notebook manufacturers add to their machines small slots (called *sockets*) that can hold credit-card–sized expansion modules for memory cards, hard disks, CD-ROMs, modems, and more.

Windows Millennium helps by recognizing your notebook's PC Card sockets (most machines have one or two), and by supporting *hot swapping,* which sounds like some sort of swinging singles party, but is really just the capability to insert and remove PC Cards

An Easier Moniker

The "PCMCIA" tongue twister is now more or less obsolete. (Yes!) In its place, most notebook folks use the phrase "PC Card," and that's what I use throughout the rest of this section.

without having to shut down the system. The next two sections demonstrate this admirable trait.

Sliding In a PC Card Device

To use a PC Card device, insert it gently and as far as it will go into any free PC Card socket. (You should feel a slight "click" at the end.) Windows Millennium recognizes that a new device is in the socket and beeps the speaker. One of two things now happens:

➤ If you've used the device before, it's ready for use within a few seconds.

➤ If you've never used the device before, you see the New Hardware Found dialog box and Windows Millennium proceeds to install the necessary software to make the device run.

After the device is up and at 'em, Windows Millennium displays a special Unplug or Eject Hardware icon on the right side of the taskbar, as shown in Figure 17.4. (Note, too, that this icon also appears if you have certain other devices—such as an external modem—plugged into the machine.)

Figure 17.4

When you wedge a PC Card device into your notebook, Windows Millennium displays this icon in the taskbar.

Unplug or Eject
Hardware icon

Popping Out a PC Card Device

This hot-swapping thing should really be called *tepid swapping* because you can't just grab a PC Card device by the scruff of the neck and drag it out of the slot. Such willy-nillyness is frowned upon. Instead, you need to tell Windows Millennium which device you're giving the heave-ho. This gives Windows a chance to shut down the device. Here's the easiest way to go about this:

Windows Wisdom

Seeing Your Devices

If you want to see a list of all your PC Card devices, double-click the **Unplug or Eject Hardware** icon. Windows Millennium displays the Unplug or Eject Hardware dialog box, which lists the devices.

1. Click the **Unplug or Eject Hardware** icon. Windows Millennium displays a list of the devices attached to your system.

2. Click the device you want to remove. Your computer beeps and then Windows Millennium displays a message telling you it's okay remove the device.

3. Click **OK** and then remove the PC Card device. (On most notebooks, you do this by pushing a button beside the socket.)

Removing the Icon

If you don't want to clutter your taskbar's system tray with the Unplug or Eject Hardware icon, you can easily remove it. To do so, select **Start**, **Settings**, **Control Panel** and then open the Control Panel's **PC Card (PCMCIA)** icon. In the dialog box that jogs in, deactivate the **Show control on taskbar** check box, and then click **OK**. (For good measure, note as well that this dialog box gives you an alternate way to shut down a PC Card gadget before removing it: highlight the device in the list and then click the **Stop** button.)

You *Can* Take It with You: Using My Briefcase

Sharing files between a desktop machine and a notebook is often fraught with difficulty because it's tough keeping everything synchronized. Sure, it's not hard to plop some files on a floppy disk, copy those files to your notebook, and then copy them back to the desktop down the road. But what if you modify only some of the documents when you work on the notebook? What if you create a *new* document on the notebook? What if the floppy disk you use contains other files? What if you make changes to the same document on both the desktop *and* the notebook?

In other words, how do you make sure that the notebook and the desktop remain *synchronized*? To help you do this, Windows Millennium offers a feature called Briefcase. To understand how it works, let's examine how you use a real briefcase to do some work at home. You begin by stuffing your briefcase full of the files and documents you want to work with. You then take the briefcase home, take out the papers, work on them, and put them back in the briefcase. Finally, you take the briefcase back to work and then remove the papers.

The Briefcase feature works in much the same way, except that you don't work with the original documents. Instead, you work with special copies called *sync copies*. A Briefcase is really a special type of folder. The basic idea is that you place the documents you want to work with inside a Briefcase, and then lug around the Briefcase using a floppy disk, Zip disk, or some other removable disk. You can then copy the

Jargon Jar

Sync Copy

A *sync copy* is a copy of a file that is synchronized with the original version of the file.

documents from the Briefcase to the notebook and work on them. The key thing is that the Briefcase "remembers" where the documents came from originally, and it automatically tracks which ones have changed. You can update the original files with just a couple of mouse clicks. There's no guesswork and no chance of copying a file to the wrong folder. It's both mussless and fussless.

Before getting started, you need to create a Briefcase. The best place to create the Briefcase is on the removable disk you'll be using to transport the files. Here are the steps to follow to create a Briefcase:

1. Insert the disk you want to use.
2. Use My Computer to display the disk.
3. To create a new Briefcase on the disk, either select **File**, **New**, **Briefcase**, or right-click the folder and then click **New**, **Briefcase**. Windows Millennium adds an icon named New Briefcase to the disk.
4. Rename the Briefcase (this is optional).

With the briefcase created, follow these specific steps to transfer and synchronize documents between a desktop and a notebook computer:

1. Copy the files you want to work with from the desktop computer to the Briefcase. (If you're using drag-and-drop, you don't have to do anything special because Windows Millennium automatically makes sync copies of the files that you drop.)

Look Out!

Don't Move or Rename the Files!

As I mentioned earlier, the Briefcase keeps careful tabs on its files: both where they came from originally on the desktop computer and where you copy them to on the notebook. Therefore, don't move or rename the files after they're safely stowed on the notebook or you'll break the synchronization.

2. The first time you copy anything to the Briefcase, Windows Millennium displays an overview of how Briefcase works. Just click **Finish** to get rid of this dialog box.
3. Remove the disk and insert it into the notebook.
4. On the notebook, use My Computer to open the removable disk and then open the Briefcase. Copy the files from the Briefcase to the notebook computer.
5. Work with the files on the notebook.
6. When you're done, insert the disk into the notebook and open the Briefcase folder. The Briefcase then checks its files with the copies you sent to the notebook. As you can see in Figure 17.5, the Briefcase's **Status** column tells you which files have been changed. (To get the various columns, activate the **View**, **Details** command.)

Figure 17.5

The Briefcase folder keeps track of which files you changed on the notebook.

This column tells you which files have been changed

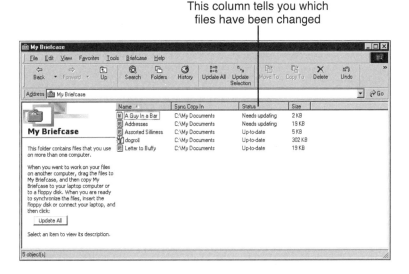

7. To update the Briefcase copies of the changed files, either select **Briefcase**, **Update All**, or click the **Update All** toolbar button. (There's also an **Update All** button on the left side of the window.) Briefcase displays a list of the files to be updated.

8. Click **Update**. Briefcase grabs copies of the changed files.

9. Insert the disk into the desktop computer and open the Briefcase folder. This time, the Briefcase compares its files with the original ones on the desktop machine. Again, the **Status** column tells you which files have been changed.

10. To update the desktop computer's original copies of the changed files, either select **Briefcase**, **Update All**, or click the **Update All** toolbar button. Once again, Briefcase displays a list of the files to be updated.

11. Click **Update**. Briefcase copies the changed files to the desktop computer.

From Laptop to Desktop and Back: Running Direct Cable Connection

In the "a chain is only as strong as its weakest link" department, the Briefcase process of emigrating files from one computer to another via floppy disk suffers from not one, but two severe limitations: Your basic floppy can hold only so much data, and floppy disk drives are notoriously slow. Zip disks are both bigger and faster, but you might not have a Zip drive on both machines.

If Both Files Were Changed

What happens if you changed the copy of the file and also changed the original? In this case, the list of files to be updated will show **Skip (both changed)** for that file. You have two ways to proceed. The first is to click **Cancel** to avoid the update altogether. Then open both files to see what changes were made. You can then edit both files by hand, if need be. The second route is to right-click the **Skip (both changed)** message and then choose one of the **Replace** commands that appear: The one with the right-pointing arrow means the Briefcase version replaces the original version; the one with the left-pointing arrow means the original version replaces the Briefcase version.

You can bypass this "sneakernet" process and overcome both problems by running Windows Millennium's Direct Cable Connection program. As its name implies, Direct Cable Connection lets you sling a bit of cable between two computers and then transfer files along that connection. You can even send documents from one computer to a printer that's attached to the other computer! It takes a bit of effort to set up, but after that's done it works pretty well.

The first thing you need is a cable. Ask the friendly geek at your neighborhood computer store for either a *null-modem cable* or a *parallel LapLink cable* (the latter is also known as a *parallel InterLink cable*). Whichever cable he gives you, be sure to ask whether it connects to your computers' serial ports or their parallel ports. Go ahead and connect the cable to the appropriate port on each machine. (If you have a choice between serial or parallel, choose the latter since it's usually faster.) To help you out, Figure 17.6 shows you a typical serial and parallel port.

To work with Direct Cable Connection, you configure one computer (usually the desktop machine) as the *host* and the other computer (usually the notebook) as the *guest*, as described in the next two sections.

Jargon Jar

Sneakernet

Sneakernet is the process of transporting files from one machine to another using a removable disk.

Figure 17.6

*What serial ports and
parallel ports look like.*

Parallel Port   Serial Port

Step 1: Configuring a Computer as the Host

Let's start with the steps for configuring the host:

1. Select **Start**, **Programs**, **Accessories**, **Communications**, **Direct Cable Connection**. The first time you do this, the Direct Cable Connection Wizard loads.

2. Activate the **Host** option, and then click **Next**.

3. The Direct Cable Connection Wizard checks the available ports on your system and displays a list of these ports, as shown in Figure 17.7. Highlight the port you want to use and click **Next**.

Figure 17.7

*Use this wizard dialog
box to choose the port you
want to use with Direct
Cable Connection.*

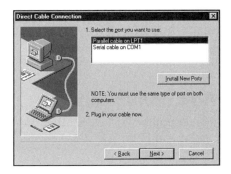

4. The wizard may now tell you that you have to use File and Print Sharing. (If not, skip to step 6.) This just means that the host computer has to *share* its files and folders so that the guest computer can work with them. If this happens, click the **File and Print Sharing** button to load the Network dialog box and then click its **File and Print Sharing** button. In the dialog box that wades in, activate the two check boxes and click **OK** to get back to the Network dialog box. Click **OK**. After a second or two, Windows Millennium tells you that you have to restart your computer. Groan inwardly and click **Yes**. When you get back to the desktop, repeat steps 1–3.

5. The wizard might admonish you for not sharing any folders. Say "Don't worry about it buster, I'll get there!" and click **Next**. See Chapter 25, "Using Windows Millennium's Networking Features," to learn how to share your stuff.

Cross Reference

To learn how to share files and folders, see "Playing Nicely with Ohers: Sharing Your Resources" p. 395.

6. The next wizard dialog box asks whether you want the guest computer to use a password to access the host. If you do, activate the **Use password protection** check box, click the **Set Password** button, enter your password (twice) in the Direct Cable Connection Password dialog box, and click **OK**.

7. Click **Finish** to complete the host configuration. The wizard now starts Direct Cable Connection, which then waits semi-patiently for a connection from the guest.

Step 2: Configuring a Computer as the Guest

Configuring the guest computer is even easier than configuring the host:

1. Select **Start**, **Programs**, **Accessories**, **Communications**, **Direct Cable Connection** to get things off the ground.

2. In the first Direct Cable Connection Wizard dialog box, activate the **Guest** option and click **Next**.

3. Highlight the port you want to use and click **Next**.

4. Click **Finish**.

Making the Connection

Now the two computers feel each other out and try to set up the connection. At this point, the guest computer may need to enter a password if the host was set up with one.

When the two machines finally see eye-to-eye, Direct Cable Connection opens a folder window on the guest computer that shows all the shared stuff on the host, as shown in Figure 17.8. If the host is attached to a larger network, the guest computer can use this window (or the Network Neighborhood) to browse and work with the network's shared resources. Note, however, that neither the host machine nor the other network computers can see the guest.

Figure 17.8

When the Direct Cable Connection session is established, the guest computer sees a folder containing the host's shared resources.

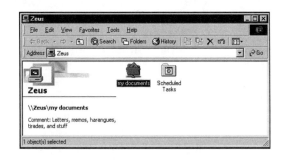

What's the Host Name?

Another connection hurdle you may have to jump is if the guest computer laments that it doesn't know the "name" of the host computer. This is the computer name that would have been entered when Windows Millennium was first installed. To see the name, right-click the desktop's **My Network Places** icon, and then click **Properties** in the shortcut menu. This gets you to the Network dialog box. Display the **Identification** tab and then make a note of what's in the **Computer name** text box. That's the name that you supply to Direct Cable Connection when connecting from the guest machine.

Note, too, that if you're not on a network, you can change the computer name to whatever you want (up to a maximum of 15 characters). If you do change the name, you have to restart your computer to put the new moniker into effect.

To shut down the connection, display the Direct Cable Connection window on one of the computers and click the **Close** button.

To reconnect, you need to do the following:

1. On the host computer, select **Start**, **Programs**, **Accessories**, **Communications**, **Direct Cable Connection**.
2. In the dialog box that appears, click the **Listen** button. Direct Cable Connection then waits for the guest computer to say hello.
3. Launch Direct Cable Connection on the guest computer.
4. In the dialog box that appears, click the **Connect** button.

Direct Cable Connection and the Briefcase

Now that you can establish a cable connection between the two computers, you can press this capability into service by using it to handle the dirty work of Briefcase file transfers. Here's a rundown of the basic Briefcase procedure from a Direct Cable Connection point of view:

1. On the host machine, make sure the folder containing the files you want to work with is either shared directly or resides in a shared folder.

2. On the guest computer, connect via Direct Cable Connection and access the shared folder.

3. Copy the files to a Briefcase folder on the guest computer.

4. Use the guest computer to work on the files from within the Briefcase folder. (This is important; don't try copying the files out of the Briefcase or you'll break the sync.) You don't need to have the connection established at this point.

5. When you're finished, reestablish the connection, if necessary, and then open the Briefcase folder on the guest computer.

6. Select **Briefcase**, **Update All**. This updates the host computer's files with the changed files in the guest computer's My Briefcase.

The Least You Need to Know

This chapter took you on a road trip to discover Windows Millennium's new notebook niceties. You learned how to monitor your battery and how to use power management to save battery life; how to use a Briefcase to keep the files on two machines in sync; how to work with PC Cards; and how to configure a direct cable connection between two computers. That's a lot of learning for such a little machine! Here's a summary of just a few of the things you crammed into your brain:

Crib Notes

➤ **Manage your power**   To maximize battery life, create a power scheme that shuts down the monitor and hard disk within a minute or two of idle time.

➤ **Lug the Briefcase**   The easiest way to use a Briefcase is to move it onto a removable disk and keep it there. You can then add files to the Briefcase, copy those files to the other machine, and use the update feature to keep the files synchronized.

➤ **Hot swap PC Cards**   You can insert a PC Card and Windows Millennium recognizes it right away (and, if necessary, installs the required files). Before removing a PC Card device, tell Windows Millennium to stop the device.

➤ **The direct connection**   String a null-modem or parallel LapLink cable between two machines and then set up one as the host and the other as the guest.

Part 4

"A Style of One's Own": Customizing Windows Millennium

A great lady (writer Margaret Oliphant) once said "Oh, never mind the fashion. When one has a style of one's own, it is always twenty times better." In your travels so far, you've seen that the "fashion" of Windows has changed. This year, a slate blue desktop is in; last year, teal was the color of choice. Next year it will be some other shade that the focus groups have cooed over. None of this surface stuff matters much if you're focused on getting your work done. But there are plenty of folks for whom viewing the standard Windows colors and configurations makes computing an even more soulless exercise. They prefer to redecorate their Windows home to suit their tastes. They want, in short, a Windows style of their own.

If you're one of those people, the four chapters here in Part 4 will suit you to a T. You learn how to customize the desktop, Start menu, and taskbar, as well as how to rearrange My Computer for better comfort and convenience. I also tell you how to install programs and devices onto your computer (and how to uninstall them, too, just in case).

Chapter 18

Refurbishing the Desktop

In This Chapter

➤ Pasting up a desktop wallpaper

➤ Redoing the desktop colors, fonts, icons, and special effects

➤ Adding stuff to the Active Desktop

➤ Monkeying around with the display's screen area and colors

➤ Working with desktop themes

➤ A cornucopia of desktop decoration treats

When discussing desktop customization at parties—well, that never happens. When discussing desktop customization with colleagues—er, um, that never happens either. Okay, when discussing desktop customization with *myself*, the point that comes up again and again is "Why bother?" Why bother tweaking something that you rarely see during the course of an average Windows session?

The answer (I tell myself) is that desktop customizing doesn't just affect the most obvious desktop features, such as the background color or the size of the icons. You can mess with those things, to be sure, but your desktop customizing can also affect features that deal with Windows Millennium as a whole. For example, you can customize all your window title bars by changing the color and font. In other words, refurbishing the desktop means not only customizing the appearance of the desktop itself, but also the appearance of many of the things that are displayed *on* the desktop. This chapter gives you the goods.

Getting Out Your Tools: Displaying the Display Properties

Most of what you do in this chapter requires the services of the Display Properties dialog box. You have two ways to get this dialog box onscreen:

➤ **The easy way**   Right-click an empty area of the desktop and then click **Properties** in the shortcut menu.

➤ **The hard way**   Select **Start**, **Settings**, **Control Panel**. In the Control Panel window, click **Display**.

Figure 18.1 shows the Display Properties dialog box.

Figure 18.1

Use the Display Properties dialog box to customize the look and feel of the desktop.

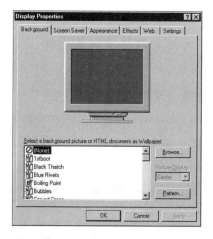

Redoing the Desktop Background

Let's start with the **Background** tab. The main purpose of this tab is to let you choose a wallpaper. *Wallpaper* is an image or design that replaces the desktop's default solid color background. (Before you ask, no, I'm not sure why Microsoft calls it "wallpaper" when you're supposed to be thinking that your screen is like the top of a desk. It's either a mixed metaphor or the Microsoft offices have a *very* strange interior designer.) You can choose one of the prefab wallpapers that come with Windows Millennium, or you can easily create your own.

Choosing One of the Windows Wallpapers

Let's start with the simplest case of picking out one of the predefined wallpapers:

1. In the **Background** tab use the **Select a background picture...** list to click one of the wallpaper names. Keep one eye peeled on the fake monitor above the list. This gives you a preview of what the wallpaper will look like. (Some of the images take a second or two to show up, so patience is required.)

2. Use the **Picture Display** list to select one of the following values:

    ➤ **Center**   Displays a single copy of the wallpaper in the center of the screen. This is a good choice for large wallpapers.

    ➤ **Tile**   Displays multiple copies of the wallpaper repeated so they fill the entire desktop. Choose this option for small wallpapers.

    ➤ **Stretch**   Displays a single copy of the wallpaper extended on all sides so that it fills the entire desktop. This is the one to use if the wallpaper image isn't quite big enough to cover the desktop. (Be careful, however: If the image is much smaller than the desktop, stretching will probably seriously distort the image and cause "wasted youth" flashbacks.)

3. Click **OK** to put the wallpaper into effect. (You also can click **Apply** if you prefer to leave the Display Properties dialog box open and ready for action.)

Creating a Wallpaper of Your Own

The images listed in the Background tab are a decent start, but what if you prefer the homegrown approach? In other words, what if you have an image you've created yourself and you want to use it as your wallpaper?

If the image is already saved as a file, copy or move the file into either the Windows folder or the Windows\Web\Wallpaper folder. The filename automatically appears in the Background tab's list of wallpapers.

If you've just created the image in Paint, you have another couple of choices on Paint's **File** menu that transform the current image into wallpaper:

➤ **Set As Wallpaper (Tiled)**   Select this command to tile the image to fill the entire desktop.

➤ **Set As Wallpaper (Centered)**   Select this command to center the image on the desktop.

Wallpaper Browsing

It isn't necessary to move the image file into the Windows folder or the Windows\Web\Wallpaper folder. Instead, click the **Browse** button in the Background tab to promote the Browse dialog box, find and highlight the image file, and then click **Open**.

Picking Out a Pattern

Windows Millennium also comes with a selection of *patterns*, which are simple black designs that cover the desktop. To use one of these patterns, click the Background tab's **Pattern** button. Use the Pattern dialog box to pick out a peachy pattern you like, and then click **OK**.

Revamping the Desktop Colors and Fonts

Now let's turn to doing Windows' colors. For this, you use the **Appearance** tab, shown in Figure 18.2. The easiest way to change Windows Millennium's colors is to select one of the predefined color schemes from the Scheme list. Here are some notes to bear in mind:

➤ These schemes control the colors of just about everything you see in Windows, including the desktop background (assuming the desktop isn't covered by wallpaper), the pull-down menus, and all the window nuts and bolts (the title bars, borders, scrollbars, and so on).

➤ The box above the Scheme list contains a couple of phony windows—one active and one inactive—and a pretend dialog box. By looking at the way your color choices affect these objects, you can see what havoc each scheme will wreak on your desktop, without actually changing anything.

➤ If your eyesight isn't what it used to be, Windows Millennium's title bar and dialog box text may be a strain on your peepers. If so, try out any of the **Scheme** items that have **(large)** or **(extra large)** in their names—such as **Rose (large)** or **Windows Standard (extra large)**.

Figure 18.2

Use the Appearance tab to select a different Windows Millennium color scheme.

These fake windows show what effect the selected scheme will have

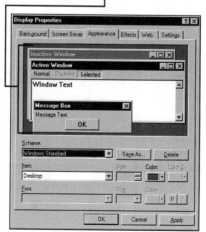

Custom Color Schemes

If you feel really brave, you can create your own color scheme. To do this, use the **Item** drop-down list to select the element you want to work with (such as Desktop or Active Title Bar). You then use the following techniques to customize the selected item:

➤ If it's possible to change the size of the item, the **Size** spin box beside the Item list will be enabled. Use this spin box to adjust the size to taste.

➤ If it's possible to change the color of the item, the **Color** button (the one beside the Item list) will be enabled. The idea here is that you click the downward-pointing arrow to drop down a color *palette*, and then click the color you want. To forge a custom color, drop down the palette, click **Other**, and use the Color dialog box to create a shade you like.

➤ Some screen elements (such as the Active Title Bar item) can display a color *gradient*, in which one color fades into another. In this case, you use the **Color** button (again, the one beside the Item list) to pick the first color, and the **Color 2** button to pick the second color. (To get a color gradient, your display must be set up to use more than 256 colors. See "Messing with the Screen Area and Color Depth," later in this chapter.)

➤ If the item has text, use the **Font** list to change the typeface. You also can adjust the font using the **Size** list, the **Color** button, and the bold and italic buttons.

Rejiggering the Desktop Icons and Visual Effects

The controls in the **Effects** tab (see Figure 18.3) deal with settings related to the desktop icons. Here's a rundown of the goodies you get on this tab:

➤ **Desktop icons**   This group lets you modify the icon used by the four basic desktop folders: My Computer, My Documents, My Network Places, and Recycle Bin (both the full and the empty versions). Highlight the icon you want to

Oodles of Icons

The Change Icon dialog box shows only a few icons. For more variety, click **Browse** and highlight either **MORICONS.DLL** or **PROGMAN**. There are also quite a few in the **SYSTEM** folder's **SHELL32.DLL** file.

Transition Effects

Transition effects are a new feature of the Windows Millennium landscape.

change, click the **Change Icon** button, choose the new icon from the Change Icon dialog box, and click **OK**. To change an icon back to its original form, highlight it and click the **Default Icon** button.

➤ **Use transition effects for menus and tooltips** With this check box activated, menus fade in and out, and ToolTips scroll in and out. (Again, you get these effects only if you're running Windows Millennium with more than 256 colors.) If these effects bug you for some reason, deactivate this check box to turn them off.

➤ **Smooth edges of screen fonts** If you activate this check box, Windows Millennium smoothes the jagged edges of large fonts, which makes them more readable.

➤ **Use large icons** Activating this check box increases the size of the desktop icons by about 50%.

➤ **Show icons using all possible colors** When activated, this check box tells Windows Millennium to use all the available colors to display the desktop icons. (Not sure how many colors your system has available? I'll show you how to find out a bit later. See "Messing with the Screen Area and Color Depth.") If you have a slower computer or video card and you find that Windows Millennium takes a long time to redraw your desktop, deactivate this option.

➤ **Show window contents while dragging** This check box toggles a feature called *full-window drag* on and off. When it's deactivated, Windows Millennium shows only the outline of any window you move with the mouse (by dragging the title bar); if you activate full-window drag, however, Windows Millennium displays the window's contents while you're dragging. If you find that your system can't update the screen fast enough during a full-window drag, deactivate this check box for better performance.

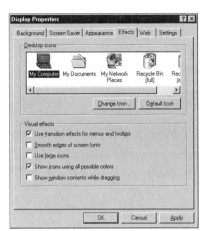

Figure 18.3

The Effects tab controls the look of the desktop icons.

Screen Saver Silliness

A screen saver is a moving pattern that displays after you haven't used your computer for a while. To set up a screen saver in Windows Millennium, click the **Screen Saver** tab in the Display Properties dialog box, and then choose the one you want from the **Screen Saver** list. Use the **Wait** spin box to set the amount of time your computer must be inactive before the screen saver starts doing its thing. You can enter a number between 1 and 60 minutes.

Desktop Dynamism: Working with the Active Desktop

The standard desktop backgrounds—wallpapers, patterns, and colors—are fine as far as they go, but they lack that element of interactivity that folks exposed to the World Wide Web have come to expect. If you're one of those folks, then I'm sure you'll get a kick out of Windows Millennium's *Active Desktop*. This variation on the desktop theme enables you to do two things:

➤ **Set a background Web page** The Active Desktop's background can be a full-fledged Web page, complete with all the images, text, and links that come with the territory.

➤ **Add "desktop items"**   You can also add things called *desktop items,* which sit on top of the desktop background. These items include other Web pages, images, and high-end geek toys such as "Java applets," and "ActiveX controls." Because these items aren't embedded in a Web page, they can be sized and moved on the desktop to achieve the look you want.

Your Desktop Disguised as a Web Page

To try out the background Web page angle, open the **Web** tab in the Display Properties dialog box. Activate the **Show Web content on my Active Desktop** check box. This gives you access to the list of items shown below the check box, which is the Web content you have available. At first, you have only **My Current Home Page**, which is the homepage defined in Internet Explorer.

As you can see in Figure 18.4, when you activate **My Current Home Page** and then click **Apply**, the desktop suddenly turns into an actual Web page with live links and everything. (If you're not online, you might just see a white block where the page is supposed to appear. To see the page, connect to the Internet, right-click the desktop, and then click **Refresh** in the shortcut menu that shows up.) Note, however, that you can't really "surf" the desktop because the links go only one level deep. That is, clicking any link changes the desktop page accordingly, but clicking subsequent links opens Internet Explorer to fetch the page.

Figure 18.4

You can turn your desktop into an honest-to-goodness Web page.

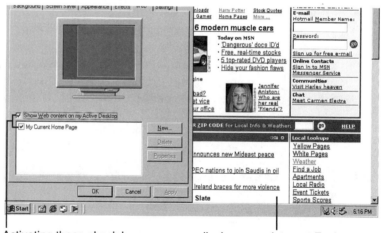

Activating these check boxes...   ...displays your Internet Explorer home page on the desktop

Adding Stuff to the Active Desktop

As I mentioned earlier, you can also plop desktop items on top of your Active Desktop background. To add an item to the desktop, follow these steps:

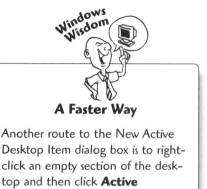

A Faster Way

Another route to the New Active Desktop Item dialog box is to right-click an empty section of the desktop and then click **Active Desktop**, **New Desktop Item**.

1. In the **Web** tab, click **New**. Windows Millennium coughs up the New Active Desktop Item dialog box, shown in Figure 18.5.

2. There are two paths you can take from here:

   ➤ **Visit Gallery**   Click this button to launch Internet Explorer and head for Microsoft's Active Desktop Gallery. This is a Web page that offers quite a few *Active Desktop items* that you can add to your system. The **Gallery Index** offers several categories to click (such as News, Sports, and Entertainment). This gives you a list of items. Click an item to see a description. From there, click the **Add to Active Desktop** button. When Internet Explorer asks whether you're sure about all this, click **Yes**.

   ➤ **Location**   Use this text box to enter the address of a Web page. This can be the full URL of a page on the Web, or the location of an HTML file on your hard disk or your network. (If you're not sure about the location of a non-Web item, click **Browse** to use the Browse dialog box to find it.)

Figure 18.5

Use this dialog box to add more Web knickknacks to the Active Desktop.

3. Whichever method you use, you eventually end up at the Add item to Active Desktop dialog box. Click **OK**. Windows Millennium downloads the content and adds the item to the desktop.

4. If you went the Location route, you'll be dropped back in the Web tab. Click **OK** or **Apply**.

The nice thing about Active Desktop items is that they can be moved and sized as required. Here's a review of the techniques to use:

➤ **To move an item**   First move the mouse pointer over the item. This gets you a border around the item, as shown in Figure 18.6. Now drag any border.

➤ **To resize an item**   Move the mouse pointer over the top border. After a couple of seconds, you get a larger bar across the top of the item, as shown in the following figure. Drag this bar to move the item.

➤ **To maximize an item**   Click the **Cover Desktop** button.

➤ **To maximize an item without affecting the desktop icons**   Click the **Split Desktop with Icons** button.

➤ **To close an item**   Click the **Close** button.

Figure 18.6

Active Desktop doodads can be moved, resized, and more.

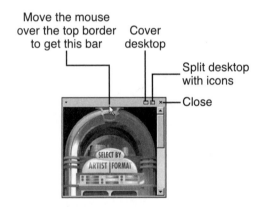

Move the mouse over the top border to get this bar — Cover desktop — Split desktop with icons — Close

Jargon Jar

Video Adapter

An internal circuit board that gets instructions about what to display from the processor and then tells the monitor what to show on the screen. Also known as the *video card* or *graphics card*.

Messing with the Screen Area and Color Depth

The next bit of desktop decoration I'll put you through relates to various display settings. Again, these are options that apply not just to the desktop, but to everything you see on your screen. You find these settings in the Settings tab of the Display Properties dialog box, shown in Figure 18.7.

Let's begin with the Display area. This line shows you two things:

➤ **Your monitor**   This tells you the name of your monitor, or sometimes just the type of monitor you have.

➤ **Your video adapter**   This tells you what type of video adapter resides inside your system.

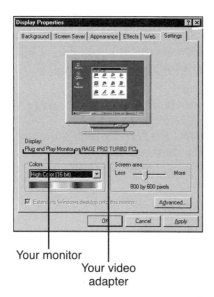

Figure 18.7

The Settings tab lets you muck around with your display.

Your monitor

Your video adapter

These two chunks of hardware determine the values you can select in the Settings tab's other two groups: Colors and Screen area.

The **Colors** group consists of a single list. The items in this list specify how many colors Windows Millennium can use to display stuff. Video jocks call this the *color depth*. Here are some notes:

➤ In general, the more colors you use, the sharper your screen images will appear.

➤ If you work with graphics programs regularly, use as many colors as possible.

➤ On the other hand, if you find that your screen display is sluggish, then you should consider reducing the number of colors.

The **Screen area** slider determines the number of pixels used to display stuff on the screen. I've mentioned pixels before, but it's worth repeating here: A *pixel* is an individual pinpoint of light. All the colors you see are the result of thousands of these pixels being activated on your monitor and set to display a specific hue.

The lowest screen area value is 640×480. This means that Windows Millennium uses pixels arranged in a grid that has 640 columns and 480 rows. That's over 300,000 pixels for your viewing pleasure! The number of higher screen area values you can pick depends on your monitor and on your video adapter. Here are some notes:

➤ The more pixels you use (that is, the higher you go on the Screen area slider), the smaller things will look on the screen. However, because things are smaller, you also see more stuff onscreen, so you've effectively enlarged your viewing area.

➤ You might be able to go to a higher screen area value only by using a smaller number of colors. Video adapters have only a certain amount of memory, so you often have to trade off one value for the other. Windows Millennium, ever on the lookout for illegal behavior, won't let you choose a color depth/screen area combination that your video adapter doesn't support.

➤ In general, you should tailor the screen area value to the size of your monitor. If you have a tiny monitor (13 inches or less), use 640×480; if you have a standard 14- or 15-inch monitor, try 800×600; for 17- or 19-inch monitors, head up to 1,024×768; if you're lucky enough to have a 21-inch behemoth, go for 1,280× 1,024 or even 1,600×1,200 (if your video adapter will let you).

Colors Versus Bits

The Colors list is confusing because it has one value in colors—256 Colors—and the rest use bits—such as High Color (16-bit). This is actually consistent, but you'd never know it. You see, Windows Millennium uses a specified number of bits (on/off values) for each screen pixel (see my discussion of the Screen area setting on the previous page). The lowest number of bits is 8, and because 2 to the power of 8 is 256, that's the minimum number of colors you can choose. Other typical bit values are 16 (65,536 colors), and 24 (16,777,216 colors). There's also 32-bit color, but that's the same as 24-bit (the extra 8 bits are used by some applications for "masking" existing colors so that they appear transparent).

When you've made your changes, click **OK** or **Apply**. If you changed the number of colors, Windows Millennium will likely display the Compatibility Warning dialog box shown in Figure 18.8. In most cases, you can get away with activating the **Apply the new color settings without restarting?** option and clicking **OK**.

Figure 18.8

After you change the number of colors, Windows Millennium wonders whether you want to restart your computer.

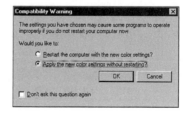

Look Out!

Wonky Display? Don't Touch Anything!

If your display goes haywire when Windows Millennium applies the new settings, it probably means that you tried some combo that was beyond the capabilities of your adapter/monitor team. Your screen probably will be unreadable, but don't panic. Windows Millennium will automatically reset the display after 15 seconds.

Wholesale Changes: Applying Desktop Themes

Earlier I showed you how to select schemes that govern the look of various objects, including menu bars, window borders, title bars, icons, and more. Windows Millennium takes this idea a step further with desktop *themes*. A theme is also a collection of customizations, but it covers more ground than a simple scheme. Each theme specifies various settings for not only windows and dialog boxes, but also a screen saver, wallpaper, mouse pointers, sounds, desktop icons, and more.

To choose a desktop theme, follow these steps:

1. Select **Start**, **Settings**, **Control Panel**. If you don't see an icon named Desktop Themes, click the **view all Control Panel options** link.

2. Launch the **Desktop Themes** icon. Windows Millennium tacks the Desktop Themes dialog box onto the desktop, as shown in Figure 18.9.

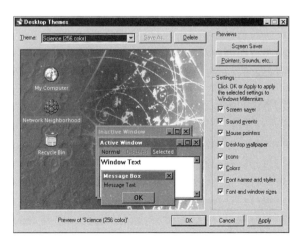

Figure 18.9

Use the Desktop Themes dialog box to choose one of the wild desktop themes that come with Windows Millennium.

293

Look Out!

Watch Your Colors

Many of the desktop themes tell you how many colors they require (usually either 256 colors or high color—65,356 colors). If you choose one of these themes, make sure your display is set up with at least that many colors, as described in the previous section.

3. Use the **Theme** drop-down list to choose the theme you want to use. The window that takes up the bulk of the dialog box shows you a preview of the theme. You see not only how the theme will affect the various window objects, but also the wallpaper and desktop icons the theme uses.

4. To preview other theme features, click the **Screen Saver** button and then the **Pointers**, **Sounds**, **etc.** button.

5. The **Settings** group contains check boxes for each object contained in the theme. To remove an object from the scheme, deactivate its check box.

6. When you're done, click **OK**.

Windows Wisdom

Themes Supreme

If the Windows Millennium collection of themes has you hankering for more, don't fret because there are thousands of them available on the Internet. Here are three great places to start:

Windows Update: `http://windowsupdate.microsoft.com/`

ThemeWorld: `http://www.themeworld.com/`

TUCOWS Themes: `http://themes.tucows.com/`

If you've got a real theme jones going, there are many more sites out there. Check out the following Yahoo! page for a long list of them:

`http://dir.yahoo.com/Computers_and_Internet/Software/Operating_Systems/Windows/Desktop_Themes/`

The Least You Need to Know

This chapter showed you a number of ways to redo the desktop. You learned how to select a wallpaper and create your own wallpaper, specify a pattern, modify the desktop colors and fonts, and change a few visual effects. I also showed you how to take advantage of Windows Millennium's Active Desktop and how to change two display settings: the color depth and the screen area. I closed by showing you how to pick out a desktop theme. Time to check out a few reverse-angle replays.

Crib Notes

➤ **Displaying the Display Properties**   Either right-click the desktop and then click **Properties**, or select **Start**, **Settings**, **Control Panel**, and then launch the **Display** icon.

➤ **Wallpaper options**   Most wallpaper images are small, so you need to use the **Tile** option to get the full effect. For larger images, use either **Center** or **Stretch**.

➤ **Raise your colors**   To get the most out of Windows Millennium's visual effects, set up your system to use more than 256 colors.

➤ **Tailor your pixels**   Try to use a screen area value that matches your monitor. For most monitors, 800×600 is ideal.

➤ **Dare to theme**   To apply a theme that covers colors, desktop settings, pointers, sounds, and more, select **Start**, **Settings**, **Control Panel**, click the **view all Control Panel options** link (if necessary), and then launch the **Desktop Themes** icon.

295

LET'S GET SOME CURTAINS UP THERE!!

Chapter 19

Remodeling the Start Menu and Taskbar

In This Chapter

➤ Quick taskbar tweaks

➤ Creating handy custom taskbar toolbars

➤ Changing Start menu settings

➤ Adding your own shortcuts to the Start menu

➤ Useful strategies for taking control of the bottom part of your screen

Microsoft has invested millions of dollars in its "usability labs," which is where they test the Windows "look and feel" on unsuspecting subjects. A person—usually an ordinary computer-using Joe or Josephine—sits at a computer while researchers clad in white coats (at least that's how I imagine them) watch how the person works. Tendencies are tracked, inefficiencies are noted, and questions are asked. All this data—suitably normalized, bell-curved, and otherwise statisticized—is studied and converted into ideas for the Windows "user interface" (the stuff you click and select).

You might think, with all this testing and data, that they'd get it right. Nope. For example, why is the hugely important ScanDisk program buried four menus deep? Why did they make it *harder* to get to some crucial Control Panel icons? Why do the taskbar buttons get so tiny when you open a few programs?

Yes, the sad news is that Windows Millennium in its right-out-of-the-box getup has configured the taskbar and Start menu a bit stupidly so they may not be right for you. Fortunately, you'll find no shortage of options and settings that will help you remake these features in your own image. That's just what this chapter shows you how to do.

Tweaking the Taskbar

The taskbar—that solid-seeming strip that acts as a kind of underline for the desktop—appears to be an unalterable aspect of the Windows Millennium scenery. Not so. As the next few sections show, you can readily alter the taskbar in many useful and practical ways.

Moving the Taskbar Hither and Yon

The taskbar, recumbent on the bottom of the screen, seems quite comfy. However, that position might not be comfy for *you*, depending on the ergonomics of your desk and chair. Similarly, you might have a program in which you need to maximize the available vertical screen space, so you might not appreciate having the taskbar usurp space at the bottom of the screen. These are mere molehills that can be easily leapt over by moving the taskbar to a new location:

1. Point the mouse at an empty section of the taskbar.
2. Hold down the left mouse button and move the pointer toward the edge of the screen where you want the taskbar situated. As you approach an edge, the outline of the taskbar suddenly snaps into place.
3. When the taskbar is on the edge you want, release the mouse button.

Resizing the Taskbar for a Better Icon Fit

Although you probably only work with, at most, a few programs at once, Windows Millennium's multitasking capabilities sure make it tempting to open a boatload of applications. The problem, however, is that it doesn't take long for the taskbar to become seriously overpopulated. As you can see in Figure 19.1, with 10 programs on the go, the taskbar buttons become all but indecipherable. ("Hey, Vern! What's this here 'Ph...' program supposed to do?") If you can't figure out what a particular taskbar button represents, point your mouse at the button that puzzles you, and after a couple of seconds a banner appears telling you the full name of the program.

Figure 19.1

An example of taskbar overcrowding.

If you prefer to take in everything at a glance and you don't mind giving up a little more screen area, you can expand the taskbar to show two or more rows of buttons. To give 'er a go, follow these steps:

1. Point your mouse at the top edge of the taskbar. When it's positioned properly, the pointer changes into a two-headed arrow.

2. Drag the edge of the taskbar up until you see the outline of a second row appear in the taskbar area, and then release the mouse button. You should now see the taskbar buttons on the bottom row and the Quick Launch icons on the top row.

3. Point your mouse at the left edge of the taskbar buttons. Again, the pointer changes into a two-headed arrow (pointing horizontally, this time).

4. Drag the taskbar buttons up into the second row and drop them to the right of the Quick Launch icons. The buttons should now be arranged as shown in Figure 19.2.

The Flaky Taskbar

Frustratingly, these steps may not work every time and you may find that the taskbar buttons refuse to populate the bottom row. Grrr. To fix this, you follow the same steps, except in step 2 you drag the taskbar up to a *third* row. After step 4, drag the taskbar down so that it's two rows again.

Figure 19.2

With two rows, the buttons have some breathing room.

Taskbar Options You Should Know About

The next round of taskbar touchups involves a small but useful set of properties, which you can plop onto the desktop by using either of the following methods:

➤ Select **Start**, **Settings**, **Taskbar and Start Menu**.

➤ Right-click an empty section of the taskbar and then click **Properties**.

Windows Millennium displays the Taskbar and Start Menu Properties dialog box, shown in Figure 19.3.

Three of the check boxes in the General tab deal specifically with the taskbar (I talk about the others a bit later in this chapter):

➤ **Always on top**   When this option is activated, the taskbar remains in view even if you maximize a window. That's usually a good thing. However, if you really need that extra bit of screen room, deactivate this check box. This means that a maximized window takes up the entire screen. The downside is that it takes a bit more work to get at the taskbar.

Figure 19.3

Use the Taskbar Properties dialog box to renovate the taskbar and Start menu.

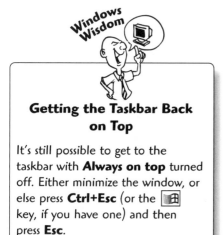

Getting the Taskbar Back on Top

It's still possible to get to the taskbar with **Always on top** turned off. Either minimize the window, or else press **Ctrl+Esc** (or the ⊞ key, if you have one) and then press **Esc**.

➤ **Auto hide** If you activate this check box, Windows Millennium shrinks the taskbar to a teensy gray strip that's barely visible along the bottom of the screen. This gives a maximized window more room to stretch its legs. When you need the taskbar for something, just move the mouse pointer to the bottom of the screen. Lo and behold, the full taskbar slides into view. When you move the mouse above the taskbar, the taskbar sinks back whence it came. On the negative side of the ledger, Auto Hide can be annoying because it sometimes means that the taskbar shows itself when you're trying to get at something else near the bottom of the screen.

➤ **Show clock** Deactivating this check box hides the clock that normally resides to the right of the taskbar's system tray.

Making the Quick Launch Toolbar Your Own

The Quick Launch toolbar is a great innovation because it's handy (it's always visible) and easy (single-click the icons to launch them). Unfortunately, Windows Millennium deposits a mere quartet of icons in this section, which seems like a waste of a precious resource. Forget that. As you'll soon see, it's not that hard to add as many icons as you like to the Quick Launch area.

The secret is that the Quick Launch icons are really just files (two of them are shortcuts) in a folder named Quick Launch. Therefore, if you add your own shortcuts to the Quick Launch folder, the icons show up in the Quick Launch toolbar and you're set.

There are two methods you can use to add shortcuts to the Quick Launch folder:

➤ **The easy method**   Open My Computer, drag the program file you want to add, and drop it inside the Quick Launch toolbar. (You can also drag an icon from any Start menu and drop it inside the Quick Launch toolbar.)

➤ **The hard method**   Right-click an empty section of the Quick Launch toolbar (this is a bit hard to do because there's not that much empty space) and then click **Open** to open the Quick Launch folder window. Click the **Folders** button to get the Folder list, and then drag shortcuts into the Quick Launch folder.

Whichever method you use, note that the Quick Launch toolbar doesn't expand automatically to accommodate the new icons. To see everything, you need to resize the Quick Launch toolbar using the same taskbar technique that I outlined earlier. (See "Resizing the Taskbar for a Better Icon Fit.")

Displaying and Tweaking Taskbar Toolbars

I've used the phrase "Quick Launch toolbar" a few times so far in this book. What's all this about a *toolbar*? It's no big secret. In the same way that some programs have toolbars to give you one-click access to features, the taskbar has its own collection of toolbars for one-click wonderment. Quick Launch is one such taskbar toolbar, but there are others. To view them, first right-click an empty spot on the taskbar. In the shortcut menu that unfurls, click **Toolbars** to get a submenu that includes the following commands:

➤ **Links**   This command toggles the Links toolbar on and off. This toolbar is the same as the Links bar in Internet Explorer.

➤ **Address**   This command toggles the Address toolbar on and off. This toolbar is a version of the Address bar that appears in Internet Explorer (as well as Windows Millennium's folder windows). You can use it to type in Web addresses. When you press **Enter**, Internet Explorer fires up and loads the specified page.

➤ **Desktop**   This command toggles the desktop toolbar on and off. The icons in this toolbar are the same as the icons on the Windows Millennium desktop. This is useful if you normally run your programs maximized and rarely see the desktop.

➤ **Quick Launch**   This command toggles the Quick Launch toolbar on and off.

If you activate any of these extra toolbars, you'll probably need to increase the number of taskbar rows (as explained earlier) to accommodate everything comfortably.

Each of these toolbars also boasts a few customization options that can help reduce the clutter on the taskbar. To see these options, right-click an empty section of the toolbar you want to work with. The resulting shortcut menu contains a bunch of commands, but we care only about the following three:

301

➤ **View**   This command displays a submenu with two options: **Large** and **Small**. These options determine the relative size of the toolbar icons.

➤ **Show Text**   This command toggles the icon captions on and off. (These captions are bits of text that sit beside each icon and tell you the icon name.) If you can recognize an icon from its image alone, turning off the text will enable you to fit many more icons on a given chunk of toolbar real estate.

➤ **Show Title**   This command toggles the toolbar title (which appears on the left side of the toolbar) on and off. Again, you can give your toolbar icons a bit more elbowroom by turning off the title.

Move Those Toolbars

You can move any of these toolbars by using the same technique that I showed you earlier for the taskbar. On my own system, I have the Address toolbar and the taskbar along the bottom of the screen, the Quick Launch toolbar along the right side of the screen, and the Links toolbar along the left side of the screen. It's busy, but boy, is it efficient!

Reconstructing the Start Menu

Even if you have all kinds of taskbar toolbars on the go and you populate the Quick Launch toolbar with shortcuts to your favorite programs, you'll still probably find yourself trudging through the Start menu system a lot during the course of a day. To help keep this trudging from becoming true drudgery, you need to customize some Start menu settings and the arrangement of the menus to suit the way you work. The rest of this chapter shows you a number of ways to do just that.

Start Menu Settings

Most of the settings I yammer on about in this section are new to Windows Millennium.

Toggling Some Start Menu Settings On and Off

Windows Millennium's Start menu boasts a number of new settings that you can turn on and off. These settings enable you to, among other things, add the Favorites list as a submenu, display the Control Panel icons as a submenu, turn off the personalized menus, and more.

To get to these settings, you have to return to the Taskbar and Start Menu Properties dialog box:

➤ Select **Start**, **Settings**, **Taskbar and Start Menu**.

➤ Right-click an empty section of the taskbar and then click **Properties**.

The General tab, shown earlier in Figure 19.3, has two Start menu check boxes to play with:

➤ **Show small icons in Start menu**   If you light up this option, the Start menu goes on a diet: It loses the "Windows Me Millennium Edition" banner along the side and it uses smaller, cuter versions of its icons. This is useful if you find that some Start menus are too big for the screen.

➤ **Use personalized menus**   This setting controls the new personalized menus feature (which I told you about back in Chapter 3, "Making Your Programs Do What You Want Them to Do"). If you don't like this feature, you can turn it off by deactivating this check box.

Cross Reference

See "Now You See 'Em, Now You Don't: Personalized Menus," p. 35.

There's a whole bunch of other Start menu fun to be had on the Advanced tab, which is shown in Figure 19.4.

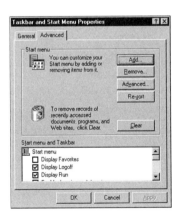

Figure 19.4

The Advanced tab is chock full of Start menu customization settings.

What you're dealing with here is the list of check boxes in the Start Menu and Taskbar group. Each one toggles a particular Start menu feature on and off. Here's a quick summary of the features:

➤ **Display Favorites**   Activate this check box to toss the Favorites submenu onto the main Start menu. I told you about Windows Millennium's Favorites feature back in Chapter 8, "It's a Small Web After All: Using Internet Explorer."

See "The Favorites Folder: Sites to Remember," p. 123.

➤ **Display Logoff**   Deactivate this setting to force Windows Millennium to remove the Log Off *User* command from the main Start menu (where *User* is the name of the user who's currently logged on).

➤ **Display Run**   Deactivate this check box to remove the Run command from the main Start menu.

➤ **Enable Dragging and Dropping**   When this setting is activated, it means you can rearrange most of the Start menu items by using your mouse to drag them to and fro. I explain how this handy technique works in the "More Ways to Monkey with the Start Menu" section later in this chapter.

➤ **Expand Control Panel**   Turn on this option to display all the Control Panel icons in a submenu when you select **Start**, **Settings**, **Control Panel**. If you use Control Panel frequently, you'll find the submenu route is faster than opening the Control Panel window and then launching an icon.

➤ **Expand Dial-Up Networking**   Activate this check box to display a submenu listing your Dial-Up Networking connection icons when you select **Start**, **Settings**, **Dial-Up Networking**. (See Chapter 26, "Remote Network Connections with Dial-Up Networking.")

➤ **Expand My Documents**   If you activate this check box, Windows Millennium displays a submenu containing your My Documents files when you select **Start**, **Documents**, **My Documents**.

➤ **Expand My Pictures**   Activate this check box to display a submenu containing your My Pictures files when you select **Start**, **Documents**, **My Pictures**.

➤ **Expand Printers**   I think you know the drill by now. Activating this check box displays a menu of your installed printers when you select **Start**, **Settings**, **Printers**.

➤ **Scroll Programs**   This setting determines what Windows Millennium does if the Programs menu contains so many items that the entire menu can't fit into the height of the screen. When this setting is off, Windows Millennium displays Programs as a two-column menu. When this setting is on, Windows Millennium displays Programs as a single menu with up and down arrows on the top and bottom, respectively. You click these arrows to scroll through the menu.

To put the new settings into effect, click **OK** or **Apply**.

Adding to the Start Menu I: The Create Shortcut Wizard

When you install a program, it's usually decent enough to add an icon for itself to your Start menu. Most DOS-based programs wouldn't know the Start menu from a

Denny's menu, however, and they won't create Start menu icons for themselves. DOS programs, Windows-ignorant savages that they are, have an excuse, but you may come across a few ornery Windows-based programs that won't do it, either. That means you have to add these programs to the Start menu manually (ugh).

To make this easy for you, Windows Millennium provides the Create Shortcut Wizard. As an example, let's see how you add a Start menu icon for the MS-DOS Editor, a text-editing program that boasts a few more features than the humble Notepad text editor. Here's what you do:

1. Select **Start**, **Settings**, **Taskbar and Start Menu** to return to our old friend the Taskbar and Start Menu Properties dialog box (if it isn't still onscreen from the previous section).

2. In the **Advanced** tab, click **Add**. The Create Shortcut Wizard makes an entrance.

3. Use the **Command line** text box to enter the location of the document or the file that launches the program. Be sure you include the disk drive, folder, and filename. Alternatively, click **Browse** and use the dialog box to pick out the file. For our example, click **Browse**, open drive C (assuming that's where Windows Millennium was installed; note that this drive will likely be opened be default), open the WINDOWS folder, and then open the COMMAND folder. Highlight EDIT and click **Open**. Figure 19.5 shows the initial dialog box with the location filled in.

Figure 19.5

The Create Shortcut Wizard takes you step-by-step through the process of adding an icon to the Start Menu.

4. Click **Next**. The wizard wonders which Start menu folder you want to use.

5. You have two choices:

   ➤ If you want to use one of the existing folders, click it to highlight it.

   ➤ If you prefer a fresh folder, first highlight the folder in which you want the new folder created. Now click **New Folder**, enter the folder name, and press **Tab**.

6. Click **Next**. The final wizard dialog box suggests a name for the new icon.

7. Adjust the name, if necessary, and then click **Finish**.

Taking Stuff Off the Start Menu

What about the opposite procedure, when you need to get rid of something on the Start menu? I'm glad you asked:

It's Okay to Delete Shortcuts

Remember, the icons you delete are only shortcuts that point to the original program file or document. You're not deleting the originals.

1. Select **Start**, **Settings**, **Taskbar and Start Menu** to open the Taskbar and Start Menu Properties dialog box.

2. In the **Advanced** tab, click **Remove**. The Remove Shortcuts/Folders dialog box sprints onto the screen.

3. Highlight the icon or folder you want to rub out.

4. Click **Remove**. Windows Millennium asks whether you're sure.

5. Click **Yes**. Windows Millennium deletes the item and returns you to the Remove Shortcuts/Folders dialog box.

6. Click **Close**.

Adding to the Start Menu II: The Start Menu Folder

The Start menu submenus are actually folders on your hard disk. In fact, the entire Start menu structure (with the exception of the set-in-stone items on the main Start menu) can be found within the following folder:

```
C:\Windows\Start Menu\
```

What good does it do you to know this? You can use all the basic file and folder techniques from Chapter 6, "Using My Computer to Fiddle with Files and Folders," to add, rename, and delete items, and to make the overall Start menu structure more efficient.

To get to the Start Menu folder collection, you can use My Computer to get there on your own. However, Windows Millennium offers two potentially faster methods:

➤ Right-click the **Start** button and then click **Explore**.

➤ In the **Advanced** tab, click **Advanced**.

Figure 19.6 shows the Start Menu folder with the Programs folder highlighted. For the most part, you use the exact same techniques for moving, renaming, and deleting files and folders as you learned in Chapter 6. To create new Start menu items, please keep the following two points in mind:

➤ To add icons to any Start menu, be sure you always create a shortcut. Never move a document or program file into the Start Menu folders. To ensure that you always create a shortcut, right-drag the document or program file, drop it inside the Start Menu folder you want to use, and then click **Create Shortcut(s) Here** in the submenu that appears.

➤ If you create a folder within the Start Menu folder, it becomes a submenu on the Start menu.

Most of the Start menu stuff can be found within these folders

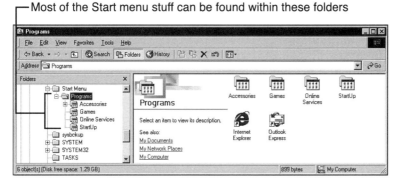

Figure 19.6

For maximum flexibility, use the Start Menu folder to work with the Start menu icons and submenus.

More Ways to Monkey with the Start Menu

To close out your look at customizing the Start menu, here are a few tips and techniques that can make this part of your life even easier:

➤ **Right-click convenience** You can perform many maintenance chores right from the Start menu itself. Right-click a start menu shortcut or submenu and you'll get a menu with all kinds of useful commands, including Cut, Copy, Delete, and Rename.

➤ **Quick Start menu shortcuts** If you want a shortcut on the main Start menu, drag it from My Computer and drop it on the **Start** button.

➤ **Drag-and-drop rearranging** Speaking of dragging and dropping, you can also display the Start menu and then use your mouse to drag the commands directly. You can drop them higher or lower on the same menu or even drop them onto another menu altogether.

➤ **Sorting an out-of-sorts menu** If you've been dragging Start menu items hither and yon, you might end up with menus that are no longer in alphabetical order. If that offends your inner neat freak, it's easy enough to fix. Just right-click the offending menu and then click **Sort by Name**. To get all the menus back in shape, return to the **Advanced** tab and click the **Re-sort** button. Note

307

that in both cases, Windows Millennium places the folders at the top of the menu (sorted alphabetically) and then it displays the shortcuts (again, sorted alphabetically).

➤ **Wiping out the Documents menu**   As you probably know, the Documents menu (**Start**, **Documents**) contains a list of the last 15 documents you worked on. If you don't want anyone else to see this list, you can scrub it clean by returning to the **Advanced** tab once again and clicking the **Clear** button.

The Least You Need to Know

This chapter showed you how to customize both the taskbar and the Start menu. For the taskbar, I began by showing you how to move and resize it. From there, you learned about some taskbar options, how to customize the Quick Launch toolbar, and how to display and customize other taskbar toolbars. For the Start menu, you first learned about Windows Millennium's new personalized menus. I then showed you how to toggle some options on and off (including those personalized menus), how to create your own Start menu shortcuts, and how to work with Start menu items directly from the Start menu.

Crib Notes

➤ **Start menu and taskbar options**   These are available by selecting **Start**, **Settings, Taskbar and Start Menu,** or by right-clicking an empty stretch of the taskbar and then clicking **Properties**.

➤ **Moving and sizing the taskbar**   Drag an empty section of the taskbar to move it; drag the top edge of the taskbar to size it.

➤ **Quick Launch customizing**   The easiest way to add icons to the Quick Launch toolbar is to drag program files and drop them onto the toolbar.

➤ **Adding Start menu stuff**   Display the **Advanced** tab and click **Add**. Alternatively, use My Computer to work with the C:\Windows\Start Menu folder directly.

➤ **Direct Start menu modifications**   Display the Start menu and then right-click any command.

Chapter 20

Renovating My Computer

In This Chapter

➤ Messing with the My Computer window

➤ Changing the file and folder view

➤ Sorting files and folders

➤ Creating custom Web views for folders

➤ All kinds of useful options and settings designed to help you make My Computer your own

My Computer, being perhaps the dullest of the Windows Millennium programs, would seem an unlikely candidate for any kind of customizing, much less a full chapter's worth. You'd be surprised. It turns out that My Computer (along with it's kissin' file cousin, Windows Explorer) is one of the most flexible programs in the Windows Millennium collection. You can rearrange the My Computer window, change how My Computer displays files and folders, sort files and folders, and even customize things such as the folder background. This chapter fills you in on these and other customizations that will help you put the "My" in My Computer.

Points of View: Changing the My Computer View

Let's begin the My Computer renovations with a few methods for changing the view. I'll divide this into four areas: changing the layout of the My Computer window, customizing the toolbar, switching how file and folders are displayed in the content area, and sorting files and folders.

Toggling My Computer's Bars On and Off

My Computer is awash in bars: the menu bar, the toolbar, the Address bar, and the status bar. And those are just the ones you see by default. Plenty of other bars are lurking beneath the surface. So, to start things off on an easy note, this section shows you how to display the various My Computer bars, as well as how to hide those you don't use.

The commands you need are on the **View** menu. Let's start with the **Toolbars** command, which shoves out a submenu that has four commands corresponding to My Computer's four available toolbars. (I talk about the Customize command in the next section.) In each case, you display a toolbar by activating its command (so that it has a check mark beside it), and you hide a toolbar by deactivating its command. Here's a summary of the four toolbars:

➤ **Standard Buttons**   This toolbar is displayed by default and it's the one that you see under the menu bar. See the next section, "Customizing the Standard Buttons Toolbar," to learn how to control the look of this all-important toolbar.

➤ **Address Bar**   This toolbar is displayed by default and it appears under the Standard Buttons toolbar. It displays the name of the current folder and you can use it to navigate to other folders (or even to Web page addresses).

➤ **Links**   This is the Links bar that you normally see only in Internet Explorer. If you display it here, clicking any button in the Links bar displays the corresponding Web page within the My Computer window.

➤ **Radio**   This is a toolbar that enables you to listen to a radio station piped in over the Web. This is useful only if you have a fast connection to the Internet and if you have that connection established while you work within My Computer.

Speedy Toolbar Toggling

You also can toggle a toolbar on and off by right-clicking any displayed toolbar and then clicking the toolbar name in the shortcut menu that shows up.

Next up on the **View** menu is the **Status Bar** command. This command toggles the status bar at the bottom of the window on and off. I recommend that you leave the status bar as-is because it offers some semi-useful info:

➤ If you highlight a menu command, a short description of the command appears in the status bar.

➤ Each time you open a folder, the status bar tells you how many files and subfolders ("objects") are in the folder and how much hard disk space the files take up.

➤ If you select one or more files, the status bar tells you how many files you selected and their total size.

The **View** menu's **Explorer Bar** command also spits out a submenu. In this case, the submenu offers a number of commands that toggle five bars on and off within the Explorer bar:

➤ **Search**   Toggles the Search bar on and off. You use the Search bar to find files on your hard disk. I covered searching back in Chapter 6, "Using My Computer to Fiddle with Files and Folders."

➤ **Favorites**   Toggles the Favorites bar on and off. You use the Favorites bar to display your list of favorites. These are normally Web sites, but you also can define a folder as a favorite. The details on favorites can be found in Chapter 8, "It's a Small Web After All: Using Internet Explorer."

➤ **History**   Toggles the History bar on and off. The History bar displays a list of the folders that you've visited each day for the past 20 days. It works the same as the History bar used by Internet Explorer.

➤ **Folders**   Toggles the Folders bar on and off. The Folders bar gives you a bird's-eye view of your disks and folders, which makes it much easier to navigate your system (see Figure 20.1). I highly recommend turning on this Explorer bar and leaving it on full time.

Jargon Jar

Explorer Bar

The *Explorer Bar* is a pane that shows up on the left side of the My Computer window, which is used to display bars (such as the handy Folders bar).

Cross Reference

See "Finding a File in That Mess You Call a Hard Disk," p. 90, for the details.

See "The Favorites Folder: Sites to Remember," p. 123.

For the goods on the History bar, see "The Way You Were: Using the History List" section, p. 125.

Figure 20.1

For easier navigation, always display the Folders bar in My Computer.

Folders bar

➤ **Tip of the Day** This command toggles the Tip of the Day bar on and off. As its name implies, this bar displays a brief Windows Millennium tip each day. This bar is a bit different in that it appears along the bottom of the My Computer window.

Explorer Bar Shortcuts

Three of the Explorer bars offer shortcut methods for toggling themselves on and off:

➤ **Search** Click **Search** in the Standard Buttons toolbar, or press **Ctrl+E**.

➤ **Favorites** Click **Favorites** in the Standard Buttons toolbar, or press **Ctrl+I**.

➤ **History** Click **History** in the Standard Buttons toolbar, or press **Ctrl+H**.

Customizing the Standard Buttons Toolbar

The Standard Buttons toolbar (which I just call "the toolbar" from now on) is a bit of an odd duck. Some buttons have text (such as the Back button) and some don't (such as the Forward button). Also, it doesn't include buttons for three commonly used commands: Cut, Copy, and Paste. You can fix this idiosyncratic behavior by tweaking the toolbar.

To begin, select **View**, **Toolbars**, **Customize**. (If you're so inclined, you also can right-click the toolbar and then click **Customize** in the shortcut menu.) My Computer lobs the Customize Toolbar dialog box your way, as shown in Figure 20.2.

Toolbar Customization

The ability to customize the Standard Buttons toolbars is a welcome new addition to Windows Millennium.

The extra toolbar buttons that you can display The toolbar buttons that are currently displayed

Figure 20.2

Use this dialog box to knock some sense into My Computer's main toolbar.

Here's a summary of the techniques you can use:

Adding an extra button to the toolbar Highlight it in the **Available toolbar buttons** list and then click **Add**. Use the **Separator** item to add a vertical bar to the toolbar. This is used to separate groups of related buttons.

Removing a button from the toolbar Highlight it in the **Current toolbar buttons** list and then click **Remove**.

Changing the order of the buttons Highlight any button in the **Current toolbar buttons** list and click **Move Up** or **Move Down**.

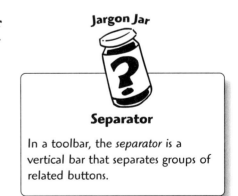

Separator

In a toolbar, the *separator* is a vertical bar that separates groups of related buttons.

"De-Customizing" the Toolbar

If you make a mess of the toolbar, you can return it to square one by displaying the Customize Toolbar dialog box again and clicking **Reset**.

Controlling the button text Use the **Text options** list:

➤ **Show text labels** This option adds text to every button. This makes the buttons much easier to figure out, so I recommend going with this option.

➤ **Selective text on right** This is the default option, and it displays text on only some buttons. As I've mentioned, this is a pretty dumb way of doing things.

➤ **No text labels** This option displays every button using just its icon. If you already know what each icon represents, selecting this option gives you a bit more room because the toolbar takes up the least amount of room vertically.

Controlling the size of the icons Use the items in the **Icon options** list. Select either **Small icons** (this is the default) or **Large icons**.

Click **Close** to put your new settings into effect.

Views You Can Use: Changing How Folders and Files Are Displayed

In the standard My Computer view, each file and folder is displayed using a big, fat icon. However, there are also several other views you can try on for size. You access these views either by pulling down the **View** menu or by clicking the **Views** button in the toolbar. In most folders, there are five possibilities:

➤ **Large Icons** This is the default honkin' big icon view.

➤ **Small Icons** This view displays files and folders using slightly smaller versions of the icons.

➤ **List** This view also displays the files and folders using small icons, but everything is arrayed in multiple columns, as shown in Figure 20.3.

➤ **Details** This view displays the files and folders using a four-column list, as shown in Figure 20.4. For each file and folder, you see its Name, its Size, its Type (such as WordPad Document), and the date and time it was last Modified. However, these aren't the only columns available. There's actually a truckload of them, and you can see the complete list by selecting **View, Choose Columns**. (This command is around only when you're in Details view.) In the Column Settings dialog box, use the check boxes to toggle columns on and off.

Figure 20.3
My Computer in List view.

Click these column headings
to sort the folder contents

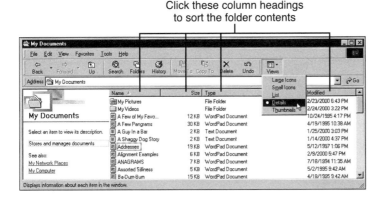

Figure 20.4
My Computer in Details view.

➤ **Thumbnails**   This view displays previews—called *thumbnails*—of all the image files in the current folder. If you have any HTML files in the folder (these are files that contain Web page data), a thumbnail of the Web page is shown. (I showed you what this view looks like back in Chapter 15, "Image Is Everything: Windows Millennium's Graphics Tools." Take a look at Figure 15.8 in that chapter.)

Ordering My Computer Around: Sorting Files

To complete your reading of My Computer's views news, let's see how you sort the files and subfolders in the current folder. By default, file and subfolders are sorted alphabetically by name, with the subfolders displayed first, and then the files. You can change this by selecting the **View**, **Arrange Icons** command, which reveals a submenu with five choices:

➤ **by Name**   This is the default sort order.

➤ **by Type**   This command sorts the folder alphabetically by the type of document.

315

➤ **by Size**   This command sorts the folder numerically by the size of each file.

➤ **by Date**   This command sorts the folder according to the date and time when each item was last modified.

➤ **Auto Arrange**   Selecting this command toggles the Auto Arrange feature on and off. When it's on, My Computer automatically re-sorts the folder (using the current sort choice) whenever you add, rename, or delete a file or folder. Note, however, that this command is only available when you've cajoled My Computer into using the Large Icons, Small Icons, or Thumbnails view.

Savvy Sorting

If you're in Details view, you can sort a folder by clicking the column headers (as pointed out earlier in Figure 20.4). For example, clicking the **Size** column header sorts the folders by size. Clicking the header again switches the sort between ascending (smallest to largest) and descending (largest to smallest).

The Long View: Applying a View to All Folders

The view options—specifically, the icon view (Large Icons, Small Icons, and so on) and the sort order—you set for one folder are immediately jettisoned when you leap to another folder. If you want to use one set of options for *all* your folders, you can tell Windows Millennium to make it so. Here are the steps to follow:

1. Set up a folder just the way you like it.
2. Select **Tools, Folder Options**. The Folder Options dialog box skids into the screen.
3. Display the **View** tab.
4. Click **Like Current Folder**. Windows Millennium asks you to confirm.
5. Click **Yes** to get back to the Folder Options dialog box.
6. Click **OK**.

If you grow tired of these view options and you want to go back to the original look and feel, display the **View** tab again and click **Reset All Folders**.

A Folder Face-Lift: Customizing a Folder

Besides changing how subfolders and files are displayed within a folder, My Computer also offers a few other folder customizations: adjusting the background and text, adding a comment, and changing the Web view options. The next three sections fill you in on the gory details.

Refurbishing the Folder Background and Text

Back in Chapter 6, I told you a bit about this newfangled Web integration business, and I showed you what havoc it wreaks on the My Computer window. This includes displaying each folder as though it were a Web page.

One of the things that a Web designer can do to a page is change the background on which the page text is displayed, and to change the color of the text to match that background. You can do the same things with your folders. So if you're tired of the plain white background and boring black text you get in the standard view, follow these steps to try something with a little more oomph:

1. In My Computer, display the folder that you want to customize.

2. Select **View**, **Customize This Folder**. The Customize This Folder Wizard parachutes into the fray.

3. The first dialog box doesn't have anything interesting to say, so click **Next** to get to a more useful dialog box named Customize This Folder.

4. Be sure the **Modify background picture and filename appearance** check box is the only check box that's activated, and then click **Next**. The wizard changes shirts to show you the dialog box in Figure 20.5.

5. Use the **Select a background picture from the list below** list to choose the background image you want to use. (If you have some other image that you'd rather use, click **Browse** to pick out the file by using a dialog box.)

Cross Reference

For a refresher course on Web integration, see "My Computer and Web Integration," p. xxx. (ch 6)

Windows Wisdom

No Command?

Windows Millennium has several "No Trespassing" signs scattered around to protect what it calls "system" folders. One such "sign" is the lack of a Customize This Folder command on the View menu. If you don't see the command, it means you can't customize the folder.

Figure 20.5

Use this dialog box to revamp the current folder's background and text.

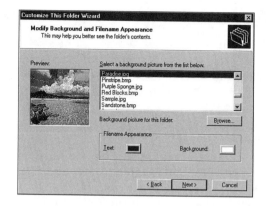

6. To change the color of the text used to display file and folder names, click the **Text** button. Use the color palette that pops up to click the color you want to live with.

7. To change the color of the background used by file and folder names, click the **Background** button to pick out the color you want from the palette that appears.

8. Click **Next**. The wizard customizes the folder and then displays the last of its dialog boxes.

9. Click **Finish**.

Adding a Folder Comment

You've seen how a folder's Web view displays an information area to the left of the folder contents. This area displays the title of the folder, info on whatever file is currently selected, and messages from the Windows Millennium powers-that-be. Interestingly, you also can add your own two cents' worth by inserting a *comment* that gets displayed in the information area when no file or folder is selected. Here's how:

1. Use My Computer to display the folder that you want to customize.

2. Select **View, Customize This Folder** to get the Customize This Folder Wizard going, and then click **Next**.

3. Activate the **Add folder comment** check box. (Also, be sure to deactivate the other check boxes, if necessary.) Click **Next** when you're ready for more action. The Add folder comment dialog box appears.

4. Use the **folder comment** text box to enter the text you want to display. Figure 20.6 is a composite image that shows some text I entered and how that text looks in the information area. Here are some notes to bear in mind:

➤ If you know HTML, feel free to augment your text with any tags that strike your fancy.

➤ This brain-dead text box doesn't give you any way to start a new line. Instead, you need to add the
 (line break) tag, as shown in the figure.

➤ If you have Internet access, you can add links to Web pages. The general format to use is <A HREF="*address*">*Link text*</A>. Here, *address* is the full address of the page, and *Link text* is the text you click.

➤ If you don't have Internet access (or even if you do, for that matter), you can create links that point to folders on your hard disk. You use the same format, except you use the folder location as the address. Here's an example: <A HREF="C:\My Documents">Go to My Documents</A>.

These words and tags...

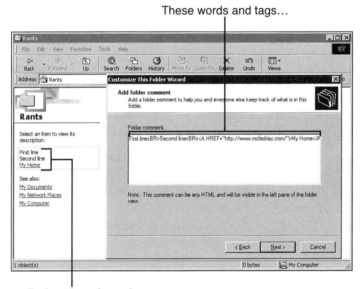

...are displayed as shown here

Figure 20.6

Use this wizard dialog box to add text and HTML tags to display in the information area.

5. Click **Next** to get to the last wizard dialog box.
6. Click **Finish**.

Changing the Web View Folder Template

The layout of a folder when it's in Web view is determined by something called a *folder template*. This is a file that tells Windows Millennium "Okay, put the contents here and the information area there, and then add in these other doodads." Windows Millennium actually ships with four different templates, so you can play around with them and pick one you like. Here's what you do:

1. Use My Computer to display the folder that you want to customize.

2. Select **View**, **Customize This Folder** to start up the Customize This Folder Wizard, and then click **Next**.

3. Activate the **Choose or edit an HTML template for this folder** check box. (Again, be sure to deactivate any other check boxes that are active.) Click **Next** and the wizard's Change Folder Template dialog box bursts through the door, as shown in Figure 20.7.

Figure 20.7

Use this wizard dialog box to select a folder template.

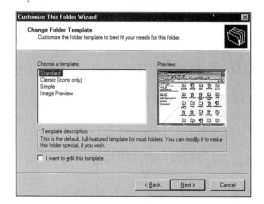

4. Use the **Choose a template** list to, well, choose a template. The **Preview** box gives you some idea of what the selected template does, and the **Template description** box tells you a bit more about the template.

5. If you know HTML and are feeling your oats, you might want to take a stab at customizing the template by hand. If so, activate the **I want to edit this template** check box. Otherwise, leave this check box deactivated.

6. Click **Next**.

7. If you elected to monkey with the template, Windows Millennium opens it up in Notepad. Make your changes to the text and the HTML tags, save the file, and then exit Notepad.

8. Click **Finish**.

The Least You Need to Know

This chapter gave you the goods on customizing various aspects of My Computer. You learned how to change the view, which included toggling Explorer bars on and off, customizing the toolbar, changing the icons, and sorting stuff. You also learned how to customize a folder, which included changing the background and text, inserting a folder comment, and changing the Web view template. Here are some things to chew on before moving ahead:

Crib Notes

➤ **Toggling toolbars**   Select **View, Toolbars** (or right-click a displayed tool-bar) to see a list of toolbars that can be toggled on and off.

➤ **Displaying the Folders bar**   Activate the **View, Explorer Bar, Folders** command, or activate the **Folders** button in the toolbar.

➤ **Customizing the toolbar**   Select **View, Toolbars, Customize** (or right-click the toolbar and then click **Customize**).

➤ **Changing the icon view**   Choose one of the following commands on the **View** menu (or the toolbar's **Views** button): **Large Icons, Small Icons, List, Details,** or **Thumbnails.**

➤ **Sorting files and folders**   Select **View, Arrange Icons** and then select a sort order. You also can sort in Details view by clicking the column headings.

➤ **Getting a global view**   Set up a folder the way you want it, select **Tools, Options**, display the **View** tab, and click **Like Current Folder**.

➤ **Customizing a folder**   Select **View, Customize This Folder**, click **Next**, and then select a customization option.

CLACK
CLACK
CLACK

Chapter 21

Installing and Uninstalling Programs and Devices

In This Chapter

➤ Installing and uninstalling chunks of Windows Millennium

➤ Installing and uninstalling software programs

➤ Step-by-step procedures for installing all kinds of devices

➤ Installing specific devices such as printers, modems, joysticks, and scanners

➤ Saying adios to devices you no longer need

➤ A treasure trove of techniques for renovating your Windows Millennium house

The smarty-pants in the labs have been developing many new devices that they say will lead us into the "post-PC" era. These newfangled machines typically are dedicated to a single task, such as reading email, surfing the Web, or being as annoying in public as possible. And I suppose if those tasks are all you do most of the day, then these machines would suit you just fine. Most of us, however, don't have such one-note workdays. We email and we surf and we write memos and we cobble together spreadsheets, so we need different programs to accomplish all of that. We also print and connect to the Net and scan documents and play games, so we need different peripheral devices in our lives, such as printers, modems, scanners, and joysticks.

So far, the only device on the planet capable of handling such a wide range of software and hardware is the PC. So if you're at a cocktail party and some nerd starts ranting about the "post-PC era," tell him *I* said he was dead wrong.

Of course, it's one thing to understand that the PC is a versatile beast that can handle all kinds of different programs and devices, but it's quite another to actually install the stuff. This chapter will help by showing you exactly how to install Windows Millennium components, software programs, and devices on your machine. For good measure, you also learn how to uninstall all those things, just in case they don't get along with your computer.

The Welcome Wagon: Installing a Program

You've seen so far that Windows Millennium comes stocked with a decent collection of programs, some of which are first-rate (such as Internet Explorer and Outlook Express) and some of which are merely okay (such as Paint and WordPad). Also, most PC manufacturers are kind enough to stock their machines with a few extra programs.

However, it's a rare computer owner who's satisfied with just these freebies (or even wants them in the first place). Most of us want something better, faster, *cooler*. If you decide to take the plunge on a new program, this section shows you how to install it in Windows Millennium. To get you started, the next section shows you how to install new Windows Millennium components.

Installing a Windows Millennium Component

Like a hostess who refuses to put out the good china for just anybody, Windows Millennium doesn't install all its components automatically. Don't feel insulted; Windows is just trying to go easy on your hard disk. The problem, you see, is that some of the components that come with Windows Millennium are software behemoths that will happily usurp acres of your precious hard disk land. In a rare act of digital politeness, Windows bypasses these programs (as well as a few other non-essential tidbits) during a typical installation. If you want any of these knickknacks on your system, you have to grab Windows Millennium by the scruff of its electronic neck and say "Yo, bozo! Install this for me, will ya!"

That's all well and good, Author Boy, but this is the first I've heard about Windows Millennium having a neck. Don't I just rerun the installation program?

Nope. The good news about all this is that Windows Millennium comes with a handy Windows Setup feature that enables you to add any of Windows Millennium's missing pieces to your system without having to trudge through the entire Windows installation routine. Here are the steps to follow:

1. Select **Start**, **Settings**, **Control Panel** to rustle up the Control Panel window.

2. Click the **Add/Remove Programs** link. Windows Millennium tosses the Add/Remove Programs Properties dialog box onto your screen.

3. Select the **Windows Setup** tab, shown in Figure 21.1. (Note that Windows Millennium takes inventory of the currently installed components, so this tab takes a few seconds to appear.)

Figure 21.1

The Windows Setup tab lets you add the bits and pieces that come with Windows Millennium.

4. The **Components** box lists the various chunks of Windows Millennium that are already installed as well as those you can add. You have two ways to proceed:

   ➤ To add an entire component, activate its check box.

   ➤ To add only part of a component (assuming that it has multiple parts), click the component name to highlight it, click **Details**, use the dialog box to activate the check boxes for the subcomponents you want to install, and click **OK**.

5. Click **OK**.

6. Depending on the components you add, Windows Millennium might ask you to restart your computer. If it does, click **Yes** to let Windows Millennium handle this for you. When the restart is complete, the new components are ready to roll.

Interpreting the Check Boxes

Here's a translation of what the various check box states mean in the Windows Setup tab:

Unchecked The component is not installed. If the component comes in several pieces, none of those pieces is installed.

Checked with a gray background The component is partially installed. That is, the component has multiple chunks, but only some of those chunks reside on your system.

Checked with a white background The component is installed. If the component comes in several pieces, all of those pieces are installed.

To find out how many of the component's pieces are installed, check out the **Description** box; below the component description, you'll see something like `1 of 2 components selected`. This tells you that the component consists of two programs and only one of them is installed on your system.

Bringing a New Program into Your Computer Home

The built-in Windows Millennium programs do the job as long as your needs aren't too lofty. However, what if your needs *are* lofty, or if you're looking to fill in a software niche that Windows Millennium doesn't cover (such as a spreadsheet program, a database, or an action game)? In that case, you need to go outside the box and purchase the appropriate program.

After you have the program, your next chore is to install it. This means you run a "setup" routine that makes the program ready for use on your computer. Most setup procedures perform the following tasks:

➤ Create a new folder for the program.

➤ Copy any files that the program needs to run to the new folder and to other strategic folders on your hard disk.

➤ Adjust Windows Millennium as needed to ensure that the program runs properly.

How you launch this setup routine depends on how the program is distributed:

➤ **If the program is on a CD**   In this case, you might not have to do much of anything. Most computer CDs support a feature called *AutoRun*. This means when you insert the disc into your CD-ROM (or DVD-ROM) drive for the first time, the setup routine gets launched automatically.

AutoRun

AutoRun is a feature that automatically launches a program's setup routine (or, later, the program itself) after you insert its CD–ROM or DVD–ROM disc.

➤ **If you downloaded the program from the Internet**   In this case, you end up with the downloaded file on your hard disk. Be sure this file resides in an otherwise-empty folder and then double-click the file. This either launches the setup routine or it "extracts" a bunch of files into the folder. If the latter happens, look for an application file named **Setup** (or, more rarely, **Install**), and then double-click that file.

Handling Zip Files

The programs you download from the Internet will occasionally come in the form of "zip" files. (You can recognize such a file animal by its name, which ends with .zip, as in program.zip. If you don't see the ".zip" part, you can still recognize a zip file by its icon, which looks like a regular folder icon with a zipper running down the middle.) This is an unusual type of file in that it actually consists of multiple files that have been scrunched (*compressed,* in the vernacular) into a single file for easier and faster downloading. To get at those files, highlight the zip file and then select **File, Extract All**. Use the Extract Wizard to select a location for the files and click **Next** to get the show on the road.

For all other cases—a CD-based program that doesn't start automatically or a program distributed on floppy disks—your best bet is to get Windows Millennium to launch the setup routine for you. Here's how:

1. Select **Start**, **Settings**, **Control Panel** to fire up the Control Panel window.

2. Click the **Add/Remove Programs** link to connect with the Add/Remove Programs Properties dialog box.

3. Make sure the **Install/Uninstall** tab is displayed.

4. Click the **Install** button. The dialog box that appears asks you to insert the first installation disk or the program's CD-ROM.

5. Insert the appropriate disk and click **Next**. The wizard checks all your floppy and CD-ROM drives, searching desperately for any installation program it can find:

A Pause for the CD Cause

After you insert a CD into its drive, it takes the disc a few seconds to get up to speed. Therefore, in step 5, wait until you see the CD-ROM drive light stop blinking before clicking Next.

➤ If the wizard locates a likely candidate, it displays it in the **Command line for installation program** text box, as you can see in Figure 21.2.

➤ If it doesn't find an installation program, the wizard asks you to enter the appropriate command in the **Command line for installation program** text box. If you know where the installation program is located, type the drive, folder, and filename (for example, E:\Install\setup.exe). You can also click **Browse** to use a dialog box to pick out the program.

6. Click **Finish**. Windows Millennium launches the installation program.

Figure 21.2

Windows Millennium can hunt down your software's installation program automatically.

From here, follow the instructions and prompts that the setup routine sends your way. (This procedure varies from program to program.)

Avoiding Installation Aggravation

Many setup programs offer what is known in the trade as a "forehead install." That is, the installation is so easy that you can run through the whole thing by simply tapping the Spacebar with your forehead when each new dialog box is presented. Although I don't suggest that you actually do this, I do recommend that you accept the default values offered by the install program (unless you *really* know what you're doing). In particular, if the program gives you a choice of a "typical" or a "custom" installation, go the "typical" route to save yourself time and hassle.

The Bum's Rush: Uninstalling a Program

Most programs seem like good ideas at the time you install them. Unless you're an outright pessimist, you probably figured that a program you installed was going to help you work harder, be more efficient, or have more fun. Sadly, many programs don't live up to expectations. The good news is that you don't have to put up with a loser program after you realize it's not up to snuff. You can *uninstall* it so that it doesn't clutter up your Start menu, desktop, hard disk, or any other location where it might have inserted itself.

Uninstalling a Windows Millennium Component

You've seen how the Windows Setup feature makes it easy to bring Windows Millennium components in from the cold of the CD-ROM to the warmth of your hard drive. What happens, however, if you grow tired of a particular component's company? For example, the artistically challenged might want to get rid of that Paint program they never use, or the hopelessly unwired might be itching to expunge HyperTerminal from their systems.

Jargon Jar

Uninstall

Uninstall completely removes a program from your computer.

329

Happily, with Windows Setup, showing these and other Windows Millennium components to the door is even easier than installing them. And as an added bonus, lopping off some of Windows' limbs serves to free up precious hard disk space, giving you more room for *really* important games—uh, I mean, applications. As you might expect, removing Windows Millennium components is the opposite of adding them:

1. Select **Start**, **Settings**, **Control Panel** to display the Control Panel window.
2. Click the **Add/Remove Programs** link.
3. Click the **Windows Setup** tab.
4. Deactivate the check boxes for the components you want to blow away. For multiprogram components, click **Details** to see the individual programs, deactivate the check boxes for those you want to nuke, and then click **OK** to return the Windows Setup tab.
5. Click **OK**. Windows Millennium removes the components you specified without further delay.
6. Depending on the components you removed, Windows Millennium may ask to restart your computer. If so, click **Yes** to make it happen.

Giving a Program the Heave-Ho

If you have a Windows application that has worn out its welcome, this section shows you a couple of methods for uninstalling the darn thing so that it's out of your life forever. The good news is that Windows Millennium has a feature that enables you to vaporize any application with a simple click of the mouse. The bad news is that this feature is only available for some programs.

To check whether it's available for your program, follow these steps:

1. Display the Control Panel by selecting **Start**, **Settings**, **Control Panel**.
2. Click the **Add/Remove Programs** link.
3. Make sure that the **Install/Uninstall** tab is visible.
4. As shown in Figure 21.3, the bottom half of the Install/Uninstall tab displays a list of the programs that Windows Millennium knows how to remove automatically. If the program you want to blow to kingdom come is on this list, highlight it and then click the **Add/Remove** button.
5. What happens next depends on the program. You may see a dialog box asking you to confirm the uninstall, or you may be asked whether you want to run an "Automatic" or "Custom" uninstall. For the latter, be sure to select the **Automatic** option. Whatever happens, follow the instructions on the screen until you return to the Install/Uninstall tab.
6. Click **OK** to wrap things up.

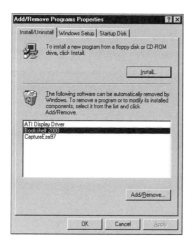

Figure 21.3

The Install/Uninstall tab maintains a list of programs that you can annihilate automatically.

Didn't see the program on the Install/Uninstall tab? All is not lost because there's still one more place to check: the program's home base on the Start menu. Select **Start**, **Programs** and then open the program's menu (if it has one). Look for a command that includes the word "Uninstall" (or, less likely, "Remove"). If you see one, great: Click it to launch the uninstall procedure.

For those applications that can't be uninstalled automatically, you need to roll up your sleeves and do the whole thing by hand. Here's what to do:

1. Use Windows Explorer or My Computer to display the program's folder.

2. Check to see whether the folder contains any data files you want to preserve. If you spent any time at all creating documents (or whatever) in the application, it's a wise precaution to save them for posterity. For one thing, you might want to use them in another application; for another, you might change your mind six months from now and decide to reinstall the application. If you want to save your data, highlight the files and then *move*

Incomplete Uninstalls

Don't be surprised if the uninstall routine doesn't wipe out absolutely everything for a program. If you created any documents, customized the program, or moved its Start menu items to a new location, the uninstall program leaves behind a few scraps.

Not sure how to delete a folder? See "Deleting a File or Folder," p. 88.

331

To learn how to delete items from the Start menu, see "Taking Stuff Off the Start Menu," p. 306.

(not copy) them to another folder (that you can use for storage), or to a floppy disk.

3. With that out of the way, go ahead and delete the application's folder.

4. Erase any traces of the program from your Start menu.

5. If the program added any shortcuts to the desktop, delete them, too.

6. To be safe, exit and then restart Windows Millennium.

Device Advice I: Installing Hardware

Software installation is usually a painless operation that often requires just a few mouse clicks on your part. Hardware, however, is another kettle of electronic fish altogether. Not only must you attach the device to your machine (which might even require that you remove the cover to get inside the computer), but you also have to hope that the new device doesn't conflict with an existing one.

The latter is less of a problem thanks to Windows Millennium's support for something called *Plug and Play*. This enables Windows Millennium to immediately recognize a new device and to configure that device automatically. It's a kind of hardware nirvana that makes it easy for the average bear to upgrade the physical side of his or her computer. To make it work, however, you need two things:

Jargon Jar

Plug and Play

Plug and play is a hardware technology that enables Windows Millennium to automatically recognize devices and configure them to play nicely with others.

➤ **Devices that support Plug and Play** Most new hardware doodads are Plug and Play friendly. However, to be safe, check the box to be sure it says "Plug and Play" before buying anything. Note that the newfangled USB (Universal Serial Bus) devices support Plug and Play. However, your computer needs to have one or more USB ports to use them.

➤ **Devices that are compatible with Windows Millennium** Windows Millennium, finicky beast that it is, won't work with just any old device. Again, before buying a device, check the box to see whether it says anything about being compatible with Windows Millennium. (Devices that are compatible with Windows 95 or Windows 98 ought to work fine as well.)

Understanding Hardware Types

Although thousands of devices are available, and dozens of device categories, I like to organize devices according to how you attach them to the computer. From this point of view, there are four types to worry about:

➤ **External plug-in devices** These are devices that use some kind of cable to plug into a *port* in the back of the PC. These devices include keyboards, mice, joysticks, modems, printers, speakers, and monitors. These kinds of devices are easy to install if you remember one thing: The computer's ports each have a unique shape, and the cable's plug has a shape that matches one of those ports. So, there's usually only one possible place into which any cable can plug.

➤ **PC Card (PCMCIA) devices** These types of devices are the easiest to install because they simply slip into any one of the computer's PC Card slots (or *sockets*, as they're called). Note, however, that these slots are almost always found only on notebook computers.

Windows Wisdom

Two Identical Ports?

The exception to this is if the back of the computer has two ports with identical configurations. That just means your machine offers two of the same port type, so you can plug your device into either one.

➤ **Internal disk drives** These are the toughest devices to install, not only because you have to get inside your computer, but also because there are many steps involved. Here's the basic procedure:

1. Shut down your computer (using **Start**, **Shut Down**), unplug the power cable, and then remove the front cover. (Note that you also might need to remove the computer's main cover to do this.)

2. Use screws (usually provided with the drive) to attach the "rails" to the sides of the disk drive. (These are usually long, skinny bits of plastic with several holes in them.)

3. The front of your computer should have several *drive bays* (places where the hard drive makes its home) open. Insert the disk drive into one of these bays, and use screws to attach the rails to the chassis of the computer.

4. Attach a power supply cable to the back of the disk drive. (The power supply cable is a multicolored collection of thin cables that runs into a single plug. Most computers have a number of such plugs available.)

Makin' It Fit

If the front cover won't quite fit, then you need to adjust the position of the drive within the bay. Try different screw positions to shift the drive up or down. If that doesn't work, try adjusting the position of the rails on the side of the drive.

5. Attach a data cable to the back of the drive. The data cable should have been supplied with the disk drive. You then attach the other end of the cable to the appropriate port inside the computer. (You'll need to read your device documentation to find out the correct way to go about this.)

6. If you're inserting a CD-ROM or DVD-ROM drive, you probably also need to run an audio cable (supplied with the drive) from the back of the drive to your sound card (again, read your device documentation).

7. Put the front cover back on the computer (and the main cover, if you took that off, as well). Before doing this, you probably need to remove the plate that previously blocked the drive bay you used.

8. Plug the power cable back in and turn the computer on.

➤ **Internal circuit boards** These are cards that plug into slots inside your computer. There are circuit boards for all kinds of things, including sound cards, graphics cards, network cards (see Figure 21.4), and video decoder cards (which usually come with DVD-ROM drives nowadays). These kinds of devices have always seemed intimidating to nongeeks, but anyone with a minimum of coordination can install them. Here are the basic steps:

Get Grounded

Before delving in to your computer's innards, touch something else that's metal to ground yourself and reduce the risk of static shocks (that could damage your computer).

1. Shut down your computer (using **Start**, **Shut Down**), unplug the power cable, and then remove the main cover.

2. Find an empty slot for your circuit board and remove the backplate (the metal plate beside the slot on the back of the computer).

3. Orient the circuit board so that the plug part is lined up with the slot inside the computer, and the board's backplate is toward the back of the computer.

334

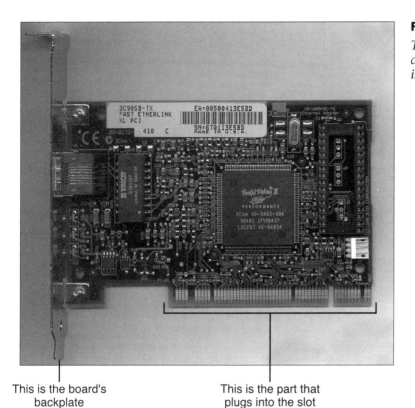

Figure 21.4

This is a typical PCI circuit board that slips inside a computer.

This is the board's
backplate

This is the part that
plugs into the slot

Which Slot Do You Use?

Inside the machine, you'll see a series of long, thin, slots. On most modern PCs, there are three types of slots: The shortest are the AGP slots, and they're usually black; slightly longer are the PCI slots, which are usually white or beige; quite a bit longer are the ISA slots, which are usually black. So what you need to do is find an empty slot that fits the plug part of your circuit board (see Figure 21.4).

4. Using gentle but consistent pressure, maneuver the board's plug into the slot. Be sure you insert the board as far as it will go. (Tip: The easiest way to tell whether the board is inserted all the way is to look at the board's backplate. If the part where you insert the screw is flush with the screw hole, then the board is inserted fully.)

5. Screw the board's backplate to the computer chassis.

6. If the board requires any internal cables (see the board's documentation), plug them in.

7. Put the computer cover on.

8. Plug the power cable in and turn the computer on.

Running the Add/Remove Hardware Wizard

Your device and your computer are now shacked up, but they're not married yet. To get a full relationship going, Windows Millennium has to install a tiny bit of software called a *device driver*. This miniprogram has the code that operates (drives) the device, so it acts as a kind of middleman between the device and Windows Millennium.

In the best of all possible worlds, after you've attached the device (and, if necessary, restarted your computer), Windows Millennium recognizes the new limb and displays the New Hardware Found dialog box. (This is my favorite dialog box because it means I have little if any work to do from here. An under-your-breath "Yes!" is the appropriate reaction to seeing this dialog box.) Windows Millennium then proceeds to install the device driver and any other software required to make the device go. This is automatic, for the most part, but you may occasionally be asked a few simple questions to complete the setup. In particular, you might see the Add New Hardware Wizard, which leads you through the installation of a device driver. (The process is similar to upgrading a driver, so see "Upgrading a Device Driver," later in this chapter.)

If, for some reason, Windows Millennium doesn't automatically recognize your new device, all is not lost. That's because Windows Millennium comes with a hardware helper called the Add New Hardware Wizard, which scours every nook and cranny of your system to look for new stuff. Here's how it works:

1. Select **Start**, **Settings**, **Control Panel** to crack open the Control Panel window.

2. Click the **view all Control Panel options** link, and then launch the **Add New Hardware** icon. The Add New Hardware Wizard wipes the grease from its hands and comes out to meet you.

3. The initial dialog box just tells you some things you already know, so click **Next**.

4. The next wizard dialog box tells you that the wizard will now search for new Plug and Play devices. Click **Next** and the wizard goes about its business.

5. If the wizard didn't find a new Plug and Play device, skip to step 6. Otherwise, you see various messages onscreen telling you that Windows has found a new device and is installing the software for it. Depending on the device, the wizard might display a list of the installed devices and present you with two options:

   ➤ **Yes, I am finished installing devices**   Activate this option and click **Next** to exit the Add New Hardware Wizard. (You can skip the rest of these steps too, of course.)

   ➤ **No, I want to install other devices**   Activate this option and click **Next** to install a non-Plug and Play device.

6. The next wizard dialog box asks whether you want Windows to detect your new hardware automatically. This is the best way to go; make sure to activate the **Yes (Recommended)** option, and then click **Next**. (I tell you a bit later how to specify hardware yourself.)

7. Windows Millennium tells you that it's ready to look for new hardware (and gives you a scary-sounding warning about how this process "may cause your computer to stop responding." Yikes!). Click **Next** once again to continue. Your computer will now make some strange crickets-on-speed noises for a few minutes. This is perfectly normal. It just means that Windows Millennium is scouring every nook and cranny of your system to look for new devices.

8. If the Add New Hardware Wizard doesn't find any new hardware, it tells you so. If that happens, click **Cancel**, shut down your computer (make sure that you use the **Start**, **Shut Down** command), check to see whether you attached the new device correctly, and then try again. If it's still a no-go, try installing the hardware by using the instructions given later in this section.

9. More likely, however, the wizard will tell you that it's finished detecting and is ready to install the support files for the device. To make sure the wizard was successful, click the **Details** button to eyeball what the wizard found.

10. Now click **Finish** and follow the instructions that show up if any. You might also be asked to restart your computer to put the changes into effect.

If the wizard failed in its quest to find your device, you can stick Windows Millennium's nose in it, so to speak, by specifying exactly which device you added. To get started, you have two choices:

➤ If you're starting the Add New Hardware Wizard from scratch, follow the preceding steps 1–5. Then, in step 6, be sure you activate the **No, I want to select the hardware from a list** option, and click **Next**.

➤ If you're still in the wizard at the dialog box that tells you Windows didn't find any new devices, click **Next**.

Either way, you now follow these steps:

1. The wizard displays a whack of device categories in the **Hardware types** list. Highlight the category that applies to your device, and then click **Next**.

2. The wizard takes a few seconds to gather its thoughts, and then it displays a list of device manufacturers and devices. For example, Figure 21.5 shows the dialog box that appears for the Network adapters category. You have two ways to proceed from here:

   ➤ Highlight the device maker in the **Manufacturers** list, then highlight the name of your device in the other list.

   ➤ If your device is nowhere to be found, it's likely that you received a disk inside the device package. Insert the disk and then click **Have Disk**. In the Install from Disk dialog box, enter the location of the disk (type the drive letter followed by a colon (:) and a slash (\), such as **A:**) and click **OK**. (If Windows Millennium complains about not being able to find anything on the disk, click **Browse** and look for a subfolder on the disk, usually with some form of "windows" label.) You'll eventually see a list of models that can be installed. Highlight your model.

Figure 21.5

Use this dialog box to pick out the device manufacturer and model.

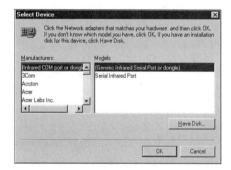

3. Click **Next**. The wizard tells you that it will now install the drivers for the device.

4. Click **Next**. The wizard, true to its word, installs the device drivers. Note that you might need to insert your Windows Millennium CD at this point.

5. When all is said and done, click **Finish** to close the wizard. If Windows Millennium asks if you want to restart your computer, click **Yes**.

Installing Specific Devices

Just to keep everyone thoroughly confused (which a cynic might describe as Windows' *real* job), Windows Millennium offers different installation routes for certain types of devices. These include perennially popular items such as printers, modems, joysticks, scanners, and digital cameras. Here's a quick look at what you have to do to install these types of devices:

➤ **Installing a printer**   Select **Start**, **Settings**, **Printers** to get to the Printers window, and then run the **Add Printer** icon. This conjures up the Add Printer Wizard to take you through the process. Along the way, you get asked how your printer is attached (choose **Local printer**), the manufacturer and model, and the printer port (this is almost always **LPT1**).

➤ **Installing a modem**   Select **Start**, **Settings**, **Control Panel**, click **view all Control Panel options** (if necessary), and then launch the **Modems** icon. This unleashes the Install New Modem Wizard. (If, instead, you see the Modems Properties dialog box, it means your modem is already installed and should be shown in the list. If it's not, or if you want to install a different modem, click **Add**.) This wizard scours your computer's ports to see if a modem is attached to one of them.

Entering Location Information

When you crank up the **Modems** icon, the first thing you might see is the Location Information dialog box. If so, use this dialog box to select the country/region that you're in and to enter your area code. You also specify the number that must be dialed to get an outside line and whether your system uses **Tone dialing** or **Pulse dialing**. Click **Close** when you're done.

➤ **Installing a game controller**   To Windows Millennium, a joystick or other device you use for gaming is called a *game controller*. To install one, select **Start**, **Settings**, **Control Panel**, click **view all Control Panel options** (if necessary), and then launch the **Gaming Options** icon. In the Gaming Options dialog box, click **Add**.

➤ **Installing a scanner or digital camera**   Select **Start**, **Settings**, **Control Panel**, click **view all Control Panel options** (if necessary), and then launch the **Scanners and Cameras** icon. In the Scanners and Cameras dialog box, launch the **Add Device** icon to send in the Scanner and Camera Installation Wizard.

Device Advice II: Removing Hardware

If a device suddenly becomes tiresome and boring, or if you get a better device for your birthday, you need to remove the old device from your computer and then let Windows Millennium know that it's gone. The exception to this is if the device supports Plug and Play. If it does, then Windows Millennium recognizes that the device is gone and it adjusts itself accordingly. Otherwise, you need to do it by hand:

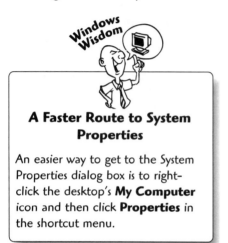

A Faster Route to System Properties

An easier way to get to the System Properties dialog box is to right-click the desktop's **My Computer** icon and then click **Properties** in the shortcut menu.

1. Select **Start**, **Settings**, **Control Panel**, click **view all Control Panel options** (if necessary), and then launch the **System** icon. Windows Millennium arranges a meeting with the System Properties dialog box.

2. Display the **Device Manager** tab.

3. Click the plus sign (+) beside the hardware category you want to work with. For example, if the soon-to-be-toast device is a network adapter, open the **Network adapters** branch as shown in Figure 21.6.

4. Click the device and then click **Remove**. Windows Millennium states the obvious and tells you that you're about to remove the device.

Figure 21.6

Use this dialog box to pick out the device you want to remove.

5. Say "Duh!" and click **OK**. Windows Millennium wastes no more of your time and removes the device from the list.

6. Click **Close**.

7. If the device is an internal component, shut down your computer (use **Start**, **Shut Down**) and then remove the device. Otherwise, just unplug the device.

340

The Least You Need to Know

This chapter showed you how to welcome new guests to your computer, and how to kick them out after the party's over. On the software side, you learned how to install Windows Millennium components and third-party programs and how to uninstall them. On the hardware side, you learned how to install the various device types and how to run the Add New Hardware Wizard to let Windows Millennium know about the device. You also learned how to install specific devices and how to remove a device.

Crib Notes

➤ **Automatic CDs**   Most computer CD-ROM (and DVD-ROM) discs support AutoRun, so the installation program runs automatically after you insert the disc.

➤ **Installing and uninstalling made easy**   Use Control Panel's **Add/Remove Programs** icon to help you install and uninstall Windows Millennium components and third-party programs.

➤ **Best hardware bets**   To ensure the easiest hardware configuration, buy only devices that are both Plug and Play-compatible and Windows Millennium-compatible.

➤ **Peruse the ports**   When installing an external device, remember that its cable can plug into only a single, complementary port on the back of the computer.

➤ **Hardware helper**   If Plug and Play doesn't work, use Control Panel's **Add New Hardware** icon to help you install and uninstall devices.

Part 5

When Good Data Goes Bad: Millennium Maintenance and Repair

The data on your computer seems real enough. After all, you can cut, copy, and paste text, move files around with your mouse, and read emails from all over the planet. It all seems quite substantial until the day your hard disk or some other vital cog goes belly up. That's when you realize that all your data was nothing but a pile of fragile electrons. It was just a bit of luck and a lot of engineering skill that kept everything so apparently permanent for so long.

This gloomy scenario can be mitigated somewhat by doing two things. First, you can put off problems and give your data a longer shelf life by performing some regular maintenance on your system, which I show you how to do in Chapter 22, "Smooth System Sailing: Wielding the System Tools." Second, you can prepare yourself for future disasters by making regular backup copies of your data, and that's the subject of Chapter 23, "Getting a Good Night's Sleep: Backing Up Your Precious Data."

Smooth System Sailing: Wielding the System Tools

Like the proverbial death and taxes, computer problems seem to be one of those constants in life. But that doesn't mean you just have to sit back and wait for trouble. Believe me, a few minutes of protection now (what I like to call "ounce of prevention mode") can save you hours of grief down the road ("pound of cure mode"). And therein lies the good news: Avoiding trouble really does take only a little extra work. Why, with just a few simple techniques and the easy-to-use system tools that come with Windows Millennium, you can set up some powerful preventative measures in no time at all. This chapter tells you everything you need to know.

The Three Hard Disk Musketeers: Some Useful Disk Tools

Let's begin with a look at three programs that tend to that most vital of computer components: your hard disk. The preeminence of the hard disk in the computing pantheon shouldn't be surprising. After all, it's your hard disk that bears the burden of storing your priceless data. To help you keep your hard disk affairs in order and to help preserve your data, the next three sections discuss Windows Millennium's Disk Cleanup, ScanDisk, and Disk Defragmenter programs.

The Electronic Yard Sale: Using Disk Cleanup to Get Rid of Junk Files

If you find that your hard disk space is running low, one reason may be that it's littered with unnecessary files. This can happen if you turn off your computer before shutting down Windows Millennium, or if some sloppy program didn't clean up after itself.

How can you tell if your hard disk space is running out? The easiest way is to fire up My Computer and then highlight the hard disk. As shown in Figure 22.1, the left side of the window shows you how much free space is left on the disk.

Figure 22.1

Highlight your hard disk in My Computer to see how much disk real estate is left to be developed.

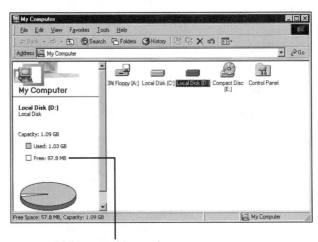

Make sure this number
doesn't get too low

Here's how Windows Millennium can help you tidy things up a bit:

1. Select **Start**, **Programs**, **Accessories**, **System Tools**, **Disk Cleanup**. A dialog box asks you which disk drive you want to clean up.

2. Use the **Drives** list to select the drive, and then click **OK**. This launches the Disk Cleanup program, which proceeds to look for files that can be safely chucked. When it's finished, you see a Disk Cleanup dialog box similar to the one shown in Figure 22.2.

Figure 22.2

Use the Disk Cleanup utility to get rid of unnecessary files that are just taking up valuable hard disk space.

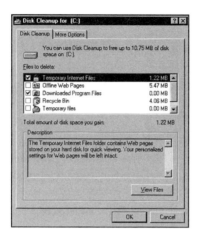

How Low Is Low?

What do I mean by "low" hard disk space? The answer depends on the disk. If it's the disk where Windows Millennium is stored (usually drive C), then you should never let that disk get much below 100MB of free space. If it's some other disk that you use to store programs and files, then you should start getting worried when the free space drops below 50MB.

3. Activate the check boxes next to the types of files you want to expunge (note that you might not see all of these options on your system):

   ➤ **Temporary Internet Files**   These are files that your Web browser keeps handy for faster viewing. They can be safely deleted, but some Web pages may take a bit longer to load the next time you view them.

   ➤ **Offline Web Pages**   These are the files that Internet Explorer stores on your system if you set up one or more pages as offline favorites. Removing these files will prevent you from viewing the pages offline and will require you to resynchronize the pages.

➤ **Downloaded Program Files** These files, which get downloaded from the Internet for temporary use in certain Web pages, can be nuked.

Cross Reference

To get the goods on the Recycle Bin, see "Deleting a File or Folder," p. 88.

➤ **Recycle Bin** As you may remember, the Recycle Bin stores the files you "delete." If you're sure you don't need to restore any of these files, activate this check box.

➤ **Temporary files** These are stray files that programs use to store data temporarily. Although most programs are civil enough to get rid of these files when they're no longer needed, some programs don't bother. These files can be deleted without remorse.

➤ **Temporary PC Health files** The "PC Health" feature maintains copies of important files just in case something messes up on your system. If you activate this check box, Disk Cleanup deletes older copies of these files that are no longer needed by the system and so are safe to blow away.

➤ **Delete Windows uninstall information** These are copies of your old Windows files that are stored if you installed Windows Millennium as an upgrade. They're used to "uninstall" Windows Millennium. If you and Windows Millennium are getting along famously and you're sure you want to keep using it, then you can save lots of disk space by deleting these files.

4. Click **OK**.

5. When Disk Cleanup asks whether you're sure, click **Yes**.

Using ScanDisk to Avoid Hard Disk Hard Times

You've seen throughout this book that your hard disk acts as a sort of "safe house" for your documents. Open and unsaved files are accidents waiting for a place to happen, but after you save the files to your hard disk, you know that you can breathe easier. Your hard disk isn't infallible, however. Although most folks get years of good service from their faithful hard disk servants, these drives are subject to the general wear-and-tear that affects all electronic components.

To help prevent your hard disk from going south before its time, you should run Windows Millennium's ScanDisk program frequently. ScanDisk scours your hard disk for chinks in its armor and can even repair those chinks before they lead to further trouble.

Here are the ScanDisk steps:

1. Select **Start, Programs, Accessories, System Tools, ScanDisk**. You see a ScanDisk window similar to Figure 22.3.

Figure 22.3

Use the ScanDisk window to pick out the hard disk you want to check.

2. In the **Select the drive(s) you want to check for errors** list, click the disk drive you want to work with. (ScanDisk won't complain if you select multiple disks. To do so, hold down **Ctrl** and click each disk.)

3. Use the **Type of test** group to pick out the ScanDisk test you want to run. The one you choose depends on how much time you have to kill, how patient you are, and how paranoid you are about your hard disk having a nervous breakdown:

   ➤ **Standard**   This test runs various checks to ensure the integrity of your hard disk's files and folders. It should take less than a minute to perform this test. I recommend running this test once a week.

   ➤ **Thorough**   This test delves deeper and checks not only your hard disk's files and folders, but also the surface of the hard disk itself. Depending on the size of your hard disk, this test can take 15 minutes or more. You probably only need to run this test once a month.

4. Now you have to decide whether you want ScanDisk to automatically fix any errors it finds. This is handy if, for example, you want to perform the lengthy Thorough test and head off to a three-martini lunch while it's running. To have ScanDisk fix any errors, activate the **Automatically fix errors** check box.

5. Click the **Start** button. ScanDisk begins nosing around in your hard disk's private parts and displays its progress at the bottom of the window.

6. If ScanDisk finds a problem (and you didn't tell it to fix errors automatically), a dialog box appears that gives you instructions on how to proceed (which vary depending on the error). If you're not sure what to do at this point, just click **OK** and let ScanDisk figure things out for itself. (If ScanDisk reports that it can't fix the error, then you may have a serious hard disk problem on your hands. Your best bet here is to take your computer in to a qualified PC repair shop and let them take a crack at it.)

7. When ScanDisk's labors are complete, it displays the ScanDisk Results dialog box to let you know what happened. This dialog box is jam-packed with stats and numbers that are best left unread by the likes of you and I. Nod your head knowingly and click **Close** to return to the ScanDisk window.

Automatic ScanDisk Scans

Way back in Chapter 2's "Quittin' Time: Shutting Down Windows" section, I told you that turning off your computer before exiting Windows Millennium was a major no-no. If this does happen, however, Windows Millennium is smart enough to recognize it and it will run ScanDisk automatically the next time you start your computer.

How Often Should I Defragment?

How often you defragment your hard disk depends on how often you use your computer. If you use it every day, you should run Disk Defragmenter about once a week. If your computer doesn't get heavy use, you probably only need to run Disk Defragmenter once a month or so.

Disk Defragmenter: The Digital Neat Freak

You can use Windows Millennium's Disk Defragmenter program to *defragment* the files on your hard disk. Defragmenting sounds pretty serious, but it's just Windows Millennium's way of tidying up a messy hard disk. It puts your files in order and does a few other neat-freak chores. (Don't worry: Disk Defragmenter doesn't change the contents of the files, and they still appear in the same places when you look at them in Windows Explorer or My Computer.)

Before you use Disk Defragmenter, you need to do a little preparation:

➤ Use the Disk Cleanup utility described earlier in this chapter to delete any files that you don't need from your hard disk. Defragmenting junk files only slows down the whole process.

➤ Check for hard disk errors by running ScanDisk as outlined in the previous section. You should probably run a Thorough test, just to be safe.

After you've completed these preliminary chores, you're ready to use Disk Defragmenter. Here's how it works:

1. Shut down all your running programs.

2. Select **Start, Programs, Accessories, System Tools, Disk Defragmenter**. Windows Millennium displays the Select Drive dialog box.

3. Choose the disk drive that you want to work with and click **OK**. Disk Defragmenter starts pounding away at the chosen disk.

4. When Disk Defragmenter finally completes its labors (it may take up to an hour, depending on the size of your disk, how cluttered it is, and how fast your computer is), your computer beeps, and a dialog box tells you that defragmentation is complete and asks whether you want to exit Disk Defragmenter. If you do, click **Yes**. Otherwise, click **No** to continue with Disk Defragmenter, and then repeat steps 3 and 4 until you're done.

Staying Regular: Using the Maintenance Wizard

You've seen quite a few handy tools so far. The crucial thing to keep in mind about all these programs is that they're only useful if you run them at regular intervals. Running them once a year or just whenever simply won't cut the system-maintenance mustard. Does that mean you have to plaster your monitor with sticky notes to remind yourself to run ScanDisk and friends? Fortunately, no. Windows Millennium comes with a wizard that will do all the remembering for you. Not only that, but this wizard even sets things up so that all these system tools run automatically.

Here's how it works:

1. Select **Start**, **Programs**, **Accessories**, **System Tools**, **Maintenance Wizard**. The wizard walks onto the screen and its first dialog box gives you a choice (click **Next** when you've made your choice):

   ➤ **Express**   If you choose this option, the wizard will do all the scheduling for you. If you don't feel like messing around with this stuff, the Express route is the way to go.

   ➤ **Custom**   If you choose this option, you can set up custom schedules for the various maintenance tools, and even skip some tools you don't want (such as Disk Defragmenter).

Maintenance Wizard Heads Up

After the first time you use the Maintenance Wizard, each subsequent time you start the program a dialog box shows up to ask whether you want to run the maintenance now or change your maintenance settings.

2. The wizard now displays the Select a Maintenance Schedule dialog box so that you can pick out when the maintenance programs should be scheduled to run. For example, if you leave your computer on all the time, select the **Nights** option. Click **Next** when you've made your choice. If you chose the Express option in step 1, skip to step 6.

3. The rest of the Maintenance Wizard's dialog boxes are related to the various hard disk maintenance tools you saw in the first part of this chapter. For example, the Speed Up Programs dialog box, shown in Figure 22.4, is related to the Disk Defragmenter utility. In the rest of the Maintenance Wizard dialog boxes, you see the same two option buttons:

   ➤ **Yes**   Activate this option to schedule the task.

   ➤ **No**   Activate this option to bypass the task.

Figure 22.4

The rest of the Maintenance Wizard's dialog boxes help you schedule the system maintenance tools.

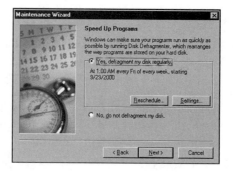

4. If you activate **Yes**, you can also work with the following buttons:

   ➤ **Reschedule**   This button displays the Reschedule dialog box, which you can use to specify a custom schedule for the task.

   ➤ **Settings**   This button displays a dialog box that contains settings related to the underlying program.

5. Here's a summary of the rest of the Maintenance Wizard dialog boxes that will come your way:

   ➤ **Speed Up Programs**   This dialog box is a front-end for Disk Defragmenter.

   ➤ **Scan Hard Disk for Errors**   This dialog box enables you to schedule a ScanDisk check.

   ➤ **Delete Unnecessary Files**   This dialog box sets up a schedule for the Disk Cleanup program.

6. The last Maintenance Wizard dialog box displays a summary of the options you chose. Click **Finish** to schedule the tasks.

The Scheduled Tasks Folder

The Maintenance Wizard only schedules the system tools to run at certain times. The actual dirty work of launching the programs at the specified times is the province of Windows Millennium's Scheduled Tasks folder. If you want to see the schedule, select **Start, Programs, Accessories, System Tools, Scheduled Tasks**. Alternatively, double-click the Task Scheduler icon in the taskbar's system tray.

Just in Case: Creating an Emergency Startup Disk

If something goes awry with your hard disk, you can regain control of your computer by inserting an *emergency startup disk* in drive A and rebooting. When your computer detects that drive A has a startup disk, it bypasses your hard disk altogether and boots instead to drive A. (That is, you see the **A:\>** prompt instead of the usual Windows Millennium screen.)

To create one of these disks:

1. Select **Start, Settings, Control Panel** to get the Control Panel window onscreen.

2. Open the **Add/Remove Programs** icon to display the Add/Remove Programs Properties dialog box.

3. Select the **Startup Disk** tab.

4. Click the **Create Disk** button. After a few seconds, you're prompted to insert a disk in drive A.

5. Pick out a disk that doesn't have any files on it that you need (Windows Millennium will obliterate all the current info on the disk), insert it, and click **OK**. Windows Millennium chugs away for a minute or two while it creates the startup disk. When it's finished, it returns you to the Add/Remove Programs Properties dialog box.

6. Click **OK** to return to the Control Panel, and then close the Control Panel window.

7. Remove the disk, label it so that you know what it is, store it in a safe place, and keep your fingers crossed that you never have to use it!

To be safe, you should probably give the startup disk a whirl to make sure that it works properly. To do this, follow these steps:

1. Make sure the startup disk is in drive A.

2. Select **Start, Shut Down** to display the Shut Down Windows dialog box.

3. Select the **Restart** option and then click **OK**.

4. Windows Millennium shuts down and then restarts the system. After a while, you see the following menu:

```
Microsoft Windows Millennium Startup Menu
=================================

    1. Help
    2. Start computer with CD-ROM support.
    3. Start computer without CD-ROM support.
    4. Minimal Boot

Enter a choice:
```

5. If you have a CD-ROM drive, press **2**. Otherwise, press **3**.

6. Press **Enter**. You eventually end up at the A:\> prompt.

7. Remove the startup disk.

8. Press **Ctrl+Alt+Delete** to restart your machine and get back to Windows Millennium.

No A:\> Prompt?

If an error prevents the computer from getting to the A:\> prompt, there may be something wrong with the floppy disk. Remove the disk, restart your computer, and then create a new emergency startup disk using a different floppy disk.

DriveSpace

Unlike earlier incarnations of DriveSpace, the one that comes with Windows Millennium only works on removable disks such as floppy disks and Zip disks.

Is That All There Is? Windows Millennium's Other System Tools

While accessing the **Start**, **Programs**, **Accessories**, **System Tools** menu, you no doubt have noticed that it includes all kinds of scary-sounding programs that I didn't cover. The ones we looked at in this chapter are the most useful, but here's a quick look at some of the other tools, just so you know what's available:

➤ **DriveSpace** This little marvel can effectively double the capacity of a disk by squeezing the files down to about half the size they are now. It's all perfectly safe and, aside from being a tad slower, the disk will look and act the way it always has.

➤ **Resource Meter** This utility adds an icon to the taskbar that shows you the current level of *system resources* available to Windows Millennium. System resources are small chunks of memory used by Windows and Windows programs, and problems can result if you run out of these resources. As long as the Resource Meter shows green, you're safe. If it turns yellow, then you need to start shutting down programs.

➤ **System Information** This program supplies you with a ton of data about your computer. The vast majority of the info is "geeks only" stuff, but it does give you semi-interesting tidbits such as the Windows Millennium version, how much memory is on your system, and more.

➤ **System Monitor** This program lets you monitor certain settings, such as the percentage of your computer's main processor that is being used at any one time.

➤ **System Restore** This new Windows Millennium feature creates periodic snapshots (called *restore points*) of your system. If you install a program or device and your system goes haywire, you can use System Restore to revert Windows back to a previously working state.

Getting the Latest and Greatest from the Windows Update Web Site

When Microsoft releases a new version of Windows, the programmers take a day or two off and then get right back to work on the next version. (No flies on those folks!) In the past, whatever new goodies were being implemented for the new version were kept under wraps and unveiled only when everything else was ready for prime time a couple of years down the road. That all changed with the release of Windows 95. Microsoft started making bug fixes, updates, and new features available right away on its World Wide Web site. That was good news for the geeks who were willing to hunt down and install these new baubles, but the whole process was out of the league of the average user.

New Knickknack

System Restore

System Restore is a new addition to the Windows Millennium box.

When Windows 98 came out, Microsoft brought these updates and enhancements down to earth. They implemented a feature called Windows Update, which uses a World Wide Web site as the starting point for all upgrades. From this site, a program examines your system and displays a list of the components for which newer versions are available. You can then select the items you need—and a couple of mouse clicks later the upgrades are downloaded and installed automatically!

Cross Reference

If you don't have an Internet connection up and running, refer to Chapter 7, "Getting Yourself Online," p. 99.

Getting to the Windows Update Web Site Directly

I'm happy to report that Windows Update is still around in Windows Millennium. Assuming that you have an Internet connection up and running, you can get to the Windows Update site by following these steps:

1. Select **Start**, **Windows Update** to load Internet Explorer and display the Windows Update home page. You can also dial the following Web address into your browser:

   http://windowsupdate.microsoft.com/

2. Click the **Product Updates** link.

3. Windows Update may ask if you want to install some software. This is a good idea, so click **Yes**.

4. Windows Update asks permission to scour your system to see which Windows Millennium components are already installed on your system. Click **Yes**. (Don't worry, they're not tracking you.) After a while, you eventually see a list of all the available updates, which will look something like Figure 22.5.

Figure 22.5

After the scan of your system is finished, this page shows you a list of the available updates.

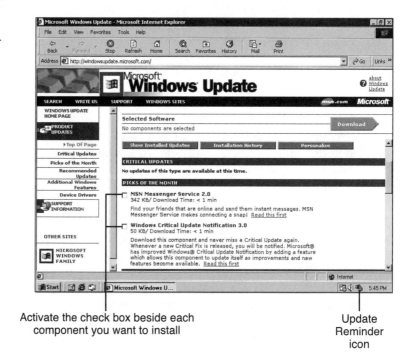

Activate the check box beside each component you want to install

Update Reminder icon

5. To install an update, activate its check box. (Note that some updates have to be installed on their own, so you may not be able to select any others at this point.)

6. When you're done, click **Download**. The next page gives you a list of the components you chose.

7. Click **Start Download**. (If you see a License Agreement at this point, studiously ignore the legalese and click **Yes**.) Windows Update downloads the component and then installs it automatically. Note that in some cases you may have to restart your computer after the upgrade is complete.

Using the New Automatic Updates Feature

After Windows Millennium sees that your computer has Internet access, you eventually see yet another icon in your taskbar's system tray. This is the Update Reminder icon (see figure 22.5) and its job is to let you know when Windows Update has something new to install.

Before you can use this feature, you have to run through a brief setup procedure:

1. Click the **Update Reminder** icon. A welcome message appears.

2. Click **Next**. Now a message from Microsoft's lawyers comes your way.

3. Activate the **I accept the agreement** option (assuming you do, of course) and then click **Next**.

4. Click **Finish**.

New Knickknack

Automatic Updates

The Automatic Updates features is new in Windows Millennium.

After that's done, the Automatic Updates feature runs in the background and checks for new components for your computer automatically. If you're connected to the Internet and a new component is available, Automatic Updates downloads it behind the scenes. When the download is complete, the Update Reminder icon displays a message letting you know that you have a new component to install. To install the component, click the icon, which gets you to the Ready to Install dialog box, shown in Figure 22.6.

Figure 22.6

*After a component has been downloaded, click the **Update Reminder** icon to get to this dialog box.*

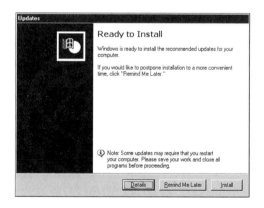

You have three choices from here:

➤ **Details**   Click this button to see what the heck was downloaded. Note that each item has a check box beside it. If you prefer not to install an item, deactivate its check box.

➤ **Remind Me Later**   Click this button to bypass the installation for now. The Update Reminder icon will pester you about it again later on.

➤ **Install**   Click this button to install the new component. Note that if you need to disconnect from the Internet while downloading the update, click the Update Reminder icon and then click Pause. To continue the download, click the icon again and then click Resume.

Taking Control of Automatic Updates

If you don't like the idea of Windows Millennium downloading stuff without your permission (who can blame you?), you can put the Automatic Updates feature in its place. To do so, select **Start**, **Settings**, **Control Panel** and then open the **Automatic Updates** icon. Windows Millennium introduces you to the Automatic Updates dialog box. In the **Options** group, activate the **Notify me before downloading...** option to force Windows Millennium to ask your permission before downloading a component. If you prefer to go to Windows Update yourself, activate the **Turn off automatic updating...** option.

The Least You Need to Know

This chapter showed you how to keep your system running smoothly by using Windows Millennium's system maintenance tools. You learned how to use Disk Cleanup to trash unnecessary files; how to use ScanDisk to scope out hard disk errors; and how to use Disk Defragmenter to be sure your files hang together on your hard disk. I was also happy to show you how to use the System Maintenance Wizard to set up a regular maintenance schedule and how to create an emergency startup disk. I closed by showing you how to use the Windows Update Web site to grab what's new and improved with Windows Millennium. Here's some important stuff to remember:

Crib Notes

➤ **Disk Cleanup**   Use this program to expunge various types of junk files from your hard disk. Select **Start**, **Programs**, **Accessories**, **System Tools**, **Disk Cleanup**.

➤ **ScanDisk**   Use this program to check for and repair hard disk wounds. Select **Start**, **Programs, Accessories, System Tools, ScanDisk**.

➤ **Disk Defragmenter**   Use this program to put your hard disk files into apple-pie order. Select **Start**, **Programs**, **Accessories**, **System Tools**, **Disk Defragmenter**.

➤ **Automatic maintenance**   Use the Maintenance Wizard to set up a maintenance schedule. Select **Start**, **Programs**, **Accessories**, **System Tools**, **Maintenance Wizard**.

➤ **Windows Update**   This Web site alerts you to new and improved Windows Millennium components. Select **Start**, **Windows Update** or use the new Automatic Updates feature.

➤ **What's the frequency, Kenneth?**   You should run Disk Cleanup every couple of weeks, ScanDisk every week (and the Thorough check every month), and Disk Defragmenter every week (every month if your machine gets only light use). You should check in with the Windows Update Web site once a month or so.

Chapter 23

Getting a Good Night's Sleep: Backing Up Your Precious Data

In This Chapter

➤ Installing and running Microsoft Backup

➤ Going through the backup steps

➤ Understanding backup jobs

➤ Restoring backed-up files

➤ The Better-Safe-Than-Sorry Department

A few years ago, I turned on my computer in anticipation of another day's writing fun. I heard a couple of alarming beeps and then saw a Hard disk configuration error message on my screen. Yup. My hard disk had died a horrible death and there was nothing I could do about it. The worst part of it was that I had hundreds of documents on the disk that were now gone for good because I was too lazy to back up my files. It took me weeks to recover from that disaster, and I've been a rabid backer-upper ever since.

I found out the hard way that there are two types of computer users: those who back up their documents and those who eventually wish they had. If you learn anything at all from this book, I hope it's this: Someday, sometime, somewhere, some sort of evil will befall your computer and all your data will be trashed. So be prepared by using the ever-so-easy backup program that comes with Windows Millennium. This chapter shows you how it works.

Installing Microsoft Backup

Microsoft does many unfathomable things, but to my mind the height of its unfathomableness is its dogged insistence on making the Windows backup program—it's called Microsoft Backup—so hard to find. In Windows 95 and Windows 98, Backup wasn't part of the so-called "Typical" installation so most folks had to run Control Panel's Add/Remove Programs feature to install it. Now, in Windows Millennium, the situation is even worse because Backup isn't a part of *any* of the various installations, and it's nowhere to be found if you run Add/Remove Programs. Hunh!?

It turns out that Backup is still around, but now it's squirreled away in an obscure nook of the Windows Millennium CD. That's right, one of the most important Windows Millennium tools is hidden away where few people are likely to find it. Unfathomable and very, very dumb.

Microsoft now makes you jump through these hoops to install the Backup program:

1. Insert the Windows Millennium CD.
2. Use My Computer to display the CD. Then open the **add-ons** folder and the **MSbackup** folder.
3. Launch the file named **msbexp**. Windows Millennium scurries about, installing various files. When it's done, it throws up a dialog box to let you know.
4. Click **OK**. Windows Millennium now tells you that you need to restart your computer.
5. Say "Grrrr" and click **Yes**.

Backing Up: A Few Things to Keep in Mind

Other than a few people who insist on living in It-Can't-Happen-to-Me Land, I think most folks get the "why" part of backing up. They just don't get the "how" part. That is, they want to run backups, but it's such a time-consuming pain in the you-know-what, that it just doesn't seem worth the hassle. "Sorry, I'd like to do a backup, but I have to call the IRS to schedule an audit."

If backing up seems like too much of a bother, you can do plenty of things to make it easier:

Forget floppy disks Backing up to floppy disks is a bad way to go because it requires about 70 disks to back up just 100MB. If you're like most people, you probably have hundreds of megabytes to protect, so backing up to dozens of floppy disks is no one's idea of fun, I'm sure.

Switch Guard Operation

In response to requests from our customers, APC has added a removable switch guard to the SurgeStation to ensure positive activation of the On/Off switch.With the switch guard installed, the switch may be activated with your finger. If you would like to be able to use your foot or toe to turn the unit on or off, the switch guard should be removed.

To remove the switch guard:
1. Place your finger through the hole in the center of the switch guard and depress the switch.
2. Hook your finger around the lip of the hole and pull straight back.
   Note: The switch guard is designed to fit securely. It may be necessary to exert a moderate amount of force in order to remove the guard.

To re-attach switch guard:
1. Position the switch guard so that the right mounting tab is inserted into the slot at the right edge of the On/Off switch.
2. With your finger through the hole in the center of the switch guard, insert the left mounting tab into the slot at the left edge of the On/Off switch.
   Note: It may be necessary to flex the guard slightly in order to engage both tabs.

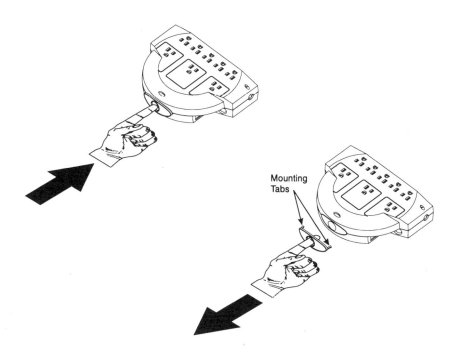

Mounting
Tabs

Use better backup destinations   For easiest backups, use a medium that has a relatively large capacity. That way, you won't spend great gobs of time shuffling disks in and out. Windows Millennium supports all kinds of backup and storage devices, but here are a few to bear in mind:

➤ **Zip disks**   These hold 100MB (the latest ones hold 250MB), which is a heckuva lot better than a floppy disk (usually 1.44MB).

➤ **Jaz disks**   These come in 1GB and 2GB flavors, so they have plenty of capacity (but cost a pretty penny; about U.S. $100).

➤ **Tape drives**   These typically come in multigigabyte capacities and are fairly cheap, so they're the most common choice used by backup aficionados.

➤ **Hard disks**   This is a great choice if you happen to have a second hard disk in your system. (Be sure it's a second disk, and not just a single disk that's been divided in two.)

➤ **Network locales**   If you have a small network at home or in a small office, you might consider turning one machine's large hard disk into a backup destination. On larger networks, see whether your system administrator has set aside space for you on a server.

Back up your documents first   The only things on your system that are truly irreplaceable are the documents that you've created with the sweat of your own brow. So, if backup space is at a premium, include only your documents in the backup job. You can always install your programs again later, if need be.

Organize your documents   If you're going to go the documents-only route, you can make your life immeasurably easier if you store everything in subfolders that all reside within a single folder (such as My Documents). That way, when you're telling Windows Millennium which files to back up, you need only select the main folder. Another plus for this approach is that any files you add to this folder will be included automatically the next time you run the backup.

Jargon Jar

Backup Job

This is a file that specifies a few particulars about your backup: the files you want backed up, the location where the files will be backed up, and any backup options.

Back up your downloaded programs   If you've downloaded programs and files from the Internet, it can be a lot of trouble to get new copies of that stuff if your system goes down for the count. You should include downloaded files as part of your backup job.

Take advantage of backup types   After you've decided on all the files that should be part of the backup, don't waste time backing up every single one of those files each time you do a backup. Instead, you can use *backup types* to tell Windows Millennium to back up only those files that have changed. Windows Millennium supports three backup types:

➤ **Normal**   Backs up each and every file, each and every time. (Note that by "each and every file," I mean "each and every file in the backup job.") All files are marked to indicate they've been backed up.

➤ **Incremental**   Backs up only those files that have changed since the most recent Normal or Incremental backup. This is the fastest type because it includes only the minimum number of files. Again, the files are marked to indicate they've been backed up.

➤ **Differential**   Backs up only those files that have changed since the most recent Normal backup. The files are *not* marked to indicate they've been backed up, so if you run this type of backup again, the same files get backed up (plus any others that have changed in the meantime).

Archive Flags and Other Backup Trivia

How does the Backup program mark files that have been backed up? Well, each file has what's known in the trade as an *archive flag* (sometimes called an *archive bit* or an *archive attribute*). When you make changes to a file, that flag gets raised. (This happens behind the scenes, so it isn't something you see or have to worry about.) This is the file's way of saying "Yo, Backup Boy! I need backing up!" When you include a file in a Normal or Incremental backup, the flag is lowered to indicate that the file has been backed up. However, a Differential backup does *not* lower the flag.

Create a backup strategy   Finally, you should come up with a backup strategy that makes sense for you, and then you should stick to that strategy no matter what. A typical strategy might go something like this:

➤ Do a full backup of all your documents once a month or so.

➤ Do a differential backup of modified files once a week.

➤ Do an incremental backup of modified files every day.

Running the Backup Program

To get things going at long last, select **Start**, **Programs**, **Accessories**, **System Tools**, **Backup**.

The first time you start Backup, it checks your system to see whether you have any "backup devices" installed. (What Windows Millennium calls a backup device, the rest of us call a tape drive.) If you don't, Backup displays a dialog box asking whether you want to run the Add New Hardware Wizard to install a device. If you do have a backup device on your system, click **Yes** and use the wizard to specify the device. (Restart your computer when you're done.) Otherwise, click **No** to continue.

Each time you start Backup, you see the Microsoft Backup dialog box shown in Figure 23.1. You have these choices:

➤ **Create a new backup job**   If you activate this option and click **OK**, the program launches the Backup Wizard to take you step-by-step through the process of creating a backup job. I explain how this wizard works in a second.

➤ **Open an existing backup job**   If you've already defined a backup job, activate this option and click **OK**. In the Open Backup Job dialog box that appears, highlight the backup job you want to work with, and then click **Open**.

➤ **Restore backed up files**   If you've already run a backup job, activate this option to restore files from that backup job. (See "If Worst Comes to Worst: Recovering Backed Up Files," later in this chapter.)

If you don't want to run any of these choices right now, click **Close** to get to the Microsoft Backup window.

Figure 23.1

Backup presents you with this dialog box at startup.

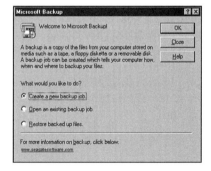

Creating a Backup Job

To reiterate (that is, to repeat myself), in Backup lingo, a *backup job* is a file that defines your backup. It includes three things:

➤ A list of the files you want to include in your backup

➤ The Backup options you selected, including the type of backup you want to use

➤ The destination drive and folder for the backed-up files

Backup Basics

Choosing the **New and changed files** option tells the program to use the differential backup type. If you want to run an incremental backup, you have to create the backup job yourself, as described in the next section.

You define a backup job either by using the friendly Backup Wizard, or by cobbling together the various job pieces by hand. The next two sections take you through both scenarios.

Using the Backup Wizard

The Backup Wizard's role is to give you a step-by-step method for setting up a new backup job. Here's what happens:

1. You start the Backup Wizard using either of the following methods:

   ➤ In the startup Microsoft Backup dialog box, activate **Create a new backup job** and click **OK**.

   ➤ In the Microsoft Backup window, select **Tools, Backup Wizard**.

Either way, you see the first of the wizard's dialog boxes. You have two choices:

➤ **Back up My Computer**   Activate this option and click **Next** to perform a complete backup of your hard drives. If you choose this option, skip to step 4.

➤ **Back up selected files, folders, and drives**   Activate this option and click **Next** to choose the files you want to include in the backup job. This is the option I recommend in most cases because you can use it to back up just your precious documents.

3. If you decided to back up only selected files, you use the next wizard dialog box to choose those files. This dialog box is reminiscent of the My Computer window, with one important difference: In the Backup window, all the disk drives, folders, and files have a check box next to them. The basic idea, illustrated by the example in Figure 23.2, is that you activate the appropriate check box for each drive, folder, and file you want to include in the backup. Click **Next** when you're done.

Figure 23.2

Activate the check boxes beside the drives, folders, and files you want to include in the backup job.

4. The wizard next asks whether you want to back up **All selected files** or **New and changed files**. The latter means only those files that you've created or changed since the last time you did a backup. Make your choice and click **Next**.

5. Now the wizard wonders where you want the selected files backed up. Depending on your system, you see one or both of the following (click **Next** after you've made your choice):

   ➤ **File**   Select this option to back up your files to a single backup file. The wizard adds an extra text box so that you can specify the name and location of this backup file.

   ➤ **Backup device**   Select this option (the name of which varies depending on the backup device you have installed) to use your backup device as the destination.

6. Now the wizard presents the following options (click **Next** when you've made your choice):

   ➤ **Compare original and backup files to verify data was successfully backed up**   If you activate this check box, Backup checks each backed-up file against its original to make sure that the backup archived the file without any errors. This ensures an accurate backup, but it effectively doubles the backup time.

   ➤ **Compress the backup data to save space**   If you activate this check box, Backup compresses the backed-up files. The backed-up files will take up approximately half the space of the originals.

7. In the next wizard dialog box, use the text box to enter a name for your new backup job, and then click **Start** to get things under way.

8. Backup might ask you for a unique name for the backup media. If so, enter a name and click **OK**. It might also warn you that the "media" already contains "backup sets." If so, click **Append** to add your backup job. (If you don't care about the other backup sets, click **Overwrite**, instead.)

9. During the backup process, the Backup Progress window lets you know how the backup is going. When the operation is complete, Backup displays a dialog box to let you know. Click **OK**, and then click **OK** in the Backup Progress window.

Creating a Backup Job with Your Bare Hands

The Backup Wizard ensures that you don't forget anything, but it's a bit of a long haul to get from A to Backup. You can usually speed up the entire process by creating a backup job by hand. To give this a whirl, display the **Backup** tab, as shown in Figure 23.3. (If you've just started Backup, click **Close** to get rid of the Microsoft Backup dialog box.)

Figure 23.3

Instead of using the Backup Wizard, you can set up a backup job from the Backup tab.

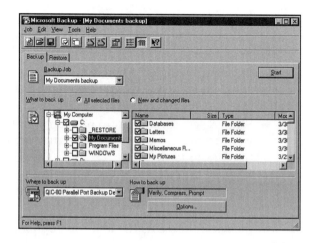

To create the backup job, use the following controls:

➤ **What to back up**   First choose either **All selected files** or **New and changed files**. Then use the lists below to activate the check boxes beside the files, folders, and disk drives you want to include in the backup.

➤ **Where to back up**   Use this list to select the type of backup media you're using. If you choose **File**, use the text box to enter the name and location of the file.

➤ **How to back up**   Click **Options** to rendezvous with the Backup Job Options dialog box (see Figure 23.4). You use this dialog box to configure various Backup options.

Figure 23.4

Use the Backup Job Options dialog box to customize some settings for your backup job.

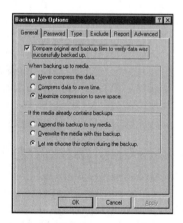

Let's take a minute or two to investigate the most useful settings in the Backup Job Options dialog box. First, in the **General** tab, use the **Compare original and backup files to verify data was successfully backed up** check box to toggle the verification process on or off.

The **When backing up to media** group contains the following three options:

➤ **Never compress the data**   Activate this option to turn off Backup's compression setting.

➤ **Compress data to save time**   This option compresses the data but doesn't use full compression, which speeds things up a bit.

➤ **Maximize compression to save space**   If the backup media is low on space, activate this option to use full compression on the backed up files. This reduces the size of the backup, but takes longer.

The **If the media already contains backups** group contains these option buttons:

➤ **Append this backup to my media**   This option adds your backup to the existing backups on the media.

➤ **Overwrite the media with this backup**   Activate this option to replace the old backup data with your new backup data.

➤ **Let me choose this option during the backup**   When this option is activated, Backup prompts you to append or overwrite the existing backup.

If you're backing up to a network drive or other public location, you can protect your backup from snoops by activating the **Protect this backup with a password** check box in the **Password** tab. Enter your password in both the **Password** and **Confirm password** text boxes.

You use the **Type** tab to choose the type of backup you want to run. For a full backup of every file in the backup job, activate the **All selected files** option. Otherwise, activate the **New and changed files only** option and then choose one of the following:

➤ **Differential backup type**   Backs up only those files that have changed since the last full backup. (This is the same as choosing the **New and changed files** option in the Backup tab.)

➤ **Incremental backup type**   Backs up only those files that have changed since the last full or differential backup.

After all that's out of the way, click **Start** to get the backup going.

Backing Up the All-Important Registry

If you're doing a full backup of your system, then you should include the *Windows Registry files* in the backup. These are crucial files that hold all your Windows Millennium configuration data. To include them in your backup job, display the **Advanced** tab in the Backup Job Options dialog box, and activate the **Back up Windows Registry** check box.

Saving and Reusing Backup Jobs

Because you'll be backing up regularly (right?), you'll almost certainly run the same backup job again in the future. To avoid reinventing the backup job wheel, you should save your settings for later use. To do this, be sure the **Backup** tab is displayed and then select **Job**, **Save**. In the Save Backup Job As dialog box, enter a **Job Name** for the job and then click **Save**.

To reuse a backup job down the road, display the **Backup** tab and select **Job**, **Open**. Use the Open Backup Job dialog box to highlight your backup job and then click **Open**.

If Worst Comes to Worst: Recovering Backed Up Files

If some unforeseen disaster should occur, you'll need to restore your data from the backups. Happily, Backup has another wizard that takes you step-by-step through the process of restoring previously backed-up data. And as with backing up, you can also elect to restore your data by hand.

Using the Restore Wizard

Here's the low-down on the Restore Wizard's workings:

1. Start this wizard using either of the following methods:
   - ➤ In the startup Microsoft Backup dialog box, activate **Restore backed up files** and click **OK**.
   - ➤ In the Microsoft Backup window, select **Tools, Restore Wizard**.

2. In the first wizard dialog box, select the device or file that contains the backup job and then click **Next**.

3. The wizard then displays a list of the backups found on the media. Activate the check boxes beside each backup job you want to restore, and then click **OK**.

4. Now the wizard creates a list of the drives, folders, and files in the chosen backup jobs. When it's finished, it displays a dialog box much like the one shown earlier in Figure 23.2. Activate the check boxes beside the items you want to restore, and then click **Next**.

5. The wizard next asks where you want the files restored. You can select either **Original Location** or **Alternate Location**. If you choose the latter, a new text box appears so that you can specify the new location. Click **Next** when you're ready to proceed.

Handling Multiple, Overlapping Backups

If you want to restore multiple backup jobs that contain some (not all) of the same files, restore the backup jobs separately, starting with the earliest and ending with the latest. This ensures that you end up with the most up-to-date files.

6. Now the wizard asks what it should do if a file with the same name already exists in the restore destination. Here are your choices:

   ➤ **Do not replace the file on my computer** If you activate this option, Backup won't replace any files on the destination drive or folder with backed-up files that have the same name. This is usually the best choice because it means the restore won't overwrite files that you've worked on since the backup.

   ➤ **Replace the file on my computer only if the file is older** If you activate this option, Backup only replaces files on the destination drive or folder with backed-up files of the same name that have a later date.

   ➤ **Always replace the file on my computer** If you activate this option, Backup replaces any files on the destination drive or folder with backed-up files that have the same name.

7. Click **Start** to get the restore operation under way. If Backup prompts you for the backup media, insert the media and click **OK**.

8. The Restore Progress window appears during the restore operation so that you can keep an eye on things. When Backup is finished, it displays a dialog box to let you know. Click **OK**, and then click **OK** in the Restore Progress window.

Restoring Files by Hand

As with backing up, restoring files is a bit faster if you do everything manually. To get started, display the **Restore** tab, shown in Figure 23.5. If Backup asks if you want to refresh the view, click **Yes**. In the Select Backup Sets dialog box, activate the check box beside the backup job you want to use, and then click **OK**.

Figure 23.5

For a wizardless restore, use the Restore tab.

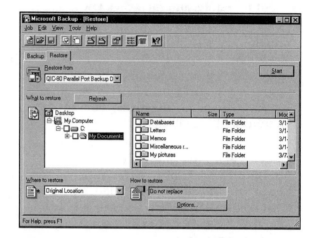

Now use the following controls to set up the restore:

➤ **Restore from**   Use this list to select the type of backup media you're using. If you choose **File**, use the text box to enter the name and location of the file.

➤ **What to restore**   Use the lists to activate the check boxes beside the files, folders, and disk drives you want to restore.

➤ **Where to restore**   Use this list to specify where you want the files restored: **Original Location** or **Alternate Location**. For the latter, use the text box that materializes to specify the new location.

➤ **How to restore**   Click **Options** to powwow with the Restore Options dialog box. Use the items in the **General** tab to specify what Backup should do if files with the same name exist in the folder to which you're restoring (as described in the previous section).

To get the restore operation underway, click the **Start** button. If Backup prompts you for the backup media, insert the media and click **OK**.

The Least You Need to Know

This chapter gave you one less thing to worry about by showing you how to use Windows Millennium's Backup program to make backups of your precious files. I began by showing you how to install Backup from the Windows Millennium CD.

I then ran through a few suggestions for making the whole backup process easier and faster. From there, you learned how to back up both with the Backup Wizard and by hand. Should a problem arise, you also learned how to restore backed-up files. Here are a few backup pointers to remember:

Crib Notes

➤ **One last bit of proselytizing**   Your hard disk is an accident waiting for a place to happen, so start backing up your files right away.

➤ **Easier backups**   To make backups something to look forward to, avoid floppy disks, use a destination with a lot of space, keep all your documents in one spot, and use backup types.

➤ **Follow a backup strategy**   Run an Incremental backup each day, a Differential backup each week, and a Normal backup each month.

Part 6

Networking with Windows Millennium

Networking—using cables to connect a group of computers so that users can share equipment, data, and office gossip[md]has been around a long time, and is by now standard fare in most businesses. Unfortunately, networking in earlier flavors of Windows always seemed like something that was bolted on at the last minute with no thought about how non-geeks would fare in such an arcane world. Even if you had some inkling about what you were doing, the networking setup was tedious and complex, and the network features weren't as friendly as they should have been. Tired, I guess, of all the complaints, Microsoft decided to do something about this sad state of networking affairs. The result is that networking in Windows Millennium is a notch or two better than it was in Windows 95 or Windows 98. Getting a machine network-ready is easier thanks to the Home Networking Wizard, and the network tools are all a bit nicer to deal with.

I tell you all about these and other networking features here in Part 6. If you're looking to create a small network in your home or office, check out Chapter 24, "Using Windows Millennium to Set Up a Small Network." I cover general networking techniques in Chapter 25, "Using Windows Millennium's Networking Features." And I tell you how to connect to your network from remote locales in Chapter 26, "Remote Network Connections with Dial-Up Networking."

Using Windows Millennium to Set Up a Small Network

In This Chapter

➤ Understanding the various hardware bits and pieces that you need

➤ Learning the easiest way to put your network together

➤ Using the new Home Networking Wizard to get your computers ready for their networking chores

➤ Proof positive that setting up a small network is *way* easier than you think

---

Networking sounds like one of those topics that must surely contravene Idiot's Guide bylaw 47C-8: "The party of the first part (hereafter known as the AUTHOR) shall not attempt to explain hopelessly technical subjects to the party of the second part (here-after known as the READER)." And, yes, it's certainly true that networking is more complicated to explain than, say, Notepad. (Although explaining how to boil water is harder than explaining how to use Notepad.) But having had my own computers here at home networked for many years, I've learned something crucial: 95% of network-ing know-how is pure hooey. That's right, most of what you *can* know about network-ing isn't anything that you *need* to know to set up your own network.

How can this be? The secret is that most networking flapdoodle is geared only to IT jocks running humongous corporate or government networks. Their world is stuffed full of things like routers and switches and packets and layers that give warm, fuzzy, feelings only to electrical engineering graduates.

Jargon Jar

IT

This stands for Information Technology, the corporate computing department overseen by a kind of priesthood and staffed by acolytes who spend their days kneeling before the Great Mainframe and sacrificing members of the mailroom staff.

However, setting up a little network for a small office or home office (the SOHO thing) requires only the teeniest subset of all that networking malarkey. You just need to know about a few pieces of equipment and one or two ways to configure that equipment, and you're off and networking. It's all well within the capabilities of most folks, and that includes *you*, as you see in this chapter.

Networking Advantages

A *local area network* (LAN) is a group of computers that are relatively close together (for example, in the same office or in the same house) and that are connected via a cable that plugs in to special hardware inside each machine. (For variety, I use the terms *LAN* and *network* interchangeably in this chapter.)

What's the point of such connections? One word: *sharing*. Having your computers lashed together in a network opens up a whole new world for sharing things:

➤ You can send data along the network cables, so it's criminally easy to fire off a file to another machine, or to grab a file you need (assuming, of course, that you have the necessary permission to do so).

➤ Peripherals—such as a printer or CD-ROM—on one machine can be made visible to the rest of the network. This means the other computers can print to that one printer, for example.

➤ A single Internet connection—whether it's via a regular modem, a cable modem, or a digital subscriber line (DSL)—can be shared with everyone on the network.

➤ If a computer happens to have a lot of empty hard disk space, it can be shared with the network and thus used as a convenient (and fast) location for backups.

A network will make your computing life more convenient, which probably isn't too surprising. However, it will also make your computing life cheaper because you need fewer peripherals (such as printers and tape drives for backups) and you can share a single Internet account.

Stuff You Need: Understanding Network Hardware

In a sense, setting up a network is all about setting up the appropriate hardware. This is particularly true of Windows Millennium, which (as you see a bit later) does a great job of installing whatever networking software is required after it detects (or is told about) the presence of networking hardware. Therefore, it's no exaggeration to say that the key to getting your network configured with the least amount of fuss is to research and purchase the correct hardware bric-a-brac up front. The next few sections tell you everything you need to know.

The Connection Point: The Network Interface Card

Networking begins and ends (literally) with a component called the *network interface card*, or NIC, for short. (Depending on the geek you're talking to, a NIC can also be called a *network adapter* or a *network card*.) The network cable (see the next section) that connects all the computers actually plugs in to the back of a NIC that resides in each machine. Therefore, the NIC is each machine's connection point to the network.

NICs come in three basic configurations:

See "Understanding Hardware Types," p. 333.

➤ **Circuit board**   This is the most common type of NIC, and it plugs into a slot inside the computer. Prices vary widely, but you can get good boards between $80 and $130 (U.S.). I gave you instructions for installing circuit boards back in Chapter 21, "Installing and Uninstalling Programs and Devices."

➤ **PC Card (PCMCIA)**   This type of NIC comes in the credit card-size PC Card format and it plugs into a PC Card socket on a notebook computer or a docking station. These are handy for notebook users, but they're slightly more expensive—$100 to $150 (U.S.).

➤ **Universal Serial Bus (USB)**   This is a relatively new type of NIC, and it plugs into a USB connector in the back of the PC. (Most new PCs come with a couple of USB connectors.) This is, obviously, easier to install than the circuit board type, and they're reasonably priced—$90 to $130 (U.S.).

After you decide on the basic type (or types) of NIC you want, here's a checklist to run through to help you narrow your search a bit further:

➤ Be sure the NICs support something called *Ethernet*. (This is a type of network architecture, and it's the one used by the vast majority of networks.) There are two varieties: standard Ethernet—which boasts a network speed of 10 megabits per second (Mbps) and is less expensive—and Fast Ethernet—which runs at a speedy 100Mbps but is slightly more expensive. Note, too, that there are "10/100" NICs that support both types.

➤ Be sure the NICs have the appropriate cable ports. As I explain in the next section, there are two basic types of cable, so you have to be sure that the NICs you choose have a port for the type of cable you decide to use. (Some NICs have ports for both types. Note, too, that a few NICs come with a third type of port—called an AUI port—that's rarely used.)

➤ For easiest installation, get NICs that support Plug and Play.

➤ For fastest performance in a circuit-board NIC, get the type that plugs into a PCI slot inside the computer.

NICs and High-Speed Internet Connections

Many people are migrating their Internet accounts to the high-speed connections offered by cable modems and DSL. If you're thinking of doing the same thing, note that you need to install *two* NICs in your computer: one for the network and another for the high-speed connection. Make sure you know which NIC does what because it will be important later on when you configure the computer to share the connection over your network.

The Connection: The Network Cable

Although wireless networks are possible, they're slow and flaky. As a result, the majority of networks use cables to connect the various machines. As I mentioned earlier, your NICs and cables have to match because the cable connects to a port in the back of the NIC, so the port and cable jack must be compatible. Fortunately, although many cable types are available, you need to consider only two when setting up your small LAN: twisted-pair and coaxial.

Twisted-pair cable is the most common type. (It's called twisted-pair because it consists of two copper wires twisted together.) Each end of the cable has an *RJ-45 jack*, which is similar to (but a bit bigger than) the jacks used on telephone cables (which are called RJ-11 jacks, in case you're interested). Figure 24.1 points out the RJ-45 jack and shows a twisted-pair cable plugged into a NIC. Here are some other notes:

➤ This type of cable is most commonly used in the "star" network structure. See "The Star Structure" later in this chapter.

➤ Always ask for "category 5" twisted-pair cable. This is the highest quality and it's suitable for all types of Ethernet networks. It costs a bit more, but it's definitely worth it.

➤ Cables come in various lengths, so be sure you buy cables that are long enough to make the proper connections (but not so long that you waste your money on cable you don't use).

RJ-45 port

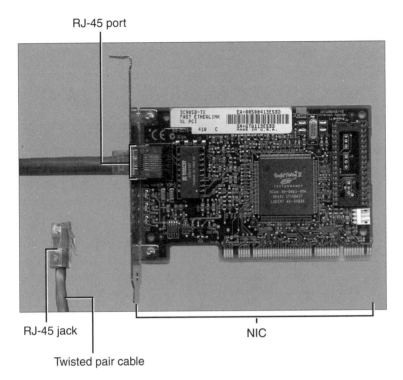

RJ-45 jack   NIC

Twisted pair cable

The other type of cable is *coaxial cable* (some network nerds refer to it as *thinnet cable*). It's somewhat reminiscent of the cables used with cable television connections, but network coaxial cable has "bayonet-style" connectors at each end. (They're called bayonet-style connectors because you plug them into the port and then give them a twist to lock them in place. This is similar, I suppose, to the way you connect a bayonet.) To use this type of cable, your NICs must have a corresponding BNC port in the back. Figure 24.2 shows an example of a coaxial cable, a NIC with a BNC port, and some other hardware you need.

Notice in Figure 24.2 that the coaxial cable doesn't plug directly into the NIC. Instead, the cable plugs into a BNC port on the T-connector, and the T-connector plugs into the BNC port on the NIC. The idea is that you'd then plug another coaxial cable into the T-connector's other BNC port (for now, you can ignore the terminator shown in the figure), and then run that cable to another NIC on the network. Here are some notes:

➤ If you're not too clear about how to hook up your network using coaxial cable, I discuss this in more detail later on when I discuss the "bus" network structure. See "The Bus Structure" later in this chapter.

➤ Coaxial cable can't go any faster than 10MBps, so you can't use it with Fast Ethernet.

➤ Again, be sure you purchase cables that are the correct length.

Figure 24.2

The coaxial cable's bayonet-style connector plugs into a T-connector, which then plugs into the corresponding BNC port on the NIC.

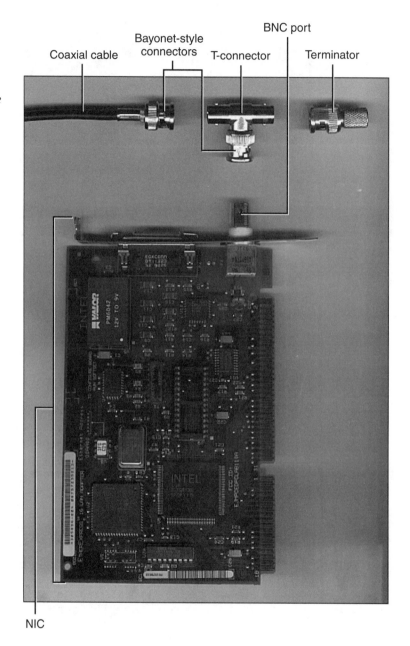

NIC

If you're not sure which cable type to go with, don't sweat it just now. As I said, each type of cable is associated with a different network structure, so you should check out those structures before deciding on the cable.

Deciding How to Structure Your Network

The last thing you have to consider before getting down to the short strokes is the overall network structure. The structure determines how each machine is connected to the network. (Networking jockeys use the highfalutin' phrase *network topology*.) Many structures are possible, but luckily for you only two are suitable for small LANs: star and bus.

The Star Structure

In the *star* structure, each NIC is connected to a *hub*, which serves as a central connection point for the entire network. A hub is a small box that has several (typically 4, 6, or 8) RJ-45 ports. Hubs vary widely in price from simple 10Mbps units that cost under $100 (U.S.) to massive machines costing in the thousands of dollars. For your small network, you shouldn't have to spend more than about $200 (U.S.).

For each computer, you run twisted-pair cable from the NIC to a port in the hub, as shown in Figure 24.3.

Get the Right Hub, Bub

Your hub must match the type of Ethernet you're using. For example, if you go with Fast Ethernet, then your hub must also support 100Mbps.

Figure 24.3

In the star structure, each machine is connected to the network by running twisted-pair cable from the NIC to the hub.

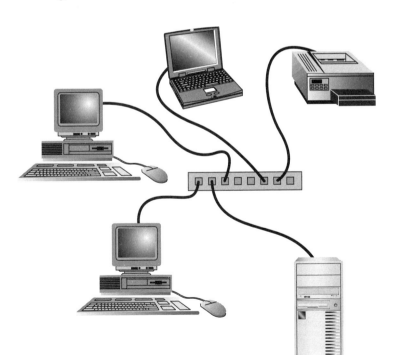

The Bus Structure

In the *bus* structure, each NIC is connected directly to another NIC using coaxial cables, T-connectors, BNC ports, and all that other stuff I mentioned earlier. Figure 24.4 illustrates how this works. As you can see, you run the cable from one T-connector to the next. Note that you can't form a "circle" by attaching a cable from the last NIC to the first NIC. Instead, you have to put special connectors called *terminators* on the T-connectors of the first and last NICs (refer to Figure 24.2).

Figure 24.4

Here's the basic bus struc-ture where you connect NICs using coaxial cable. Note the terminators on the first and last NICs.

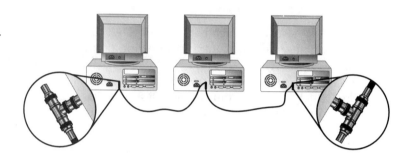

Decisions, Decisions: What Route Should You Take?

I've given you a lot of choices to mull over so far, so there's a good chance your head is spinning a bit with all the permutations and combinations. Actually, you really have to consider only two configurations:

➤ NICs with RJ-45 ports arranged in a star structure that uses twisted-pair cable to connect each computer to a central hub. Here are the pros and cons of this con-figuration:

   Pros   It's easy to add and remove computers from the network (just plug them in and out of the hub); the network isn't affected if one of the com-puters goes down; it can be very speedy if you go with Fast Ethernet; it's the most common configuration, so you have a greater selection of NICs and hubs.

   Cons   It's more expensive because it requires a hub; it requires more cable because each cable must run from the NIC all the way to the hub.

➤ NICs with BNC ports arranged in a bus structure that uses coaxial cable to con-nect each computer directly. Some pros and cons to consider:

   Pros   This is the least expensive route; it requires less cable because each connection has to reach only to the next computer.

Cons It's harder to add and remove computers from the network because each change requires changing the cabling on one or two other machines; the entire network goes down if one machine goes down; it's limited to 10Mbps; it has a lesser selection of NICs.

Of these two configurations, the former is the one I prefer, and it's the one I used to put together the test network that serves as an example throughout the chapters here in Part 6, "Networking with Windows Millennium."

Setting Up Your Network

After you've made your decision about what network hardware to purchase, and after you've installed that hardware, your next task is to set up each machine for networking.

Throughout the rest of this chapter (as well as the next chapter), I use the word "workgroup" a lot, so let's take a second here to be sure you know what I'm blathering on about. In network lingo, a *workgroup* is a small collection of related computers on a network. In a large corporate network, for example, there might be one workgroup for the Accounting department and another for the Marketing department. For your small LAN, you have just a single workgroup for all your computers.

There are two more points to bear in mind before you get started:

Networking and the Windows Millennium Setup

If you're installing Windows Millennium on one or more of the would-be LAN computers, the Setup program eventually asks you for a few bits of network-related info, including a computer name and a workgroup name. See the steps in the next section for descriptions of these tidbits.

➤ Make sure you've installed and connected all your network hardware.

➤ If you want to share an Internet connection among all the computers, set up that connection on one of the machines. This computer will be known as the *Internet Connection Sharing host*. Also, be sure to run the Home Networking Wizard on that machine first (as described a bit later; see "Setting Up a Network With Internet Connection Sharing") so that Windows Millennium's Internet Connection Sharing feature is properly set up and ready to go for the other computers.

Your companion on the network setup journey is the new Home Networking Wizard, which takes great pains to ensure that your network is properly configured. The rest of this chapter takes you through all the steps required.

Home Networking Wizard

The Home Networking Wizard is a new piece of the Windows networking puzzle.

Another Route to the Wizard

Another way to start the Home Networking Wizard is by selecting **Start, Programs, Accessories, Communications, Home Networking Wizard**.

Using the Home Networking Wizard to Set Up Your Network

In previous versions of Windows, getting your computers configured to handle the burdens of networking was unpleasant, to say the least. It involved wrestling with innumerable dialog boxes, puzzling over esoterica such as "clients" and "protocols," and scratching the hair off your head trying to figure out why things didn't work.

So I'm sure you'll be quite pleased to hear that all that network nincompoopery is a thing of the past thanks to Windows Millennium's new Home Networking Wizard. This wizard takes you through the entire network setup process one step at a time, and it handles most of the technical stuff behind the scenes where it belongs. Here's how the wizard works:

1. Double-click the desktop's **My Network Places** icon and then double-click the **Home Networking Wizard** icon. Windows Millennium hires the Home Networking Wizard, which promptly shows up for work.

2. The initial dialog box is merely an overview, so click **Next** to get to something more useful.

3. The wizard asks if this computer connects to the Internet. If not, activate **No, this computer does not use the Internet**, click **Next**, and then fast forward to step 6. Otherwise, activate **Yes** and proceed to step 4.

4. If you chose **Yes** in step 3, the wizard promotes a couple of option buttons as shown in Figure 24.5. You use them to specify how this computer connects to the Internet:

   ➤ **A connection to another computer on my home network...**
   Choose this option if you're setting up a machine that will use a shared Internet connection from another computer. If you go this route, click **Next** and skip to step 6.

   ➤ **A direct connection to my ISP using the following device**
   Activate this option if the machine connected to the Internet is the same machine you are using to run this wizard. Use the list to choose the Internet connection "device" the machine uses. If you get online using a modem connection, select the **Dial-Up Networking** item; if you get online using a cable modem or DSL line, select the network adapter you use for that connection. Click **Next**.

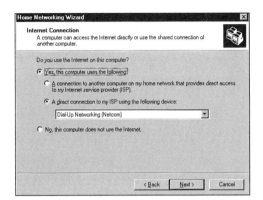

Figure 24.5

*If you activate **Yes**, use the option buttons to tell the wizard how the machine connects to the Internet.*

5. If you chose **A direct connection to my ISP using the following device** in step 4, the wizard now asks if you want to share that Internet connection with the network. Once again, you have two choices (and, once again, you click **Next** when you're done):

➤ If you're setting up the Internet Connection Sharing host computer, activate **Yes**. Then use the list to select the device that the computer uses to connect to the network (that is, your network adapter).

➤ If you don't want to share the connection with other computers on your network, activate **No, I do not want to share my Internet connection**.

6. The next wizard dialog box, shown in Figure 24.6, asks you for two crucial bits of information (click **Next** when you're ready to continue):

➤ **Computer Name** This is the name that other people on the LAN will see for the computer, so enter an appropriate (and unique) moniker. It's standard in small networks to use the first or last name of the person who'll be wrestling with the computer, but feel free to be a little creative. The name can be up to 15 characters long (don't use any spaces), and it can include any of the following symbols:

` ! @ # $ % ^ & ( ) - _ { } .

➤ **Workgroup Name** This is the name of your workgroup. The Home Networking Wizard suggests, MSHOME (dull!), but you can change that by activating the **Use this workgroup name** option and then typing in the new name.

Look Out!

Workgroup Names Must Be Universal

For your LAN to work successfully (and simply), all the computers *must* use the same workgroup name.

387

Figure 24.6

Use this dialog box to set the computer's network name and the name of your workgroup.

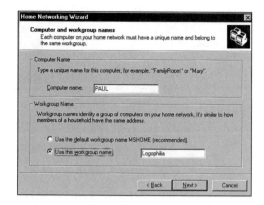

7. Now the wizard wants to know about sharing files and printers, as shown in Figure 24.7. *Sharing* means that you give other people on the network access to some or all of the files and folders on your computer, as well as to your printer (if the machine has one attached). Activate the **My Documents folder and all folders in it** check box to let other people see and use files in your My Documents folder. You then need to protect this folder with a password by clicking the **Password** button beside the check box, entering the password (twice), and clicking **OK**.

Passwords Are a Must!

Why bother with a password if only your family or trusted work colleagues will be rifling through the folders? One simple reason: If you don't set a password, then it's entirely possible that someone on the Internet could also access your shared folders! This sounds bizarre, I know, and the reasons behind it are eye-glazingly technical. The short answer is that the "language" your computer uses to "talk" to the other computers on the network is identical to the one used by all the computers on the Internet. So if a nefarious hacker located your machine while it was online (another not-too-far-fetched scenario), then it would be easy for him to talk your computer into giving up its secrets.

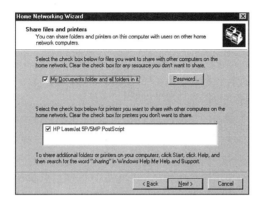

Figure 24.7

Use this dialog box to share some folders and your printer.

8. If you have a printer installed and you want to share it, make sure the check box beside it is activated. When you're done with this dialog box, click **Next**. (You don't have to decide about any of this sharing business right now because it's easy to share folders and printers after the network is assembled. See Chapter 25 for more information.)

9. The wizard now muses about the possibility of there being any Windows 95 or Windows 98 computers on your network. If your network does have such creatures, then you need to create a Home Networking Setup disk. The purpose of this disk is to run a copy of the Home Networking Wizard on those primitive versions of Windows. This ensures that all your computers will work together with some semblance of harmony. You have two choices (click **Next** after you pick one):

Cross Reference

To learn how to share folders and drives, see "Playing Nicely with Others: Sharing Your Resources," p. 395.

   ➤ **Yes, create a Home Networking Setup disk**   Activate this option if you have Windows 95 or Windows 98 computers attached to your network. To learn how to set up those machines, see "Dealing with Non-Millennium Machines" later in this chapter.

   ➤ **No, do not create a Home Networking Setup disk**   Activate this option if your workgroup is pure Windows Millennium. Skip to step 11.

10. If you elected to create the disk, insert a disk (make sure it doesn't contain any data you need) and click **Next**.

11. The wizard lets you know that it has finished the interrogation and is ready to make your machine network-ready. Remove the Home Networking Setup disk (if you created one) and click **Finish** to make it so.

12. When the wizard asks if you want to restart your computer, click **Yes**.

Changing the Network Configuration

If you ever need to make changes to your network setup, just run the Home Networking Wizard again. To do so, either select **Start**, **Programs**, **Accessories**, **Communications**, **Home Networking Wizard**, or open the My Network Places folder and double-click the **Home Networking Wizard** icon.

Dealing with Non-Millennium Machines

If you want to set up networking on a Windows 95 or Windows 98 machine, follow these steps:

1. Grab the Home Networking Setup disk that you created earlier and slide it into the Windows 95 or Windows 98 machine's floppy disk drive.

2. Select **Start**, **Run** to open the Run dialog box.

3. In the **Open** text box, type `a:\setup.exe` and then click **OK**. (I'm assuming that the machine's floppy disk is in drive A; if it's drive B, instead, type `b:\setup.exe`.) The Home Networking Wizard gets installed and then makes a guest appearance.

4. Follow the steps from the previous section to run through the various wizard duties.

One Last Chore: Setting Up the Shared Internet Connection

If you set up the host computer to share its Internet connection, you need to set up the other computers to use that shared connection. Here's how:

1. Double-click the **Connect to the Internet** icon if it's still on the desktop. If it's not, select **Start, Programs, Accessories, Communications, Internet Connection Wizard**.

2. In the first wizard dialog box, activate the **I want to set up my Internet connection manually...** option and click **Next**.

3. Activate the **I connect through a local area network (LAN)** option and click **Next**.

See "Manually Setting Up an Existing Internet Account," p. 104

4. Make sure the **Automatic discovery of proxy server (recommended)** check box is turned on, and then click **Next**.

5. Follow the rest of the Internet Connection Wizard's prompts, as described in Chapter 7, "Getting Yourself Online."

The Least You Need to Know

This chapter gave you the know-how you need to create a network suitable for a small office or home office. After a brief discussion of the benefits of a network, I took you on a tour of network hardware, including network interface cards and network cables. I then showed you the two basic network structures: star and bus. The rest of the chapter looked at network setup using Windows Millennium's new Home Networking Wizard.

Crib Notes

➤ **The nicest NICs**   Get NICs that support Ethernet (Fast Ethernet is best), are compatible with your network cable, and support Plug and Play.

➤ **The cable conundrum**   If you plan on using a star structure, you need twisted-pair cable (I highly recommend category 5 cable); if the bus structure is more your speed, go for coaxial cable.

➤ **The need for network speed**   Networks can travel at two different speeds: 10Mbps and 100Mbps. Equipment designed for the latter costs a bit more, but it's definitely worthwhile if you can afford it. Remember, however, that the coaxial cables can only handle 10Mbps.

➤ **Workgroup names**   Be sure that all the machines in your network use the same workgroup name.

➤ **Ready the host**   If you're looking to share an Internet connection across the network, decide which machine will be the host and then set up that connection on the computer. After that's done, run the Home Networking Wizard on that computer so that Internet Connection Sharing is running for the other network machines.

Chapter 25

Using Windows Millennium's Networking Features

In This Chapter

➤ Getting to know the My Network Places folder

➤ Graciously sharing your resources with the network

➤ Greedily accessing shared network resources

➤ Handy techniques that help you put all your hard (net)work to good use

The word "networking" has gone through something of a renaissance in recent years. For a while it was on everyone's Linguistic Pariah list because it was associated with the shallow excesses of the 1980s. Back then the word meant "Social interaction with the goal of using each other shamelessly for profit and personal aggrandizement." Book clubs and art galleries and the like were suggested as excellent networking spots. That was true, I suppose, but no one ever seemed to give a darn about the books or the art!

Nowadays, thankfully, network connections are associated more with computers than cocktail parties. So you'll no doubt be pleased to hear that this chapter has nothing whatsoever to do with the "I'll-scratch-your-back-if-you'll-scratch-my-back" variety of networking. Instead, this is more of an "I'll-share-my-stuff-if-you'll-share-your-stuff" chapter. That's because I spend most of the chapter talking about *shared resources*: disk drives, folders, printers, and even Internet connections that have been set up so that people on the network can access and use them. You also learn a few other network techniques that will help you take advantage of this networked beast that you've built.

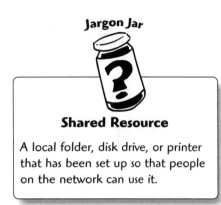

Jargon Jar

Shared Resource

A local folder, disk drive, or printer that has been set up so that people on the network can use it.

Your Starting Point: The My Network Places Folder

Most of your network travels set sail from a special folder called My Network Places. Windows Millennium offers several ways to get there:

➤ Launch the desktop's **My Network Places** icon.

➤ Open My Computer and click the **My Network Places** link in the information panel on the left.

➤ Display My Computer's Folders bar, if it's not already visible (click the **Folders** button), and highlight **My Network Places** in the tree.

Whichever method you prefer, you end up with the My Network Places window staring back at you, as shown in Figure 25.1.

Figure 25.1

The My Network Places folder is the starting point for your network meandering.

Network places
(folders shared by other computers)

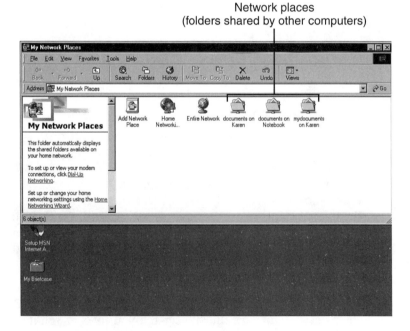

In its default guise, My Network Places shows you three things:

➤ **Add Network Place**   You use this icon to set up another computer's shared resource for use from your machine. See "Setting Up Network Places" later in this chapter.

➤ **Home Networking Wizard**   You use this icon to get reacquainted with the Home Networking Wizard and make changes to your network setup.

➤ **Entire Network**   This icon represents the network as a whole. On your small network, this is the same thing as your workgroup. (In larger networks, however, opening this icon would display all the defined workgroups.)

➤ **Network places**   The rest of the icons represent folders that have been shared by other computers on the network.

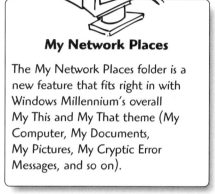

New Knickknack

My Network Places

The My Network Places folder is a new feature that fits right in with Windows Millennium's overall My This and My That theme (My Computer, My Documents, My Pictures, My Cryptic Error Messages, and so on).

Playing Nicely with Others: Sharing Your Resources

The lifeblood of any good workgroup network is the resources that have been shared by the various computers in the group. To see why, just consider the variety of things that can be shared:

➤ **Folders**   You can set up common folders so that some or all of the network users can access files and documents.

➤ **Disk drives**   You can give users access to entire drives, including Zip and Jaz drives.

➤ **CD-ROM drives**   Speaking of drives, you can set up a shared CD-ROM drive so that another user who doesn't have one can still run a program or access data.

➤ **Printers**   By sharing a printer, you save either the expense of supplying each user with his own printer, or the hassle of moving a printer from one machine to another.

Look Out!

Making Network CDs Work

Unfortunately, not all programs will run from a shared network CD-ROM. However, you can coax some of these recalcitrant programs into running by "mapping" the shared CD-ROM drive. See "Making Network Folders Look Like Drives on Your Computer" later in this chapter.

Cross Reference

See "Setting Up Your Network,"
p. 385.

➤ **Internet connections** You can set up an Internet connection on one machine and the other computers in the workgroup can then use that connection to access the Internet. I explained how to share an Internet connection in Chapter 24, "Using Windows Millennium to Set Up a Small Network."

The next couple of sections take you through the specifics of sharing resources.

Sharing Folders and Disks

The first thing you need to decide is how you want to share your resources. For each drive or folder you share, Windows Millennium gives you three choices (called *access rights*):

➤ **Read-Only** At this level, someone else who accesses one of your shared drives or folders can only copy, open, and view files. They can't move, modify, rename, delete, or add files.

➤ **Full** This anything-goes level gives others complete access to the files in the shared drive or folder. They can move, copy, open, view, modify, rename, delete, fold, spindle, and mutilate files, and they can even create new files.

➤ **Depends on Password** This level enables you to assign separate passwords for read-only and full access.

Windows Wisdom

Eyeballing the Comments

To see the comments associated with each shared resource, change My Network Places to Details view by activating the **View**, **Details** command.

Follow these steps to share a disk drive, CD-ROM drive, or folder:

1. In My Computer, highlight the disk drive or folder that you want to share.

2. Select the **File**, **Sharing** command (or right-click the drive or folder and then click **Sharing** in the shortcut menu). Windows Millennium displays the Sharing tab. Figure 25.2 shows a completed example.

3. Activate the **Shared As** option button.

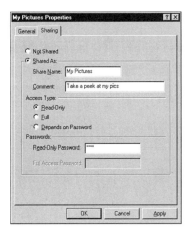

Figure 25.2

Use the Sharing tab to share a drive or folder with your workgroup pals.

4. The **Share Name** text box shows either the letter of the disk drive or the name of the folder. This is the name that people see in the My Network Places folder, so you should probably change it to something reasonably descriptive. (I say "reasonably" because the share name can only be a maximum of 12 characters.) You can also enter a brief description of the resource in the **Comment** text box. (Something like "Hard disk" or "CD-ROM drive" or "Crucial workgroup files" is sufficient.)

5. Select the type of access you want for this resource: **Read-Only**, **Full**, or **Depends on Password**.

6. If you want others to enter a password to access the shared drive or folder, enter the appropriate password in either the **Read-Only Password** or the **Full Access Password** text box. If you selected **Depends on Password**, you need to enter a password in both text boxes.

7. Click **OK**. If you entered a password, Windows Millennium asks you to confirm it. If that happens, reenter the password and click **OK**.

Look Out!

Spread the Password

If you do enter a password, don't forget to let the appropriate people in your group know what it is! This may sound obvious, but it always seems to be the one thing people forget when setting up their shares.

When you return to My Computer, you see that Windows Millennium has tacked on a little hand under the folder's usual icon, as shown in Figure 25.3. This reminds you that you've shared the folder.

Figure 25.3

When you share a folder or drive, Windows Millennium superimposes a hand icon under the regular icon.

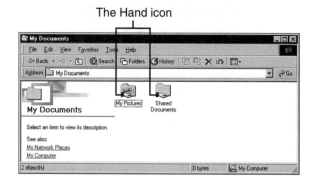

Sharing a Printer

You'll be happy to hear that sharing a printer is pretty much the same as sharing a file or folder. Here's what you do:

1. Select **Start**, **Settings**, **Printers** to open the Printers folder for business.

2. Highlight the printer you want to share, and then select **File**, **Sharing**. (On the other hand, you might feel like right-clicking the printer and then clicking **Sharing**.) The printer's Properties dialog box appears, and the Sharing tab is conveniently picked out from the herd.

3. Activate the **Shared As** option.

4. Change the **Share Name**, if you feel like it.

5. Enter a brief **Comment** that describes the printer.

6. If you want to restrict who uses the printer, enter a **Password**.

7. Click **OK**.

8. If you specified a password, reenter it in the Password Confirmation dialog box and then click **OK**.

Checking Out the Workgroup's Shared Resources

With your workgroup machines generously sharing their folders, drives, and printers, it's now time to see just how to get at those resources. There are four ways to go about this:

➤ **Access the resources directly** You do this by opening **My Network Places** and then double-clicking any of the shared resources that are shown. If the resource is protected by a password, you see the Enter Network Password dialog box shown in Figure 25.4. Enter the appropriate **Password** and click **OK**.

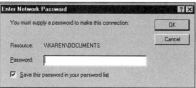

Figure 25.4

You see this dialog box if the shared resource is protected by a password.

➤ **Define a network place**   A network place is an icon that resides in the My Network Places folder, and it points to a shared resource. You saw earlier that the Home Networking Wizard sets up a few of these icons for you. However, you can also add your own icons. See "Setting Up Network Places," later in this chapter.

➤ **Map a shared folder or drive**   This takes a shared folder or drive and assigns it to an available drive letter on your system. For example, if your hard disk is drive C and your CD-ROM drive is drive D, then you could set up a shared folder or drive as drive E. This gives you even easier access to the shared resource. See "Making Network Folders Look Like Drives on Your Computer" later in this chapter.

➤ **Install a network printer**   This enables you to print from your machine and have the hard copy appear on the network printer. (You have to pick it up yourself, however. Networks are convenient, but they're not *that* convenient.) Check out "Printing Over the Network" a bit later.

Avoiding Password Drudgery

To avoid getting sick of constantly entering the same share passwords, make sure you leave the **Save this password in your password list** check box activated in the Enter Network Password dialog box. This tells Windows to enter the password for you automatically. If you're a bit paranoid about some interloper gaining access to a network share this way, deactivate the check box.

Setting Up Network Places

Here are the steps involved in creating a network place for a shared folder or drive:

1. In the **My Network Places** folder, launch the **Add Network Place** icon. The Add Network Place Wizard takes charge.

2. Click **Browse** to arrive at the Browse For Folder dialog box.

3. Open the **Entire Network** branch, followed by your workgroup branch, followed by the branch of the computer you want to work with. You should now see a list of the shared folders and drives on that computer (see Figure 25.5).

Figure 25.5

Open the branches until you get to the computer that has the shared folder you're hankering to get at.

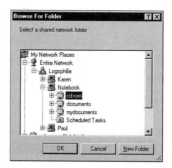

4. Click the shared resource you want, and then click **OK**. You're dropped off back at the Add Network Place Wizard.

5. Click **Next**. The last of the wizard's dialog boxes suggests a name for the new network place, which takes the form *Share Name* on *Computer Name*. Edit the name, if you're so inclined, and then click **Finish**.

6. If the resource is locked behind a password, you see the Access Denied dialog box. Type in the **Password**, say "Oh yeah, well deny *this!*", and click **OK**.

You end up with a new icon in My Network Places for the shared resource. Windows Millennium is also kind enough to open a window for the resource automatically. In the future, you open the same window by launching the resource's icon in My Network Places.

Viewing a Computer's Shared Stuff

If you want to take a peek at all the resources a workgroup is sharing, you need to open the computer using the Entire Network icon. Here's how:

1. Open the **My Network Places** folder.

2. Double-click the **Entire Network** icon. In the Entire Network window that comes into view, you should see a single icon for your workgroup.

3. Double-click the workgroup icon. The window changes again—this time you see icons for the computers in your workgroup, as shown in Figure 25.6.

Figure 25.6

When you open your workgroup, you see an icon for each computer.

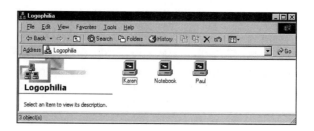

4. Double-click the icon of the computer you want to work with. Windows Millennium forks over a list of resources that the computer is sharing, as shown in Figure 25.7.

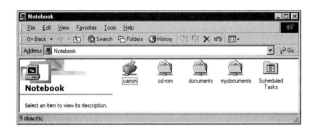

Figure 25.7

When you open a work-group computer, you see all the resources that it's so generously sharing.

Making Network Folders Look Like Drives on Your Computer

You can avoid the My Network Places folder altogether if you map a network folder or drive so that it takes up a drive letter on your system. This is called *mapping* the folder. Here's how you do it:

1. Use the steps from the previous section to open the computer that has the folder you want to map.

2. Highlight the shared folder or drive you want to map, and then select **File**, **Map Network Drive**. (As you might have guessed by now, you also can right-click the folder or drive and then click **Map Network Drive**.) Up pops the Map Network Drive dialog box, shown in Figure 25.8.

Figure 25.8

Use this dialog box to map a network resource to a drive letter on your computer.

3. Windows Millennium defaults to the first available drive letter. If you prefer another, use the **Drive** list to choose it.

4. If you want the resource to get mapped again automatically the next time you crank up Windows Millennium, activate the **Reconnect at logon** check box.

5. Click **OK**.

6. If the resource is password-protected, you see the Enter Network Password dialog box. Type in the **Password** and click **OK**.

Windows Millennium connects to the resource, creates a new drive letter on your system, and then displays a window that shows the contents of the resource.

Printing Over the Network

After you connect to a network printer, you use it as though it was attached directly to your computer. Windows Millennium offers a couple of methods for connecting to a network printer.

The easiest way is to use the steps outlined earlier to open the computer that has the shared printer (see "Viewing a Computer's Shared Stuff"). Highlight the printer, and then select **File**, **Connect**. (You also can right-click the printer and then click **Connect**.) Windows Millennium installs the printer lickety-split using the remote machine's printer driver files.

If you like using a wizard for these kinds of things, you can do it using the Add Printer Wizard:

1. Select **Start**, **Settings**, **Printers** and launch the **Add Printer** icon to get the Add Printer Wizard to the top of the pile.

2. Click **Next** to get past the introductory dialog box.

3. In the next dialog box, activate the **Network printer** option and click **Next**.

4. The wizard now asks you to enter the printer name, but forget that. Instead, click **Browse** and use the **Browse for Printer** dialog box to highlight the network printer you want to use. (Open **Entire Network**, then your workgroup, and then the computer.) Click **OK** to return to the wizard.

5. Click **Next**. From here, you complete the wizard normally.

Accessing a Shared Internet Connection

If you configured one of your workgroup machines to share its Internet connection, it's a no-brainer to get the other computers to use that connection:

If at First You Don't Succeed...

If the host computer takes too long to connect, the other computer's Web browser may "time out" and tell you that it can't access the Web site. Mutter a few choice epithets under your breath and press F5 to tell the browser to reload.

➤ If the host computer uses a cable modem or DSL line, the connection is "on" full-time, so the other computers just access the Internet willy-nilly.

➤ If the host computer uses a dial-up connection and that connection is active, again the other computers can go right ahead and start playing on the Net.

➤ If the host computer uses a dial-up connection and that connection is *inactive*, the other computers won't be able to connect to the Internet right away. Instead, they have to wait a minute or two while the host computer makes the connection.

➤ If the non-host computer already had an Internet connection set up, Windows Millennium may try to use that connection when you first try to connect to the Internet. So if you see the Connect dialog box the first time you try to get online, close it and Windows Millennium will then get online using the host's shared connection.

The Least You Need to Know

This chapter made the previous chapter's network configuration toil worthwhile. I began by showing you the My Network Places folder. From there, you learned how to play nicely and share your folders, drives, and printers with your workgroup cohorts. Next up were a few lessons on working with shared resources, including setting up network places, mapping network folders and drives, and setting up a network printer. I closed by showing you how to use a shared Internet connection. Here's a review of some of the things you learned along the way:

Crib Notes

➤ **Getting to the network** Double-click the desktop's **My Network Places** icon. You can also highlight **My Network Places** in My Computer's Folders list.

➤ **Sharing your stuff** To share a resource, highlight it, select **File**, **Sharing**, and then activate the **Share As** option.

➤ **Creating a network place** In the **My Network Places** folder, run the **Add Network Place** icon.

➤ **Viewing other workgroup computers** In My Network Places, double-click the **Entire Network** icon and then double-click the icon for your workgroup.

➤ **Mapping a network folder or drive** Open the workgroup computer, highlight the folder or drive, and then select **File**, **Map Network Drive**.

➤ **Using a network printer** Open the network computer, highlight the shared printer, and then select **File**, **Connect**.

Chapter 26

Remote Network Connections with Dial-Up Networking

In This Chapter

➤ Configuring a computer to answer incoming calls

➤ Setting up a computer to dial up the network

➤ Connecting to the network from a remote locale

➤ Handling area codes, calling cards, and long-distance providers

➤ How to stay in the loop when you're out of town

There's an old saying that "Far folks fare well." No, I don't know what it means, either. However, folks who are far away from their network can still fare well by using Windows Millennium's Dial-Up Networking program. This feature enables you to use a modem to establish a connection to your network lifeline when a physical connection just isn't physically possible (say, when you're out of town on business).

This chapter does two main things:

➤ If you've used the past couple of chapters to create your own small network, this chapter shows you how to set up a computer to accept incoming calls.

➤ It shows you how to configure and use Dial-Up Networking to connect remotely to your network.

If you're looking to connect to a larger corporate network, the principles of connecting may still be the same. (However, you should talk to your system administrator about all this to make sure. Some corporate networks have extra security hoops that you have to jump through before you can connect.) You'll also appreciate the section at the end of the chapter that deals with dialing "locations" that enable you to set up connections with calling cards, long-distance providers, area codes, and other telephonic bric-a-brac.

A Mercifully Brief Introduction to Dial-Up Networking

Most of the malarkey that I go on and on about in this chapter is related to a Windows Millennium component called Dial-Up Networking (DUN). The name more or less sums up what it does, which is enable you to place a phone call through your modem to connect to and use your network. In other words, instead of connecting to your network through a cable, you connect to it through a phone line.

Gee, it's kind of the same as connecting to the Internet, isn't it?

An extra piece of cake for you because, yes, it *is* very much the same as a dial-up Internet connection. In fact, that's precisely what the Internet Connection Wizard does: It creates a Dial-Up Networking *connection*—an icon that specifies the particulars of getting online through your Internet service provider. (Some geeks use the term "connectoids" for these connections, but you won't catch me using such an off-the-scale ugly word.) You can find the Internet Connection Wizard details in Chapter 7, "Getting Yourself Online."

Cross Reference

See "The Step-By-Step Net: Using the Internet Connection Wizard," p. 101.

These connection icons reside, and can be created, within the Dial-Up Networking folder. Windows Millennium gives you a couple of different ways to get to this folder:

➤ Select **Start**, **Settings**, **Dial-Up Networking**.

➤ If you have the Folders list displayed in My Computer (if not, click the **Folders** button), open the **Control Panel** branch and then click **Dial-Up Networking**.

At this point, Windows Millennium may launch the Make New Connection Wizard automatically. I show you how the wizard works later on, so click **Cancel** for now. Figure 26.1 shows the Dial-Up Networking window. The Make New Connection icon should be there, and you may see another icon for your Internet connection, if you have one. After you create a dial-up connection to your network, its icon will appear here, as well.

Figure 26.1

The Dial-Up Networking window is where you spend most of your time in this chapter.

Create button

Dial button

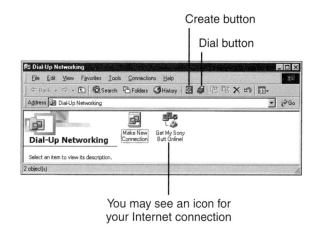

You may see an icon for
your Internet connection

Setting Up a Network Computer to Accept Incoming Calls

You can't dial up your network unless you have something to dial up *to*. If you deal with a large, corporate network, the super-geeks in the IT department will have already set things up properly, so you can skip this section. If you're dealing with your own small net, however, your first chore is to convert one of your workgroup computers into a machine that's only too happy to accept incoming calls. The next couple of sections show you how it's done.

Getting the Dial-Up Server Ready to Serve

Part of the Dial-Up Networking work crew is a component called Dial-Up Server. Its job is to monitor the computer's modem and listen for incoming calls. When the modem rings, it connects the remote caller, verifies her password, and then gives her access to the shared resources on the network.

Here are the steps to follow to get Dial-Up Server up and serving:

1. In the Dial-Up Networking folder, select the **Connections**, **Dial-Up Server** command. The Dial-Up Server dialog box dances in (see Figure 26.2).

Jargon Jar

Server

A *server* is a computer that gives other computers access to network resources. (It might help to picture the machine serving up those resources on the electronic equivalent of a platter.)

407

Figure 26.2

Use Dial-Up Server to let workgroupies dial up your computer.

2. If you happen to have multiple modems installed, the dialog box shows a tab for each one. Display the tab for the modem you want to use for incoming calls.

3. Activate the **Allow caller access** option.

4. If you want to protect the dial-up with a password (a *very* good idea), click the **Change Password** button to slap up the Dial-Up Networking Password dialog box. Ignore the **Old password** text box (because there's no old password to speak of), enter your password in the **New password** and **Confirm new password** text boxes, and click **OK**.

5. Click **Apply**. Dial-Up Networking adds the Dial-Up Server icon to the system tray and begins monitoring the modem for incoming calls.

Monitoring the Connected User

With the Dial-Up Server configured, the **Status** box displays **Monitoring** to indicate that it's looking for incoming calls. When a call comes in, the **Status** line tells you who it is and when she connected, as shown in Figure 26.3. You can disconnect the user at any time by clicking the **Disconnect User** button.

Figure 26.3

Watch the Status box to see who's connecting.

Look Out!

Dial-Up Server Hogs the Phone

Dial-Up Server is a bit pushy, which means that it muscles in on any incoming phone call and answers it right away (usually on the first ring). This means you can't accept voice calls on the same line and you can't run Dial-Up Server with any other communications software that answers incoming calls (such as a fax program).

Creating a Dial-Up Connection to Your Network

With the Dial-Up Server doing its duty, you next need to set up the computer that will be making the remote calls. Before the fun begins, you should know that I'm making two assumptions right off the bat:

➤ That your modem and computer are attached at the hip (electronically speaking, of course; the latest computers and peripherals come without hips).

➤ That you've clued Windows Millennium in on what kind of modem you have.

Given that, let's dive right into the deep end of creating a connection. You need to follow these steps:

1. Open the Dial-Up Networking folder, if you haven't done so already.

2. As I mentioned earlier, if this is the first time you've done the DUN thing, Windows Millennium starts the Make New Connection Wizard automatically. If that doesn't happen, you see the Dial-Up Networking window, instead. Curse your luck and launch the **Make New Connection** icon by hand. You use this wizard to specify the Dial-Up Networking connection

Windows Wisdom

Getting Back to Dial-Up Server

If the Dial-Up Server dialog box is no longer onscreen, you can coax it into returning by double-clicking the Dial-Up Server icon in the taskbar's system tray.

Cross Reference

To install a modem, see "Installing Specific Devices," p. 338.

409

More Ways to the Wizard

You can also fire up the wizard by selecting **Connections, Make New Connection** or by clicking the **Create** toolbar button (pointed out previously in Figure 26.1).

particulars, and each connection contains, among other things, a name, the modem to use, and the phone number to dial.

3. In the first wizard dialog box, shown in Figure 26.4, you need to fill in two things (click **Next** when you've done that):

➤ **Type a name for the computer you are dialing** Use this text box to enter a name for the new Dial-Up Networking connection.

➤ **Select a device** If you've installed multiple modems, use this drop-down list to select the modem you want to use for this connection.

Figure 26.4

Use this dialog box to enter a connection name and choose the modem to use with Dial-Up Networking.

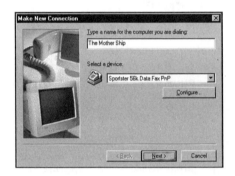

4. You use the next dialog box to enter the **Area code**, **Telephone number**, and **Country or region code** for the computer you'll be dialing. When you're finished, click **Next**.

5. That'll do it: your new connection is ready to roll. In the final dialog box, click **Finish** to shut down the wizard.

When you get back to the Dial-Up Networking window, you see a new icon for your connection, as illustrated in Figure 26.5.

Figure 26.5

The Dial-Up Networking window sprouts an icon for the new connection.

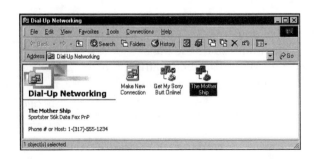

Remote Network Connecting and Disconnecting

Now you're ready to make the connection. Here are the steps to march through:

1. Make sure your modem is hooked up properly and, if you have an external modem, that it's turned on.

2. If you haven't done so already, open the Dial-Up Networking window as described earlier.

3. Double-click the connection icon you created in the previous section. Dial-Up Networking brings up the Connect To dialog box on the desktop, as shown in Figure 26.6.

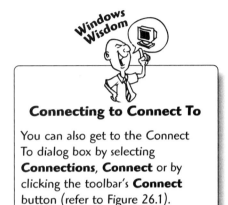

Connecting to Connect To

You can also get to the Connect To dialog box by selecting **Connections**, **Connect** or by clicking the toolbar's **Connect** button (refer to Figure 26.1).

Figure 26.6

Use this dialog box to initiate the connection.

4. Make sure your **User name** is correct (this doesn't matter so much if you're just connecting to your small network) and enter your **Password**. The dialog box also offers two convenience options:

   ➤ **Save password**   Activate this check box if you want Windows Millennium to enter your password automatically in the future.

   ➤ **Connect automatically**   Activate this check box to avoid the Connect To dialog box in future sessions. This means that Dial-Up Networking starts connecting immediately when you launch the connection icon. This is a good choice if you find that you never change anything in this dialog box.

5. Make sure the correct phone number is shown in the **Phone number** text box.

6. When you're ready, click **Connect**. Windows Millennium dials your modem and connects with the computer you set up to handle incoming calls.

7. When the connection is made, a dialog box pops up to let you know. Click **Close**. You also see a connection icon in the system tray.

Locations, Locations, Locations

Dial-Up Networking supports "locations" that enable you to specify things like different area codes you're calling from, numbers to dial for outside lines, calling cards, and much more. See "Locations: Wrangling with Area Codes, Calling Cards, and All That" later in this chapter. After you've read that section, you can change the location specifics of a call by clicking **Dial Properties** in the Connect To dialog box. If you set up alternate locations, use the **Dialing from** list to choose the location you want.

When you're connected, your computer becomes a full member of the network. You can access network resources, create network places, and others on the network can see your computer as well.

When you've finished your online work, you need to remember to disconnect to clear the line and avoid running up long distance charges (if applicable). To disconnect, you have two choices:

➤ Double-click the connection icon in the system tray and then click the **Disconnect** button in the dialog box that appears. (It's also possible to right-click the icon and then click **Disconnect**.)

➤ Open the Dial-Up Networking folder, highlight the connection icon, and select **File**, **Disconnect**. (You can also right-click the icon, and then click **Disconnect**.)

Locations: Wrangling with Area Codes, Calling Cards, and All That

You probably noticed that the Connect To dialog box has a Dial Properties button. This button enables you to specify different dialing locations, which tell Windows Millennium whether you use a calling card, the number to dial to get an outside line, and more. Locations are particularly useful for Dial-Up Networking because notebook computer users often have to connect to their networks from different places:

➤ You may need to connect from home, where you have call waiting (which needs to be disabled).

➤ You may need to connect from a client's office where you have to dial 9 for an outside line.

➤ You may need to connect from out of town, and so have to dial the number as long distance and use your calling card.

For such situations, you can change these and other location parameters by clicking the **Dial Properties** button in the Connect To dialog box. (Another possibility is to select **Start**, **Settings**, **Control Panel**, click **view all Control Panel options**, if necessary, open the **Modems** icon, and then click **Dialing Properties**.) Figure 26.7 shows the dialog box that appears.

Digital Phone Jack Alert!

If you find yourself on the road with your notebook computer and want to connect to your office network, watch out for the digital phone systems used by many hotels. Most modems aren't compatible with digital systems, and you can end up frying your modem if you attempt to connect over a digital line. Unfortunately, digital phone jacks look identical to regular analog jacks. You need to ask the hotel staff what kind of phone jacks they use.

Figure 26.7

Use this dialog box to set up dialing locations.

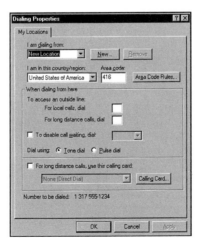

Here's a rundown of the controls in this dialog box:

➤ **I am dialing from**   This list contains all the dialing locations you've defined. To set up another location, click **New**, click **OK** when Windows Millennium tells you a new location was created, and then click inside the list to rename the location as you see fit. You then customize the rest of the dialog box fields to set up the dialing properties for the new location.

➤ **I am in this country/region**   Use this list to set the country from which you're dialing.

➤ **Area code**   Use this text box to set the area code from which you're dialing.

➤ **Area Code Rules**   Windows Millennium enables you to set up 10-digit dialing and other area code customizations. To do so, click this button to display the Area Code Rules dialog box (shown in Figure 26.8), which has two groups (click **OK** when you're done):

When calling within my area code   In some cases, the phone company requires that you use the area code even if you're calling another number in the same area code. If the call isn't a long distance number, activate the **Always dial the area code (10-digit dialing)** check box. If some of the phone number prefixes in your area code *are* long distance calls (and thus require the country code), click **New** to add the prefixes to the list.

When calling to other area codes   In some larger cities, the phone company has run out of phone numbers in the main area code. To overcome this problem, the phone company usually splits off part of the existing customer base into a new area code and requires that calls between the two areas be prefaced with the appropriate area code. Because these aren't long-distance calls, however, no country code is required. In this case, click **New** to add the area codes for which Windows Millennium shouldn't dial a 1.

Figure 26.8

Use this dialog box to set up 10-digit dialing.

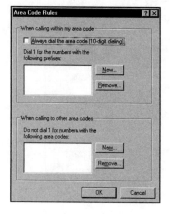

➤ **To access an outside line**   Use the **For local calls, dial** text box to enter the code that must be dialed to get an outside line for local calls (such as 9). Use the **For long distance calls, dial** text box to enter the code that must be dialed to get an outside line for long distance calls (such as 8).

➤ **To disable call waiting, dial**   To deactivate call waiting before making the call, activate this check box and then either enter the appropriate code in the text box or select one of the existing codes from the list.

Disabling Call Waiting Is a Must!

Because the extra beeps that call waiting uses to indicate an incoming call can wreak havoc on modem communications, you should always disable call waiting before initiating a data call. One of the sequences *70, 70#, or 1170 (which are the ones listed in the **To disable call waiting, dial** drop-down list) will usually disable call waiting, but you should check with your local phone company to make sure. If you need to use a different sequence, type it in the list box.

➤ **Dial using**   Select **Tone dial** or **Pulse dial**, as appropriate for your telephone line.

➤ **For long distance calls, use this calling card**   These controls enable you to set up a calling card or long-distance carrier. This procedure is explained in detail next.

Setting Up Calling Cards and Long-Distance Carriers

Although most of your phone calls are likely to be free, at times this might not be the case, and you'll want to make some other arrangements for charging the call. Two situations, in particular, might crop up from time to time:

➤ You're dialing from a hotel and want to charge the call to your calling card.

➤ You need to make a long-distance connection, in which case you might want to first dial the number of a long-distance carrier.

Windows Millennium can handle both situations. To specify either a calling card number or a long-distance carrier phone number, follow these steps:

1. Activate the **For long distance calls, use this calling card** check box in the Dialing Properties dialog box.

2. Click the **Calling Card** button to display the Calling Card dialog box.

3. Use the list box to choose the type of calling card or long-distance carrier you have (see Figure 26.9).

Figure 26.9

Use the Calling Card dialog box to enter a calling card number or select a long-distance carrier.

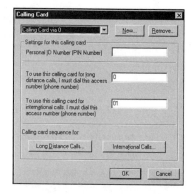

4. For a calling card, use the **Personal ID Number (PIN Number)** text box to enter your PIN.

5. Fill in the next two text boxes with the access numbers required by your calling card or carrier. The first text box is for long distance calls, and the second is for international calls.

6. To change the long distance dialing sequence for the calling card or carrier, click **Long Distance Calls** to display the Calling Card Sequence dialog box. In each step, select the appropriate **Dial** code and use the **Then wait for** list to specify which signal Windows Millennium must wait for before continuing. Click **OK** when you're finished.

7. To change the international call long distance dialing sequence, click **International Calls** and fill in the dialog box that appears.

8. Click **OK** to return to the Dialing Properties dialog box.

Adding a New Calling Card or Long-Distance Carrier

If your calling card or long-distance carrier doesn't appear in the list, follow these steps to add it:

1. In the Calling Card dialog box, click the **New** button to display the Create New Calling Card dialog box.

416

2. Enter a descriptive name for the calling card or carrier, and then click **OK**. Windows Millennium tells you that you must now enter the dialing rules for the card or carrier.

3. Click **OK** to return to the Calling Card dialog box.

4. Follow steps 4 through 8 in the preceding section to specify the dialing rules for your new card or carrier.

The Least You Need to Know

This chapter showed you how to use Dial-Up Networking to connect to your network using a modem. The first part of the chapter went through the procedure for setting up a computer to accept incoming calls. You then learned how to set up the soon-to-be-remote computer to dial up the network and how to make the connection. I closed by letting you in on a few secrets about locations. Here are some things to think about:

Crib Notes

➤ **Dial-up central** You use Dial-Up Networking to configure computers to accept and make dial-up network connections. To get to this folder, select **Start**, **Settings**, **Dial-Up Networking**.

➤ **The dial-up-ee** To set up a computer to accept dial-up connections, run the Dial-Up Networking folder's **Connections**, **Dial-Up Server** command.

➤ **The dial-up-er** To set up a computer to make dial-up connections, open the Dial-Up Networking folder's **Make New Connection** icon.

➤ **Getting connected** In the Dial-Up Networking folder, double-click the connection icon.

➤ **Getting disconnected** Either highlight the connection in the Dial-Up Networking folder and then select **File**, **Disconnect**, or right-click the connection icon in the system tray, and then click **Disconnect**.

➤ **Calling cards and other dialing data** To change how Dial-Up Networking dials the phone, set up new locations. Either click the **Dial Properties** button in the Connect To dialog box, or open Control Panel's **Modems** icon, and then click **Dialing Properties**.

The Jargon Jar: The Complete Archive

access rights   In a network, the level of access that people are assigned when they use your *shared resources*. You can assign either "read-only" access (people can view stuff, but they can't change it) or "full" access (people can do whatever the heck they please).

attachment   A file that latches onto an email message and is sent to the recipient.

Auto Hide   A feature that hides the taskbar until you move the mouse to the bottom of the screen.

AutoRun   A feature that automatically launches a program's setup routine after you insert its CD-ROM or DVD-ROM.

backplate   A piece of metal that covers a hole in the back of a computer beside an internal *circuit board* slot.

backup job   A file that specifies a few particulars about a backup: the files you want backed up, the location where the files will be backed up, and any backup options.

Bcc   A blind courtesy (or carbon) copy email message. These are copies of the message that get sent to other people, but their addresses aren't shown to the other recipients. See also *Cc*.

bit   Short for "binary digit," and it represents the most basic unit of computer information. Within your computer, data is stored using tiny electronic devices called *gates*, each of which holds a single bit. These gates can be either on (which means electricity flows through the gate) or off (no electricity flows through the gate). For the likes of you and me, the number 1 represents a gate that's on, and the number 0 represents a gate that's off.

boot   To start your computer.

bps   Stands for bits per second, and it's used to measure the speed at which the modem spews data through a phone line.

browser   See *Web browser*.

bus structure   A network structure in which each *network interface card* is connected to the network interface card in the computer "beside" it via *coaxial cable*. See also *star structure*.

byte   8 *bits* strung together, which represents a single character of data. For example, the letter "X" is represented by the following byte: 01011000. Weird, I know. Further, the mathematicians tell us that a byte can have 256 possible combinations of ones and zeros (prove it for yourself by raising 2 to the power of 8), and those combinations represent all possible characters: lowercase letters, uppercase letters, numbers, symbols, and so on.

Cc   A courtesy (or carbon) copy. These are copies of an email message that get sent to other people. See also *Bcc*.

circuit board   A device that fits into a slot inside your computer.

click   To quickly press and release the left mouse button.

coaxial cable   A cable that uses a bayonet-style connector to attach to a T-connector, which then attaches to a BNC *port* in the *network interface card*. See also *twisted-pair cable*.

color depth   The number of colors Windows Millennium uses to display stuff on your screen. See also *screen area*.

cursor   See *insertion point cursor*.

cutout   A selected section of a Paint drawing.

defragment   To rearrange the contents of a hard disk so that each file's *sectors* run consecutively. See also *fragmented*.

desktop   The sea of blue that takes up the bulk of the Windows Millennium screen. It's called a "desktop" because it's where your documents and tools appear.

device driver   A wee chunk of software that enables Windows Millennium to operate a device.

dial-up   A connection to a network (or an *Internet service provider*) that occurs via a modem over a phone line.

dialog box   A box that shows up when Windows Millennium or a program requires more information from you.

differential backup   Backs up only files in the current *backup job* that have changed since the last *full backup*. See also *incremental backup*.

digital camera   A film camera-like device that takes pictures of the outside world and stores them digitally for later downloading to a hard disk.

directory   See *folder*.

docking station   A box into which you can plug a notebook and that offers expansion room in the form of extra PC Card sockets, drive bays, plugs for external accessories, and ports for other devices.

document scanner   A photocopier-like device that creates a digital image of a flat surface, such as a piece of paper or a photograph.

double-click   To quickly press and release the left mouse button *twice* in succession.

download   To receive data from a remote computer. See also *upload*.

drag-and-drop   A technique you use to run commands or move things around; you use your mouse to *drag* files or icons to strategic screen areas and then release the mouse button to *drop* them there.

Explorer bar   A pane that shows up on the left side of the My Computer window and that's used to display bars (such as the handy Folders bar).

favorite   A *Web page* name and address saved within Internet Explorer for easy recall down the road.

fax modem   A special type of modem (although it's by far the most common type these days) that can handle fax transmissions in addition to its usual data duties.

female   A port or plug that has holes. See also *male*.

folder   A storage location for files and other folders (subfolders).

folder template   A file that tells Windows Millennium how to display a *folder* in *Web view*.

font   A style of text that includes the typeface (a unique design applied to every character), the type style (such as **bold** or *italic*), the *type size*, and possibly some type effects (such as <u>underline</u>).

fragmented   When a file is stored on the hard disk using multiple sectors that are scattered throughout the disk. See also *defragment*.

full backup   Backs up all the files in the current *backup job*. See also *differential backup* and *incremental backup*.

gigabyte   1,024 *megabytes*. Those in-the-know usually abbreviate this as "GB" when writing, and as "gig" when speaking. See also *byte*, *kilobyte*, and *megabyte*.

hard disk   The main storage area inside your computer.

hibernate   A power mode that saves the location and contents of all your open windows and programs, and then shuts down your computer. When you restart, Windows reappears very quickly and restores the saved Windows and programs.

hot swapping   Inserting and removing *PC Card* devices without having to shut down Windows Millennium.

hub   A central network connection point used in the *star structure*.

idle time   Time during which a network or Internet connection isn't used.

incremental backup   Backs up only files in the current *backup job* that have changed since the last *full backup* or the last *differential backup*.

insertion point cursor   The blinking vertical bar you see inside a text box or in a word processing application, such as WordPad. It indicates where the next character you type will appear.

Internet service provider   A company that takes your money in exchange for an Internet account, which is what you need to get online.

IP address   An address (which will look something like 123.234.45.67) that serves as the location of your computer while you're connected to the Internet.

ISP   See *Internet service provider*.

Jaz drive   A special disk drive that uses portable disks (about the size of floppy disks) that hold either 1 or 2 *gigabytes* of data. See also *Zip disk*.

Kbps   Kilobits per second, or thousands of bits per second. *Data transfer rates* are often measured this way, so the three main rates are also written as 28.8Kbps, 33.6Kbps, and 56Kbps.

kilobyte   1,024 *bytes*. To be hip, always abbreviate this to "K" or "KB." See also *megabyte* and *gigabyte*.

LAN   See *local area network*.

link   In a *Web page*, a chunk of text or an image that, when clicked, takes you to another Web page.

local area network   A group of computers located relatively close together and that are connected via network cable.

log on   To provide your *Internet service provider* with your username and password, and so gain access to the wonder that is the Internet.

mail server   A computer that your ISP uses to store and send your email messages.

male   A port or plug that has pins. See also *female*.

map   To set up a shared network folder or disk drive so that it has its own drive letter on your system. See also *shared resource*.

megabyte   1,024 *kilobytes* or 1,048,576 *bytes*. The experts write this as "M" or "MB" and pronounce it "meg." See also *gigabyte*.

message body   The text of an email message.

MIDI   See *Musical Instrument Digital Interface*.

modem   An electronic device that somehow manages to transmit and receive computer data over telephone lines. Modems come in three flavors: external, internal, and *PC Card*.

modem cable   A special data cable that connects an external *modem* to a PC. The cable attaches to a *port* in the back of the modem on one end, and to a *serial port* in the back of the computer on the other end.

multimedia   Using a computer to play, edit, and record sounds, animations, and movies.

multitasking   The capability to run two or more programs at the same time.

Musical Instrument Digital Interface   A sound file that plays music generated by electronic synthesizers.

network interface card   A *circuit board*, *PC Card* device, or *USB* device into which the network cable is plugged.

network place   A *shared resource* that has its own icon in your My Network Places folder.

newsgroup   An online discussion forum devoted to a particular topic.

NIC   See *network interface card*.

null-modem cable   A special communications cable designed for direct connections between two computers.

page   See *Web page*.

PC Card   A small, credit card-sized device that slips into a special socket on your notebook. There are PC Card devices for *modems*, *network interface cards*, hard disks, and much more.

personalized menus   A new Windows Millennium feature that displays only those Start menu commands that you use most often.

423

pixels   The individual pinpoints of light that make up a Paint drawing (and, for that matter, everything you see on your screen).

port   A receptacle in the back of a computer into which you plug the cable used by an external device. See also *modem cable*, *printer port*, and *serial port*.

post   To send a message to a newsgroup.

print job   A document for which the Print command has been issued.

print queue   The list of pending *print jobs*.

printer port   On the back of the computer, the receptacle into which you plug the printer cable. On most systems, the printer port is named LPT1.

RAM   Random Access Memory. The memory in your computer that Windows Millennium uses to run your programs.

Recycle Bin   The place where Windows Millennium stores deleted files. If you trash a file accidentally, you can use the Recycle Bin to recover it.

Registry   The crucial configuration files that are the lifeblood of Windows Millennium.

right-click   To click the right mouse button instead of the usual left button. In Windows Millennium, right-clicking something usually pops up a *shortcut menu*.

sans serif   A *font* that doesn't have cross strokes at its extremities. This type of font is most often used for titles and headings that require a larger type size. See also *serif*.

screen area   The number of columns and rows in the grid of pixels that Windows Millennium uses to display screen images. See also *color depth*.

screen saver   A feature that displays a moving pattern on your monitor after your computer hasn't been used for a while. It prevents the screen image from being "burned in" to the monitor, but most folks just like to watch the crazy psychedelic patterns they make.

screen shot   A copy of the current screen image.

sector   A storage area on your hard disk.

separator   In a toolbar, a vertical bar that separates groups of related buttons.

serial port   A plug in the back of your computer into which you insert the *modem cable*. If you have an internal modem, the serial port is built-in to the modem's circuit board, so you never have to worry about it and there's no cable to run. On most computers, the serial port is named COM1.

serif   A *font* that has small cross strokes at the extremities of each character. Serif fonts are good for regular text in a document. See also *sans serif*.

shared resource   A local folder, disk drive, or printer that has been set up so that people on the network can use it.

shortcut   A file that points to another file. Also, another name for most of the commands on the various Start menus.

shortcut menu   A menu that contains a few commands related to an item (such as the *desktop* or the *taskbar*). You display the shortcut menu by *right-clicking* the object.

signal-to-noise ratio   In a *newsgroup*, the ratio of useful, on-topic *posts* to useless, off-topic posts.

signature   A snippet of text that appears at the bottom of an email message.

spam   Unsolicited commercial email, and the scourge of the Internet. To avoid spam, don't put your real email address in your news account.

star structure   A network structure in which each *network interface card* is connected to a central *hub* via *twisted-pair cable*. See also *bus structure*.

Start Menu folder   A folder on your hard disk that holds the various Start menu shortcuts and folders. It's usually C:\Windows\Start Menu\.

Subject line   A line of text that describes what an email message is about.

surf   To jump from *Web page* to Web page using a *Web browser*.

system standby   A power mode that shuts everything down temporarily until you press a key, move the mouse, or poke the power button.

tab stop   A spot on the WordPad ruler at which the cursor stops when you press the **Tab** key.

tape drive   A device that backs up data to tape. Unless you have a spare hard disk, this is the best kind of backup medium to use.

taskbar   The gray strip along the bottom of the Windows Millennium screen that's used to switch between running programs.

text editor   A program that lets you edit files that contain only text. The Windows Millennium text editor is called Notepad.

thumbnail   A preview of an image or HTML file (*Web page*).

twisted-pair cable   A cable that uses RJ-45 jacks to connect to an RJ-45 port in the NIC. See also *coaxial cable*, *hub*, and *star structure*.

uniform resource locator   See *URL*.

uninstall   To completely remove a program from your computer.

Universal Serial Bus   See *USB*.

upload   To send data to a remote computer. See also *download*.

URL   The address of a *Web page*.

USB   A new way to connect all kinds of devices[md]including keyboards, mice, speakers, printers, modems, and network cards[md]to a PC. Most new computers have one or two USB *ports* into which these devices connect.

video adapter   An internal *circuit board* that grabs display instructions from the processor and then tells the monitor what to show on the screen.

wallpaper   An image or design that covers the screen background.

wave file   A standard Windows sound file.

waves   How sounds are transmitted through a telephone line. When you talk, you create a sound wave that vibrates a diaphragm in the phone's mouthpiece. The vibration converts the sound wave into an equivalent electromagnetic wave, which is then sent along the phone line. At the other end, the wave vibrates a diaphragm in the earpiece, which reproduces the original sound wave, and your voice is heard loud and clear.

Web browser   A program that you use to *surf* sites on the World Wide Web. The browser that comes with Windows Millennium is called Internet Explorer.

Web integration   The use of Web-like features within the Windows Millennium interface.

Web page   A document on the Web that contains text, images, and usually a few links.

Web view   A folder view that displays a folder as though it were a *Web page*.

workgroup   In a large network, a group of related computers. In a small network, all the computers.

Zip drive   A special disk drive that uses portable disks (a little smaller than a *Jaz drive* disk) which hold 100 or 250 *megabytes* of data.

Index

D

data
  compressing (Backup program), 367
  protecting Web, 134
Date/Time command (Edit menu), 223
decoder
  hardware, 255
  software, 256
Default Icon button, 286
defragmenting disks, 350
Delete command (Edit menu), 162
Delete command (File menu), 88, 168
deleting
  emails, 162
  files, 88-89
    Disk Cleanup tool, 347-348
    temporary Internet, 138
  folders, 88-89, 168
  mistakes in Paint, 238
  programs, 330
  Start menu items, 306
  text, 69
desktop, 21, 282
  active, 287-289
  color depth, 290-292
  color schemes, 284-285
  customizing, 288, 293-294
  effects, 285

fonts, changing, 285
icons, 10, 21-22, 285
Internet Explorer icon, 22
items, 287, 289
My Briefcase, 23
My Computer, 22
My Documents, 22
My Networks Places, 22
new features, 10
Online Services, 23
Outlook Express, 23
Recycle Bin, 22
screen area, 290-292
  pixels, 291
screen savers, 287
setting as Web page, 288
Windows Media Player, 23
desktop computers, synchronizing notebooks, 271-273
desktop items, adding, 289
desktop themes, applying, 293-294
Desktop Themes icon, 293
Desktop toolbar, 301
desktops, wallpaper, 246
Details view (My Computer), 314
device driver, updating, 255

Dial-up Connection dialog box, 109
Dial-Up Networking
  calling cards, 415-417
  connections, 409-412
  disconnecting, 412
  locations, 412, 414-415
  long-distance, 415-417
  modems, 409
  monitoring users, 408
  passwords, 408
Dial-Up Networking folder, 406
Dial-Up Server command (Connections menu), 407
dialog boxes, 39, 41
  Accounts, 191
  Active Desktop, 289
  Add Favorite, 124
  Add folder comment, 318
  Add/Remove Programs Properties, 325, 353
  Advanced Connection Properties, 106
  Area Code Rules, 414
  Background, 170
  Backup Job Options, 369
  Browse, 95
  Calling Card, 416
  Color, 285
  Connect To, 412-415
  controls, 41
  Copy To, 245

G

441

O

P